ALSO BY PENELOPE CASAS

The Foods and Wines of Spain

Tapas: The Little Dishes of Spain

Discovering Spain: An Uncommon Guide

These Are Borzoi Books
Published in New York by Alfred A. Knopf

¡DELICIOSO!
THE REGIONAL
COOKING
OF SPAIN

¡Delicioso!
THE REGIONAL
COOKING
OF SPAIN

PENELOPE CASAS

Photographs by Luis Casas

ALFRED A. KNOPF

New York   1996

THIS IS A BORZOI BOOK
PUBLISHED BY ALFRED A. KNOPF, INC.

Copyright © 1996 by Penelope Casas
Map copyright © 1996 by David Cain

Library of Congress Cataloging-in-Publication Data

Casas, Penelope.
    ¡Delicioso! The regional cooking of Spain / Penelope Casas. —
1st ed.
        p.   cm.
    Includes index.
    ISBN 0-679-43055-5
    1. Cookery, Spanish.   I. Title.
TX723.5.S7C3576   1996
641.5946—dc20   95-34171
                        CIP

Manufactured in the United States of America

First Edition

To Luis—

the very spirit of Spain

and my guiding light for three decades

CONTENTS

ACKNOWLEDGMENTS

In my search for the very best of Spanish regional cooking, I followed my own paths of investigation but also relied on Spanish friends and family—many of whom are chefs and restaurateurs—to tell me about dishes they have cherished since childhood and recipes that over the years have become favorites.

Mari Carmen, wife of our lifelong friend Chalo Peláez, entrusted me with a handwritten cookbook in which her mother had carefully penned her prized recipes, and Aurora, wife of our old friend Pepe Sanz, gave me a time-worn cookbook that has been in her family for generations; Reme Domínguez and Chimo Boix at Tasca del Puerto restaurant showed me how to prepare the foods of their Valencian mothers and grandmothers; Pili and Rafa Salgado directed my attention to some exceptional dishes from Mallorca; and Carmen and Pepe González—friends who go beyond the call of duty—were always on the lookout for information that might help me in my research.

Lucio Blázquez, owner of celebrated Casa Lucio in Madrid, gave me the opportunity to observe the preparation of the ever-so-simple but difficult-to-reproduce traditional dishes that emerge from his diminutive kitchen—and that made all the difference. Juan Mari Arzak, unquestionably a leader in creative cooking but equally expert at preparing exquisite renditions of age-old Basque dishes, offered suggestions and a guided tour of San Sebastián's dazzling marketplace, all of which helped me capture Basque cooking at its best. In Albarracín, Pedro Narro of modest El Chorro restaurant explained the secrets of his exceptional stews. And Fray Juan Barrera, director of the dining room at the Guadalupe monastery, graciously provided recipes that display all the refinement and keen culinary sense of Extremadura's legendary monastic cooking.

The impish brothers Antonio and Simón Tomás of Sol-Ric restaurant showed me the best Catalan dishes of the coast of Tarragona; Martí Forcada, owner of Quo Vadis, accompanied me to his favorite stands at the remarkable La Boquería market in Barcelona; and gracious, warmhearted Irene España gave me many of her fine recipes from Casa Irene in the Pyrenees.

Vicentina Gonzalo, cook and co-owner of Casa Julián on the banks of the lovely Cares River, set forth simple dishes based on exceptional Asturian produce, and Emeterio Martín and his wife, Pilar, at Tres Coronas de Silos took me into their rustic kitchen and demonstrated step-by-step the elaboration of a perfect Castilian garlic soup and unraveled some of the mysteries of earthenware cookery.

My friends in Andalucía were, as always, unsparing in their help: Fernando and Paco Hermoso provided some wonderful local dishes that they serve at Casa Bigote in Sanlúcar de Barrameda; Salvador Lucero—a man in a million—showed me how to make the simple yet uncommonly good tapas served at Bar Bahía; Gonzalo Córdoba, a restaurateur with a magic touch, took me into the busy kitchen of El Faro and led me through detailed demonstrations of dishes that interested me; and Paqui and Pepe Delfín, friends of unlimited generosity, imparted their knowledge and enthusiasm for the cooking of their beloved coast of Cádiz.

My husband, Luis, the driving force behind my writing career and my official taster, sampled each and every recipe and provided invaluable suggestions; my parents, Toni and Chick, gave me a lifetime of love and encouragement; my daughter, Elisa, and her husband, Steve, were fountains of insight and sound advice; Marsha—in all but name a family member—was the one I frequently turned to for guidance and good cheer; and Ruby Amelia, although far too young to have made any tangible contribution, will undoubtedly keep the spirit of Spain alive for yet another generation.

My thanks to Rufino López for allowing us to shoot photographs at Solera, his fine New York City restaurant and tapas bar. I thank also my friends and colleagues Pilar Vico and Jeanne Miserendino—my indispensable links to Spain in New York City; Craig Claiborne, who changed the course of my professional life; and Judith Jones, my superlative editor, who has skillfully guided me through four books and is surely the quintessential editor.

INTRODUCTION

Thirty years have passed since I first began to seriously investigate Spanish food and travel, a pursuit that has led me to write two cookbooks and a personal travel guide to Spain. Every time I returned to Spain, however, I realized how much more still needed to be explored, and I was particularly struck by the culinary legacy of Moorish Spain, which was coming to light after centuries of obscurity. Although my previous cookbooks were certainly comprehensive, I found that I had merely scratched the surface and, frankly, had greatly underestimated Spain's gastronomic ingenuity and rich culinary heritage. It was time to put all this fresh information I had found into another book.

With this book, therefore, I hope to attract not only those new to Spanish food but those who consider themselves well versed in the cooking of Spain. I have collected what I consider to be the most exceptional versions of time-honored dishes—the pillars of Spanish cooking—as well as long-forgotten recipes that I have unearthed. For the first time a full chapter is devoted to the cooking of the Canary Islands, a fascinating culinary crossbreed that I find singularly attractive, and another chapter to new tapas recipes—appropriate, I think, for a cookbook about a country in which this form of snacking is an art and where tapas come in endless varieties.

Modern-day Spain began to flourish, both culturally and economically, in the late 1970s and early 1980s, and it was a period of rapid transformation that telescoped decades of world changes, styles, and trends into a few brief years. Traditional ways were often thoughtlessly cast aside in the name of innovation and novelty. But Spaniards soon came to their senses and realized they had gone too far in the name of progress. Today Spain has once more reversed course with a renewed appreciation of its past, and traditional cooking—the very backbone of Spanish life—has made a remarkable comeback. Certainly the creative cooking of talented young chefs, which can be extraordinarily good, is here to stay and, in fact, has been a positive influence on the quality of ancestral dishes. But it is not what this book is about.

In preparing *¡Delicioso! The Regional Cooking of Spain*, I consulted centuries-old cookbooks, prized unpublished family recipe collections, and recipes kept alive in monasteries and convents (traditional repositories of fine eating). I have spoken with home cooks and restaurant chefs who continue to prepare the foods of their forefathers. After all, what is more appealing than the tried and true, the simple, heartwarming, comforting dishes of the past based on lusty Mediterranean flavors? Who indeed can resist a great garlic sauce, an accent of *alioli*, fish perfectly fried or simmered in green sauce, a spectacular paella, a tasty potato omelet (*tortilla*), or a garden fresh gazpacho? And yet the cooking of Spain is so much more. It includes dishes that one might never imagine to be Spanish, long-lost dishes like dried cod with apples, *alioli* and honey, beef stew with melon, and chicken in pomegranate sauce—all part of the sensual, sophisticated cooking of the Moors that is now reemerging and adding complex flavors to traditional fare.

When my first book, *The Foods and Wines of Spain*, was published more than a decade ago, authentic Spanish cooking was virtually unknown in America. The uninitiated automatically associated it with Mexican cooking, and I would grow weary of explaining that Spanish food was not hot and spicy and, in fact, had little in common with Latin American food. Progress has been slow, but it is now possible to find properly prepared paellas in the United States where once there were none, and tapas have been enthusiastically embraced by Americans who are enchanted with this lively Spanish version of grazing. Tapas have become part of our vocabulary, and thankfully I no longer must spell out, as I was compelled to when I wrote *Tapas: The Little Dishes of Spain*, that a tapas bar is quite different from a topless bar. I can only hope that the way we have adopted tapas will soon carry over into other areas of Spanish cooking.

La Buena Mesa: Spain's Good Table

You need look no farther than the humblest family gathering to be impressed by a Spaniard's remarkable appreciation of fine food. Even the most expensive foods are eaten with abandon by those who seem least likely to afford them. Good food and good ingredients are what count in Spain, and if sometimes the cost is high, that is quite irrelevant. *Jamón* (Spanish mountain cured ham), for example, is a national obsession, despite its extravagant price, and Spaniards turn a blind eye to what the freshest fish and shellfish sell for in the marketplace.

Why do Spaniards place such importance on food? Perhaps because eating is an ongoing social affair that provides inordinate pleasure and relaxation, and because Spain's fine foods have always been a tremendous source of pride to Spaniards. Moreover, eating in a leisurely fashion takes up a good part of each day, beginning with breakfast and followed by a midmorning snack and early-afternoon tapas. The workday grinds to a halt for the traditional three-hour lunch that has survived against all odds in an efficiency-oriented world. There are tea and pastries or more tapas in the early evening and dinner at 10:00 p.m.

Even when eating at home Spaniards would not dream of serving just one course. A meal is not a mere necessity to rush through to get on with more important matters. Perhaps it's because we are in such a hurry in America that we heap one plate with a main course, vegetables, and potatoes, whereas in Spain there is always a first course (soup, eggs, salad, or vegetables), followed by a main course that is most often served, even in restaurants, with no garnish. If there is a sauce, bread is used to sop it up. And thus, a Spanish meal, which naturally incorporates lively conversation, stretches out over several hours. When this much time and effort are spent daily in food-related activities, is it any wonder that Spaniards are focused on good food, that they have developed well-tuned palates and are willing to pay for their indulgences?

Spain's road to *la buena mesa* has indeed been a bumpy one. It was the Romans who first brought good eating to Spain, introducing wheat, wine, and olive oil, and the Moors who embellished the foods of Spain with Eastern flavors. However, five centuries ago, when Spain expelled the Moors, food lost a lot of its diversity and excitement. In the spirit of reunification and renewal, the nation sought to eradicate all traces of foreign foods and customs that had dominated the country for almost eight hundred years. As a result food became somewhat plain and unimaginative. Many wonderful dishes based on Eastern flavors disappeared, although fortunately a great deal of the Moorish influence had already been incorporated into Spanish cooking. For example, rice brought by the Moors to Spain had become a diet staple on the eastern coast; lemon and orange trees planted by the Moors thrived; Eastern spices like saffron, anise, sesame seed, nutmeg, and black pepper had become essential to Spanish cooking, and convent nuns became the guardians and promoters of the wonderful Moorish tradition of preparing sweets.

What was lost by the expulsion of the Moors was compensated for in part by the "exotic" foods that began arriving from the newly discovered Americas. Tomatoes, peppers, and potatoes (we can thank Spain for bringing these native American products to the Old World and for their subsequent incorporation into European cuisine) were such a sensation that they were soon considered among the most important ingredients in Spanish cooking. Trendy "fusion cooking" that today excites our taste buds has, in fact, been the very essence of Spanish cooking for almost two thousand years, and when I come across dishes that appear to be inventions of the fertile minds of creative contemporary Spanish chefs, they often turn out to be based on culinary unions from Spain's distant past.

Let's not overlook the effect that Spain's geography and climate have had on Spanish food. From the cool green mountainous north, where cows graze, to the delta lands of the eastern coast that produce rice and wonderful fruits and vegetables, to the high *meseta* of central Spain, where golden wheat waves in the wind and flocks of sheep are an integral part of the landscape, to the arid south, where olive trees yield some of the world's finest olive oils, to the Mediterranean and Atlantic coasts with their incredible diversity of seafood, to the vineyards all across the country that yield quality wines of every description, Spain amazingly compresses the diversity of a continent into a country about the size of Texas.

The mountains that crisscross Spain (it is the most mountainous country in Europe save Switzerland) have isolated one region from another. Without sufficient contact and with differing climates and terrains, styles of cooking and ingredients varied significantly, and that's why it is much more accurate to speak of Spanish cuisines in the plural. Despite modern communication that brings the regions closer together today, food, fortunately, has not become homogenized. It retains its local character, making it all the more important when traveling in Spain to know what to eat and where to eat it. As you will clearly see in each chapter of this book, every culinary region of Spain has different strengths. Thus, one chapter may overwhelmingly concentrate on fish, while another emphasizes meat and beans, and yet another is dominated by rice dishes.

Many of these gastronomic regions cross political boundaries but are united by their foods and their methods of food preparation. As each chapter developed, I could plainly see just what makes each of these food regions unique, and this enabled me to present Spanish food in a fresh light. The traditional Spanish delineations that designate, for example, the northern coast as the Region of the Sauces, Catalunya as the Region of the Casseroles, and the northeastern interior as the Region of the Peppers are, of course, only shorthand expressions to highlight typical cooking styles and local ingredients; certainly such descriptions cannot express the full diversity of the regions' foods.

In each chapter I introduce you to chefs and home cooks whom I admire and respect, as well as to my Spanish friends, to restaurants, both elegant and rustic, that I love, to markets that are sights to behold, and to the exceptional wines of each region. I have also shared with you some of my memorable food experiences. I hope that through these stories you will get a taste of the real Spain and that this book will be for you more than a collection of recipes—it will serve also as a food guide when you travel to Spain. I would have liked nothing better than to tell you everything I know and love about Spain well beyond its food, but, of course, this is a cookbook. For more detailed travel information, I hope you will consult my book *Discovering Spain: An Uncommon Guide*.

I wish you a pleasant journey through Spain by way of its wonderful foods. After all, what better way to understand the heart and soul of a nation than through its cooking? Take a tip from Spaniards and make eating a relaxing, all-enveloping pursuit; learn, as they say in Spain, to *vivir para comer* (live to eat) instead of *comer para vivir* (eat to live), and we will all be the better for it.

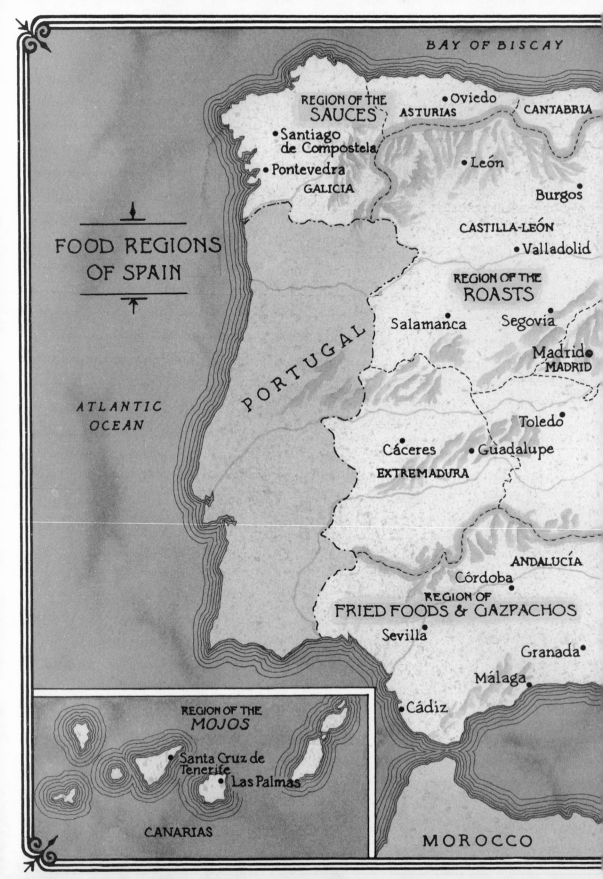

FOOD REGIONS
OF SPAIN

ATLANTIC
OCEAN

BAY OF BISCAY

REGION OF THE
SAUCES

• Oviedo
ASTURIAS   CANTABRIA

• Santiago
de Compostela
• Pontevedra
GALICIA

• León

Burgos •

CASTILLA-LEÓN
• Valladolid

REGION OF THE
ROASTS

Salamanca   Segovia •

Madrid •
MADRID

Toledo •

Cáceres   • Guadalupe
EXTREMADURA

ANDALUCÍA

Córdoba •

REGION OF
FRIED FOODS & GAZPACHOS

Sevilla •

Granada •

Málaga •

• Cádiz

PORTUGAL

REGION OF THE
MOJOS

• Santa Cruz de
Tenerife
• Las Palmas

CANARIAS

MOROCCO

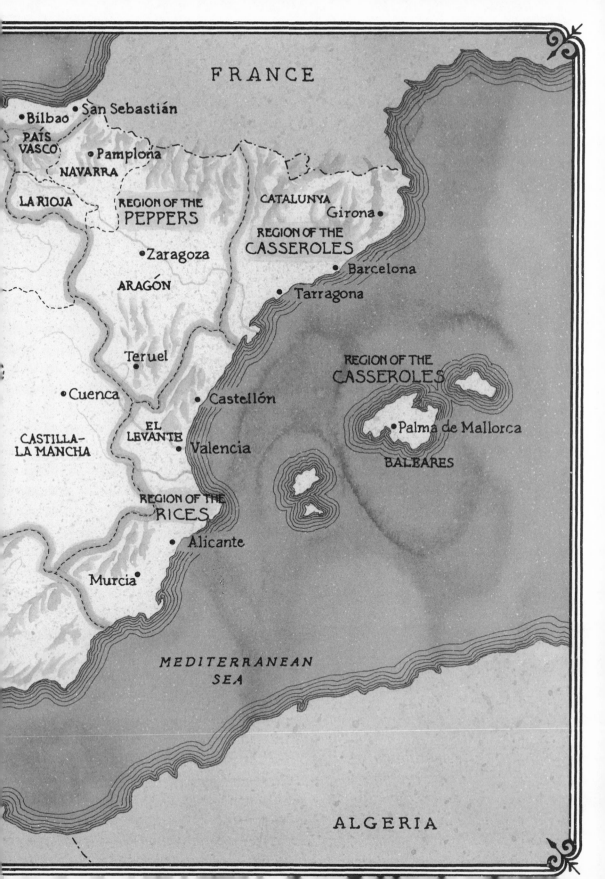

¡DELICIOSO!
THE REGIONAL
COOKING
OF SPAIN

CHAPTER I

Spain

THE COUNTRY OF TAPAS

apas in all their delicious and entertaining variety were fully explored in my book *Tapas: The Little Dishes of Spain*. And yet here I am devoting an entire chapter to them, with some sixty new recipes, proving that tapas are a never-ending feast—there are always new ones to discover. You never know what great tapa you might come across in an unknown bar in the middle of nowhere. That happened to us recently as we were traveling through the desolate Sierra Pobre (Poor Mountains) in the province of Madrid with its slate-roofed "Black Villages." There we found exceptional tapas, such as chorizo simmered in dry sherry, at the only bar in the village of Majaelrayo—in fact, it was the only business of any kind within miles. Or the delicious garlicky fresh pork and ham roll, *flamenquín cordobés*, we ate at an empty bar in the mountains of Córdoba, where, although no tapas were on display, the cook graciously prepared them to order.

Tapas, enjoyed in every region of Spain, are a national pastime; you might say they are a microcosm of traditional Spanish cooking. For those of you not yet acquainted with tapas—even though tapas bars seem to be sprouting up all across the United States—tapas are Spanish-style appetizers that go far beyond dainty little tidbits to accompany an aperitif. They are most often bite-size, but nevertheless may need a dish or small casserole if they are saucy, or perhaps a fork or toothpick. When enough tapas are served and in sufficient variety, they can easily replace a meal, and nothing is more fun—in tapas bars both here and in Spain, or in your very own home—than eating tapas-style.

Tapas represent a Spanish style of living, and there is no better way to partake in the life of the country than by participating in this time-honored tradition. Spaniards love gathering in bars before their hearty lunchtime meal (a three-hour period in which almost all business comes to a halt), and temporarily satisfying their hunger with tapas and a glass of beer, wine, or dry (*fino*) sherry. They meet with friends and associates and vigorously discuss affairs of the day (the decibel level is exceptionally high), denounce the government, tell the latest jokes, and dissect the performances of their favorite soccer players and bullfighters. At the end of the workday (about 8:00 p.m.) the bars fill once more for yet another round of tapas, drinks, and animated conversation.

Spanish cities excel at tapas, and some regions of Spain have stronger tapas traditions than others. In the Basque Country, for example, the tapas are truly mind-boggling, made up of painstakingly assembled mini mountains of ingredients, often speared together with toothpicks. You could spend a lifetime investigating tapas bars in Madrid alone, and Andalucía is undoubtedly tapas heaven. It was in Andalucía that the custom of tapas originated, for tapas are ideal accompaniments to the region's sherries and perfectly suited to the gregarious nature of Andalusians.

Based on healthy robust Mediterranean ingredients, tapas, although in the tradition of "snacking," are a far cry from junk food. Seafood salads, grilled shellfish, meatballs, potato omelets, marinated quail eggs, meat and vegetable turnovers, or tapas as straightforward as slices of nutty Spanish cured ham, tasty chorizo sausage, or unique Manchego cheese are just a few of the tantalizing possibilities.

Tapas served at home may simply accompany drinks, although some make ideal first courses, and a wide array of tapas are delightful as a meal in itself. In this case I suggest you offer tapas prepared in a variety of styles—something marinated, a tapa in sauce, another that is fried or baked, and one that has a bread or pastry base. See how enthusiastically everyone takes to this style of eating and how tapas invariably set the mood for a wonderfully enjoyable and successful party.

ACEITUNAS VERDES ESTILO ANDALUZ
(*Marinated Green Olives, Andalusian Style*)

PREPARE SEVERAL DAYS IN ADVANCE

Fragrant with herbs and spices, these green olives are without equal. The longer they marinate, the tastier they become.   *Makes about 2 cups*

About 8 ounces large green unpitted Spanish olives

¼ cup red wine vinegar

4 cloves garlic, lightly crushed and peeled

2 thin lemon wedges

1 teaspoon coriander seeds, lightly crushed

½ teaspoon ground cumin, preferably freshly ground in a mortar or spice mill

2 sprigs thyme or ½ teaspoon dried

1 sprig rosemary or ¼ teaspoon dried

1 bay leaf

½ teaspoon fennel seeds

A ½-inch piece dried red chile pepper, seeded

Lightly crush the olives with the back of a knife and place them in a jar in which they fit tightly. Add all other ingredients and enough water to cover the olives with the marinade. Close the jar and shake to blend all ingredients well. Leave overnight at room temperature, then refrigerate at least several days. The olives will keep for months. Bring to room temperature before serving.

ACEITUNAS CON MOJO ESTILO CANARIO
(*Black Olives in Paprika and Herb Marinade*)

PREPARE SEVERAL DAYS IN ADVANCE

This marinade is based on the red *mojo* (p. 401) of the Canary Islands, a versatile mix of herbs, oil, vinegar, and paprika that may be a marinade, a sauce, or a dip. Do not use California-style black olives—they are mushy and tasteless. Better to use a black olive that has already been lightly cured in brine.

Makes about 2 cups

Black Olives in Paprika and Herb Marinade (continued)

About 8 ounces unpitted black olives in brine, drained

3 cloves garlic, lightly crushed and peeled

A 1-inch piece, or to taste, dried red chile pepper, seeded and crumbled

1 tablespoon extra virgin olive oil

¼ cup red wine vinegar

¼ teaspoon ground cumin, preferably freshly ground in a mortar or spice mill

1 tablespoon minced oregano leaves or ½ teaspoon dried

1 tablespoon thyme leaves or ½ teaspoon dried

1 tablespoon minced parsley

1 teaspoon imported sweet paprika

Lightly crush the olives with the back of a knife and place in a jar in which the olives fit tightly. Add all other ingredients and enough water to cover the olives with the marinade. Close the jar and shake to blend all ingredients well. Leave overnight at room temperature, then refrigerate at least several days. The olives will keep for months. Bring to room temperature before serving.

ACEITUNAS NEGRAS ALIÑADAS
(Marinated Black Olives)

PREPARE SEVERAL DAYS IN ADVANCE

Although just about all the Spanish olives that come to America are green, black olives are of course also served in Spain as tapas. This well-seasoned marinade is one excellent way to enliven the flavor of black olives.

Makes about 2 cups

About 8 ounces small, unpitted black olives in brine, drained

1 tablespoon imported sweet paprika

1 small onion, slivered

⅓ cup red wine vinegar

2 cloves garlic, lightly smashed and peeled

¼ teaspoon dried oregano

10 peppercorns

1 lemon wedge

1 teaspoon cumin seeds

3 bay leaves

1 sprig rosemary or ¼ teaspoon dried

Few sprigs thyme or ¼ teaspoon dried

2 tablespoons olive oil

Combine all ingredients in a glass jar and add enough water to cover the olives. Shake to blend, then refrigerate for several days (they will keep for several months). Bring to room temperature before serving.

ALMOGROTE DE LA GOMERA
(Red Pepper, Cheese, and Garlic Spread)

A uniquely Canary Island mixture that is delicious simply spread on toasted bread rounds. It is also the accompaniment to Canary-Style Meatballs (p. 60).

Makes about ¾ cup

4 dried sweet red peppers or mild
    New Mexico style, seeded; or
    4 pimientos, finely chopped,
    plus 4 teaspoons paprika
A 1-inch piece, or to taste,
    dried red chile pepper
    seeded and crumbled

2 cloves garlic, peeled
¼ teaspoon salt
6 tablespoons grated cured
    Manchego, goat's milk, or
    Parmesan cheese
¼ cup extra virgin olive oil
Minced cilantro for garnish

Soak the dried peppers in warm water for 30 minutes. Drain and mince.

In a mortar or mini processor, mash to a paste the chile pepper, minced red pepper (or pimiento), garlic, and salt. Transfer to a bowl and stir in the cheese (add the paprika here if using a combination of pimiento and paprika), then gradually add the oil, beating with a fork until smooth. Transfer to a serving bowl in which the spread just fits, smooth the top with a rubber spatula, and sprinkle with cilantro.

QUESO FRESCO CON MOJO DE CILANTRO
(Fresh Cheese in Cilantro and Green Pepper Marinade)

START PREPARATION SEVERAL HOURS IN ADVANCE

An uncommonly good tapa for a party. The mild flavor of the cheese combines beautifully with the garlicky marinade in which the flavor of fresh cilantro predominates.

Serves 8–10

Fresh Cheese in Cilantro and Green Pepper Marinade (continued)

¾ cup Mojo de Cilantro
  (p. 402)
1 pound fresh cheese with a
  solid consistency, such as

fresh mozzarella or mild
goat cheese, cut in 1-inch
cubes

In a bowl gently mix together the Mojo de Cilantro and the cheese. Refrigerate several hours or overnight. Serve chilled or at room temperature.

CREMA DE CABRALES
(Blue Cheese, Apple, and Walnut Spread)

Cabrales, the assertive blue cheese of Asturias, is a classic tapa, especially when accompanied by Asturian hard apple cider. This tapa combines the cheese with apples, walnuts, and raisins and is excellent spread on crackers.

Makes enough for 16 canapés

2 teaspoons raisins
1 tablespoon medium-sweet
  sherry (*oloroso*)
¼ pound Cabrales or other blue
  cheese, at room temperature
1 tablespoon cream
2 tablespoons finely chopped
  apple

1 tablespoon finely chopped
  walnuts
1 tablespoon chopped pine nuts
¾ teaspoon thyme leaves or
  ⅛ teaspoon dried

Soak the raisins in the sherry for 20 minutes. Drain the raisins and reserve the sherry.

In a bowl, mash together the cheese, cream, and reserved sherry until smooth. Stir in the raisins, apple, walnuts, pine nuts, and thyme. Serve at room temperature.

BUÑUELOS DE QUESO Y SÉSAMO
(Cheese and Sesame Seed Puffs)

According to L. Benavides Barajas, an expert on the foods of Moorish Al-Andalus, cheese puffs such as these, coated with sesame seeds, used to be served at elaborate Moorish banquets in Sevilla. They are just as elegant today.

Makes about 16

2 tablespoons sesame seeds
½ cup plus 2 tablespoons flour
½ teaspoon baking powder
¼ teaspoon imported sweet
  paprika
⅛ teaspoon salt
Freshly ground pepper
2 eggs, separated
3 ounces Spanish Tetilla or

Fontini cheese, grated or
  finely chopped (about 1 cup)
2 tablespoons grated cured
  Manchego or Parmesan
  cheese
Oil for frying, preferably mild
  olive oil
Untoasted sesame seeds for
  coating

Lightly toast the sesame seeds on a foil-lined cookie tray in a 350°F oven for about 5 minutes.

Mix together the flour, baking powder, paprika, salt, and pepper to taste. In another bowl, beat the egg whites until stiff but not dry. Stir in the cheeses, egg yolks, sesame seeds, and the flour mixture.

Drop by rounded tablespoons onto a cookie tray lined with foil and chill until firm.

Pour the oil into a skillet to a depth of at least 1 inch (or better still, use a deep-fryer) and heat until the oil quickly browns a cube of bread. Roll the puffs in sesame seeds and fry until golden. Drain on paper towels and serve.

BERENJENA REBOZADA A LA MORISCA
(Coriander-Scented Batter-Fried Eggplant)

Eggplant, as old as civilization itself, was introduced to Spain from the Far East by the Moors, who favored it in their cooking. It continued to be an important ingredient in medieval times and appears in the sixteenth-century cookbook of Ruperto de Nola (see page 154), seasoned with such Moorish flavors as ginger, coriander, cloves, and nutmeg. In this batter-fried preparation it is the Moorish touch of crushed coriander seed that brings the mild-flavored eggplant to life.   *Serves 6*

¾ pound very small eggplants,   Kosher or sea salt
   unpeeled, in ½-inch cross-
   wise slices

BATTER

1 egg   Salt
¼ cup dry white wine   Freshly ground pepper
½ cup seltzer water   1 tablespoon minced cilantro or
1 cup flour   parsley
1 small clove garlic, mashed to   1½ teaspoons crushed corian-
   a paste   der seeds

· · ·

Oil for frying, preferably mild olive oil

GARNISH

Crushed coriander seeds   1 tablespoon minced cilantro

Arrange the eggplant slices in layers in a colander, salting each layer well. Leave for 15 minutes, then drain and dry on paper towels.

Meanwhile, in a bowl whisk together the egg and wine. Stir in the seltzer, flour, garlic, salt and pepper to taste, fresh cilantro, and coriander seeds.

Pour the oil into a skillet to a depth of at least 1½ inch (or better still, use a deep-fryer) and heat until the oil quickly browns a cube of bread. Dip the eggplant slices in the batter (if the batter has become too thick, thin with a little water until it has the consistency of a thin pancake batter) and drop into the hot oil. Fry until the eggplant is cooked and golden, turning once. (Fry in several batches if necessary.) Drain on paper towels, sprinkle with the crushed coriander seeds and fresh cilantro, and serve right away.

BROCHETA DE CHAMPIÑONES CON JAMÓN Y ALIOLI
(Grilled Mushrooms with Cured Ham and Garlic Mayonnaise)

Mushrooms, Spanish mountain cured ham, and garlicky mayonnaise combine to create an irresistible mixture of flavors. Use 7- to 8-inch skewers and serve one to a person, with a dollop of garlic mayonnaise on the side—essential to making this simple tapa something special. Homemade *alioli* is of course best, but if you begin with a good-quality commercial mayonnaise and improve it by whisking in a little extra virgin olive oil, mashed garlic, and some lemon juice, the results will be excellent. *Serves 6*

24–30 small cultivated mushrooms, stems removed, brushed clean
¼ pound Spanish mountain cured ham, capicollo, or proscuitto, sliced ⅛ inch thick, then cut into 1-inch squares
Extra virgin olive oil
Kosher or sea salt
½ recipe *Alioli* (p. 302)

Thread the mushrooms, alternating them with pieces of ham, onto 7- or 8-inch skewers. Brush well on all sides with olive oil.

Grease a stovetop griddle with olive oil and heat to the smoking point. Place the skewers on the griddle, lower the flame to medium-high, and cook until the mushrooms have softened and browned, turning and brushing with olive oil occasionally. Sprinkle with salt and serve right away, accompanied by the *alioli*.

CHAMPIÑONES Y GAMBAS A LA PLANCHA
(Sautéed Mushrooms and Shrimp)

Quick and easy to prepare with simple ingredients, but the flavor blend of mushrooms, shrimp, garlic, and parsley is outstanding. *Makes 8*

Sautéed Mushrooms and Shrimp (continued)

1 tablespoon olive oil	Salt
1 large clove garlic, minced	Freshly ground pepper
8 medium-large cultivated mushrooms, caps only, brushed clean	8 small-medium shrimp, shelled
	1 tablespoon minced parsley

In a skillet, heat the oil and lightly sauté the garlic. Remove the garlic and divide among the mushroom caps, pressing into their hollows. Sauté the mushrooms, cap side down, over a medium flame for a few minutes until brown; sprinkle with salt and pepper. Turn the mushrooms and sauté on the other side until done to taste, then turn the mushrooms again, being careful to keep the garlic in the cap. Remove to a warm platter. Scoop up any garlic left behind in the skillet and return to the mushroom caps.

Raise the heat, season the shrimp with salt, and sauté until just done, about a minute or two. Place a shrimp atop each inverted mushroom cap, securing with a toothpick. Sprinkle with parsley and serve.

ESPINACAS CON GARBANZOS A LA SEVILLANA
(Spinach and Chickpeas, Sevilla Style)

Spinach was eaten in Moorish Andalucía (the Spanish word *espinaca* is in fact of Arab origin) and has been a popular green ever since, especially in Sevilla, where when combined with chickpeas it is a staple of tapas bars. Of course, the combination is also excellent for dinner to accompany meat, poultry, or fish.

Serves 4–5

½ pound spinach leaves	¾ cup cooked chickpeas, home-made or canned
2 tablespoons olive oil	
A ¼-inch slice of bread cut from a long narrow loaf	1 teaspoon thyme leaves or ⅛ teaspoon dried
2 cloves garlic, peeled	1 teaspoon minced oregano leaves or ⅛ teaspoon dried
⅛ teaspoon salt	
½ teaspoon wine vinegar	1 teaspoon minced rosemary leaves or ⅛ teaspoon dried
¼ teaspoon imported sweet paprika	

¼ teaspoon ground cumin,
preferably freshly ground in
a mortar or spice mill

A 1-inch piece, or to taste,
dried red chile pepper,
seeded

Wash the spinach, drain well, and tear into pieces. Place in a microwave dish, cover, and cook on high 4 minutes (or simmer about 10 minutes in a pot of water on the stove). Drain and chop finely.

Heat 1 tablespoon of the oil in a skillet. Sauté the bread and garlic until they are golden on all sides. Transfer the bread and garlic to a mortar or mini processor. Add the salt and vinegar and mash to a paste.

Add the remaining oil to the skillet and heat. Quickly sauté the spinach, then add the paprika, chickpeas, the bread-and-garlic mixture, the thyme, oregano, rosemary, cumin, and chile pepper. Cook a minute, adding a little water if the mixture seems too dry. Let sit 10 minutes to blend flavors, then serve hot or at room temperature.

ENSALADA ANDALUZA DE TOMATE, ATÚN, Y PIMIENTOS
(Tomato, Tuna, and Pimiento Salad)

A delicious and refreshing blend of flavors, either as a tapa or to complement a light summer meal.   *Serves 4–6*

2 tablespoons flaked light-meat
tuna
8 small cured black olives
1 pound ripe and flavorful
tomatoes, in a ¾-inch dice
2 tablespoons chopped
pimiento, preferably homemade (p. 178) or imported
2 cloves garlic, minced

¼ cup fruity extra virgin olive
oil
4 teaspoons wine vinegar,
preferably white
Half of a small onion, slivered
Salt
Freshly ground pepper
¼ teaspoon sugar

Tomato, Tuna, and Pimiento Salad (continued)

Gently combine all ingredients in a bowl with a rubber spatula. Refrigerate 20 minutes before serving, mixing occasionally.

TORTILLA DE PATATA JOSÉ LUIS
(Potato Omelet José Luis)

José Luis is a famous tapas bar in Madrid that has been fashionable for decades and specializes in somewhat upscale and refined tapas. The man behind the name, José Luis Ruiz de Solaguren, is the reason for the bar's long-term success, for he is an energetic and indefatigable public relations man who knows how to please his clientele.

Among the elegant canapés of smoked fish, caviar, and cheese is his now-legendary potato omelet, which in fact has exactly the same ingredients as any other potato omelet, but somehow tastes even better. I remember once flying to New York with José Luis; he had brought along a meal from his restaurant that he shared with us and that included this *tortilla*. We were the envy of every Spaniard on that flight.

Serves 8–12 for tapas, 4 for supper

¾ cup olive oil

1 medium onion, very finely chopped

4 medium-large baking potatoes, peeled, in ⅛-inch slices

Salt

5 large eggs

Heat the oil in an 8- or 9-inch skillet until just hot enough to sizzle a piece of onion, and cook the onion very slowly for about 20 minutes (alternatively, the onion can be sliced and cooked with the potato without discarding). Skim off the onion and discard. Add the potato slices one at a time, making layers and salting each layer lightly. Cook slowly (in effect, "simmering" the potatoes in the oil) until the potatoes are tender (they should not brown),

(continued on page 16)

The Versatile *Tortilla Española:* A Culinary Work of Art

Spaniards have an ongoing love affair with their *tortilla española*, a potato omelet that has nothing in common with a Mexican tortilla except its name, which refers to its round shape. It is the most versatile dish imaginable, equally appropriate for breakfast, lunch, and dinner or for the tapas hour, cut either in wedges or in small squares. Its ingredients are simply potatoes, eggs, olive oil, salt, and sometimes onion, and yet there is something about the mixture and the way it is cooked that makes *tortilla española* an object of adoration among Spaniards. "It doesn't seem possible that something as simple as this can be a work of art," gushes one Spanish food writer. Indeed, I know many Americans who are also addicted to the Spanish *tortilla* and make it their weekly Sunday evening supper.

The mundane name "potato omelet" does little justice to this exceptional creation. Although the quality of ingredients (eggs from free-range hens, potatoes from Galicia, the sweetest onions, and the finest olive oil) and the personal touch of each cook can make the difference between good *tortilla* and one that is splendid, in all my years of sampling *tortillas* across Spain I have never found one I didn't like.

Tortilla is made with everyday ingredients, but the method of preparation is somewhat unusual, so follow the instructions carefully. In deference to so many of you who dislike frying, I have achieved very good results by roasting the potatoes, as in Patatas Panaderas (page 247), with slivered onions, and removing the potatoes from the oven when they are cooked but not brown. Any self-respecting Spaniard would be horrified by such unorthodoxy, and I must admit that I prefer the time-honored method. But by whatever means, be sure to try this very special dish. *Tortilla* may be eaten hot, but to my taste it improves immeasurably if cooled to room temperature and is at its best when allowed to sit a few hours before serving.

Potato Omelet José Luis (continued)

lifting and turning them as they cook (this may also be done in the basket of a deep-fryer, or see box, p. 15, for oven-roasting alternative). Drain in a colander and pat with paper towels. Reserve about 2 tablespoons of the oil. Wipe out the skillet and scrape off any stuck particles.

In a large bowl, lightly beat the eggs with a fork and add some salt. Add the potatoes and press with the back of a slotted pancake turner to immerse them in the egg. Let sit at room temperature about 10 to 15 minutes.

Heat 2 teaspoons of the reserved oil in the skillet to the smoking point. Add the potato mixture all at once and press with the back of a pancake turner to spread the mixture evenly in the skillet. Lower the heat to medium-high and cook until the *tortilla* is lightly brown underneath, shaking constantly.

Slide the *tortilla* onto a dish, cover with a second dish, and invert. Add another teaspoon or so of reserved oil to the skillet, heat again to the smoking point, slide in the *tortilla*, and continue to shake the pan until the *tortilla* has browned on the other side, tucking in any rough edges with the back of the pancake turner. Turn the *tortilla* twice more, to perfect its shape and cook it a little more (about 30 seconds on each side). It should remain juicy within. Cut into wedges or 1½-inch squares that can be speared with toothpicks. Serve warm or at room temperature (it can be made several hours in advance).

TORTILLA DE PATATA CON AJO Y PEREJIL
(Potato Omelet with Garlic and Parsley)

Although the additions of garlic and parsley to a traditional Spanish potato omelet may seem unremarkable, this is, in fact, a significant departure in a dish that, no matter where you eat it in Spain, varies only in the use of onion. Garlic and parsley make this *tortilla* subtly different.   *Serves 8–10*

½ medium onion, finely chopped

4 medium-large baking potatoes, peeled, in ⅛-inch slices

¾ cup olive oil
5 large eggs
Salt

1 clove garlic, minced
2 tablespoons finely chopped
    parsley

Sauté the onion and potatoes in the oil as described in the first paragraph of the previous recipe.

In a large bowl lightly beat the eggs with a fork and add salt to taste. Stir in the garlic and parsley. Add the drained potatoes, pressing the potatoes with the back of a pancake turner to completely immerse them in the egg. Let sit 10 to 15 minutes.

Finish cooking the *tortilla* as described in the previous recipe.

TORTILLA A LA NAVARRA
(Potato Omelet with Ham and Mint)

This version of *tortilla* from Navarra introduces two unusual elements—mountain cured ham and mint—that give it a unique flavor.

Serves 4–6

1 small onion, very finely
    chopped
4 medium-large baking pota-
    toes, peeled, in ⅛-inch slices
¾ cup olive oil for frying
5 large eggs
Salt

2 ounces mountain cured ham,
    finely diced
2 cloves garlic, minced
2 tablespoons minced parsley
1½ teaspoons chopped mint
    leaves or ¼ teaspoon dried

Sauté the onion and potatoes in the oil as described on page 14.

In a large bowl, lightly beat the eggs and a little salt with a fork, add the drained potatoes, ham, garlic, parsley, and mint, pressing the potatoes with the back of a pancake turner to completely immerse them in the egg. Let sit 10 to 15 minutes.

Finish the *tortilla* as described on page 16.

TORTILLA DE PATATA Y PLÁTANO
(Potato and Banana Omelet)

A close cousin to the traditional Spanish potato omelet but with a pleasant hint of sweetness, as is so often the case in Canary Island cooking. The Canaries, with their year-round crops, supply Spain with many fruits and vegetables, but principally with bananas. In the Gran Rey valley on the island of La Gomera the veritable carpet of banana trees is especially impressive. So it is not unusual that the islands, in their typically crossbred culinary style, would find a way to adapt the classic Spanish potato omelet to their native crops.

The Canary Islands grow a banana variety that is very small, firm, and sweet. Bananas of this kind are often available at your greengrocer, so use them if possible.   *Serves 4–6*

3 tablespoons olive oil
1 medium potato, peeled, cut in
   ½-inch cubes
Salt
¼ pound semi-ripe bananas,
preferably baby bananas,
peeled and cut in ⅛-inch
slices
4 eggs

In an 8-inch skillet, heat the oil to the smoking point; add the potato cubes and stir to coat with the oil. Sprinkle with salt and sauté the potatoes over a medium flame, stirring occasionally, until tender, about 15 minutes. Remove the potatoes from the oil, drain on paper towels, and reserve.

In the same oil, lightly brown the bananas. Drain on paper towels. Leave about 2 teaspoons of oil in the skillet and scrape off any stuck particles with a pancake turner.

In a bowl, with a fork lightly beat the eggs and add salt to taste. Stir in the potatoes and let sit 5 minutes. Stir in the bananas. Heat the oil remaining in the skillet until very hot. Quickly pour in the egg mixture and distribute evenly in the skillet. Lower the heat to medium and cook, shaking constantly until lightly browned underneath. Slide onto a plate, cover with a second plate, and invert.

If no oil remains in the skillet, add 1 more teaspoon, then slide the omelet back into the hot skillet. Lightly brown, tucking in any rough edges with the back of a pancake turner. The omelet should remain juicy within. Cut in wedges or small squares and serve warm or at room temperature.

HUEVOS DE CODORNIZ EN SALPICÓN
(Marinated Quail Eggs)

START PREPARATION SEVERAL HOURS IN ADVANCE

Hard-boiled marinated quail eggs, popular in Andalucía, are a unique and indeed delicious tapa. The eggs are usually available at Oriental markets.

Serves 6

2 dozen quail eggs

SALPICÓN DRESSING

6 tablespoons olive oil
1 tablespoon wine vinegar,
    preferably white
1 tablespoon sherry vinegar
5 tablespoons chopped dill or
    cornichon pickle
2 tablespoons drained small
    whole nonpareil capers or
    chopped larger capers

2 tablespoons minced onion,
    preferably Spanish or
    Vidalia
2 tablespoons chopped
    pimiento, homemade
    (p. 178) or imported
1 tablespoon minced parsley
Salt
Freshly ground pepper

Place the quail eggs in a saucepan with cold water to cover, bring to a boil over medium heat, and cook 4 to 5 minutes. Run under cold water, then shell, removing all membrane.

To make the Salpicón Dressing, whisk together in a large bowl the oil and vinegars, then stir in the remaining ingredients. Gently fold in the quail eggs and refrigerate several hours, or overnight.

PATATAS ALIÑADAS
(Potato Salad)

These marinated potatoes, scattered with onion, sliced egg, and tuna (light-meat tuna gives more flavor than white), are an exceptionally refreshing addition to any tapas menu. Or they may accompany a summer meal—perhaps simply grilled or broiled meat or fish. Other possible additions are diced tomato and diced or thinly sliced green pepper.   *Serves 6–8*

3 tablespoons flaked canned
  light-meat tuna
2 tablespoons plus ¾ teaspoon
  wine vinegar
2 pounds new or red waxy
  potatoes
6 tablespoons extra virgin
  olive oil

Salt
Freshly ground pepper
2 hard-boiled eggs
2 tablespoons minced parsley
Half of a small onion, slivered

In a small bowl combine the tuna with ¾ teaspoon of the vinegar. Boil the potatoes in salted water until tender. Cool briefly, peel, then cut in ¼-inch slices.

In a small bowl whisk together the oil, the remaining 2 tablespoons vinegar, salt, and pepper. Mash 1 hard-boiled egg yolk and stir into the vinaigrette. Thinly slice the egg white and the remaining hard-boiled egg.

Arrange the potatoes in 2 layers in a shallow serving bowl, sprinkling each layer with parsley, onion, tuna, the sliced egg, salt, and pepper. Drizzle the vinaigrette over the potatoes and serve chilled or at room temperature.

ENSALADILLA RUSA
(Potato and Vegetable Salad)

Why this potato salad, enlivened with bits of egg, tuna, and colorful vegetables, which has been around as long as anyone can remember, is called Russian Salad is mystifying, for it could not be more Spanish (for political purposes its name was temporarily changed by Franco's followers during the Civil War to National Salad). You can find it at almost any tapas bar; it is also a fine accompaniment to a summer barbecue.

Serves 6

1¼ pounds red waxy potatoes,
  peeled and cut in ½-inch
  cubes

2 medium carrots, trimmed,
  scraped, and cut in ½-inch
  cubes

3 tablespoons minced pimiento, homemade or imported

2 tablespoons chopped green olives

¼ cup cooked peas

3 tablespoons flaked white or light-meat tuna

1 hard-boiled egg, chopped

2 tablespoons finely chopped dill pickle

2 tablespoons extra virgin olive oil

1½ teaspoons wine vinegar

Salt

Freshly ground pepper

½ cup mayonnaise, preferably homemade (p. 302; omit garlic), thinned with water to the consistency of a thick sauce

GARNISH

Pimiento strips
Egg wedges

Thin radish and carrot slices

Over medium heat, cook the potatoes and carrots in salted water, covered, for 12 minutes, or until both are just tender. Drain, refresh with cold water, and drain again well.

In a large bowl, with a rubber spatula gently combine the minced pimiento, olives, peas, tuna, chopped egg, and pickle with the potatoes and carrots. In a cup whisk together the oil, vinegar, salt, and pepper. Fold into the potato mixture and let sit 20 minutes. Fold in the mayonnaise and transfer to a serving platter.

Garnish attractively with the pimiento strips, egg wedges, radish and carrot slices. Chill. Remove from the refrigerator a few minutes before serving—this is best if not too cold.

HOJALDRE DE QUESO Y COMINO
(Cheese and Cumin Puffs)

A delicate and delicious tapa, ideal as party finger food. Vary the amount of cumin to taste—the cheese mixture should be very well seasoned.

Makes about 16

Cheese and Cumin Puffs (continued)

1 pound puff pastry, preferably homemade (recipe follows)

¼ pound Spanish Mahón or Fontini cheese, finely grated

1 tablespoon ground cumin, preferably freshly ground in a mortar or spice mill

Freshly ground pepper

Refrigerate the puff pastry until ready to use. Mix together the grated cheese, cumin, and pepper.

Roll the puff pastry ⅛ inch thick and cut out 1½-inch circles. Place 1 teaspoon of the cheese mixture in a mound in the center of half of the pastry rounds. Wet the edges with water and cover with a second circle of pastry. Press the edges together well with your fingers then crimp with a fork (do a few at a time, keeping the remaining circles chilled—they must not soften if they are to puff properly).

Arrange the filled pastries on a cookie tray and place on an upper rack of a 425°F oven. Bake about 6 minutes, until brown. Turn off the oven and leave the pastries in the oven for a few minutes to dry the inner layers of pastry. Serve warm.

HOJALDRE
(Puff Pastry)

I have never found an easier or more foolproof way of preparing puff pastry than this method devised by Julia Child. If you do not need the full amount for a recipe, keep the rest well wrapped in your freezer for future use.   *Makes 2¾ pounds*

3 cups unbleached all-purpose flour

1 cup cake flour

1½ teaspoons salt

6½ sticks chilled unsalted butter

1 cup iced water

Mix together the all-purpose and cake flours. Stir in the salt. Cut the sticks of butter in half lengthwise, then in half again lengthwise. Now cut into ½-inch cubes and add to the flour. Rub the cubes of butter between your fingers to flatten them into flakes, incorporating them at the same time into the flour. Refrigerate the mixture 10 minutes (the butter must be kept firm throughout the process). Add the cold water and stir until the dough roughly holds together.

Turn the dough onto a lightly floured work surface. Pat into a rectangle about 18 inches long and 8 inches wide. Sprinkle the top of the dough with flour. With the aid of a pastry scraper or a wide thin knife, fold one side over the top, then fold over the other side, business-letter fashion. Lift the dough, flour the work surface again, flour the top of the dough, then roll out with a rolling pin to the previous size, making the folded sides the width and the open ends the length. (All this must be done quickly—if the butter softens, refrigerate briefly before proceeding.) Fold up a second time in the same manner, roll out again, then repeat 2 more times, flouring surfaces as necessary and ending with the dough folded. Enclose in plastic wrap and refrigerate 40 minutes. Roll and fold twice more. The dough is now ready to use or to store in the refrigerator or freezer.

BUÑUELOS DE PATATA
CON ANCHOA Y ACEITUNAS
(Potato Puffs with Anchovy and Olive)

Makes about 14

2 medium baking potatoes
2 teaspoons olive oil
2 anchovy fillets, finely
   chopped
1 hard-boiled egg, finely
   chopped
1 tablespoon finely chopped
   pimiento-stuffed green
   olives
¼ teaspoon baking powder
4 tablespoons (¼ cup) grated
cured Manchego or Parmesan cheese
2 tablespoons minced parsley
Salt
Freshly ground pepper
Dash of grated nutmeg
1 egg
Dried bread crumbs
Oil for frying, preferably mild
   olive oil

Boil the potatoes in salted water until tender. Peel and pass through a ricer or strainer into a bowl. Mix in the oil, anchovy, hard-boiled egg, olives, baking powder, cheese, parsley, salt, pepper, nutmeg, and the uncooked egg. Chill. Shape into 1½-inch balls and coat with bread crumbs. Pour the oil into

Potato Puffs with Anchovy and Olive (continued)

a skillet to a depth of at least 1 inch (or better still, use a deep-fryer) and heat until the oil quickly browns a cube of bread. Fry potato balls until golden on all sides. Drain on paper towels and serve right away.

PAN CON TOMATE MALLORQUÍN
(Mallorcan Seasoned Bread)

Here is a somewhat embellished version of the Catalan Pa amb Tomàquet (p. 179), which comes from Mallorca and includes olives, capers, thyme, and slices of tomato. It makes a wonderful tapa or accompaniment to a meal.

Serves 4–6

¾-inch-thick slices of country
    bread, cut from a large
    round loaf
½ pound ripe and flavorful
    tomatoes, skinned and cut in
    very thin slices
Fruity extra virgin olive oil

Kosher or sea salt
2 tablespoons minced cured
    black olives
½ teaspoon minced capers
1 tablespoon thyme leaves or
    ½ teaspoon dried

Cut the bread slices in half crosswise and place on a cookie sheet. Bake in a 350°F oven about 3 minutes on each side, or until the bread is crisp but not brown. Cool.

Arrange the tomato slices over the bread and press with a spatula to release the juices into the bread. Drizzle with olive oil and sprinkle with salt.

In a cup, mix together the olives, capers, and thyme and scatter the mixture over the bread.

PINCHO DE TOMATE
(Fresh Tomato and Cilantro Canapé)

START PREPARATION 1 HOUR IN ADVANCE

This uninvolved tapa was passed on to me by a Spanish food fan who lives in Atlanta. To be really good, your tomatoes must be very flavorful. Do not assemble until ready to serve or the tomato mixture will soften the toast.

Makes 20–24

6 cloves garlic, minced
5 tablespoons extra virgin olive oil
2 teaspoons sugar
3 tablespoons sherry vinegar
8 fresh plum tomatoes, peeled, seeded, and chopped

Salt
Freshly ground pepper
1 tablespoon minced cilantro
1 long narrow bread loaf, in ¼–½-inch slices
Minced cilantro for garnish

In a small bowl combine the garlic and olive oil and let sit 1 hour.

In another bowl, dissolve the sugar in the vinegar, then stir in the tomatoes, salt, pepper, and the tablespoon of minced cilantro. Remove 1 teaspoon of minced garlic from the oil and garlic mixture and stir into the tomatoes. Let sit 20 minutes. Meanwhile, toast the bread slices in a 350°F preheated oven for about 8 minutes, or until golden, turning once.

Brush one side of the bread slices with the oil and garlic mixture. Spoon the tomato mixture onto the bread, sprinkle with cilantro, and serve.

ZAPATILLA CON JAMÓN, AJO, Y TOMATE
(Flat Yeast Bread with Mountain Cured Ham, Garlic, and Tomato)

This delicious tapa is made with a flattened, elongated bread that in some gourmet shops in Madrid is also known as *chapata*. If you don't want to bake your own bread (the recipe, however, is extremely simple) use a good foccacia—not quite the same but an adequate substitute. *Serves 8–10*

Flat Yeast Bread (continued)

1 loaf *ʒapatilla* (p. 256)
2 large cloves garlic, peeled and
cut in half crosswise
About 5 paper-thin tomato
slices, cut from a very ripe
and flavorful medium-large
tomato

Fruity extra virgin olive oil
Several very thin slices Spanish
mountain cured ham or
prosciutto

Slice the bread loaf through the middle, turn the sliced sides up, and rub them with the cut garlic cloves. Arrange the tomato slices in a single layer on one side of the bread. Drizzle with the olive oil and top with 2 layers of ham. Cover with the other bread half and cut crosswise into 1½- to 2-inch-wide pieces.

CANAPÉ DE CEBOLLA FAÍN
(Onion Canapé Faín)

We have stayed at Cortijo Faín (see p. 392) on numerous occasions, but it was on my annual tour to Spain with a group of Americans that Faín's gracious owner, Soledad Gil, treated us to a cocktail party at which this excellent tapa was served.   *Makes 12*

2 very small onions, about
2 ounces each, peeled

Olive oil for brushing

WHITE SAUCE

3 tablespoons butter
3 tablespoons flour
6 tablespoons milk
6 tablespoons chicken broth
½ teaspoon lemon juice

Salt
Freshly ground pepper
Generous grating of nutmeg

· · ·

Twelve 1¾-inch bread rounds
cut from firm-textured
sandwich bread

Grated cheese (Manchego or
Parmesan), about 6 table-
spoons

Place the onions in a small baking dish, brush with oil, and bake at 375°F for 40 minutes. Cool and slice in ¼-inch rings.

To make the White Sauce, melt the butter in a saucepan, stir in the flour, and cook a minute or so. Add the milk, chicken broth, lemon juice, salt, pepper, and nutmeg (it should be very well seasoned). Cook, stirring constantly, until the sauce is thickened and smooth. Cool, stirring occasionally.

In a 350°F oven lightly toast the bread for about 5 minutes. Place the sliced onion on the bread rounds, top with about 2 teaspoons of the sauce, and sprinkle each with about ½ teaspoon cheese. Run under the broiler, about 2 inches from the flame, for about 1 minute, or until lightly golden.

TOSTADAS DE ESCALIVADA Y GARUM

(Roasted Vegetable Canapés with Anchovy and Olive Paste)

Garum, an extraordinary blend of anchovy, garlic, capers, and olives that came to Spain by way of the early Romans, gives extra zip to this canapé of peppers, eggplant, and tomato.   *Makes 8–10*

1 red bell pepper
A ¾-pound eggplant
1 small tomato, halved
Salt
Freshly ground pepper
1 tablespoon thyme leaves or
    ½ teaspoon dried

1 tablespoon fruity extra virgin
    olive oil
Eight to ten ½-inch bread slices
    cut from a long narrow loaf

GARUM

8 anchovy fillets, minced
2 cloves garlic, minced
2 teaspoons capers

12 cured black olives, minced
¼ teaspoon sherry vinegar
1 teaspoon extra virgin olive oil

· · ·

Thyme leaves or chopped
    parsley for garnish

Roasted Vegetable Canapés (continued)

Arrange the red pepper, eggplant, and halved tomato in a roasting pan and cook in a preheated 500°F oven, turning the pepper and eggplant once, for about 20 minutes, or until the skin of the pepper browns and separates from the flesh. Cool. Peel, core, and seed the pepper. Peel the eggplant, cut in half lengthwise, and scrape out most of the seeds, then dice the pepper and eggplant. Chop the tomato, removing as much skin as possible. Mix all the vegetables together in a bowl with salt, pepper, thyme, and the tablespoon of olive oil.

Arrange the bread slices on a cookie sheet and toast in a preheated 350°F oven for about 5 minutes, or until crisp but not brown. Place the ingredients for the Garum in a mortar or a mini processor and mash to a paste. Spread the Garum on the bread slices, spoon the vegetable mixture on top, and garnish with thyme.

CANAPÉ DE ESCALIVADA
(Roasted Vegetable Canapé)

A tapa that is just vegetables with a touch of fine olive oil. Healthy, low in calories, and simple to prepare, the vegetable mixture is spread on rounds of raw zucchini instead of bread.   *Serves 6*

1 small eggplant (about ½ pound)	1 tablespoon minced parsley
1 red bell pepper	1 teaspoon thyme leaves or ⅛ teaspoon dried
1 green bell pepper	Kosher or sea salt
1 medium onion, peeled	Freshly ground pepper
1 tablespoon fruity extra virgin olive oil	1 large zucchini, skin on, in ⅛-inch crosswise slices
Freshly squeezed lemon juice	

Arrange the eggplant, red and green peppers, and onion in a roasting pan. Roast in a 500°F oven for about 20 minutes, turning the eggplant and peppers once. Cool. Skin, core, and seed the peppers. Peel the eggplant, cut in half lengthwise, and scrape out most of the seeds. Cut the peppers, eggplant, and onion roughly into julienne strips about 1 inch long. Place in a bowl and gently mix in the olive oil, a few squeezes of lemon juice, the parsley, thyme, salt, and pepper.

Lightly sprinkle the zucchini rounds with salt and let sit a few minutes. Top the zucchini rounds with the vegetable mixture. Serve at room temperature.

PINCHO DE LANGOSTINO Y HUEVO
(Shrimp, Anchovy, and Egg on Garlic Toast)

I offer this typically Basque tapa, or *pincho*, as representative of the mind-boggling array of similarly delicious tapas in bars all over the Basque Country, but especially in San Sebastián. *Pinchos* usually begin with a small slice of bread, upon which such ingredients as shellfish, hard-boiled egg, and vegetables are piled high and held together with a toothpick. Vary this prototype as you wish—possible additions or substitutions are sliced pickles, olives, crabmeat, tomato, and pimiento.   *Makes 8 canapés*

2 tablespoons olive oil	8 anchovy fillets, cut in halves
2 cloves garlic, mashed to a	crosswise
paste	8 medium shrimp, cooked and
Eight ¼-inch bread slices cut	shelled
from a long narrow loaf	4 teaspoons mayonnaise
2 hard-boiled eggs	4 teaspoons minced parsley

Combine the olive oil and garlic and brush both sides of the bread slices with this mixture. Place the bread slices on a cookie tray and bake at 350°F, turning once, about 8 minutes, or until lightly browned. Cool.

Cut 1 egg into thin slices. Finely grate the other egg. Arrange two pieces of anchovy on each slice of bread. Cover with an egg slice, then the shrimp and a daub of mayonnaise. Sprinkle with the grated egg and the parsley.

TOSTADAS DE ANCHOA
(Anchovy Toasts)

Garlic, olive oil, and pimientos are the ideal complements to the strong salty taste of anchovy. The proportions in this recipe are elastic, but good-quality anchovies—firm and not overly salty—are important. I find those that are sold in small jars rather than tins are generally superior.

Makes 12 canapés

3 tablespoons fruity extra virgin olive oil
1 large clove garlic, crushed to a paste
Twelve ⅜–½-inch-thick bread slices cut from a long narrow loaf

24 small anchovy fillets
Pimientos, preferably imported or homemade (p. 178), in short thin strips
3 tablespoons minced parsley

Mix the olive oil and garlic together in a small bowl or cup. Place the bread slices on a cookie tray in a 350°F oven and bake about 5 minutes, turning once. They should be crusty but not browned. Cool and brush with the garlic and oil.

Place 2 anchovy fillets over each bread slice, topped with the pimiento strips, which should crisscross the anchovies. Sprinkle with the parsley.

CANAPÉ DE ANCHOA Y AGUACATE
(Anchovy and Avocado Canapé)

The assertive taste and firm texture of anchovy is the perfect foil for avocado, which is soft and somewhat bland. This is a house appetizer at El Drago, one of the finest restaurants in the Canary Islands, located in an old country house near Tegueste on the island of Tenerife.

Quantities are somewhat elastic; they can be varied according to taste and to the number of canapés needed.   *Makes 6 canapés*

1 tablespoon extra virgin olive oil

1 clove garlic, mashed to a paste

Six ¼-inch bread slices cut from a long narrow loaf

Mayonnaise

6 avocado rounds, about ⅛ inch thick, cut from very small avocados (the rounds should be about the same size as the bread slices)

6 pieces lettuce to fit the bread rounds

6 anchovy fillets, cut in halves crosswise

1 hard-boiled egg, finely grated

1 tablespoon minced parsley

Combine the oil and garlic in a cup and brush on both sides of the bread slices. Place on a cookie tray and bake at 350°F about 8 minutes, turning once, until lightly toasted. Cool.

Spread some mayonnaise on each bread round; follow with an avocado round, lettuce, and 2 anchovy halves. Sprinkle with the egg and parsley.

COCARRONS DE ESPINACA
(Spinach Turnovers)

These turnovers closely resemble the delicious ones I tasted from a fine bakery, Forn Fondo, in Palma de Mallorca. They were made with greens similar to collard greens, combined with raisins and pine nuts, perfumed with mint, and enclosed in a slightly sweetened dough. Although here I have recommended spinach, which is the most common filling for these turnovers in Catalunya, they are equally good made with other greens.

Makes about 30

Turnover Dough (p. 48),
    made with 1½ teaspoons
    sugar
2 tablespoons raisins
2 tablespoons olive oil
1 medium onion, finely
    chopped
2 cloves garlic, minced
¾ pound spinach leaves, well
    dried, finely chopped (or
    trimmed and finely chopped
    collard greens, escarole, or
    Swiss chard)

Salt
Freshly ground pepper
½ teaspoon imported sweet
    paprika
2 tablespoons minced parsley
1½ teaspoons minced mint
    leaves or ¼ teaspoon dried
2 tablespoons chopped pine
    nuts
1 egg, lightly beaten with
    1 teaspoon water

Prepare the Turnover Dough according to directions. Soak the raisins in warm water. Heat the oil in a skillet and sauté the onion and garlic for a minute or two. Cover and cook over low heat for 10 minutes more. Raise the heat, add the spinach, salt, pepper, paprika, parsley, mint, pine nuts, and the drained raisins, and cook 5 minutes more.

Roll out and fill the Turnover Dough as described on page 48. Brush with the beaten egg. Bake on a lightly greased cookie sheet in a preheated 350°F oven 15 to 20 minutes, or until golden.

Down with Gritty Mussels and Clams!

Many Spanish dishes, especially those from the Basque Country, incorporate live mussels and clams directly into a sauce; to avoid sand particles in your sauces (and we all know what an unpleasant experience that can be), it is of utmost importance that these mollusks be grit-free before cooking. Here is a simple procedure—just be sure to purchase your mussels and clams a day in advance.

Scrub and rinse the clams and/or mussels well and remove the beards from the mussels. Make sure all the shells close tightly without much coaxing. Mollusks that begin to relax their muscles may still be alive and not harmful to eat, but they acquire an off taste and odor. Any that refuse to close with gentle pressure must be discarded. Place the mollusks in a bowl and cover with salted cold water. Sprinkle about 1 tablespoon cornmeal or flour over the surface and refrigerate at least several hours, but preferably overnight. Rinse well, then proceed with any recipe that calls for mussels or clams.

ALMEJAS A LA MARINERA
(Clams in Garlic and Wine)

Here is one of the most classic Spanish tapas, found all around Spain's coastline and always outstanding. The main variable is the kind of clam used, but always use the smallest clam you can find. In Andalucía the dish is made with *coquinas* (bean clams), so tiny that dozens easily enter into a portion and can be eaten with such ease that the shells will be piled high in no time. The sauce is exceptional for bread dunking. *Serves 6–8*

Clams in Garlic and Wine (continued)

3 tablespoons olive oil
½ cup finely chopped onion
3 cloves garlic, minced
48 cockles or Manila clams, or
    24 very small littlenecks,
    thoroughly cleansed (p. 33)
½ cup dry white wine
1 bay leaf

3 tablespoons minced parsley
A 1-inch piece dried red chile
    pepper, seeded and
    crumbled
1 tablespoon freshly squeezed
    lemon juice
Several strands of saffron
Diluted clam juice or water

Heat the oil in a skillet and slowly sauté the onion and garlic until the onion is softened. Add the clams and cook over a high flame, shaking the pan constantly for a minute or two. Add the wine and cook most of it away. Reduce the flame to medium-high, add the bay leaf, 2 tablespoons of the parsley, the chile pepper, lemon juice, and saffron. Cook, stirring and removing the clams to a warm platter as they open, adding clam juice or water if necessary to keep some sauce in the pan. Return all the clams to the pan, sprinkle with the remaining parsley, and serve.

ALMEJAS EN SALSA DE ALMENDRA
(Clams in Almond Sauce)

Despite his somewhat patrician appearance, Herb Livesey—a first-class travel writer—likes his pleasures down-to-earth. He has taken on the daunting project of restoring a centuries-old house in the quaint village of Calaceite in Aragón and loves to spend his free time in the region. Since he has no intentions of writing a cookbook, he graciously sent me one of his favorite recipes from Bar Manolo in the nearby village of Horta de Sant Joan (which happens to be just over the border in the region of Catalunya). These clams in a delicious sauce of almonds and garlic make a wonderful tapa.

Serves 4

Three ½-inch slices bread cut
    from a long narrow loaf
20 blanched almonds

8 cloves garlic, peeled
4 tablespoons (¼ cup) minced
    parsley

Salt

2 tablespoons plus ½ teaspoon olive oil

2 cloves garlic, lightly smashed and peeled

1 cup Fish Broth (p. 175) or ¾ cup clam juice diluted with ¼ cup water

A generous grinding of pepper

½ teaspoon imported sweet paprika

3 dozen cockles or Manila clams, or 1½ dozen very small littlenecks, thoroughly cleansed (see p. 33)

Place the bread and almonds on a cookie sheet in a 350°F oven. Toast the bread until golden and crisp, about 10 minutes, and the almonds until golden, about 5 minutes. Cool.

In a mortar or mini processor, mash to a paste the 8 cloves peeled garlic, parsley, almonds, bread, ⅛ teaspoon salt, and the ½ teaspoon oil. Reserve.

In a large skillet or earthenware casserole, heat the remaining oil with the smashed garlic cloves, pressing the garlic with the back of a wooden spoon to extract its flavor. When the garlic has browned, discard. Add to the skillet the Fish Broth, pepper, and paprika. Stir in the mortar mixture, add the clams, and bring to a boil. Simmer until the clams have opened. Cover and let sit 10 minutes before serving.

ALMEJAS CON AJO Y PEREJIL
(Steamed Clams on the Half Shell with Garlic and Parsley)

Here is yet another way—from the Canary Islands—to give a great garlicky taste to clams.   *Serves 4*

A ½-inch piece, or to taste, dried red chile pepper, seeded

2 tablespoons olive oil

2 cloves garlic, minced

1 tablespoon minced parsley

¼ teaspoon lemon juice

2 tablespoons dry white wine

1 dozen very small littleneck clams, thoroughly cleansed (see p. 33)

Soak the chile pepper briefly in warm water to soften, then slice in the thinnest possible rings.

In a small skillet, slowly heat the oil with the garlic and chile pepper.

Steamed Clams on the Half Shell (continued)

When the garlic just begins to color, add the parsley, lemon juice, and wine. Cook away the wine.

Place the clams in a large skillet with ¼ cup water. Cover and cook over medium-high heat, removing the clams as they open. Add 1 tablespoon of the pan liquid to the garlic mixture. Discard half the clam shells, leaving the clam meat in the half shell. Spoon the garlic mixture over the clams and serve right away.

LAPAS CON MOJO GRATINADAS
(Limpets with Green Mojo)

Limpets—mollusks with a single shell, the open side of which clings to rocks—are common in the Canary Islands. They find little acceptance elsewhere in Spain, but I really enjoyed them in these two versions I tasted in Lanzarote and Tenerife. Here I have substituted clams in the half shell for the limpets, and both versions—the first using chopped clams mixed with bread crumbs, the second leaving the clam meat whole—use a tasty green *mojo* sauce as seasoning.

Chopped Stuffed Clams with *Mojo*

Serves 4

1 dozen small-medium littleneck clams
4 tablespoons Mojo de Cilantro
   (p. 402) or Mojo Verde de
   Perejil (p. 402)

4 tablespoons (¼ cup) dried
   bread crumbs

Place the clams in a skillet with ¼ cup water. Cover and cook over a high flame until the clams open, removing each clam as it opens. Separate the shells, remove the meat, and discard half of the shells. Mince the clam meat and in a bowl stir it together with the *mojo* and bread crumbs. Fill the 12 shells with the mixture and brown in a 450°F oven for about 10 minutes.

Broiled Clams on the Half Shell with *Mojo*

Serves 6

1 dozen small-medium little-
    neck clams
2 tablespoons Mojo de Cilantro

(p. 402) or Mojo Verde de
    Perejil (p. 402).
Dried bread crumbs

Open the clams and loosen the clam meat in each half shell, leaving it in the shells. Spoon ¼ teaspoon *mojo* over each clam. Sprinkle with bread crumbs and run under a broiler, very close to the flame, until the crumbs are browned.

TIGRES

(Stuffed Mussels with Shrimp)

START PREPARATION AT LEAST 2 HOURS IN ADVANCE

For some inexplicable reason, this exceptional shellfish tapa is typical of landlocked La Rioja and called a "tiger." The mussel shells in this version are filled with a well-seasoned mixture of chopped mussels and shrimp, then coated with a white sauce, breaded, and fried until crisp and golden. I can guarantee it will be a big hit at any tapas party.

    Tigres can be prepared in advance—indeed, they get better when made a day ahead—but bread and fry them only when ready to serve.

Makes about 14–16

1 dozen medium-size mussels,
    thoroughly cleansed (see
    p. 33)
1 tablespoon olive oil
½ cup very finely chopped
    onion
2 cloves garlic, minced
2 tablespoons minced parsley
¼ pound shrimp, shelled and
    finely chopped

2 tablespoons minced Spanish
    mountain cured ham or
    prosciutto
½ teaspoon imported sweet
    paprika
¼ teaspoon crushed red pepper
    flakes
Salt
Freshly ground pepper

Stuffed Mussels with Shrimp (continued)

WHITE SAUCE

2 tablespoons butter
1 tablespoon oil
4 tablespoons (¼ cup) flour
½ cup milk
½ cup reserved mussel broth

2 teaspoons lemon juice
Salt
Freshly ground pepper
Dash of nutmeg

. . .

1 cup dried bread crumbs
1 tablespoon grated cured
   Manchego or Parmesan
   cheese

2 eggs, lightly beaten with
   1 teaspoon water
Oil for frying, preferably mild
   olive oil

Place the mussels in a skillet with ¾ cup water and bring to a boil. Lower the heat to medium, cover, and cook, removing the mussels as they open. Reserve ½ cup of the mussel broth. Separate the mussel meat from the shell and chop finely. Save 16 half shells.

In a small skillet, heat the oil and sauté the onion, garlic, and parsley for 1 minute. Cover and cook very slowly 15 minutes. Turn up the flame and add the chopped mussels and shrimp. Cook a minute or two, stir in the ham, paprika, and red pepper flakes, and cook a minute more. Season with salt and pepper (it should be very well seasoned) and fill each reserved mussel shell with about 2 teaspoons of the mussel mixture.

To make the White Sauce: in a saucepan, melt the butter with the oil, stir in the flour, and cook 1 minute. Gradually add the milk, reserved mussel broth, and lemon juice. Season with salt, pepper, and nutmeg and cook over a medium flame, stirring constantly, until the sauce is thickened and smooth and begins to bubble. Cool, stirring occasionally.

Cover the mussels with a layer of White Sauce (about 1 tablespoon for each mussel), using the cupped side of a small spoon to bring the sauce to the edges and seal in the filling. Place on a cookie tray and refrigerate at least 2 hours, but preferably overnight.

Combine the bread crumbs and grated cheese. Dip the mussels in the beaten egg, then coat on all sides with the bread crumb mixture. Pour the oil into a skillet to a depth of at least 1 inch (or better still, use a deep-fryer) and heat until the oil quickly browns a cube of bread. Fry the mussels filled side down, until they are golden. Drain on paper towels and serve right away, or keep briefly in a 200°F oven.

GAMBAS A LA PLANCHA
(Grilled Shrimp, Spanish Style)

An ideal way to prepare shrimp, split lobster, or langoustines. Even if the shellfish has been frozen, this cooking method produces succulent full-flavored shellfish that has the taste of the grill although you may have cooked it in a skillet.   *Serves 4*

½ pound extra-large shrimp in their shells, heads on, if possible

Kosher or sea salt
Extra virgin olive oil
Freshly squeezed lemon juice

Sprinkle the unshelled shrimp on both sides with the salt and drizzle with oil. Let sit 15 minutes.

Coat a griddle or skillet with oil and heat to the smoking point. Grill the shrimp a minute or so, turning once. Sprinkle with lemon juice and cook briefly, until the shrimp have just become opaque within. Serve immediately.

GAMBAS AL AJILLO
(Garlic Shrimp)

Shrimp in garlic sauce is among the most classic Spanish tapas and admits very few variations without compromising its wonderful simplicity. When using frozen shrimp (most shrimp in fish markets have been frozen and defrosted) it is important to salt the shrimp and let them sit a few minutes before cooking to bring back their briny flavor. Garlic shrimp are typically cooked and served in individual shallow earthenware casseroles, but they can just as well be prepared in a common casserole or skillet.

Serves 4–6

Garlic Shrimp (continued)

½ pound small shrimp, shelled
Kosher or sea salt
¼ cup extra virgin olive oil
3 cloves garlic, peeled and
    coarsely chopped

1 small bay leaf
A 1-inch piece dried red chile
    pepper, seeds removed
1 tablespoon minced parsley

Sprinkle the shrimp on both sides with salt. Let them sit at room temperature for about 15 minutes.

In a small shallow casserole (preferably Spanish earthenware—see p. 168), combine the oil, garlic, bay leaf, and chile pepper and sauté over a medium-high flame until the garlic just begins to color. Add the shrimp and cook, stirring, until the shrimp are just done, about a minute or two (if the shrimp have turned opaque at the center, they are sufficiently cooked). Sprinkle with parsley and serve immediately in the casserole dish, accompanied by good crusty bread for dunking.

SALPICÓN DE MARISCO LA TRAINERA
(Shellfish Vinaigrette)

PREPARE SEVERAL HOURS IN ADVANCE

Shellfish simply marinated in vinaigrette is a staple at tapas bars where seafood is served and is one of my favorite tapas. This version from one of Madrid's finest seafood restaurants, La Trainera, was glisteningly fresh and uncommonly good. We always order it as a tapa for the table when we dine at La Trainera, although it also makes a terrific first course. Be sure the crabmeat you use is real crab—not the mix of crab, fish, and seasonings that often passes for crab.

Serves 4

1 recipe Fish Broth (p. 175)
    increasing the water to 9
    cups, or 7 cups clam juice
    diluted with 3 cups water
    and seasoned like the Fish
    Broth

A 1½-pound live lobster
¾ pound large shrimp in their
    shells

MARINADE

9 tablespoons fruity extra virgin olive oil
3 tablespoons white wine vinegar
1 tablespoon reserved broth
¼ teaspoon Dijon-style mustard
Salt
2 tablespoons diced tomato
2 tablespoons chopped dill
   pickle

2 tablespoons chopped Vidalia
   or Spanish onion
2 tablespoons chopped pimiento,
   preferably imported or
   homemade (p. 178)
2 tablespoons minced hard-
   boiled egg
1 tablespoon minced parsley

. . .

½ pound cooked chunk
   crabmeat

Bring the Fish Broth to a boil. Add the lobster, upside down and head first, return to the boil, and cook about 10–15 minutes. Transfer to a platter. Add the shrimp to the fish broth and cook very briefly until they just turn opaque. Drain and cool the shrimp, reserving 1 tablespoon of the fish broth for the marinade. (Save the rest of the broth, if you wish, for some other use.) Shell the lobster and cut into chunks. Shell the shrimp.

To make the Marinade: in a large bowl, whisk together the oil, vinegar, tablespoon of reserved broth, mustard, and salt. Stir in the tomato, pickle, onion, pimiento, egg, and parsley. Add the lobster, shrimp, and crab, cover, and refrigerate several hours. Serve chilled or at room temperature.

TORTILLITAS DE CAMARONES
(Shrimp Pancakes)

START PREPARATION 3 HOURS IN ADVANCE

Thin, crisp, and totally irresistible, these pancakes, typical of the province of Cádiz, are especially delicious in this version from owner and chef Natividad Mateos of Los Remos restaurant in Algeciras. Besides the typical ingredients of shrimp and onion, Natividad adds the special touch of chickpea flour to give additional flavor and crispness and seaweed to accentuate the taste of the sea. If you can find tiny shrimp, such as those that would be used in the south of Spain, leave them whole. If fresh seaweed is available, by all means use it, but dried seaweed, found in Oriental markets, produces excellent results.   *Makes 30*

½ cup flour	½ pound shrimp, shelled and
½ cup chickpea flour, or	chopped
another ½ cup flour	3 tablespoons crumbled dried
1 cup water	seaweed or ¼ pound fresh
¼ cup minced onion	1 teaspoon salt, or to taste
2 tablespoons minced parsley	Olive oil for frying

In a bowl, whisk together the flours and water until smooth—the mixture should have a thin pancake consistency. Stir in the onion, parsley, shrimp, seaweed, and salt. Let stand at least 3 hours in a cool place.

Thin the batter, if necessary, to its original consistency. Pour the oil to a depth of ¼ inch into a large skillet, and heat to the smoking point. Drop the batter by the tablespoon into the oil, spreading and pricking with the edge of a spoon into thin, lacy-textured pancakes. Fry until golden underneath, then flip to the other side. Drain on paper towels. Keep warm in a 200°F oven while preparing the rest of the pancakes.

Fried Squid

Here are three different ways to fry squid, all excellent but each slightly different. Squid in beer batter has a thicker coating that becomes very crisp. Those that are dipped in egg before coating with flour acquire a faint eggy taste, while those dipped just in flour (or flour mixed with a little cornmeal to make the flour more like that used in Spain) have the purest taste. Small thin-fleshed squid will produce the best results.

CALAMARES FRITOS, ESTILO CANARIO
(Fried Squid in Egg and Flour Coating)

Serves 4–6

1 pound cleaned (see p. 81)
    small, thin-fleshed squid
    with tentacles
Kosher or sea salt
2 eggs, lightly beaten with
    1 teaspoon water

¾ cup flour
Oil for frying, preferably mild
    olive oil
1 lemon, cut in wedges

Cut the squid body in ½-inch rings. If the tentacles are large, cut in half lengthwise. Sprinkle with salt and let sit 10 minutes. Dip the squid in the egg, then coat with flour. Pour oil into a skillet to a depth of at least 1 inch, and heat to the smoking point (or better still, use a deep-fryer on its highest setting). Fry very quickly—less than a minute—or the squid will toughen. Drain on paper towels and serve immediately, accompanied by lemon wedges.

CALAMARES FRITOS, ESTILO ANDALUZ
(Fried Squid in Flour Coating)

Serves 4–6

1 pound cleaned (see p. 81)
    small, thin-fleshed squid
    with tentacles
½ cup flour
¼ cup cornmeal

Salt
Oil for frying, preferably mild
    olive oil
1 lemon, cut in wedges

Cut the squid body in ½-inch rings. If the tentacles are large, cut in half lengthwise. Combine the flour and cornmeal.

    Wet the squid with water, sprinkle with salt, then coat with the flour mixture. Pour oil into a skillet to a depth of at least 1 inch, and heat to the smoking point (or better still, use a deep-fryer on its highest setting). Fry very quickly—less than a minute—or the squid will toughen. Serve with lemon wedges.

CALAMARES REBOZADOS
(Batter-Fried Squid)

Serves 4–6

1 pound cleaned (see p. 81) small, thin-fleshed squid with tentacles

Kosher or sea salt

BATTER

1 egg, lightly beaten
¾ cup beer
1 cup flour
1 clove garlic, crushed to a paste

1 tablespoon minced parsley
Salt

. . .

Oil for frying, preferably mild olive oil

1 lemon, cut in wedges

Cut the squid body in ½-inch rings. If the tentacles are large, cut in half lengthwise. Sprinkle the squid with salt and let sit 10 minutes.

In a bowl beat together the egg and beer with a fork, then gradually add the flour. Stir in the garlic and parsley and salt to taste.

Place all of the squid rings in the batter and leave them there 15 minutes. Pour oil into a skillet to a depth of at least 1 inch, and heat to the smoking point (or better still, use a deep-fryer on its highest setting). Remove the squid from the batter piece by piece and quickly transfer to the hot oil. Fry very quickly—less than a minute—or the squid will toughen. Serve with lemon wedges.

CALAMARES EN ADOBO
(Marinated Squid)

START PREPARATION 45 MINUTES IN ADVANCE

A preparation typical to the Canary Islands, these squid have a pleasant, slightly chewy texture and great flavor that comes from a mixture of garlic, paprika, vinegar, and oregano. Serve hot or at room temperature. For an authentic Canary Island presentation, accompany with "Wrinkled" Potatoes (p. 409)—delicious dipped in the squid sauce. *Serves 6*

4 cloves garlic, peeled
A 1-inch piece dried red chile pepper, or to taste, seeded and crumbled
⅛ teaspoon salt
1 tablespoon imported sweet paprika
6 tablespoons olive oil
6 tablespoons wine vinegar

1½ teaspoons minced oregano leaves or ¼ teaspoon dried
2 tablespoons minced parsley
1½ pounds small cleaned (see p. 81) squid, with or without tentacles
¾ cup clam juice diluted with ¼ cup water

In a mortar or mini processor, mash to a paste the garlic, chile pepper, and salt, then stir in the paprika, oil, vinegar, oregano, and parsley.

Split the squid lengthwise, then cut into ¾-inch strips. If using the tentacles, split lengthwise. Place the squid in a shallow flameproof casserole, stir in the mortar mixture, and marinate about 45 minutes.

Add the clam juice to the casserole and bring to a boil. Cook uncovered over medium heat until the squid is tender and most of the liquid consumed, about 30 minutes (if the liquid is gone but the squid is not done, add a little water; if the squid is done and there is still too much liquid, boil it away). Salt to taste, cover, and let sit 10 minutes before serving.

CALAMARES A LA PARRILLA EN VINAGRETA
(Grilled Squid in Vinaigrette)

This wonderful tapa can be prepared in no time—just whisk together the vinaigrette ingredients and very quickly grill the squid. The squid should be as small as possible—select those with bodies under 3 inches long

Serves 5–6

VINAIGRETTE

¼ cup extra virgin olive oil
4 teaspoons wine vinegar
2 cloves garlic, crushed to a
    paste

2 tablespoons minced parsley
Salt
Freshly ground pepper
Pinch of sugar

. . .

18 very small cleaned (see
    p. 81) squid, with or without
    tentacles

Kosher or sea salt

In a small bowl, whisk together the Vinaigrette ingredients. Sprinkle the squid with salt and let sit 10 minutes.

    Brush a stovetop griddle with olive oil and heat to the smoking point. Place the squid on the griddle and cook over very high heat about 1 minute, turning once (longer cooking will toughen them). Transfer to a serving platter and pour on the dressing, gently mixing to coat the squid.

PESCADO EN ADOBO (BIENMESABE)
(Marinated Fried Fish)

START PREPARATION 1 DAY IN ADVANCE

The people of Cádiz like to live in the streets. Although we have been visiting our friends Paqui and Pepe Delfín in Cádiz for the past fifteen years we had never before eaten in their home—a classic townhouse in the Old Quarter of the city that has been in Paqui's family for generations. Pepe loves to cook, and that summer Sunday morning he was out bright and early to the market. With an expert eye bred of a lifetime of eating fish in a city where life seems to revolve around fish, he made his selection for our meal. Pepe, despite being in his middle years, retains the cherubic rosy-cheeked face of a bouncing baby and a boyish enthusiasm for his beloved city and its remarkable seafood.

Simplicity is the key to Andalusian cooking and great care is taken never to mask the pure taste of just-caught seafood. The feast that Pepe prepared showed just that; it included succulent grilled prawns that had all the taste of the sea, and this marinated fried fish (he made it with fresh tuna), both of which typify Cádiz cookery. *Serves 4–5*

1 pound fresh tuna, shark, or swordfish steaks, 1 inch thick, cut into 1-inch cubes	1 bay leaf, crumbled
	Salt
	Flour for dusting
1 tablespoon wine vinegar	Oil for frying, preferably mild olive oil
2 cloves garlic, crushed to a paste	
2 tablespoons minced oregano leaves or 1 teaspoon dried	

In a bowl, combine the fish with the vinegar, garlic, oregano, and bay leaf. Cover and marinate in the refrigerator overnight.

Drain. Sprinkle the fish with salt and dust with flour. Pour the oil into a skillet to a depth of at least 1 inch (or better still, use a deep-fryer) and heat until the oil quickly browns a cube of bread. Fry the fish until just done—it should not take more than 5 minutes. Drain on paper towels and serve right away.

EMPANADILLAS DE ATÚN
(Tuna Turnovers)

Since these savory turnovers, combining canned tuna with pimiento, tomato, and lots of onion, do not require any special regional ingredients, you will find them in tapas bars all over Spain. They are typically fried (and better that way because the tuna does not cook) but may also be baked on a lightly greased cookie sheet in a 350°F oven, brushed with beaten egg, for 15 to 20 minutes, or until golden.   *Makes about 20*

TURNOVER DOUGH

½ cup olive oil
4 tablespoons (¼ cup) melted
    lard or vegetable shortening

½ cup water
2½ cups flour
⅛ teaspoon salt

. . .

2 tablespoons olive oil
1 medium onion, finely
    chopped
½ cup finely chopped pimiento,
    preferably homemade
    (p. 178) or imported
½ pound tomatoes, skinned,
    seeded, and finely chopped
Salt

Freshly ground pepper
1 tablespoon minced parsley
Few strands of saffron,
    crumbled
A 6½-ounce can light-meat
    tuna packed in oil, drained
    and flaked
Oil for frying

To make the Turnover Dough, mix well in a bowl all the ingredients. Turn out onto a floured board and pat into a ball. Cover with plastic wrap and reserve at room temperature while preparing the filling.

Heat the oil in a skillet and sauté the onion for a minute. Lower heat, cover, and continue cooking very slowly for 10 minutes. Turn up the flame to medium-high, add the pimiento, tomatoes, salt, pepper, parsley, and saffron; sauté 2 minutes, then cover and continue cooking over low heat for about 30 minutes. Stir in the tuna and let cool.

Roll the dough out on a floured board to the thinness of a nickel and cut into rounds of about 3¼-inch diameter. Place a tablespoon of filling in the center of each round, bring up the sides, and press the edges of the dough together lightly. Now place the turnover flat on the work surface and press the edges with a fork to seal well.

Pour the oil into a skillet to a depth of at least 1 inch (or better still, use a deep-fryer) and heat until the oil quickly browns a cube of bread. Fry the turnovers, turning once, until golden. Drain on paper towels.

EMPANADILLAS DE ATÚN CON PIÑONES
(Tuna Turnovers with Pine Nuts)

Here's another version of tuna turnovers, which includes minced hard-boiled egg and pine nuts. *Makes 20*

Turnover Dough (p. 48)
2 tablespoons olive oil
1 medium onion, finely
   chopped
¾ cup finely chopped pimiento,
   preferably imported or
   homemade (p. 178)
2 tablespoons minced parsley
Salt
Freshly ground pepper

3 tablespoons finely chopped
   pine nuts
A 6½-ounce can light-meat
   tuna, drained and flaked
¼ teaspoon imported sweet
   paprika
1 hard-boiled egg, finely
   chopped
1 egg, lightly beaten

Have the Turnover Dough prepared and rolled into a ball. In a skillet, heat the oil, sauté the onion for a minute or two, then cover and cook over a low flame for 15 minutes (the onion should not brown). Add the pimiento, parsley, salt, pepper, and pine nuts. Cover and cook 10 minutes more. Turn off the heat and stir in the tuna, paprika, and hard-boiled egg. Cool.

Roll out the dough; fill and fry the *empanadillas* according to the instructions in the preceding recipe. Or brush with the egg and bake in a 350°F preheated oven for 15 to 20 minutes, or until browned.

ATÚN EN ESCABECHE EL CAMPESINO
(Marinated Tuna El Campesino)

El Campesino restaurant on the Canary Island of Lanzarote was designed by surrealist artist and native son César Manrique, who dedicated his life to enhancing this fascinating volcanic, lava-strewn island. A starkly white undulating creation, trimmed in "Lanzarote green," El Campesino, besides being a good restaurant, features artisans at work, demonstrating their skills and selling their wares.

I particularly enjoyed this marinated fresh tuna that is not at all saucy, but very tender and unusually flavorful.

Serves 6 for tapas, 4 for dinner

1½ pounds fresh tuna steaks, in 1-inch cubes

Kosher or sea salt

¼ cup extra virgin olive oil

12 cloves garlic, peeled

½ teaspoon cumin seeds or ground cumin

2 tablespoons minced parsley

6 tablespoons Fish Broth (p. 175) or 4 tablespoons clam juice diluted with 2 tablespoons water

1 small onion, slivered

1 small green frying pepper, cored, seeded, and cut in ½-inch strips

½ teaspoon imported sweet paprika

2 teaspoons wine vinegar

1 tablespoon thyme leaves or ½ teaspoon dried

1 bay leaf

1½ teaspoons minced oregano leaves or ¼ teaspoon dried

10 peppercorns

Sprinkle the fish cubes all over with salt. Let sit 10 minutes. Heat 1 tablespoon of the oil in a skillet, sear the tuna, and remove to a warm platter. Wipe out the skillet, heat another tablespoon of the oil, and add the garlic. Give the garlic cloves a turn in the oil, without browning, and transfer to a mortar or mini processor. Add to the mortar ⅛ teaspoon salt, the cumin, and the parsley and mash to a paste. Stir in the broth.

Reheat the skillet and sauté the onion and green pepper until softened. Add the mortar mixture, the paprika, vinegar, thyme, bay leaf, oregano, and peppercorns. Stir in the remaining 2 tablespoons olive oil. Cover and cook slowly 5 minutes. Add the fish, cover, and cook 2 minutes more. Turn off the heat, cover, and let sit a few minutes, turning the fish occasionally in the sauce. Serve at room temperature, or reheat.

TORTILLITAS DE BACALAO SALVADOR
(Salvador's Cod Pancakes)

START PREPARATION 2–3 DAYS IN ADVANCE

The talented Salvador Lucero of Bar Bahía in Cádiz never ceases to surprise me with new dishes—always uncomplicated and uncommonly good—such as these crisp pancakes that are relatively light on cod but filled with plenty of parsley and onion. You could make them with fresh fish, but you would lose the special flavor that dried cod gives. *Makes about 24*

¼ pound boneless dried salt cod
Few strands of saffron
1 medium red onion, very
    finely chopped
4 tablespoons (¼ cup) minced
    parsley
1 clove garlic, minced

½ cup chicken broth
1¼ cups seltzer water
Salt
2 cups flour
Olive oil for frying

Soak the cod in cold water to cover in the refrigerator for 2 to 3 days (changing water once or twice daily), until desalted to taste. Drain the cod and chop finely. Steep the saffron in 1 tablespoon warm water for 10 minutes.

In a bowl, combine the cod, onion, parsley, garlic, saffron (with the liquid), chicken broth, seltzer, and salt to taste. Gradually stir in the flour. Cover and let sit at room temperature about 2 hours.

Thin the batter, if necessary, to its original consistency. In a large skillet, pour the oil to a depth of ¼ inch, and heat until very hot. Add the batter by heaping tablespoons, spreading and pricking with the edge of a spoon into thin, lacy-textured pancakes. Fry the pancakes until well browned on both sides. Drain on paper towels and serve (they can be kept warm for a few minutes in a 200°F oven).

BUÑUELOS DE BACALAO CON ALIOLI
(Cod and Potato Fritters with Alioli)

START PREPARATION 2–3 DAYS IN ADVANCE

The somewhat strong flavor of cod is tempered in this tapa by the addition of potato. This is an exceptional tapa to which an *alioli* dip contributes a burst of garlic. If you don't make your own garlic mayonnaise (although you can do so in a matter of minutes) use a good commercial brand and add a little extra virgin olive oil, lemon juice, and mashed garlic to taste. A *romesco* sauce is also a great accompaniment.   *Makes 50*

1 pound dried boneless salt cod
2 teaspoons olive oil
3 cloves garlic, minced
¾ pound baking potatoes, peeled and quartered
¾ cup flour
2 eggs, separated

⅛ teaspoon baking powder
2 tablespoons minced parsley
Salt
Oil for frying, preferably mild olive oil
½ recipe *Alioli* (p. 302) and/or Salsa Romesco (p. 169)

Cover the cod with cold water and soak in the refrigerator for 2 to 3 days, changing the water once or twice daily, until desalted to taste. Drain.

In a small skillet, heat the 2 teaspoons oil and the garlic and sauté slowly until the garlic just begins to color. Reserve. Boil the potatoes in salted water to cover until tender. Remove the potatoes from the water, bring the water to the boil again, and add the cod. When the water once more reaches the boil, remove and drain the cod and chop coarsely. Transfer the cod to a processor and blend until very finely chopped. Add the potatoes, the sautéed garlic (with its oil), the flour, egg yolks, baking powder, and parsley and blend well. Salt to taste.

In a bowl, beat the egg whites until stiff but not dry. Add to the cod mixture and pulse to blend. Pour the oil into a skillet to a depth of at least ½ inch (or better still, use a deep-fryer) and heat until the oil quickly browns a cube of bread. Drop by tablespoons into the hot oil, and fry until golden on all sides. Drain on paper towels and serve with *alioli* and/or *romesco*.

CROQUETAS DE BACALAO SALVADOR
(Salvador's Cod Croquettes)

START PREPARATION 3–4 DAYS IN ADVANCE

A white sauce gives these cod croquettes a creamy consistency, in contrast to the previous recipe, in which the potato produces a crunchier tapa. The amount of cod called for is small, contributing excellent flavor without being overpowering.   *Makes about 25–30*

¼ pound dried boneless salt cod
6 tablespoons olive oil
2 cloves garlic, minced
¼ cup minced onion
3 tablespoons minced parsley
¾ cup flour
2 cups milk
Generous grating of nutmeg

Salt
Freshly ground pepper
2 eggs, lightly beaten with
    1 teaspoon water
Dried bread crumbs
Oil for frying, preferably mild
    olive oil

Soak the cod in cold water to cover in the refrigerator for 2 to 3 days, changing water once or twice daily, until desalted to taste. Drain.

Shred or mince the cod. In a skillet, heat 1 tablespoon of the oil, add the garlic and onion, sauté a minute, then cover and cook slowly 10 minutes. Turn up the heat, add the cod and parsley, and sauté a minute. Reserve.

In a saucepan, heat the remaining 5 tablespoons olive oil. Stir in the flour, cook a minute or two, and gradually pour in the milk, stirring constantly. Season with nutmeg, salt, and pepper. Cook over a medium flame, stirring constantly, until the mixture is thickened and smooth and reaches the boiling point. Stir in the cod mixture and taste for salt. Remove from the heat and cool, stirring occasionally. Chill for at least 3 hours or overnight (you can speed the process by spreading the mixture in a thin layer on a plate before refrigerating).

With floured hands, shape the cod mixture into 1½-inch balls, coat with the beaten egg, and cover with bread crumbs (you can refrigerate at this point until ready to fry). Pour the oil into a skillet to a depth of at least 1 inch (or better still, use a deep-fryer) and heat until the oil quickly browns a cube of bread. Fry until the croquettes are browned on all sides. Eat immediately, or keep warm for up to 30 minutes in a 200°F oven.

ALBONDIGUILLAS DE PESCADO
(Shrimp and Hake Balls)

From the Galician seaside town of Villagarcía de Arosa with its inviting waterfront promenade come these savory fish balls flavored with almonds, garlic, and saffron.   *Serves 8*

1 pound hake or scrod
1 cup Fish Broth (p. 175) or
   ¾ cup clam juice diluted
   with ¼ cup water
¼ pound uncooked shrimp in
   their shells
3 tablespoons bread crumbs
½ cup plus 2 tablespoons dry
   white wine
1 egg, lightly beaten
Salt
Freshly ground pepper
⅛ teaspoon nutmeg
3 tablespoons minced parsley

2 large cloves garlic, minced
10 blanched almonds, chopped
Few strands of saffron, crumbled
Flour for dusting
2 tablespoons olive oil
1 tablespoon diced pimiento,
   preferably imported or
   homemade (see p. 178)
¼ teaspoon imported sweet
   paprika
2 tablespoons minced Spanish
   mountain cured ham, capicollo, or prosciutto
1 hard-boiled egg, chopped

Place the scrod and the Fish Broth in a saucepan. Shell the shrimp, add the shells to the saucepan, and bring to a boil. Simmer until the scrod is just done, about 8 minutes to each inch of thickness. Drain the fish, and strain the broth. Mince the scrod and finely chop the uncooked shrimp. In a bowl soak the bread crumbs in 1 tablespoon of the reserved broth and 2 tablespoons of the wine. Mix in the fish and shrimp, along with the beaten egg, salt, pepper, and nutmeg.

In a mortar or mini processor, mash to a paste 1 tablespoon of the parsley, a pinch of salt, half the minced garlic, the chopped almonds and the saffron. Add this to the fish mixture.

Shape the mixture into 1-inch balls and dust with flour. Heat the oil in a large shallow flameproof casserole, and brown the fish balls on all sides over medium-high heat. Lower the heat to medium and sprinkle in the remaining minced garlic and the pimiento and cook a minute. Stir in the paprika, then add the remaining ½ cup wine and ½ cup of the reserved broth, and a tablespoon of the parsley. Season with salt and pepper. Bring to a boil, cover, and simmer 20 minutes. Sprinkle with the ham, chopped egg, and remaining parsley and serve.

PINCHO MORUNO
(Marinated Pork Kabobs)

START PREPARATION 24 HOURS IN ADVANCE

Even the name of this enormously popular tapa of pork marinated in a variety of Eastern spices, then skewered and grilled, reflects its Moorish origins. The Moors, of course, must have used lamb, but today this tapa is almost always made with pork. I also like these kabobs for dinner—cut in larger cubes—accompanied by Ensaladilla Rusa (p. 20).

Serves 8 for tapas, 4 for dinner

MARINADE

2 tablespoons olive oil
2 tablespoons lemon juice
8 cloves garlic, minced
2 tablespoons minced parsley
1 teaspoon fresh ginger, minced
1½ teaspoons ground cumin,
    preferably freshly ground in
    a mortar or spice mill
1 teaspoon crushed coriander
    seeds
¼ teaspoon turmeric

½ teaspoon imported sweet
    paprika
¼ teaspoon dried crushed hot
    red pepper
¼ teaspoon freshly ground
    black pepper
1½ teaspoons minced oregano
    leaves or ¼ teaspoon dried
Several threads of saffron
½ teaspoon salt

. . .

1 pound lean pork, in 1-inch
    cubes

Combine in a shallow bowl all Marinade ingredients. Add the pork and mix with a rubber spatula to coat the meat well. Cover and refrigerate 24 hours, turning occasionally.

Marinated Pork Kabobs (continued)

Thread the meat onto small skewers, about 8 inches long, using 1 skewer per portion. Grill, preferably over hot coals, or on a greased griddle, until browned and just cooked through.

FLAMENQUÍN CORDOBÉS
(Rolled Pork Cutlet with Ham and Garlic)

We were famished and unwilling to search any farther for a place to have a light lunch, so we entered what appeared to be a most unpromising bar in the province of Córdoba and ordered a variety of tapas, among them this typical Cordobés appetizer. The ingredients are so straightforward and the results so juicy and delicious that I always thought there had to be a secret ingredient. There is not—the tapa is prepared in the same manner all over Córdoba.   *Makes six 3-inch rolls*

2 ounces Spanish mountain cured ham, capicollo, or prosciutto, in thin slices	2 tablespoons minced parsley
	2 eggs, lightly beaten with 2 teaspoons milk
6 pork cutlets (about ½ pound), pounded thin and cut in 5 x 3 inch rectangles	Dried bread crumbs, plain or seasoned
2 cloves garlic, minced	Oil for frying, preferably mild olive oil

Place a slice of ham over each cutlet. Mix together the garlic and parsley, and sprinkle over the cutlets. Roll up from the short end and secure with toothpicks. Dip in the egg, then coat with the crumbs. Pour the oil into a skillet to a depth of at least ½ inch (or better still, use a deep-fryer) and heat until the oil quickly browns a cube of bread. Fry the rolled cutlets until golden on all sides. Drain on paper towels. The rolls can be sliced into bite-size pieces for serving.

LOMO ADOBADO CON PIMIENTO
(Marinated Pork with Pimiento)

You simply can't go wrong ordering a marinated pork tapa anywhere in Spain, but the best version I have ever eaten was at one of the renowned Mallorca gourmet shops in Madrid, a place for breads, pastries, jams, candies, olive oil, prepared foods, and tapas at a bar with an astonishing variety of things to choose from. It was served here with pimiento on a homemade mini roll, but is just as good on a slice of bread.   *Serves 6–8*

Lomo de Cerdo en Adobo (p. 271)

Bread sliced about ½ inch thick, from a long narrow loaf

Pimiento strips, preferably from *piquillo* peppers (p. 127)

Marinate the pork loin as directed, slicing the meat ⅛–¼ inch thick. Coat a skillet or griddle with olive oil and heat to the smoking point. Brown the meat quickly on both sides, until just done. Place each meat slice on a piece of bread and garnish with pimiento.

CHORIZO OCEJÓN
(Chorizo Simmered in Sherry)

The dry sherry added to this appetizer gives the chorizo additional flavor and a certain complexity. It is one of the great tapas we sampled at an unexpectedly fine bar in the remote hills of Guadalajara province (see p. 248). A well-cured chorizo works best—if yours is too fresh, hang it overnight to dry at room temperature.   *Serves 6*

½ pound sweet chorizo, split lengthwise

Dry Spanish sherry (*fino*)

Place the chorizo in a small skillet and cover with sherry. Bring to a boil, then simmer, uncovered, 10 minutes. Remove the chorizo and serve on bread, cutting the bread and chorizo into smaller pieces if you wish.

MORCILLA CON PASAS Y PIÑONES
(Black Sausage with Raisins and Pine Nuts)

A tapa that I enjoyed at the classic Taberna de Antonio Sánchez (see p. 280) in Madrid. Black sausage, especially the Burgos variety (in the United States often called Colombian-style and found in Hispanic markets) that incorporates rice, has always been one of my very favorite tapas. I like it sliced and sautéed, but here, raisins and pine nuts bring an interesting and most compatible new taste. In the Canary Islands there is a black sausage mixture similar to this, but made with a typical Canary addition of mashed sweet potato.

Makes enough for 8–10 canapés

1½ tablespoons raisins
1 teaspoon olive oil
½ pound *morcilla* (black
   sausage), preferably made
   with rice

1½ tablespoons pine nuts
Eight to ten ¼-inch bread
   rounds, cut from a long
   narrow loaf

Soak the raisins in warm water to cover for about 20 minutes. Drain.

Heat the oil in a skillet and sauté the *morcilla* until it browns and gives off its fat. Drain the *morcilla* on paper towels and pour off the fat from the skillet. Skin the *morcilla*, mash with a fork, and return to the skillet. Cook a minute, then stir in the raisins and pine nuts and cook another minute. Serve on bread rounds.

ALBÓNDIGAS CON PICADA DE ALMENDRA
(Meatballs in Almond, Garlic, and Parsley Sauce)

My husband and I are insatiable meatball eaters, always looking for the ultimate in meatballs, but quite content with those that are merely good. I submit these as among the best I have ever tasted—deliciously seasoned, moist, and light. In Andalucía, *albóndigas* (from an Arab word meaning ball) are so common as tapas and as part of home cooking that some regional cookbooks devote entire chapters to their preparation. Judging from the typically Spanish ingredients in these meatballs, however, they could be from just about any region. This recipe serves 4 to 6 for tapas or 2 or 3 as a main course.

Makes 20–25

MEATBALLS

⅓ cup dried bread crumbs
⅓ cup chicken broth
1 pound ground veal or a mix-
    ture of ground beef, veal,
    and pork, in equal parts
1 tablespoon minced parsley
2 cloves garlic, minced

½ teaspoon lemon juice
2 tablespoons minced Spanish
    mountain cured ham, capi-
    collo, or prosciutto
½ teaspoon salt
Freshly ground pepper
1 egg, lightly beaten

. . .

Flour for dusting
2 tablespoons olive oil
3 tablespoons minced onion
2 tablespoons skinned, seeded,
    and finely chopped tomato
¼ cup dry white wine
½ cup chicken broth
1 small bay leaf
Salt
Freshly ground pepper

1 tablespoon minced parsley
2 cloves garlic, minced
Few strands of saffron,
    crumbled
1 tablespoon chopped blanched
    almonds
¼ teaspoon imported sweet
    paprika
2 tablespoons fresh or frozen
    peas

To make the Meatballs, in a large bowl soak the bread crumbs in the broth. Lightly mix in all the other meatball ingredients, then shape into 1½-inch balls.

Dust the meatballs with flour. Heat the oil in a shallow flameproof casserole and brown the meatballs on all sides over medium-high heat. Lower the heat, add the onion, and cook until it has wilted, then add the tomato and cook another minute. Stir in the wine, broth, and bay leaf. Season with salt and pepper, cover, and simmer 30 minutes.

Meanwhile, mash to a paste in a mortar or mini processor the parsley, garlic, ⅛ teaspoon salt, saffron, almonds, and paprika. Add this mixture, along with the peas, to the meatballs and cook 15 minutes more.

ALBÓNDIGAS CANARIAS CON ALMOGROTE

(Canary-Style Meatballs with Red Pepper Dip)

These meatballs are not cooked in a sauce, but dipped in the distinctive cheese-and-red-pepper mixture from the Canary Islands called *almogrote*. Do not overcook—the meatballs should be cooked through but still moist.

Serves 4–6

3 tablespoons dried bread crumbs
¼ cup chicken broth
1 pound ground beef
¼ pound Spanish mountain cured ham or prosciutto, minced
3 cloves garlic, minced
2 tablespoons minced parsley
¾ teaspoon minced oregano leaves or ⅛ teaspoon dried
¾ teaspoon salt, or to taste

1 tablespoon grated cured Manchego or Parmesan cheese
1 egg, separated
Flour for dusting
Dried bread crumbs
3 tablespoons olive oil
1 recipe Almogrote de la Gomera (p. 7), thinned with about 3 tablespoons chicken broth to a dipping consistency

In a cup mix the bread crumbs with 2 tablespoons of the broth. Combine in a bowl the ground beef, ham, garlic, parsley, oregano, salt, grated cheese, egg yolk, and the remaining 2 tablespoons broth.

Lightly beat the egg white with 1 teaspoon water in a shallow bowl. Shape the meat mixture into 1½-inch balls and dust with flour. Dip in the egg white, then coat with bread crumbs.

Heat the oil in a skillet and sauté the meatballs until golden and cooked through, shaking frequently to prevent sticking. Serve with the *almogrote* dip.

CHAPTER 2

Northern Coastal Spain

REGION OF THE SAUCES

I t was a sunny spring morning in San Sebastián, the sophisticated Basque city on La Concha bay that became famous at the turn of the century when the Spanish royal family summered there. I had arranged to meet my good friend Juan Mari Arzak, celebrated chef and owner of Arzak restaurant, to accompany him on his daily shopping rounds at the city's sensational La Brecha market. A familiar and revered figure who sports a big boyish grin, Juan Mari is always anxious to please, and on this day he was unable to progress more than a few steps without pausing to acknowledge delivery men and produce sellers who shouted greetings. He frequently stopped to inspect the market's exceptional produce. Scooping up a handful of lustrous black beans offered by a country woman, he declared, "These are the best black beans in the market," and the woman beamed. We proceeded to the market's upper level—a huge space worthy of a cathedral, devoted entirely to fish, and it was a sight to behold: hake, bass, tuna, squid, cuttlefish, langoustine, lobster—up to sixty varieties of fish and shellfish all lovingly displayed and of a freshness beyond compare.

You would naturally expect Juan Mari's three-star Michelin restaurant to use only the finest ingredients, but all along the northern coast of Spain, from the Basque Country to Cantabria, Asturias, and Galicia, Spaniards from every walk of life demand the best and will settle for nothing less. "We all shop in the same market," says the ebullient owner of Alotza, a modest restaurant in the Old Quarter of San Sebastián, "and although Arzak is without question a phenomenal restaurant, his fish can't possibly be better than mine. My clients are tough critics who really know and appreciate quality food. It is what they eat at home—and I must meet their expectations."

The designation of the entire northern coast of Spain as a gastronomic entity is admittedly broad; each of its four regions was shaped by diverse historical and cultural influences and has a distinctive appearance as well. Even when it comes to food there are significant differences, but a common thread is a keen interest in fine food and an emphasis on seafood, typically prepared in a sauce. But first, I'll concentrate on what makes each of these regions unique.

In Galicia fjord-like estuaries, called *rías*, bring the Atlantic Ocean inland and create magnificent coastal scenery, while the interior is gentle and lushly green. Early Celtic tribes crossing into Spain from Europe stopped when they reached the western coast of Galicia and the Atlantic Ocean (Galicia's Cape Finisterre, literally "the end of the earth," was so named because here the known world ended), and the Celtic legacy is still seen in blue-eyed blond Galicians and heard in the sound of bagpipes played at traditional festivals. Perhaps Celtic influences are also the reason for the popularity of the Galician *empanada,* a pizza-size double-crusted savory pie of meat or fish, and for the flaming *queimada,* a potent drink made from a grappa-like spirit called *orujo* mixed with apples and sugar. Grazing land is plentiful in Galicia, and cows are everywhere. Galician beef is held in highest esteem for its fine flavor and exceptional tenderness.

The outdoor market in the delightful city of Santiago de Compostela in Galicia is a far more rustic affair than the San Sebastián market but no less impressive. Here country folk arrive with farm cheeses like creamy piquant Tetilla, freshly made country bread loaves made from rye and corn flour, and glistening fresh vegetables grown on small family plots, including famous *pimientos de Padrón*—tiny green peppers, some sweet, others fiery—and *grelos,* greens similar to Swiss chard and collards, used in stews and soups, none more renowned than *caldo gallego.* The farmers set up their wares in the Plaza de Cervantes, not far from the cathedral where the tomb of Saint James has been the object of pilgrimages since the Middle Ages.

Asturias shares its western border with Galicia, but its early history and culture relate to the role of Asturias in the expulsion of the Moors from northern Spain, the region's unique pre-Romanesque architecture, and the importance of Asturias as guardian of the Christian faith in a country otherwise dominated by the Moors. Asturian terrain is spectacularly rugged and crowned by the awesome mountains of the Picos de Europa. Here Cabrales cheese, a pungent blue cheese unlike other blues, is aged in mountain caves. Apart from seafood, beans are a culinary highlight, and the signature dish of Asturias is *fabada,* a bean stew made special by the extraordinary quality of Asturian beans and the assertive flavor of Asturian chorizo and black sausage, with which the beans are cooked.

The region of Cantabria, edged by long stretches of fine sand beaches and luxuriantly green in its stunning mountain interior, was for centuries politically part of Castile and therefore had less contact with its coastal neighbors and fell short of developing a distinctive style of cooking. Turning inward to ample pastures, Cantabrians concentrated on dairy production (the region is known for its excellent butter and desserts based on fresh cheeses) and they also make a fine chickpea stew (*cocido montañés*) using inland products that is closely related to the *cocido* of the central plains.

In the Basque Country grassy cliffs dip abruptly to the fertile fishing grounds of the Bay of Biscay, and rolling emerald green hills punctuated by quaint country houses provide grazing land for cows and sheep (the region is known for its smoked sheep's milk cheese called Idiazábal). Basques are a mysterious people with a language unrelated to any other. Their proximity to France reflects on Basque cooking and attitudes toward food. Cooking is more creative, and men-only eating societies, bastions of fine food and good times that are unique to the Basque Country, have been fixtures of Basque life for generations.

Climate and geography along the northern coast, nevertheless, are more similar than different, and the fish that dominates the traditional diet is generally prepared in similar ways. A strong connection is the use of sauces (always more popular in cool damp regions such as these) that tend to be light and gently seasoned, never masking the fresh taste of the sea. In Galicia such sauces are often made with local dry fruity Albariño wines and paprika; in Asturias, where climate does not permit wine production, dry hard cider may be the sauce base; in the Basque Country it is the young "green" wine, *txakolí,* but with the Basques' knack for ingenuity there are much more unusual sauces as well, such as dried red pepper and onion sauce (*vizcaína* style), an ingenious creamy emulsion of olive oil and cod gelatin (*pil pil* style), and squid in ink sauce (*en su tinta*).

Some kinds of seafood are eaten all along the coast (hake is especially appreciated), although each area has certain favorites. Basques adore dried cod (perhaps a taste related to the historic Basque prowess in sailing the seas to Newfoundland in search of cod) and *angulas*—elvers (tiny eels) the size of matchsticks that are caught at the mouths of rivers as they arrive from their incredible journey from their spawning grounds in the Sargasso Sea across the Atlantic (see box, p. 87). In Cantabria the preference is for sardines, anchovies, and large squid (*rabas*); in Asturias *centollo* (spider crab), fresh tuna, and *pixín* (monkfish) are favorites, while in Galicia it is *pulpo* (octopus), served on wooden plates, spiny lobster, *nécora* crabs, scallops in their shells (long a symbol of pilgrimage to Santiago), and goose barnacles, grotesque creatures that despite their somewhat unappetizing appearance capture the very essence of the sea. The cooking of the northern coast is indeed based on an extraordinary ability to take a wealth of seafood and prepare it simply yet brilliantly without ever compromising its pure fresh taste.

Notes on Regional Wines and Liquors

The young, delicate, and fruity Albariño white wines from the western coast of Galicia with the Rías Baixas appellation of origin are rapidly gaining fans in America. Look for As Laxas, Fefiñanes, Valdamor, and Martín Códex. A popular after-dinner liqueur all over Spain, most often made in Galicia, is the powerful orujo, *made from grape skins and somewhat similar to grappa. It is typically served chilled.*

There is little wine-making along Spain's northern coast, but sidra, *a hard dry apple cider from Asturias, and* txakolí, *is a dry fruity "green" wine made around the town of Guetaria in the Basque Country, are popular with regional seafood. Txomín Etxániz txakolí is a well-regarded label. The interior Basque province of Álava does, however, produce fine red wines under the Rioja Alavesa appellation of origin, such as Remelluri and Marqués de Arienzo.*

Salads ❧ Soups ❧ Meals-in-a-Pot Vegetables ❧ Egg Dishes

ENSALADA DE BERROS
(Watercress Salad)

The essential partner for Watercress Meatballs (p. 111) and excellent as well with a variety of meat and fish dishes.   *Serves 4*

2 bunches watercress, thick
    stems trimmed, cut in pieces

6 medium-large radishes, very
    thinly sliced

DRESSING

¼ cup extra virgin olive oil
4 teaspoons freshly squeezed
    lemon juice
½ teaspoon Dijon-style mustard

1 clove garlic, mashed to a
    paste
1 tablespoon minced parsley
Salt
Freshly ground pepper

In a salad bowl toss together the watercress and radishes. In a small bowl whisk together the Dressing ingredients and mix into the salad.

CALDO GALLEGO
(Galician Meat, Potato, Greens, and Bean Soup)

START PREPARATION I DAY IN ADVANCE

There is remarkably little variation from one cook to the next in the preparation of Caldo Gallego, the famous soup that has traveled the world with Galician émigrés. Only one ingredient, chorizo, is a point of contention. Purists reject it, yet many traditional recipes include it; it does, in fact, produce a richer, more flavorful soup. The kinds of greens may also vary, although *grelos*—closely akin to collard greens—are most typical. Caldo Gallego is hearty enough to be a meal, but you may choose to serve it in smaller portions as a first course or as an accompaniment to a light supper.

Serves 4–6

½ pound medium dried white beans

1 tablespoon olive oil

2 cloves garlic, minced

1 teaspoon imported sweet paprika

7 cups water

1 pound boneless beef chuck

1 beef or ham bone

¼ pound Spanish mountain cured ham, prosciutto, or capicollo, in a thick chunk

A 2-ounce piece slab bacon or salt pork

1 leek, well washed

½ pound collard greens, Swiss chard, or kale, thick stems trimmed and coarsely chopped (about 4 cups)

¾ pound small (about 2-inch diameter) new or waxy red potatoes, peeled

¼ pound sweet chorizo

Salt

Soak the beans overnight in water to cover. Drain.

In a small skillet, heat the oil and garlic and sauté a minute (the garlic should not color). Turn off the flame and add the paprika. Stir in a tablespoon or two of water.

Add to a soup pot the water, beans, beef, bone, ham, slab bacon, leek, and garlic mixture from the skillet. Bring to a boil, cover, and simmer about 2 hours, or until the beans are almost tender.

Add the greens, potatoes, chorizo, and salt to taste, cover, and continue cooking until the potatoes are done, about 30 minutes.

Remove and cut up the beef, ham, bacon, leek, and chorizo and return to the pot. Discard the bone. Cover and let sit 10 minutes before serving. Reheat if necessary.

MARMITAKO
(Basque Tuna Soup)

Tuna and bread were the original ingredients of this soup made on board Basque fishing vessels at sea. The Basques, fearless fishermen who brave the tempestuous waters of the Bay of Biscay, are, as they have been for generations, lovers of fine food. The mere fact of being in high seas is not likely to deter them from a good meal, even if the task of cooking aboard ship in rough waters can be somewhat precarious.

The word *marmitako* is thought to derive from a Basque word, *ameike-tako*, which refers to a midmorning meal. *Marmitako* was greatly enriched when peppers, potatoes, and tomatoes arrived from the New World, all of which became essential to the preparation of the soup as we know it today.

Serves 5–6

3 dried sweet red peppers or mild New Mexico style, seeded; or 3 medium pimientos, finely chopped, and 1 tablespoon paprika

3 tablespoons extra virgin olive oil

2 medium onions, finely chopped

4 cloves garlic, minced

1 pound green frying peppers, cored, seeded, and finely chopped

2 tablespoons minced parsley

1 tablespoon imported sweet paprika

2 tablespoons brandy

1½ pounds potatoes, preferably new or red waxy, peeled and cut in ¾-inch cubes

¾ pound tomatoes, skinned, seeded, and chopped

5½ cups Fish Broth (p. 175) or 4¾ cups clam juice diluted with ¾ cup water

½ cup dry white wine

1 large carrot, trimmed, scraped, and cut crosswise in 4 pieces

1 medium leek, well washed

1 dried red chile pepper, or to taste, cut in half crosswise and seeded

Salt

Freshly ground pepper

Twelve ¼-inch slices good-quality bread, cut from a long narrow loaf

1½ pounds tuna steaks, in ¾-inch cubes

Basque Tuna Soup (continued)

Soak the dried peppers in warm water for 20 minutes. Drain. Heat the oil in a large shallow casserole and sauté the onions, garlic, green peppers, and parsley (if using pimiento instead of dried peppers, add here) for about 5 minutes. Cover tightly and cook very slowly for 30 minutes.

Uncover and stir in the paprika (1 tablespoon if using dried sweet red peppers, 2 tablespoons if using pimiento). Raise the heat, add the brandy, and flame. When the flame dies, stir in the potatoes and sauté a minute, then add the tomatoes and cook 2 minutes more. Pour in the broth and wine and add the carrot, leek, and chile pepper. Scrape the flesh from the dried red peppers (if using) and add to the pot. Season with salt and pepper to taste. Bring to a boil, then simmer about 30 minutes, or until the potatoes are almost tender.

Meanwhile, place the bread slices on a cookie sheet and toast in a 350°F oven about 8 minutes, or until lightly golden, turning once. Reserve.

Discard the leek, carrot, and chile pepper and add the tuna to the soup. Taste again for salt, and simmer 3 minutes. Cover and let sit 5 minutes. Serve in bowls with the toasted bread floating in the soup or served on the side.

ALUBIAS ROJAS DE TOLOSA CON BERZA
(Red Beans with Cabbage)

START PREPARATION 1 DAY IN ADVANCE

A dollop of cabbage, placed in each bowl of beans, is a delicious complement to this bean stew based on the outstanding red beans that grow in Tolosa in the Basque province of Guipúzcoa along the banks of the Oria River. You can use any kind of red bean to make this dish, but the results will be best with Tolosa, Adzuki, or other dark red beans, sometimes available at food specialty shops.   *Serves 4*

1 pound small, deep-red dried beans	1 small leek, well washed
1 medium onion, peeled and cut in half crosswise	A ¼-pound piece slab bacon, preferably fresh (otherwise cured)
1 large carrot, scraped and cut in half crosswise	¼ pound sweet chorizo
	2 tablespoons olive oil

1 medium onion, finely
   chopped
6 cloves garlic, minced

2 teaspoons imported sweet
   paprika
Salt to taste

SAUTÉED CABBAGE

3 tablespoons olive oil
¼ cup onion
2 cloves garlic, minced
1 small head cabbage, coarsely
   chopped

Salt
Freshly ground pepper

Soak the beans overnight in water to cover. Drain, then combine in a large pot with 6 cups fresh water and bring to a boil. Reduce the heat, add the onion, carrot, leek, bacon, and chorizo. Cover and simmer 1 hour.

Meanwhile, heat the olive oil in a large skillet, add the chopped onion and garlic, and sauté slowly until the onion has wilted. Stir in the paprika, then add to the beans. Season with salt, cover, and continue cooking about 30 minutes more, or until the beans are just tender. Wipe out the skillet.

While the beans are cooking, prepare the cabbage. Heat the oil in the skillet and sauté the onion and garlic until the onion has wilted. Add the cabbage, salt, and pepper and stir-fry about 10 minutes. Cover and continue cooking until done to taste.

Serve the beans in soup bowls, accompanied by crusty country bread. Heat the cabbage, transfer to a serving bowl, and pass separately. Typically, a spoonful or two of cabbage is placed in the soup bowl, off to one side—not mixed into the beans.

FABADA LA MÁQUINA
(*Asturian Bean Stew La Máquina*)

START PREPARATION 8 HOURS IN ADVANCE

I always wondered why the family-run roadside restaurant La Máquina, just outside of Oviedo, asks for a precise reservation time for a dish that I imagined could be cooked up in advance in a big pot. It is just about the only thing the restaurant serves, and I thought it was just reheated as orders reached the kitchen. Wrong! Once I obtained the recipe of cook María García Ro-dríguez, I understood why. She is a perfectionist when it comes to this dish that is the pride of all Asturias but especially of this restaurant, known as the "grand temple of *fabada*," and a place of "pilgrimage." Few travel this way without stopping in.

María tells you every detail that goes into the preparation of the ab-solutely perfect, quintessential *fabada*. You will have to be less fussy than she, since the *fabe* beans of Asturias, which command top pesetas and which the restaurant personally selects for its *fabada*, cannot generally be found here, and the meat products are homemade. Nevertheless, even without using the optimum products and without following all of María's admoni-tions (some of which I have included in italics), this will be an exceptional bean stew.   *Serves 4–6*

1 pound large white beans, preferably Asturian *fabes*	A 2-ounce piece slab bacon
Several strands of saffron	¼ pound sweet or spicy chorizo
½ pound cured ham hocks	¼ pound black sausage, prefer-ably Spanish *morcilla*
A 2-ounce piece Spanish moun-tain cured ham or prosciutto, cut from the narrow end, or capicollo	2 tablespoons olive oil
	Salt

Soak the beans not more than 8 hours in cold water. Drain. Toast the saffron in a very small ungreased skillet for a minute or two over a medium flame. Transfer to a mortar and crush.

Put the beans in a wide shallow casserole (*do not use a deep stew pot*) and pour in enough water so that there is an inch of water covering the beans. Bring to a slow boil over a medium-high flame and skim off any foam that comes to the surface. Stir in the saffron.

Add the ham hocks and the pieces of ham and bacon, making room for them at the bottom of the casserole (*so they don't damage the beans*). Cook 5 minutes, covered. Skim off the foam. Add the chorizo and black sausage (*it must be well sealed at the ends so it doesn't break up into the stew, or it will be the sure ruin of the dish—use toothpicks to close the ends if necessary*). Boil 5 min-utes more and skim the foam again (*the black sausage must always be on top so that it doesn't break up*).

Lower the flame to a simmer. Add the oil, check to be sure there is ½ inch of liquid over the beans, cover, and cook slowly 2 to 3 hours, depending on the beans, maintaining ½ inch of liquid over the beans (*if more liquid is necessary, add only cold water to "frighten" the beans*). Shake occasionally to prevent sticking. When the beans are done, taste for salt and adjust if necessary. Let sit at least 30 minutes, during which time the liquid will thicken (*if too thin, mash 6 to 10 beans, combine with a little of the cooking liquid, and return to the pot, giving a quick boil to incorporate it*).

Serve the beans and present the meats, cut into serving pieces, on a separate platter. (*Let guests serve themselves, adding the meats to their soup bowls or eating the meat separately, as is the old custom.*)

SETAS EN SALSA DE AVELLANAS
(Wild Mushrooms in Hazelnut Sauce)

The blend of garlic, hazelnuts, onion, and parsley gives these mushrooms a wonderfully subtle flavor. Serve with simply cooked meats.   *Serves 4*

2 cloves garlic, minced
10 hazelnuts, shelled, skin on
2 tablespoons minced parsley
Salt
1 tablespoon olive oil
1 small–medium onion,
    slivered

1 pound wild mushrooms, such
    as shitake, or a mix of wild
    and small cultivated mush-
    rooms, brushed clean, thick
    stems removed
Freshly ground pepper

In a mortar or mini processor mash to a paste the garlic, hazelnuts, parsley, and ⅛ teaspoon salt.

Heat the oil in a skillet and sauté the onion a minute or two. Cover and cook over low heat for 10 minutes. Add the mushrooms and sauté 2 minutes. Season with salt and pepper, then add the mortar mixture and continue cooking slowly until the mushrooms are cooked to taste.

JUDÍAS VERDES REHOGADAS CON JAMÓN
(Green Beans Sautéed with Cured Ham)

Whenever we stay in Niserias in Asturias (as we often do, since my husband loves to trout-fish in the Cares River) we dine at Casa Julián (see p. 113), where co-owner and cook Vicentina produces simple Asturian fare with an expert hand. My favorite first course is her sautéed green beans, seasoned with garlic and generously sprinkled with mountain ham.   *Serves 4*

Salt
½ small onion
1½ pounds broad green beans,
    ends snapped off
2 tablespoons olive oil
4 cloves garlic, lightly smashed
    and peeled

2 ounces Spanish mountain
    cured ham or prosciutto, in
    small cubes or thin squares
    (about ¼ cup)
Freshly ground pepper

Bring a pot of salted water to a boil, add the onion and green beans, return to a boil, then cook uncovered at a slow boil for about 20 minutes, or until cooked as desired. Discard the onion and drain the green beans in a colander. Refresh with cold water.

In a skillet, heat the oil with the garlic, pressing the garlic with the back of a wooden spoon to release its flavor, until the garlic is golden on both sides. Add the beans and the ham, season with salt and pepper, and sauté, stirring, over a medium flame, until the beans are hot.

PURÉ DE PATATAS A LA VASCA
(Creamy Potato Purée)

While in other regions of Spain sautéed or fried potatoes are favorites, the Basques, with their penchant for subtle, delicate flavors, often prefer puréed potatoes that are thin and creamy. You can, of course, vary the consistency of the potatoes by increasing or decreasing the amount of milk added; if you are serving the potatoes on their own, rather than as a bed for fish (as on p. 96) or meat, you may wish to make them slightly thicker.   *Serves 4*

2 pounds baking potatoes,
   peeled and halved
1 clove garlic, peeled
About 1 cup hot milk

Salt
6 tablespoons butter
1 small egg yolk

Place the potatoes and the garlic in a saucepan with a mixture of water and
¼ cup of the milk to cover. Season with salt. Bring to a boil, then cover and
cook over a medium flame until the potatoes are tender, about 40 minutes.

    Drain the potatoes (do not discard the garlic). Pass the potatoes and gar-
lic through a ricer or strainer and back into the saucepan. Stir in the butter
and enough hot milk to make the potatoes the consistency of mayonnaise.
Add the egg yolk and beat with a wooden spoon until the mixture is smooth.
Taste for salt.

PATATAS AL HORNO CON PIMIENTOS
(Roast Potatoes with Peppers)

Tasty, tender, and moist potatoes that are a great accompaniment for any
simple, sauceless meat preparation. *Serves 4*

4 large scallions
3 tablespoons olive oil
4 medium potatoes, peeled, in
   ¼-inch slices, each slice cut
   in half
1 green bell pepper, cored and
   seeded, in julienne strips

2 cloves garlic, minced
1 small onion, thinly sliced
1 tablespoon minced parsley
Salt

Trim any tough or bruised ends from the scallions and cut in 1½-inch
lengths. Split the white portion lengthwise.

    Heat the oil in a shallow casserole, then add the potatoes, green pepper,
garlic, and onion. Sauté over a medium-high flame for 10 minutes, turning
occasionally. Sprinkle with the parsley and salt to taste. Cover with foil and
bake in a 350°F oven for 15 to 20 minutes, or until the potatoes are done.

REVUELTO DE JAMÓN Y SETAS
(Soft-Set Eggs with Cured Ham and Wild Mushrooms)

"Scrambled" eggs in the Spanish style are not beaten, just stirred together with the other ingredients. And what could taste better with eggs than garlic, mushrooms, and ham? You must work quickly once the eggs are added so they do not overcook.   *Serves 1*

1 tablespoon extra virgin
 olive oil
2 ounces wild mushrooms, such
 as shitake, brushed clean,
 thick stems removed, and
 coarsely chopped
About 1 ounce Spanish
 mountain cured ham or

prosciutto, in ¼-inch
 dice (2 tablespoons)
1 clove garlic, minced
1 tablespoon minced parsley
2 eggs
Salt

Heat the oil in a small skillet and sauté the mushrooms, ham, garlic, and parsley over a medium flame until the mushrooms begin to soften. Increase the heat to medium-high. Break in the eggs and stir rapidly, removing the skillet from the flame almost immediately. Season with salt and continue stirring until the eggs are no longer liquid and have just begun to set. Transfer immediately to a plate to prevent further cooking.

Shellfish ❀ Fish

ENSALADA DE LUBRIGANTE CON BERROS
(Lobster and Watercress Salad)

A specialty of Galicia and found at the excellent El Náutico restaurant in Cedeira, a charming, immaculately kept town at the mouth of the idyllic Cedeira estuary. This main-course salad blends the wonderfully complementary flavors of lobster and watercress.   *Makes 4 dinner portions*

2 recipes Fish Broth (p. 175) or
    10 cups clam juice diluted
    with 4 cups water
Two 2-pound lobsters
1 pound red waxy potatoes
2 medium white turnips
Salt
2 bunches watercress (about
    ¼ pound each), thick stems
    trimmed

1 clove garlic, peeled
8 black or white peppercorns
4 mint leaves, finely chopped
½ teaspoon Dijon-style
    mustard
¼ cup freshly squeezed lemon
    juice
½ cup fruity extra virgin
    olive oil
4 radishes, thinly sliced

Bring the Fish Broth to a boil in a large pot, add the lobsters upside down and headfirst, and boil about 15 minutes. Cool. Remove from the shell; cut the tail in thick slices and the rest in large pieces.

Meanwhile, cook the potatoes and turnips in boiling salted water until tender. Cool and cut in ½-inch slices.

Mince enough watercress leaves to make 3 tablespoons. In a mortar or mini processor, mash to a paste the garlic, peppercorns, minced watercress, and mint with ⅛ teaspoon salt. Stir in the mustard and lemon juice, transfer to a small bowl, and whisk in the oil. Taste for salt.

Arrange the remaining watercress on a platter, scatter the radish slices over, sprinkle with salt, and place the lobster pieces over the salad at the center. Arrange the sliced turnips and potatoes around the rim of the platter. Pour the dressing over everything and serve.

VIEIRAS DE SANTIAGO
(Scallops with Onions and Cured Ham)

This is one of the two most popular ways (the other is with tomato sauce) to prepare scallops in Galicia. If you are fortunate enough to find scallops in their shells, save the roe and sauté it with the onion and garlic.

Makes 8 first-course portions

2 tablespoons plus 1 teaspoon
 olive oil
¾ cup minced onion
1 clove garlic, minced
4 tablespoons (¼ cup) finely
 chopped Spanish mountain
 cured ham or prosciutto
1½ pounds bay scallops or
 halved sea scallops

¼ cup dry white wine
Salt
Freshly ground pepper
½ cup dried bread crumbs
2 tablespoons minced parsley
Freshly squeezed lemon juice

Heat 1 tablespoon of the oil in a skillet and sauté the onion, garlic, and ham for a minute or two. Cover and continue cooking slowly 15 minutes. Add the scallops and wine and boil away the liquid. Season with salt and pepper.

Divide the scallop mixture into 8 greased scallop shells. In a small bowl combine the bread crumbs, parsley, salt, a squeeze or two of lemon juice and the remaining oil. Bake at 400°F 10 minutes, or until the crumbs are golden.

VIEIRAS ESTOFADAS
(Sautéed Scallops and Onions)

Casa Simón is a highly regarded Galician restaurant near the town of Cangas de Morrazo, and all the extraordinary seafood of this Atlantic coastline is prepared in a huge open kitchen. Scallops, of course, are typical of Galicia and prepared in the simplest ways possible so that their delicate taste is never overpowered by conflicting flavors. *Serves 4*

1½ pounds sea scallops

Kosher or sea salt

2 tablespoons olive oil

½ cup minced onion

4 tablespoons (¼ cup) minced parsley

Few strands of saffron

4 tablespoons (¼ cup) diced Spanish mountain cured ham or prosciutto

5 tablespoons dry white wine

Freshly squeezed lemon juice

Sprinkle the scallops with salt. In a skillet, heat the oil to the smoking point. Brown the scallops quickly over a high flame, shaking the pan frequently, for about 1 minute. Remove the scallops to a warm platter (they will cook more later). Return the skillet to the flame and sauté the onion until wilted. Stir in the parsley and saffron, then return the scallops to the pan and add the ham and wine. Cook briefly until the scallops are done, about 2 to 3 minutes. Sprinkle with lemon juice and serve, accompanied if you like by Saffron Rice with Pine Nuts (p. 297).

VIEIRAS CON ALGAS
(Scallops and Shrimp with Seaweed)

Patxiku Quintana, burly chef and owner of a restaurant of the same name in San Sebastián, demonstrates his exceptional culinary talents in this delicious and quickly made mixture of scallops and shrimp in wine sauce. The dish acquires extra character by the addition of seaweed, which can be purchased dried in Oriental food markets (soak 3 or 4 minutes to reconstitute). If you wish, you can serve the seafood over rice instead of in scallop shells.

Serves 4

2 tablespoons olive oil

4 medium-size shallots, peeled and slivered

2 small, well-washed leeks, white part only, in julienne strips

1 pound bay scallops or sea scallops, cut in halves

16 large shrimp, shelled

¼ cup dry white wine

¼ cup heavy cream

4 tablespoons (¼ cup) fresh or reconstituted seaweed, well dried, in julienne strips

Salt

Scallops and Shrimp with Seaweed (continued)

In a skillet, slowly heat the oil with the shallots and leeks until the vegetables have softened. Add the scallops, shrimp, wine, cream, and seaweed, turn up the flame, and cook until the scallops and shrimp are done and the liquid is reduced and slightly thickened, about 3 to 4 minutes. Season with salt. To serve, divide into 4 scallop shells.

ALMEJAS CON ARROZ
(Clams with Rice)

"Clams with rice," as opposed to "rice with clams," signals which is the dominant ingredient in this Basque dish which has suddenly appeared on the menus of Spain's most fashionable restaurants.

A similar dish is made in Andalucía, adding crisp garlic bread cubes. Because of the crunch the bread lends to the rice, it is called "rice with sand." To make this version, prepare as directed below, make the bread cubes (see p. 246), and sprinkle over the rice just before serving.   *Serves 4*

1 recipe Saffron Rice with Pine Nuts (p. 297), substituting clam juice for the chicken broth and omitting the pine nuts and saffron	clams, or 2 dozen very small littlenecks, thoroughly cleansed (see p. 33)
5 large garlic cloves, minced	¼ teaspoon paprika
A few strands of saffron	½ cup dry white wine
6 tablespoons minced parsley	1 tablespoon freshly squeezed lemon juice
Salt	Freshly ground pepper
¼ cup olive oil	A 1-inch piece dried red chile pepper, seeded
4 tablespoons (¼ cup) minced onion	2 bay leaves
4 dozen cockles or Manila	Fish Broth (p. 175) or diluted clam juice

While the rice is baking, combine in a mortar or mini processor the garlic, saffron, 5 tablespoons of the parsley, and a pinch of salt. Mash as finely as possible. When the rice is done and while it is resting, heat the oil in a skillet and slowly sauté the onion until tender.

Drain and rinse the clams, then increase the flame to high, add the clams, and stir in the paprika, wine, lemon juice, pepper, chile pepper, and bay leaves. Stir constantly, removing the clams to a warm platter as they open and adding some Fish Broth as the liquid evaporates. Add the mortar mixture and more Fish Broth if necessary to make a sauce that is just slightly thickened. Simmer a minute.

Spoon the rice into the center of a platter or onto individual dishes. Arrange the clams around the rice and pour the sauce over the clams and rice. Sprinkle with the remaining parsley and serve immediately.

CREPES DE TXANGURRO CON SALSA MARINERA
(Crabmeat Crepes in Wine Sauce)

Txangurro is the name of a Basque dish made from flaked and well-seasoned *centolla*—the spider crab found off Spain's northern coast. In this outstanding version, the crab mixture is enclosed in crepes (which have long been traditional in the north for desserts) and covered with a *marinera* sauce (which in Spanish cooking does not imply a tomato sauce).

If you prefer to prepare the crab in the classic manner, eliminate the crepes, combine the sauce and the crabmeat mixture, and divide into 4 scallop shells (or if possible into crab shells) and bake at 400°F for about 10 minutes.

Makes 4 first-course portions

CREPES

1 egg	1 cup flour
½ cup milk	⅛ teaspoon salt
½ cup water	

. . .

1 tablespoon olive oil	2 tablespoons very finely
2 tablespoons well-washed,	chopped carrot
very finely chopped leeks,	½ pound fresh crabmeat, flaked
white part only	2 tablespoons brandy
2 tablespoons very finely	Salt
chopped onion	

Crabmeat Crepes in Wine Sauce (continued)

SALSA MARINERA

1 tablespoon olive oil	1 bay leaf
1 small onion, finely chopped	2 tablespoons flour
1 small tomato, skinned, seeded, and finely chopped	½ recipe Fish Broth (p. 306), boiled down to 2 cups, or 2 cups clam juice
¼ cup dry white wine	
1 teaspoon thyme leaves or ⅛ teaspoon dried	Salt

To make the Crepes, combine in a processor the egg, milk, water, flour, and salt and mix until smooth. Grease and heat a 5- to 6-inch skillet or crepe pan. Swirl in just enough batter (about 1 tablespoon) to coat the pan. When the crepe is set (it should not brown), turn and briefly cook the other side. Keep the crepes stacked and separated with pieces of wax paper until ready to use.

To make the crab filling, heat the oil and sauté the leeks, onion, and carrot for a minute. Cover and cook very slowly about 15 minutes, or until the vegetables are softened. Stir in the crabmeat, then add the brandy and flame. Cook another minute, taste for salt, and reserve.

To make the Salsa Marinera, heat the oil in a sauté pan and sauté the onion slowly until softened. Stir in the tomato and cook until the tomato liquid evaporates. Add the wine, thyme, and bay leaf and boil down to half. Stir in the flour, cook a minute, then pour in the Fish Broth. Simmer, uncovered, 30 minutes. Strain and measure out 1 cup. Taste for salt.

Place 2 tablespoons of the crab filling down the middle of each crepe and roll up tightly. Arrange in a greased baking pan and pour on the sauce. Bake at 400°F for 10 minutes.

The Eminently Edible Squid

Despite squid's somewhat menacing appearance, it is an inexpensive high-protein food that continues to gain in popularity. There was a time when fishermen near our shores would dump squid that became entrapped in their nets; squid had little following in America, although it has long been an everyday food in Europe. What a dramatic turn-around squid has made, featured today on so many restaurant menus.

Perhaps the "cleanest" animal of the deep, the squid has an external digestive system and no skeletal structure except a vestigial cartilage (it is technically a mollusk); unlike other fish, which lose about half of their weight when cleaned, more than 75 percent of the squid is edible. In general, small squid are better—more tender and less chewy. Note, however, that for squid to be tender it must be quick-cooked or subjected to long, slow cooking; any other way, the squid toughens.

Squid move by jet-style propulsion, ejecting ink to confuse their predators. This ink was once used for writing and drawing (sepia photographs take their name from the brownish color of the ink of the related cuttlefish, called *sepia* in Ancient Greek and in Spanish). Squid ink is essential to several of Spain's most celebrated dishes, such as stuffed squid in ink sauce and black rice. It gives any dish a striking appearance, while it lends subtle flavor and acts as a thickener.

Cleaning squid is a thankless chore, better left to your fishmonger. But if you can't find squid ink (it comes in vacuum-sealed packets and is sold in fish markets or specialty food shops—see Marketing Sources, p. 428) and a recipe requires it, clean the squid yourself.

To clean squid, remove the outer membrane, then grasp the squid body in one hand and with the other hand pull out the head and tentacles. Cut off the tentacles, but keep them attached to one another. Locate the silvery ink sac and gently peel it off, being careful to keep it intact. Discard the remaining waste material. Turn the body of the squid inside out, rinse under cold water, removing the cartilage and any other waste material. Turn right side out and use as directed.

CHIPIRONES RELLENOS EN SU TINTA
(Stuffed Baby Squid in Ink Sauce)

While the Spanish word *calamar* generally refers to large squid, *chipirón* in the Basque Country means baby squid; for any squid dish requiring slow cooking, they are far superior because of their more delicate flesh. This dish is another brilliant example of the Basque genius for taking the simplest ingredients and transforming them into works of art. If you order squid in ink at the most sophisticated or humblest restaurant or bar in the Basque Country, it will invariably be excellent, with hardly a difference of ingredients or technique, although in restaurants where price is no object *chipirones de pincho*—hooked by hand rather than netted—will be featured. In a region where every subtlety is noted and appreciated, the difference is significant.

The traditional and perfect accompaniment to this dish is white rice, which should be molded—into a half ball or into a ring around the squid (Spanish-style rice is slightly sticky and molds easily). Recently, vacuum-sealed packets of squid ink have become available and greatly reduce the bother associated with emptying squid ink sacs. They are found here at some food specialty markets (see Marketing Sources, p. 428). Otherwise you will need uncleaned squid and some extras to obtain the necessary ink (to clean the squid, see box, p. 81).   *Serves 4*

2 pounds very small cleaned (p. 81) squid with tentacles (the body should be no more than 3 inches long), adding 1 pound large uncleaned squid if not using the ink packets

Two 4-gram packets squid ink or the ink from the squid ink sacs
¼ cup dry red wine
¼ cup Fish Broth (p. 175) or 3 tablespoons clam juice diluted with 1 tablespoon water

STUFFING

2 tablespoons olive oil
2 medium onions, very finely chopped
3 cloves garlic, minced

3 tablespoons minced parsley
Salt
Freshly ground pepper

. . .

1 tablespoon olive oil
2 medium onions, finely
   chopped
4 cloves garlic, minced
½ pound green frying peppers,
   cored, seeded, and finely
   chopped

½ pound tomatoes, skinned,
   seeded, and finely chopped
2 sprigs parsley
Salt
Freshly ground pepper

Remove the soft swimming fins from the squid and chop them and the tentacles finely. In a small bowl combine the squid ink with the wine and Fish Broth (if using ink sacs, pass the ink, wine, and broth through a strainer several times). Set aside.

To make the Stuffing, heat the oil in a skillet and sauté the chopped fins and tentacles, the onions, garlic, parsley, salt, and pepper over low heat about 10 minutes. Cool, then fill the squid bodies with the mixture, about 2 teaspoons to each squid (do not overstuff since the squid will shrink during cooking). Close with toothpicks.

In a shallow casserole, heat the oil and sauté the onions, garlic, peppers, tomatoes, and parsley for 5 minutes. Cover and cook very slowly 15 minutes. Raise the heat, add the stuffed squid, and simmer about 5 minutes, or until the squid become opaque. Stir in the ink mixture, season with salt and pepper, cover, and cook at a slow simmer 1½ to 2 hours, or until the squid is tender. Remove the squid to a warm platter. Strain the sauce, pressing with the back of a wooden spoon to pass as much of the solid matter as possible (the sauce should be quite thick). Return the sauce to the casserole with the squid, taste for salt, cover, and cook 20 minutes more, stirring occasionally to prevent sticking.

If serving with white rice, use the recipe on page 297 but omit the pine nuts, parsley, thyme, and saffron and use 1½ cups water and ½ cup chicken broth. Mold the rice into a half ball, or into a ring, placing the squid and its sauce at the center.

BEGI AUNDIS A LA PARRILLA CON CEBOLLA, PIMIENTO, Y TINTA
(Grilled Cuttlefish with Onions, Peppers, and Ink Sauce)

START PREPARATION 1 DAY IN ADVANCE

This is one of the most exquisite dishes imaginable, created by Spain's foremost chef, Juan Mari Arzak, who has received worldwide acclaim and achieved a coveted three stars from Michelin for Arzak, his restaurant in San Sebastián. But fame has never gone to the head of Juan Mari—his restaurant is the same roadside establishment begun by his mother in the very house where he was born. Of course, today the restaurant is elegantly appointed and the kitchen a marvel of modern efficiency.

Juan Mari relies upon the extraordinary produce of the Basque Country, and his preparation of classic regional fare is done to perfection. However, when he sets out to create, he is in a class of his own, as this dish attests. Although I have taken care to present only traditional cooking in this book, I make an exception in this case because the dish is so special and because it is, in essence, nothing more than a brilliant rearrangement of ingredients basic to Basque cuisine and that are in fact all found in the classic rendition of this dish called Chipirones Rellenos en su Tinta (p. 82).

Although there are several separate operations involved here, none are difficult. Use cuttlefish, certainly not as popular as its close cousin squid (it is thicker than squid and generally considered less refined than squid); if you can't find it, large squid are a good substitute. And if squid ink packets are not available to you (see Marketing Sources, p. 428), buy the cuttlefish or squid uncleaned and extract the ink yourself (buy a few extra fish to ensure enough ink, and save the extra fish for use in another recipe).

Be very careful not to overcook the fish, since cuttlefish and squid toughen rapidly. The ink sauce, the bed of vegetables, and the vinaigrette can all be made in advance, leaving only a quick grilling of the fish at the last minute. *Serves 4*

4 cuttlefish or 4 very large squid, about ¾ pound each, uncleaned, or 6 ounces each, cleaned, with tentacles
½ cup extra virgin olive oil

3 large shallots minced
4 tablespoons minced
    parsley

Salt

VEGETABLE BED

3 tablespoons olive oil
2 medium onions, finely chopped
¾ pound green frying peppers,
cored, seeded, and finely
chopped

INK SAUCE

Two 4-gram packets squid ink,
    or ink from the fish ink sacs
¾ cup dry red wine
3 tablespoons extra virgin olive
    oil
2 onions, chopped
2 cloves garlic, minced
½ pound green frying peppers,
    cored, seeded, and chopped

½ pound tomatoes, skinned,
    seeded, and chopped
1 tablespoon fresh rosemary or
    ½ teaspoon dried
2 sprigs parsley
Salt

VINAIGRETTE

2 tablespoons red wine vinegar
2 tablespoons white wine
    vinegar, preferably
    herbal-scented

1 clove garlic, mashed to a
    paste
1 tablespoon brandy
Salt

Slit open the cuttlefish lengthwise, and clean (see p. 81), reserving the tentacles and the ink sacs (if ink packets are not available). Remove and reserve the soft swimming fins. With a thin sharp knife, lightly score the outer side of the cuttlefish in a crisscross pattern, being very careful not to cut all the way through. Place in a single layer with the tentacles on a tray or in a shallow bowl. Pour on the oil, then sprinkle with shallots, 3 tablespoons of the parsley, and salt. Cover and refrigerate overnight.

    To make the Vegetable Bed, heat the oil in a shallow casserole with the onions and peppers. Sauté a minute or two, cover, and cook very slowly 30 minutes. Transfer to a shallow bowl and wipe out the casserole.

Grilled Cuttlefish (continued)

To make the Ink Sauce, place the contents of the ink packets or the ink sacs, including the extra ones, in a strainer over a small bowl. Press with a wooden spoon to pass the ink through the strainer. Pour the wine through the strainer. Pass the liquid from the bowl through the strainer several times more, until most of the ink color is removed from the strainer. Set aside. Heat the oil in the casserole and sauté the onions, garlic, peppers, tomatoes, rosemary, parsley, salt, and reserved swimming fins for a minute or two. Cover and cook very slowly 15 minutes. Add the ink and wine mixture and salt to taste, then cook at a slow boil for about 10 minutes. Strain, pushing through as much of the solid matter as possible with the aid of a wooden spoon. The sauce should be quite thick.

Whisk together the Vinaigrette ingredients. Heat a greased stovetop griddle to the smoking point. Remove the fish from the marinade (let some of the oil and seasonings cling to the fish) and place on the griddle, scored side down. Cook over a high flame—1 minute for cuttlefish, 30 seconds for squid. Turn, pour on the vinaigrette, and cook the cuttlefish 1 minute more (30 seconds for the squid). Remove the fish to a warm platter, leaving the tentacles to grill about 1 minute more.

Warm the Vegetable Bed and the Ink Sauce. Arrange the vegetables in the center of 4 dinner dishes. Cover with the fish. Place the tentacles slightly under the upper edge of the fish (making it look somewhat like a whole fish again) and spoon the ink sauce around the other three sides of the fish. Sprinkle with the remaining tablespoon of minced parsley.

Baby Eels: A Spanish Delicacy

Angulas—baby eels or elvers—have been compared to short spaghetti strands with eyes, among other unappetizing descriptions. But to Spaniards *angulas* are manna from heaven and worth every peseta of their extravagant price.

Eons before Europe "discovered" America, the European eel had been making its amazing five-month journey across the Atlantic to spawning grounds in the Sargasso Sea. In this seaweed-covered body of water between Bermuda and Puerto Rico, which is roughly the site of the infamous Bermuda Triangle, the eels mingle with their American counterparts, deposit immense numbers of eggs, and die. For the offspring of the European eel, however, a treacherous return voyage awaits, and these transparent larvae, no more than ¼ inch long, are carried by the Gulf Stream some 4,000 miles across the Atlantic to their ancestral rivers.

Untold numbers are consumed by predators along the way, and yet swarms of them arrive—albeit a full three years later—at the mouths of European rivers along the Atlantic and Mediterranean shores. By now they have grown to about 3 inches and acquired some pigmentation. In northern Spain fishermen await the prized catch with large metal sieves. Since eels have a remarkable ability to wriggle about out of water, they are killed by plunging them into water that has been deoxygenated with an infusion of tobacco and later parboiled in salt water. For this reason, you will never find truly "fresh" *angulas,* although in season (late October through February) they are rushed to fine restaurants, especially in the Basque Country, and eaten before freezing becomes necessary.

Indeed it was the Basques—fine fishermen and gastronomes that they are—who made *angulas* a highlight of their cooking and elevated them to culinary stardom in Spain (*angulas* are found, but rarely appreciated, elsewhere in the world). The final cooking of *angulas* requires exceptional restraint, for their flavor is so subtle (it is difficult to identify the taste as fish) that it can be lost altogether if *angulas* are

Baby Eels (continued)

combined with unsuitable or overpowering ingredients. There is nothing quite like the simple traditional Basque method of cooking *angulas* (see recipe below)—sizzled in individual earthenware ramekins (*cazuelitas*) in olive oil with garlic and a touch of chile pepper and then eaten with small wooden forks. Certainly chefs bent on creative cooking have abused *angulas,* scattering them about on salads and over fish as little more than an expensive garnish.

Angulas are commonly served in Spanish restaurants in the United States and are sold here (see Marketing Sources, p. 428) frozen (because they have been parboiled they freeze remarkably well). Don't even consider using tinned *angulas.* If you are wondering why the elvers that travel to American rivers are not captured and consumed, it is because their journey from the Sargasso Sea is significantly shorter and thus they are too small to cook with any success. If a larger market existed, the elvers could of course be fattened in fish farms and be every bit the equal of their European cousins. As for now, however, *angulas* remain a rare treat, and I have never met an adult or child who has not instantly fallen in love with them.

ANGULAS A LA BILBAÍNA
(Baby Eels in Oil and Garlic Sauce)

If you are fortunate enough to find baby eels (see box, p. 87, and Marketing Sources, p. 428) in this country, you will be sampling one of the world's great delicacies. The preparation takes a matter of seconds.

Makes 2 first-course portions

¼–½ pound baby eels
6 tablespoons extra virgin olive
    oil
2 cloves garlic, peeled and
    sliced

Four ½-inch pieces dried red
    chile pepper, seeded

If the eels are frozen, as they are most likely to be, it is very important to defrost them in the refrigerator overnight—never at room temperature or they will shrivel and dry out. Dry them well between paper towels.

In each of two 4½-inch *cazuelitas* (flameproof earthenware ramekins) heat 3 tablespoons of the oil, a sliced clove of garlic, and two pieces of the dried red chile pepper over a high flame. When the garlic just begins to turn golden, quickly add the baby eels, divided equally between the two ramekins, immediately remove from the heat, and cover each ramekin with a small plate. Serve right away, uncovering the *angulas* when they are brought to the table and giving them a quick stir.

REO CON ALMEJAS
(Salmon Trout with Clams)

Utterly simple, delicately flavored, and prepared in no time. Needless to say, the freshest fish is a necessity. The dish comes from one of Galicia's fine restaurants, Vilas, in the historic city of Santiago de Compostela, which has been a place of pilgrimage since the Middle Ages because it is here that the Apostle Saint James is said to be interred (see my book *Discovering Spain: An Uncommon Guide* for more information about the city and Saint James).

Serves 4

½ cup dry fruity white wine, preferably Galicia's Albariño, or Spanish sparkling wine (*cava*)
½ teaspoon Dijon-style mustard
2 teaspoons butter
2 tablespoons olive oil
2 pounds salmon trout or other trout fillets, skin removed

2 cloves garlic, minced
Salt
24 cockles or Manila clams or 12 small littlenecks, thoroughly cleansed (see p. 33)
Fish Broth (p. 175) or clam juice diluted with ¼ part water, as needed
1 tablespoon minced parsley

In a cup, combine the wine and mustard. Heat the butter and oil in a skillet and very lightly sauté the trout on both sides. Remove to a warm platter (the fish will be partially cooked). In the same skillet put the garlic, the wine mix-

Salmon Trout with Clams (continued)

ture, salt to taste, and the clams and simmer, removing the clams as they open. Return the clams and fish fillets to the skillet and continue cooking until the fish is done (a total time, including the sauté, of 5 minutes for each ½ inch of thickness), adding some Fish Broth as needed to maintain a small amount of sauce in the skillet. Spoon the sauce over the fish, sprinkle with parsley, and serve.

MERLUZA FRITA A LA ROMANA
(Egg-Coated Fried Hake)

You can find hake prepared in this simple manner all over Spain, but it is the small details and the quality of the fish that make all the difference. I have found that the hints provided by Patxiku Quintana, a white-bearded Basque who is owner and chef of a fine restaurant of the same name in the Old Quarter of San Sebastián, make the fish (be it hake or scrod) exceptionally succulent and flavorful. Some of his secrets are salting the fish before cooking, adding garlic to the cooking oil, and using a small skillet in which the fish fits snugly. The egg coating locks in moisture.   *Serves 4*

Four 1-inch hake or scrod steaks	Flour for dusting
Kosher or sea salt	2 eggs, lightly beaten with 1
¼ cup olive oil	teaspoon water
2 large unpeeled garlic cloves,	Lemon wedges
lightly crushed	

Sprinkle the fish well on both sides with salt and let sit at room temperature for 30 minutes.

Heat the oil and garlic over a medium-high flame in a small skillet in which 2 fish steaks will just fit, until the oil is hot but has not reached the smoking point. Lightly dust 2 of the fish steaks with flour, coat with the egg, and place directly into the hot oil. Cook over moderate heat, turning once, until lightly golden, about 4 minutes to a side (be careful not to overcook). Drain and keep warm, then repeat for the remaining fish steaks (or use 2 skillets and prepare all 4 steaks at the same time). Serve with lemon wedges.

MERLUZA A LA VASCA
(Hake with Clams in Wine and Parsley Sauce)

One of the great dishes of Spanish cuisine, and, as is usually the case with Spanish cooking, simplicity itself. Its distinctiveness results from using the finest ingredients—extra virgin olive oil and just-caught fish from the Bay of Biscay—plus employing a few techniques that produce a magnificently light but slightly thickened sauce. There are many variations on this dish, like the addition of peas and asparagus, but here it is in its purest—and I think its best—form. *Serves 4*

½ cup Fish Broth (p. 175) or 6 tablespoons clam juice diluted with 2 tablespoons water

½ cup dry white wine

2 pounds hake or scrod, in 1-inch steaks

Kosher or sea salt

6 tablespoons extra virgin olive oil

6 cloves garlic, minced

Two 1-inch pieces, or to taste, dried red chile pepper, seeded

1 tablespoon flour

4 tablespoons (¼ cup) minced parsley

24–28 cockles or Manila clams or 12–16 very small littlenecks, thoroughly cleansed

In a small saucepan boil the Fish Broth and wine down to half.

Sprinkle the fish on both sides with salt. Let sit 15 minutes. In a shallow earthenware casserole or a skillet in which the fish fits closely (the size is important for best results), slowly heat the oil, garlic, and chile pepper until the garlic is lightly colored. Add the fish, sprinkle with the flour and 2 tablespoons of the parsley, and cook a minute over medium heat. Add the clams and the broth, a little at a time, cooking 2 minutes more and gently shaking the casserole all the while.

Carefully turn the fish and cook another 5 minutes, continuing to gently shake the casserole. Continue cooking until the clams open and the fish is done, about 5 more minutes. If some of the clams have not opened, remove the fish, cover the casserole, and cook briefly. Serve, spooning the sauce over the fish and arranging the clams around each dish. Sprinkle with the remaining parsley.

MERLUZA A LA BILBAÍNA
(Hake with Olive Oil, Garlic, and Chile Pepper)

Here's a twist on a well-known Basque fish preparation that is little more than olive oil, garlic, dried red chile pepper, and exquisitely fresh fish. This version from a Basque restaurant in Madrid, Taberna Gaztelupe, adds a touch of vinegar and soaks the chile pepper to reduce its fire.

Serves 4

Two 2-inch pieces dried red
   chile pepper, seeded
2 pounds hake, scrod, or monkfish, about 1 inch thick
Kosher or sea salt
¼ cup extra virgin olive oil
4 cloves garlic, peeled and cut
   in thin slices

2 teaspoons wine vinegar,
   preferably white
2 tablespoons minced parsley
4 teaspoons Fish Broth (p. 175)
   or diluted clam juice

Soak the chile pepper in warm water until softened, about 10 minutes. Drain and cut in very thin crosswise slices. Sprinkle the fish on both sides with salt and let sit.

In a small skillet heat the oil with the chile pepper and the garlic and cook over a medium flame until the garlic is lightly colored. Stir in the vinegar, parsley, Fish Broth, and salt to taste. Remove from the flame.

Grease a stovetop griddle with oil and heat to the smoking point. Grill the fish over medium-high heat, about 10 minutes, or until done, turning once. Reheat the garlic sauce and pour over the fish.

MERLUZA A LA SIDRA
(Fresh Hake in Hard Cider Sauce)

Oven-baked fish dishes from the north of Spain are often served over a bed of sliced potatoes, slowly fried in oil before they are combined with the fish. In my efforts to limit the oil in dishes such as this one, I have microwaved the potatoes, with hardly any oil, and find the texture and taste to be surprisingly similar to the original method.

In Asturias, where this dish is popular, hard dry apple cider is often used in cooking, but I have not found a similar cider in America. Therefore, it is best to substitute Spanish *cava* (sparkling wine) or a dry fruity white wine.

Serves 4

3 tablespoons olive oil
2 medium potatoes, peeled and
    cut in ⅛-inch slices
Salt
Freshly ground pepper
2 pounds boneless hake or
    scrod, about 1½ inches
    thick, cut into 4 portions
Flour for dusting
4 cloves garlic, minced
1 onion, finely chopped
1 teaspoon flour
3 tablespoons minced parsley

2 teaspoons imported sweet
    paprika
A 1-inch piece dried red chile
    pepper, seeded
2 cups dry Spanish cider,
    sparkling wine, or white
    wine
¼ cup peeled chopped apple
1 bay leaf
2 dozen fresh cockles or Manila
    clams or 1 dozen very small
    littleneck clams, thoroughly
    cleansed (see p. 33)

Grease a shallow microwave-safe casserole (large enough to hold the fish in one layer) and arrange the potato slices in layers, sprinkling each layer with salt and pepper and drizzling with olive oil (a total of about 1 tablespoon oil). Spoon 2 tablespoons water over the potatoes, cover, and cook on high for 8 minutes. Turn the potatoes, cover, and continue cooking for about 6 minutes. The potatoes should be almost tender. Alternately, the sliced potatoes can be drizzled with oil (eliminate the water) and cooked in a greased shallow casserole, tightly covered with foil, in a 350°F oven for about 45 minutes, or until almost tender.

Sprinkle the fish with salt and pepper and dust with flour. Heat 1 tablespoon of the oil in a skillet and quickly brown the fish on both sides (the fish will continue to cook in the oven) and place over the potatoes. Wipe out the skillet. Add the remaining tablespoon of oil, heat, and sauté the garlic and onion until the onion has wilted. Stir in the teaspoon of flour, 2 tablespoons of the parsley, the paprika, and the chile pepper, then add the cider, apple, bay leaf, salt, and pepper. Simmer 5 minutes, then

Hake in Hard Cider Sauce (continued)

pour over the fish and potatoes. Arrange the clams around the fish, cover, and transfer to a 350°F oven for about 25 minutes, or until the fish reaches an internal temperature of 140° to 145°F. Sprinkle with the remaining parsley.

MERLUZA ENCEBOLLADA
(Hake Smothered in Onions)

An excellent dish popular along Spain's northern coast. A large amount of very slow-cooked onions makes the fish succulent and exceptionally flavorful. The onions can be prepared in advance; final preparation takes just 15 minutes.   *Serves 4*

3 tablespoons extra virgin olive
  oil
2 medium onions, slivered
2 tablespoons minced scallions,
  white part only
¾ cup hard dry cider or dry
  fruity white wine, sparkling
  or still

Salt
Freshly ground pepper
2 pounds hake or scrod, in
  1-inch steaks
4 teaspoons bread crumbs
1 clove garlic, minced
2 tablespoons minced parsley

Heat the oil in a shallow ovenproof casserole, and sauté the onions and scallions a minute or two. Cover and cook over low heat for 10 minutes. Add the cider, turn up the flame, and cook away most of the liquid. Season with salt and pepper. Remove from the heat.

Sprinkle the fish with salt and pepper and add to the casserole. Spoon some of the onion mixture over the fish, sprinkle with the bread crumbs, garlic, and parsley and drizzle with olive oil. Bake in a 400°F oven for about 15 minutes, or until the fish is done.

PIMIENTOS RELLENOS DE MERLUZA JOSETXO
(Fish-Filled Pimientos)

When July 7 arrives in Pamplona, the week-long madness of the Running of the Bulls begins, and the city is transformed from a quiet, quite ordinary provincial capital into a center of insanity, as Spaniards and foreigners alike flock to the city for the annual rite that you will find described at length in my book *Discovering Spain: An Uncommon Guide*. The city's bars and restaurants are filled to capacity at lunch and dinner time, and Restaurante Josetxo, before it moved, was at the heart of the excitement, right on Estafeta Street, where the bulls run free with those who choose to tempt fate.

I remember when owner Felisa Burgui would give us front-row seats to watch the charging bulls, enveloped by the fast-moving crowds, from the safety of her first-floor balcony; it was truly a memorable sight. Since then Josetxo has relocated to more elegant and peaceful quarters where it continues as one of the city's finest restaurants. Among the excellent Navarra dishes served there are these fish-filled *piquillo* peppers (see box, p. 127) so popular in Navarra, La Rioja, and the Basque Country. They may be served in a fresh tomato sauce, although I also like them with a puréed pimiento sauce (see p. 152).   *Serves 6*

TOMATO SAUCE

3 tablespoons olive oil
1 clove garlic, minced
1 medium onion, finely
  chopped
1 small leek, well washed and
  finely chopped

1 pound tomatoes, peeled,
  seeded, and chopped
Salt
¼ cup brandy

Fish-Filled Pimientos (continued)

. . .

12 very small elongated fresh
    red frying peppers, or 24
    pimientos del piquillo
2 tablespoons olive oil
1 medium onion, finely
    chopped
2 cloves garlic, minced
½ pound green frying peppers,
    finely chopped

2 tablespoons minced parsley
2 ounces Spanish mountain
    cured ham or prosciutto,
    minced
¾ pound hake or scrod, in
    ½-inch cubes
Salt
Freshly ground pepper
Minced parsley for garnish

To make the Tomato Sauce, heat the oil in a shallow casserole and sauté the garlic, onion, and leek a minute or two. Cover and cook very slowly 15 minutes. Add the tomatoes, salt, and brandy and cook uncovered 15 minutes more. Transfer to a food processor and purée. Strain and reserve.

If you are using fresh red peppers, hold them over a high flame or better still, rest them on a burner diffuser over a high flame or on a charcoal grill until they are thoroughly blackened. Place in a paper bag until the skins have softened, then remove the skins with wet hands. Core and seed the peppers but otherwise leave them intact.

Heat the oil in a shallow casserole and sauté the onion, garlic, green peppers, parsley, and ham for a minute or two. Cover and cook very slowly for 15 minutes. Add the fish, season with salt and pepper (it should be well seasoned), and cook about 5 minutes, or until the fish is opaque. Cool.

Fill each *piquillo* pepper with 1 to 1½ tablespoons of the fish mixture (about 2 tablespoons when using fresh red peppers). Return the Tomato Sauce to the casserole and add the filled peppers. Cover and simmer about 10 minutes. Sprinkle with parsley and serve.

RAPE ALIÑADO SOBRE UN LECHO DE PURÉ DE PATATA
(Garlic-Brushed Monkfish on a Bed of Creamy Mashed Potatoes)

I always remember this dish—a paragon of simplicity—that I ate at Karlos Arguiñano, a restaurant and small deluxe hotel in Zarautz with magnificent sea vistas. Its chef, Karlos Arguiñano, has become a household word in Spain because of his enormously popular television series, which features simple-to-make, tasty foods, made special by the subtle touches of a fine chef. His restaurant is today a required stop for anyone passing through Zarautz.

This beautifully presented grilled monkfish was served over thin, almost sauce-like puréed potatoes and garnished with just-caught prawns and the first asparagus of spring.

Serves 4

6 tablespoons extra virgin olive oil
1 tablespoon lemon juice
2 cloves garlic, minced
3 tablespoons minced parsley
Kosher or sea salt
4 monkfish (or other firm-textured fish like swordfish or halibut) steaks, about 1 inch thick
½ recipe Creamy Potato Purée (p. 72)
Cooked shrimp and asparagus spears for garnish (optional)

In a small bowl combine the olive oil, lemon juice, garlic, parsley, and salt. Reserve. Sprinkle the fish on both sides with salt and let sit while preparing the potatoes. When the potatoes are made, keep them warm while cooking the fish.

Coat a stovetop griddle or skillet with oil and heat to the smoking point. Grill the fish about 5 minutes to a side, or until done. Spoon the potatoes onto dinner plates and place the fish over the potatoes. Brush the fish generously with the olive oil mixture and serve, garnished if so desired with the optional shrimp and asparagus.

LISA A LA PARRILLA
(Grilled Mullet with Anchovy Sauce)

This is a delicious way to grill almost any kind of whole fish—brushed with a sauce of garlic, anchovy, oil, and vinegar. I like to fillet the fish before serving—simply run a knife with a thin blade along the length of the bone.

Serves 4

Grilled Mullet with Anchovy Sauce (continued)

Whole fish, such as mullet or red snapper, either four ¾-pound or two 1½-pound fish, cleaned, heads on or off	2 tablespoons lemon juice
	9 anchovy fillets, minced
	3 cloves garlic, minced
	2 tablespoons minced parsley
	¼ teaspoon dried crushed hot red pepper
Salt	3 tablespoons wine vinegar
Freshly ground pepper	
½ cup extra virgin olive oil	

Place the fish in a shallow bowl and sprinkle both sides with salt and pepper. In a small bowl whisk together 4 tablespoons of the oil and the lemon juice. Pour over the fish, turn to coat, cover, and refrigerate for at least 1 hour.

Meanwhile, in a mortar or mini processor mash to a paste the anchovy, garlic, parsley, and crushed red pepper. Stir in the vinegar and the remaining 4 tablespoons oil.

Heat a grill or stovetop griddle, brush it with oil, and grill the fish 10 minutes to each inch of thickness, turning once and basting occasionally with the anchovy mixture. Fillet the fish, leaving the skin on, brush with the remaining anchovy mixture, and serve.

ATÚN A LA ASTURIANA
(Tuna Steaks with Onion and Vinegar)

Sautéed onion and garlic and a splash of vinegar combine to enhance a simple tuna steak.   *Serves 4*

2 pounds tuna steaks, about 1 inch thick	1 medium onion, slivered
	4 cloves garlic, minced
Salt	2 teaspoons imported sweet paprika
Freshly ground pepper	
2 cloves garlic, mashed to a paste	2 tablespoons wine vinegar
	Pinch of sugar
4 tablespoons minced parsley	2–3 tablespoons Fish Broth (p. 175), diluted clam juice, or water
1 tablespoon olive oil	

Rub the tuna steaks on both sides with the salt, pepper, and mashed garlic, and sprinkle with 2 tablespoons of the parsley. Let sit 20 minutes.

Heat the oil in a skillet and slowly sauté the onion until it has wilted. Add the minced garlic, cook a minute, then stir in the paprika, vinegar, salt, pepper, sugar, the remaining 2 tablespoons parsley, and the Fish Broth. Cover and cook very slowly for 8 to 10 minutes, adding more broth if necessary.

Meanwhile, heat a greased griddle or grill and cook the tuna until just done, about 8 to 10 minutes, turning once (do not overcook). Serve, spooning the onion mixture over the tuna.

ATÚN A LA BILBAÍNA
(Grilled Tuna with Red Pepper Sauce)

A purée of pimientos, seasoned with garlic, onion, and plenty of paprika, is lovely in combination with tuna. It is best to grill the tuna over hot coals— the charcoal adds yet another dimension of flavor.

Serves 4

2 pounds tuna steaks, about 1 inch thick
Salt
3 tablespoons extra virgin olive oil
2 cloves garlic, mashed to a paste
4 tablespoons minced parsley
1 medium onion, slivered
4 cloves garlic, minced

2 tablespoons imported sweet paprika
4 medium pimientos, home-made (p. 178) or imported, chopped
1¼–1½ cups Fish Broth (p. 175) or 1–1¼ cups clam juice diluted with ¼ cup water
Freshly ground pepper

Sprinkle the fish on both sides with salt. Mix together in a cup 2 tablespoons of the oil, the mashed garlic, and 2 tablespoons of the parsley. Brush this mixture on the fish and let sit.

Heat the remaining tablespoon of oil in a skillet and sauté the onion and minced garlic for a minute or two. Cover and continue cooking very slowly for 10 minutes. Stir in the paprika, the pimientos, the remaining 2 table-

Grilled Tuna (continued)

spoons parsley, ¾ cup of the Fish Broth, and salt and pepper to taste. Simmer 5 minutes.

Transfer the pimiento mixture to a food processor and purée. With the motor running, drizzle in more of the broth, until the mixture has a fairly thick sauce consistency. Return to the skillet and slowly simmer while preparing the fish.

Grill the tuna over hot coals or on a greased stovetop griddle, allowing 4 to 5 minutes on each side. Spoon the sauce onto dinner plates and place the fish on top.

Cooking with Salt Cod: A Tradition as Old as Civilization Itself

A good argument can be made attributing the spread of civilization to the trade in codfish. At a time when there was no refrigeration and most products were available only in their season, cod—dried and salted—was one of the few year-round foods, and was marketed throughout the known world. When Christianity in medieval times mandated meatless meals on certain days and times of the year, the demand for fish skyrocketed. For the poor and for those far from the sea, this meant eating dried cod. Why cod rather than other kinds of fish? Because dried cod has the remarkable ability to last for long periods without spoiling or changing significantly in quality.

Cod's long association with penitence and abstinence and its totally unappetizing appearance when dried have often made it an object of contempt. Reinforcing this impression are the nailed wooden crates, resembling coffins, in which cod is packed. And yet when properly handled and prepared, salt cod is food for the gods.

Cod seeks out cold waters, hence it is found in the North Atlantic, from the Bay of Biscay to Boston (the cod that lives farthest to the north is said to have the finest quality). It was the Basques, fearless fishermen accustomed to braving fierce storms and open waters, who by the fifteenth century were fishing as far from home as Newfoundland. They pursued whales and cod, and in the waters around that island found fish in such abundance that they merely lowered their nets, then raised them, overflowing with fish. When fish is found in such quantity, fishermen know a larger body of land cannot be far away (cod in particular congregate in relatively shallow waters), and it was the profusion of fish observed around Newfoundland and in the Grand Banks that extend to Massachusetts (Cape Cod was so named because its waters teemed with cod) that may have caused Columbus and other early explorers to theorize that a continent was nearby. Cod was therefore in part responsible for the discovery of the New World.

Dried cod can suffer a host of indignities and emerge relatively unscathed. To consider salt cod in the same category as fish is somehow misleading, for it is a food unto itself with a lore and tradition unique among sea creatures. A common Spanish expression, *"el que corta el bacalao"* (he who cuts the cod), refers to a person of great influence and prestige and indicates the high regard for cod in Spain, where it is found in all regional cooking. It has a firm texture, a singular taste, and it combines effortlessly with vegetables, fruit, and beans, in all sorts of sauces, a trait which makes it an appealing and practical fish in cooking.

But it was the Basques who had the wisdom to take cod and magically transform it into a culinary wonder. The preparation of salt cod in the Basque Country reaches rarefied heights, and nothing is more representative of Basque cooking than dried cod, despite the incredibly high quality of the fresh fish found in Basque markets.

All salt cod is not created equal. Its worth depends first on the quality of the fresh cod from which it is made and also on the drying process and the conditions under which the fish is stored. Desalting is an art unto itself, and even some of the finest Basque chefs entrust the soaking procedure to their fishmongers, whose sixth sense tells them when the cod has reached its optimum moment.

When buying dried cod, shop in fish markets or food stores that

Cooking with Salt Cod (continued)

cater to a demanding ethnic clientele with a passion for dried cod, such as the Portuguese, Spanish, and Italians. During the Christmas holidays, I have found my local Italian delicatessen to be the best place to buy cod. Look for cod that is very white, with some occasional streaks of yellow, and very well dried.

When desalting, seek the proper balance—the fish should not be salty, nor, on the other hand, bland. The best method is to cover the cod with cold water and refrigerate 2 to 3 days, changing the water once or twice a day. Occasionally break off a piece and taste, until it is desalted to your liking. If the cod is very thick or of irregular thickness, it is best to slice it into pieces of equal thickness so it can desalt more evenly.

BACALAO A LA VIZCAÍNA
(Dried Cod in Onion and Red Pepper Purée)

START PREPARATION SEVERAL DAYS IN ADVANCE

This dish is a masterpiece of Basque cookery—a unique sauce, assertive yet subtle, of slow-cooked onions and the flesh of dried red peppers. It takes hours of slow cooking to prepare Bacalao a la Vizcaína properly. Don't look for shortcuts if you want to create a superlative dish. And try your best to use dried sweet red peppers—the suggested alternative will not give the same results.

This slightly refined version is the recipe of the Basque chef Genaro Pildain of Guría restaurant, who is known for the miracles he works with this desiccated cod. It is typically served in a shallow earthenware casserole, or *cazuela*.   *Serves 4*

1¼ pounds boneless dried salt cod of uniform thickness (about ½ inch)

5 tablespoons olive oil
3 cloves garlic, minced
1¼ pounds red onions, chopped

¼ pound Spanish mountain
    cured ham or prosciutto,
    finely chopped
2 tablespoons minced parsley
4 medium dried sweet red
    peppers or mild New Mexico
    style, or a mixture of
    4 medium pimientos,
    finely chopped, and 4 tea-
    spoons paprika

1 tablespoon tomato sauce (op-
    tional)
A 1-inch piece, or to taste,
    dried red chile pepper, seeds
    removed
1 teaspoon butter
Salt
Freshly ground pepper
2 cloves garlic, peeled

Soak the cod in cold water to cover in the refrigerator for 2 to 3 days, chang-ing the water once or twice daily, until desalted to taste. Drain and dry on paper towels.

Heat the oil in a large shallow casserole and sauté the minced garlic, onions, ham, and parsley a minute or two. Cover and cook over a very low flame for 2½ hours.

Place the dried peppers in a saucepan and fill with water. Bring to a boil, then remove from the flame. Drain off the water, refill with cold water, and bring to a boil again. Repeat this 3 more times. Cut open the peppers and re-move the seeds. Scrape off the flesh with a knife—you should have about 4 tablespoons (¼ cup).

When the onion mixture is done, drain off as much of the oil as possi-ble, reserving 1 tablespoon. Add the flesh of the peppers (or the pimiento and paprika mixture) and cook slowly 15 minutes. Strain, pushing through as much of the solid matter as possible. Return to the casserole, add the tomato sauce (if using), chile pepper, butter, salt, and pepper. Simmer 5 min-utes.

In another shallow casserole, preferably earthenware, heat the reserved tablespoon of oil and brown the whole garlic, pressing with the back of a wooden spoon to extract its flavor. Discard the garlic. Add the cod and cook very slowly for 15 minutes, turning once. Spoon the sauce over the cod and heat over a low flame 5 minutes more before serving.

BACALAO CON PIMIENTOS Y MANZANA PATXIKU QUINTANA

(Salt Cod in Red Pepper Sauce with Apples)

START PREPARATION SEVERAL DAYS IN ADVANCE

Another unusual Basque preparation of salt cod that may sound odd but works beautifully, from master chef Patxiku Quintana (see p. 90) of San Sebastián.

Serves 4

1½ pounds dried boneless salt cod, in a ½-inch-thick piece (if it is thicker, split)
Flour for dusting
3 tablespoons olive oil
1 large onion, finely chopped
1 clove garlic, minced
½ pound tomatoes, skinned, seeded, and finely chopped
2 dried sweet red peppers, or mild New Mexico style, seeded and cut in pieces, or 2 pimientos plus 2 teaspoons paprika
¼ pound green frying peppers, cored, seeded, and finely chopped
1 Golden Delicious apple, skinned, cored, and cut in ½-inch wedges
Salt

To desalt the cod, place in cold water to cover. Refrigerate 2 to 3 days, until the cod is desalted to taste, changing the water once or twice daily. Drain and dry on paper towels and reserve ¾ cup of the liquid.

Dust the cod with flour. Heat the oil in a shallow casserole, add the cod, and brown lightly on both sides. Remove to a warm platter and leave 2 tablespoons of the oil in the casserole. Add the onion and garlic and slowly sauté until the onion has softened. Add the tomatoes, dried red pepper (or pimiento and paprika), green peppers, and apple. Cover and simmer 15 minutes. Add the reserved cod liquid and cook 15 minutes more. Transfer the contents of the casserole to a food processor and purée. Strain, pressing with the back of a wooden spoon to pass as much of the solid matter as possible. Return to the casserole, and add salt to taste. Place the cod over the sauce and simmer 5 minutes before serving.

BACALAO AL PIL PIL
(Dried Cod in Creamy Garlic Sauce)

START PREPARATION SEVERAL DAYS IN ADVANCE

A supreme creation of Basque cookery, and a dish that is magic to watch as it takes shape. No one in the Basque Country does cod quite like Genaro Pildain of Guría in Bilbao, and for that reason he is known throughout Spain as the Codfish Wizard. Don't pass up an opportunity to visit him in Bilbao; his absolutely masterful rendition of this dish is unrivaled anywhere.

Bacalao al Pil Pil begins simply as salt cod and olive oil, but gradually is transformed into a succulent cod with a creamy white sauce that is a product of the emulsion of the oil with the gelatinous juices of the fish.

Follow instructions precisely—like mayonnaise, this sauce emulsifies only if properly made; otherwise you will have a nice oil and garlic sauce, but nothing more. The tricks to achieve this act of sorcery are the thickness of the cod, its slow cooking, the constant shaking of the pan, and the very gradual addition of the oil, as for a mayonnaise.

If, however, the sauce fails to emulsify, it can be salvaged by dissolving 1 envelope (¼ ounce) gelatin in 2 tablespoons cold water. Stir into the sauce and continue to shake the pan until the sauce is creamy.   *Serves 4*

1 pound dried boneless salt cod, about 1 inch thick	A 1-inch piece, or to taste, dried red chile pepper, seeded and broken into
½ cup extra virgin olive oil	several pieces
4 cloves garlic, sliced	

Soak the cod in cold water to cover in the refrigerator for 2 to 3 days, changing the water once or twice daily, until desalted to taste. Drain and dry between paper towels.

In a skillet or earthenware casserole in which the cod pieces just fit (this is important), very slowly heat the oil with the garlic and chile, until the garlic just begins to color. Remove and reserve the garlic and chile. Add the cod and cook over medium-low heat for 8 to 10 minutes, turning once (the fish really simmers rather than sautés and should just sizzle lightly around the edges). Remove the cod to a warm platter. Drain the oil into a small bowl and

Dried Cod in Creamy Garlic Sauce (continued)

reserve. Pass a metal spatula over the bottom of the pan to be sure there are no stuck particles.

Return the fish to the pan and over the same low heat, add 1 tablespoon of the reserved oil, constantly shaking the pan back and forth and in circular motions until the oil emulsifies to a white creamy consistency. Add the rest of the oil, not more than a tablespoon at a time, and don't add more until the previous addition has emulsified. Continue until all the oil has been incorporated.

Transfer the fish to a serving platter or individual dinner plates, spoon on some sauce, and garnish with the garlic and chile.

Poultry ✻ Meats
Stuffed Vegetables

CHIMBOS A LA BILBAÍNA
(Sautéed Small Birds with Crumb Topping)

This recipe from Bilbao calls for *chimbos,* a loose term for small birds such as sparrows that are gastronomically prized. The preparation is as simple as can be, but delicious, and works just as well with Cornish hen, quail, or chicken.

Serves 4

2 Cornish hens, quartered
Salt
Freshly ground pepper
2 tablespoons olive oil

2 tablespoons bread crumbs
2 cloves garlic, minced
2 tablespoons minced parsley

Sprinkle the Cornish hen pieces with salt and pepper. Heat the oil in a shallow casserole, add the Cornish hen pieces, and sauté quickly until golden on both sides. Cover and continue cooking over a medium-low flame until cooked through, about 25 minutes.

Meanwhile, in a small bowl mix together the bread crumbs, garlic, and parsley. When the Cornish hens are done, remove to a warm platter. Add the bread crumb mixture to the skillet and sauté briefly until the crumbs are crisp. Spoon over the Cornish hens.

ZORZA CON HUEVOS FRITOS
(Marinated Ground Pork with Fried Eggs)

START PREPARATION I DAY IN ADVANCE

A wonderfully satisfying home-style dish that comes from Galicia and can be found at Mesón de Alberto in the ancient walled city of Lugo. The meat is marinated overnight in plenty of paprika (Galicians love to use substantial amounts of paprika in their cooking), then sautéed and served with boiled new potatoes and fried eggs. *Serves 4*

1 pound lean ground pork
4 teaspoons imported sweet
   paprika
½ teaspoon hot paprika
½ teaspoon salt
8 large cloves garlic, minced

¼ cup chicken broth or water
4–8 small new potatoes (not
   more than 2 inches in
   diameter)
1 tablespoon olive oil
4–8 eggs

In a bowl, mix the meat with the sweet and hot paprikas, salt, garlic, and broth. Cover and refrigerate overnight.

Boil the potatoes, in their skins, in salted water until tender. Meanwhile, heat the oil in a skillet, add the meat mixture, and sauté, breaking up the meat as it cooks, until lightly browned.

Once the meat and potatoes are done, fry the eggs—to taste, or better still, in the Spanish style (see p. 254). Peel the potatoes. Divide the meat onto dinner plates, and arrange the potatoes around the meat. Place the fried eggs over the meat and serve right away.

EMPANADA GALLEGA DE RAXÓ
(Galician Pork and Peppers Pie)

START PREPARATION 2 HOURS IN ADVANCE

I have never found a filling that is tastier and more succulent than this one for Galicia's classic savory pie. *Empanadas,* however, may be filled with many other mixtures, from tuna, scallops, and sardines to rabbit and chicken. The dough also varies according to the cook, from a real bread dough to a much more refined modified puff pastry. Here I have provided my favorite puff pastry *empanada* dough from *Tapas: The Little Dishes of Spain,* but when I do not have the time or inclination to make my own pastry, I go to my local pizzeria and buy an uncooked pizza dough. The *empanada* comes out just like those of Galicia based on bread dough.

Empanadas cut in small wedges or squares make excellent tapas, and in larger portions, accompanied by a salad, make a most enjoyable light meal. I think they are at their best freshly baked but at room temperature.

Makes about 4 dinner or 8–10 tapas portions

Puff Pastry for Empanadas (p. 109) or 1½ pounds pizza dough

3 cloves garlic, peeled

2 tablespoons minced parsley

1½ teaspoons minced oregano leaves or ¼ teaspoon dried

Several strands of saffron

1½ teaspoons thyme leaves or ¼ teaspoon dried

¼ cup olive oil

3 tablespoons dry white wine

¾ pound boneless pork loin, cut in ⅛-inch slices, then in ½-inch strips

1 large onion, preferably Vidalia or Spanish, slivered

¾ pound green frying peppers, cored, seeded, and cut in long narrow strips

2 teaspoons imported sweet paprika

¼ pound tomato, skinned, seeded, and chopped

4 tablespoons (¼ cup) finely diced Spanish mountain cured ham, prosciutto, or capicollo

Salt

Freshly ground pepper

1 hard-boiled egg, sliced

1 pimiento, imported or homemade (p. 178), cut in strips

1 egg, lightly beaten with 1 teaspoon water

If using homemade dough, prepare according to instructions.

In a mortar or mini processor, mash to a paste the garlic, parsley, oregano, saffron, and thyme. Mix in 1 tablespoon of the oil and the wine. Transfer to a bowl and mix in the strips of pork, coating them well. Marinate 2 hours. Drain the meat and reserve the marinade.

In a shallow casserole, heat 2 tablespoons of the oil and slowly sauté the meat until it just loses its color. Return the meat to the reserved marinade. Add the remaining tablespoon of oil to the casserole and sauté the onion and peppers a minute or two. Cover and cook very slowly for 15 minutes. Stir in the paprika, then turn up the heat, add the tomato, and cook 5 minutes. Add the pork with its marinade and the ham and season with salt and pepper.

Roll the dough into a 14- by 28-inch rectangle. Divide into two 14-inch squares, then trim the corners to make two 14-inch circles. Place one of them on a cookie sheet (dampened if using pastry dough, sprinkled with cornmeal or flour if using pizza dough) and arrange the pork mixture to within 1 inch of the edge. Scatter on the egg slices, top with the pimiento strips, and cover with the second dough circle. Roll up the edges and press well to seal. Make several slits in the dough, brush with the beaten egg, and bake at 350°F for about 30 to 35 minutes, or until browned. Cool a few minutes before serving or serve at room temperature.

MASA HOJALDRADA PARA EMPANADAS
(Puff Pastry for Empanadas)
Makes dough for 1 large savory pie

3 cups unbleached flour
1½ teaspoons salt
¾ cup cold water
4½ teaspoons vinegar

2 egg yolks
1 cup lard or vegetable shortening, softened

Mix the flour in a large bowl with the salt, then incorporate the water, vinegar, and egg yolks and work the dough with your hands until the dough forms a smooth ball. Let sit for 30 minutes covered with plastic wrap.

Roll the dough into a 10- by 15-inch rectangle. With a rubber spatula spread ⅓ cup of the lard over the dough. With the aid of a knife, fold one side over the top, then fold over the other side, business-letter fashion.

Puff Pastry for Empanadas (continued)

Enclose again in plastic wrap and refrigerate for 15 minutes. Repeat, using another ⅓ cup of the lard, refrigerating 15 minutes more. Repeat a third time, leaving the dough refrigerated this time for 1 hour. The dough is better if refrigerated overnight, and it may also be frozen.

CEBOLLAS RELLENAS DE CARNE
(Meat-Filled Baked Onions)

I think these onions make a lovely meal that is delicate, light, and quite elegant.

Serves 6

12 medium onions
3 tablespoons olive oil
3 cloves garlic, minced
1½-pound mixture of ground
    beef, veal, and pork in equal
    parts
2 tablespoons finely chopped
    Spanish mountain cured
    ham, prosciutto, or
    capicollo
3 tablespoons minced parsley
Salt
Freshly ground pepper

1 tablespoon thyme leaves or
    ½ teaspoon dried
3 tablespoons seeded and finely
    chopped tomato
6 tablespoons finely chopped
    pimiento, preferably im-
    ported or homemade
    (p. 178)
2 hard-boiled eggs, finely
    chopped
½ cup dry white wine
½ cup chicken broth

Remove the tough outer layers of the onions, trim the ends, and hollow out the onions, leaving a shell of ¼ inch. Finely chop and reserve 2 cups of the onion that has been removed.

Heat 2 tablespoons of the oil and sauté 1 cup of the reserved onions and 2 minced garlic cloves until the onions have softened. Add the ground meat and cook, stirring, until the meat loses its color. Stir in the ham, 2 table-spoons of the parsley, salt, pepper, and the thyme, then add 2 tablespoons of the tomato and 4 tablespoons of the pimiento. Turn off the flame and stir in the eggs.

Fill the onions with the meat mixture, packing tightly. Place in a shallow baking dish.

Heat the remaining tablespoon of oil in a skillet and sauté the remaining cup of chopped onions and clove of minced garlic. Add the remaining 2 tablespoons pimiento, 1 tablespoon tomato, and 1 tablespoon parsley. Stir in the wine and broth, and season with salt and pepper. Pour over the onions, cover, and cook slowly about 1½ hours. Serve, spooning the sauce over the onions.

ALBÓNDIGAS CON BERROS
(*Watercress Meatballs*)

You will rarely find watercress in Spanish cooking, except along the northwestern coast in Galicia and Santander and in the Canary Islands, where this leafy green enters into salads and soups. In this dish watercress lends an interesting flavor to meatballs that is accentuated by the Watercress Salad on page 65. The salad should be considered part of the dish, since the meatballs have no sauce, although of course the salad can be served with many other dishes.   *Makes 3–4 dinner portions*

1 pound lean ground beef
1 egg, lightly beaten
2 slices bread, crusts removed,
    soaked in water and
    squeezed dry
1 tablespoon minced parsley
½ cup minced watercress
    (trimmed of thick stems)

About 1½ teaspoons salt
Freshly ground pepper
2 tablespoons olive oil
1 medium onion, finely
    chopped

In a bowl combine the meat, egg, bread, parsley, watercress, salt, and pepper (it should be well seasoned).

Heat 1 tablespoon of the oil in a skillet, sauté the onion a minute or two, then cover and cook slowly 15 minutes. Cool slightly and add to the meat mixture. Shape into 1½-inch balls or 4 to 6 patties.

Wipe out the skillet, and heat the remaining oil. Sauté the meatballs over medium-high heat, until browned on all sides and cooked through. Serve on a bed of Watercress Salad.

PIMIENTOS RELLENOS A LA ASTURIANA
(Stuffed Peppers, Asturian Style)

You may use either red or green peppers, or a combination of both, for these meat- and rice-filled peppers, although I think the red peppers give a nicer flavor.   *Serves 3–4*

1¼ pounds mixture ground
  beef, veal, and pork in equal
  parts
2 tablespoons minced Spanish
  mountain cured ham, prosciutto, or capicollo

2 cloves garlic, mashed to a
  paste
Salt

SAUCE

1 tablespoon olive oil
1 small onion, finely chopped
1 clove garlic, minced
1 small carrot, trimmed,
  scraped, and finely chopped
1 small tomato, skinned,
  seeded, and chopped

1 tablespoon minced parsley
1 cup chicken broth
Few strands of saffron
1 bay leaf
½ cup dry white wine
Salt
Freshly ground pepper

. . .

1 tablespoon olive oil
1 medium onion, finely
  chopped
Freshly ground pepper
2 tablespoons minced parsley
1 small tomato, skinned,
  seeded, and chopped

¼ cup uncooked rice, preferably short-grain
1 tablespoon dry white wine
6–8 medium-large red and /or
  green bell peppers

In a bowl, mix together the ground meat, ham, garlic, and 1 teaspoon salt. Let sit while preparing the Sauce.

To make the Sauce, heat 1 tablespoon oil in a shallow casserole and sauté the onion, garlic, and carrot until the onion has wilted. Stir in the tomato and parsley and cook a minute or two, then add the broth, saffron, bay leaf, wine, salt, and pepper. Bring to a boil, cover, and simmer 15 minutes.

To finish making the meat filling, heat 1 tablespoon oil in a skillet and sauté the onion until wilted. Add the meat mixture, breaking it up as it loses its color and seasoning with salt, pepper, and parsley. Cook until the meat is lightly browned. Stir in the tomato, cook a minute, then add the rice and wine. Cook 5 minutes more.

Cut the tops off the peppers, scoop out the membrane and seeds, and fill loosely with the meat mixture. Cover the peppers with their caps and arrange in the casserole—upright or on their sides. Transfer to a 350°F oven and cook about 1 hour, or until the peppers have softened, spooning the sauce over them as they cook.

PATATAS RELLENAS CASA JULIÁN
(Meat-Filled Potatoes)

Casa Julián is a small family-run restaurant and hotel in Asturias, set on the banks of the glorious Cares River. During trout and salmon season it is a mecca for fly fishermen and those merely interested in enjoying the magnificent mountain scenery of the Picos de Europa. Guests feel right at home here, thanks to the hospitality of owner Julián and his sons and the exceptional cooking of his wife, Vicentina. These small potatoes, hollowed out and filled with ground meat, are one of her specialties.   *Serves 3–4*

2 tablespoons olive oil
1 medium onion, finely
   chopped
1 clove garlic, minced
1 pound mixture of ground
   beef, veal, and pork in equal
   parts
Salt
Freshly ground pepper
½ pound tomatoes, skinned,
   seeded, and finely chopped
2 tablespoons minced pimiento,

preferably homemade
   (p. 178) or imported
2 tablespoons minced parsley
16 small (about 2-inch
   diameter) potatoes
2 tablespoons finely chopped
   Spanish mountain cured
   ham, prosciutto, or capicollo
1 teaspoon flour
1¼ cups chicken broth
¼ cup dry white wine

Meat-Filled Potatoes (continued)

In a shallow casserole, heat 1 tablespoon of the oil and sauté the onion and garlic until the onion has wilted. Remove and reserve 2 tablespoons of the mixture for the sauce. Add the ground meat to the casserole, breaking it up as the meat cooks, and sauté until the meat loses its color. Season with salt and pepper, add the tomatoes, pimiento, and parsley, and cook slowly 10 minutes more.

Peel and hollow out the potatoes with a small spoon or melon scoop, leaving a shell about ⅜ inch thick. Fill each potato with about 1 tablespoon of the meat mixture, and cover with a scrap of potato.

Wipe out the casserole, heat the remaining tablespoon of oil, and add the reserved onion mixture, the ham, and the flour. Stir in the broth and wine, then arrange the filled potatoes in the casserole and spoon some of the sauce over them. Cover and simmer until the potatoes are tender, about 1 hour, basting occasionally with the sauce.

XARRETE GUISADO
(Veal Stew with Potatoes and Onions)

START PREPARATION 6–8 HOURS IN ADVANCE

A specialty at La Tacita d'Juan restaurant in the historic Galician city of Santiago de Compostela, this stew is a delight on a cold winter's evening. The meat is uncommonly tender and the sauce assertively seasoned. The large amount of garlic lends flavor but loses its garlicky taste with long cooking.   *Serves 4*

3 pounds veal shank, in 2-inch
    slices
Salt
Freshly ground pepper
1 small head garlic, separated
    into cloves, peeled and
    minced
1¼ cups dry white wine

Flour for dusting
3 tablespoons olive oil
½ pound small white onions,
    peeled
1 pound small potatoes (about
    1½-inch diameter), peeled
Chicken broth

Place the meat in a shallow bowl, and sprinkle with salt, pepper, and the garlic. Pour the wine over, cover, and marinate in the refrigerator for 6 to 8 hours. Scrape the garlic off the meat (return it to the marinade), drain, and dry the meat on paper towels. Reserve the marinade.

Dust the veal with flour. Heat the oil in a shallow casserole and sauté the meat and onions until the meat is browned on both sides. Add the marinade, sprinkle the meat with salt and pepper, cover, and simmer 45 minutes.

Add the potatoes and sprinkle them lightly with salt. Cover the casserole and transfer to a 350°F oven. Cook until the potatoes are tender, about 1 hour, adding chicken broth if the marinade evaporates. Serve, spooning sauce over the meat.

CARNE ESTOFADA A LA ASTURIANA
(Beef Stew, Asturian Style)

The ingredients in this beef stew are not at all unusual, but they create a very tasty sauce.　　　　　　　　　　　　　　　　　　　　　　　*Serves 4*

2 pounds boneless beef chuck, in 1½-inch cubes	2 tablespoons olive oil
2 cloves garlic, mashed through a garlic press	1 large onion, chopped
	1 bay leaf
6 cloves garlic, peeled	2 teaspoons imported sweet paprika
2 tablespoons minced parsley	A 1-inch piece, or to taste, dried red chile pepper
Salt	
1 cup dry white wine	

In a bowl combine the meat with the mashed garlic. Let sit 30 minutes. In a mortar or mini processor mash to a paste the garlic cloves, parsley, and ⅛ teaspoon salt. Stir in the wine.

In a deep casserole, heat the oil and sauté the meat until it is well browned. Add the onion and sauté until softened, then add the bay leaf, paprika, chile pepper, and the wine mixture. Bring to a boil, cover, and simmer 1½ to 2 hours, or until the meat is tender.

Desserts

ARROZ CON LECHE CASA LUCIO
(Rice Pudding, Asturian Style)

"You must try our rice pudding," the waiter at Madrid's Casa Lucio insisted. "It's sensational." Indeed, it was—creamy and seemingly rich—although it had no eggs, no cream, and was not overly sweet. It was probably the purest-tasting rice pudding I had ever had, even though rice pudding in Spain is always excellent. The region of Asturias is in particular famous for its rice pudding, and this recipe is prepared in the Asturian manner.

Be sure your milk is absolutely fresh. Short-grain rice is essential, for it produces a creamier consistency and when refrigerated does not harden, as long-grain rice does. You may serve the pudding with or without the crackling sugar coating. *Serves 8*

¾ cup short-grain rice
8 cups whole milk
⅛ teaspoon salt
1 cinnamon stick

½ cup plus 2 tablespoons sugar, plus ½ cup for the sugar coating

Rinse the rice in a strainer and drain well. Place in a deep pot with the milk, salt, and cinnamon and bring to the boiling point, watching carefully. Lower the heat and cook at the slowest simmer possible for 3 hours, stirring frequently, or until the mixture has the consistency of a soft custard. Stir in ½ cup plus 2 tablespoons of the sugar, simmer 15 minutes more, then cool, stirring occasionally.

Pour the rice pudding into 8 dessert bowls, preferably flat-bottomed earthenware. Refrigerate until cold, or keep at room temperature.

To make the caramelized sugar coating, sprinkle 1 tablespoon sugar over each rice pudding. Heat a salamander or a small heavy saucepan filled with a few tablespoons of water until red hot (or use a blow torch sold for this purpose). Rest the salamander over the sugar, moving it over the surface until the sugar is caramelized and crackling. Repeat for the remaining puddings, reheating and wiping clean the salamander after each application. Serve right away (the sugar will soften if left more than a few minutes).

CREMA DE ESPINACAS EN CANUTILLOS
(Sweet Spinach Custard in Puff Pastry Horns)

At the beginning of the century, this most unusual dessert of custard and spinach was popular in Bilbao; it continues to be featured at some of the city's finest restaurants, either in a tart shell or as a filling for pastry horns. It is said to be a vestige of the medieval custom of sweetening just about every kind of food imaginable in an effort to make ingredients of doubtful freshness more palatable.

Jolastoki, in a lush garden setting in nearby Neguri, where at the turn of the century Bilbao's elite built astonishingly vast gingerbread-style summer homes several stories high on surprisingly small plots, serves this dessert as a tart with crisscrossed pastry strips on top. At Bilbao's acclaimed Guría restaurant chef Genaro Pildain prefers to spoon the custard into pastry horns, and I have used his method here. To make the tart version, see instructions below.   *Filling for 30 pastry horns*

About 1 pound puff pastry, purchased or, preferably, homemade (p. 22), chilled	Peel of ¼ lemon
	2 eggs
	⅛ teaspoon salt
2 ounces spinach leaves (about 1 cup, loosely packed)	½ cup granulated sugar
3 tablespoons cornstarch	Confectioners' sugar
2 cups plus 2 tablespoons milk	1 egg yolk, lightly beaten with 1 teaspoon water

If making your own puff pastry, prepare it at least 1 hour in advance and keep chilled. Place the spinach in a microwave-safe dish (if the spinach is damp, no water is necessary; otherwise sprinkle lightly with water); cover and cook on high 4 minutes. (Or simmer on the stove in a pot of water for about 10 minutes.) Drain well, then wrap in paper towels and squeeze out any liquid. Chop finely.

Dissolve the cornstarch in 2 tablespoons of the milk and reserve. Heat

Sweet Spinach Custard in Puff Pastry Horns (continued)

the remaining 2 cups milk in a saucepan with the lemon peel, bring to a boil, and simmer 10 minutes.

In another saucepan, whisk together the eggs, salt, granulated sugar, and the cornstarch mixture. Discard the lemon peel and stir in the hot milk. Cook over medium heat, stirring constantly, until the mixture begins to thicken. Add the spinach and continue cooking until the custard begins to bubble. Remove immediately from the heat and cool without stirring (stirring will thin the custard).

Roll out the puff pastry dough according to instructions to a scant ⅛ inch. Cut into ½-inch-wide strips and wrap in slightly overlapping circles around 4-inch baking horn molds. (If more than 1 strip is needed to complete a horn, seal the seam well with the egg yolk.) Place on a cookie tray lined with foil, seam side down, and bake at 425°F on an upper rack about 5 minutes, or until the horns are golden. Turn off the oven and leave the pastries in the oven to dry the inner layers of dough. Carefully remove the molds and cool the pastries. Fill each horn with about 4 teaspoons of the custard, sprinkle with confectioners' sugar, and serve warm or at room temperature.

To make the tart version, roll about half of the puff pastry as described above and cut in a circle large enough to cover the bottom and sides of a 9-inch tart pan. Pierce all over with a fork and bake in a 425°F oven on an upper rack until golden, pricking occasionally to deflate the pastry.

While the tart shell is baking, roll the remaining dough and cut into six ½-inch-wide strips 9 inches long. Refrigerate.

Spoon the custard into the tart shell and cover with 3 strips of dough. Interweave 3 more strips through the others. Brush with beaten egg yolk and return to the oven for 10 minutes, or until the pastry strips are golden. Serve at room temperature.

GALLETAS DE REINOSA
(Crisp Butter Cookies)

When traveling by car through Spain, we always purchase a package of Chiquilín brand cookies to ward off hunger attacks in the late morning. These cookies, imprinted with a design, are not too sweet and very crisp (this kind of cookie is a *galleta,* in contrast to short, richer cookies called *pastas*), and although they are commercially made, we thoroughly enjoy them. They are based on the traditional butter cookies of the town of Reinosa, in the mountains of Santander, an area known for its fine-quality butter.

Reinosa is today one of the principal cookie-producing centers of Spain, and yet the town retains its quaint streets and charming mountain architecture. The following is my re-creation of these famous cookies.

Makes about 35

1¾ cups flour	½ cup plus 2 tablespoons sugar
⅛ teaspoon salt	¼ pound (1 stick) unsalted
2 tablespoons cornstarch	butter
½ teaspoon baking soda	1 egg
½ teaspoon cream of tartar	1 tablespoon honey
1 teaspoon powdered malted	1 teaspoon grated coconut
milk	¼ teaspoon vanilla

Mix together in a bowl the flour, salt, cornstarch, baking soda, cream of tartar, malted milk, and sugar. Cut in the butter.

In a small bowl, whisk together the egg, honey, coconut, and vanilla. Stir into the flour mixture. Work with your hands to form a dough.

On a floured surface, roll the dough ¼ inch thick. To imprint the cookies, you can cut a design partway through the cookies with the dull side of a knife (or better still, press an imprinted rolling pin, of the kind used to make springerle cookies, over the dough, then cut with a knife to separate into individual cookies, following the imprinted lines). Otherwise, cut into 1¾- by 2-inch rectangles. Arrange on a foil-lined, greased cookie sheet and bake at 300°F about 15 to 18 minutes, turning the tray frequently from back to front and side to side to brown evenly. The cookies should be a very deep golden color. Cool on a rack.

TARTA DE ALMENDRA O MERLO
(Galician Almond Cake O Merlo)

There is hardly a restaurant in Galicia that does not offer the region's traditional almond cake, often called *tarta de Santiago* because the cross of Spain's patron saint, Santiago, is usually emblazoned in the cake with caramelized sugar.

Santiago, known in English as the apostle Saint James, was said to have traveled to Spain to preach the Gospel, and after he was martyred in Jerusalem his body miraculously reappeared in Galicia in a field that gradually developed into the glorious city of Santiago de Compostela (see my *Discovering Spain: An Uncommon Guide* for the full story). Santiago de Compostela became a place of mass pilgrimage in medieval times as millions of Europe's faithful made the arduous journey on foot to reach the shrine of the Apostle. One of Galicia's most enduring symbols is the distinctive cross of Santiago.

Tarta de almendra is a single-layer almond cake, simple and moist. Although served as a dessert in Galicia, we would probably consider it more appropriate as a tea cake. One of the best I have eaten comes from Alfonso Merlo, the owner and chef of O Merlo, in the provincial capital of Pontevedra, a restaurant specializing in tapas that are often meal-size. It is a great place to eat when here to visit the city's quaint Old Quarter and delightful old squares.   *Makes one 8-inch cake*

6 ounces blanched almonds	¾ cup sugar
(about 1 cup)	3 eggs
6 tablespoons flour	Confectioners' sugar

In a processor, coarsely chop 2 ounces (about ⅓ cup) of the almonds with the flour. Remove from the processor and reserve. Now add to the processor the remaining almonds and ¼ cup of the sugar, and grind the almonds as fine as possible.

In a bowl, with an electric mixer beat the eggs until foamy. Add the remaining ½ cup sugar and beat until the mixture is light-colored and thick. Then beat in the sugar-and-almond and flour-and-almond mixtures. Pour into a greased and floured 8-inch springform pan and bake at 350°F for about 35 to 40 minutes, or until the cake springs back slightly to the touch. Cool, then remove the rim of the pan and sprinkle the cake heavily with confectioners' sugar.

To burn the traditional cross in the sugar, heat a thin metal skewer (protect your hand with a pot holder) over a flame until the lower portion is red-hot. Press the skewer over the center of the cake to caramelize the sugar. Wipe off the skewer, reheat, and repeat to form a cross.

FRIXUELOS RELLENOS DE SALSA DE MANZANA

(Thin Rolled Pancakes Filled with Cinnamon Apple Sauce)

Dessert pancakes have always been traditional in Asturias, where they are called *frixuelos,* and in Galicia, where they are known as *filloas.* Loosely rolled and sautéed in butter or oil, they can be served on their own, with a sprinkle of sugar or perhaps a dash of anisette, filled with pastry cream, or, as here, in the style of Asturias, where apple trees flourish, filled with applesauce.

I sampled these *frixuelos,* among other well-prepared Asturian specialties, at La Tahona, a charming, cozy country inn sponsored by the regional government and set in a remote corner of the awesome Picos de Europa mountains.   *Makes about 14*

Crepes (p. 79), adding 1 teaspoon sugar to the batter
1¾ cups applesauce, homemade or good-quality jarred, or 3 recipes Mermelada de Melocotón (p. 217), made with apples
1 teaspoon cinnamon

¼ teaspoon nutmeg
½ teaspoon grated lemon peel
1 tablespoon melted butter
Sugar to taste
1 tablespoon vegetable oil
Sugar and cinnamon for sprinkling

Make the Crepes according to instructions. In a bowl, mix together the applesauce, cinnamon, nutmeg, grated lemon peel, and melted butter. Stir in the sugar—the amount will depend on whether the applesauce has already been sweetened or not. In any case, since only a small amount fills each pan-

Pancakes Filled with Applesauce (continued)

cake and it is being used as a dessert filling, the applesauce should be sweeter than customary—figure adding about 2½ extra tablespoons of sugar.

Spoon about 2 tablespoons of the applesauce down the middle of each crepe. Fold over one side, then the other. Heat the oil (you could use butter if you prefer) in a medium skillet and add as many *frixuelos* as will comfortably fit, seam side down. Cook over a medium flame until lightly golden, turn, and lightly brown the other side. Serve right away, sprinkled with sugar and cinnamon.

CORBATAS DE UNQUERA
(Frosted Puff Pastries)

Just about everyone who passes through the town of Unquera, near the northern coast of Cantabria, stops in one of its many pastry shops or bars to purchase *corbatas* or to relax over a cup of coffee accompanied by one of these fine pastries. A *corbata* is literally a necktie—in this case a bow tie— and these airy pastries, lightly frosted and twisted at the center like the knot of a tie, take their name from this resemblance.   *Makes 10–12*

½ pound puff pastry, prefer-   ¼ cup honey
    ably homemade (p. 22)   ¼ cup sugar
1 egg white

Roll the puff pastry ⅛ inch thick and cut into 5- by 1½-inch rectangles, being sure the dough stays chilled (refrigerate briefly if necessary). Twist half of each rectangle 180 degrees so that the dough pieces look like bow ties. Place on a cookie sheet lined with foil and bake on an upper rack of a 425°F oven until the pastries are golden, about 10 minutes. Turn off the oven and leave the pastries in the oven to dry the inner layers of dough. Cool.

To make the frosting, beat the egg white in a small bowl with an electric mixer until it forms soft peaks—it should not be too stiff. In a small saucepan, heat the honey and sugar, stirring occasionally, until the mixture comes to a boil. Simmer 5 minutes. Add the egg white and stir until smooth, then spread over each pastry, using about 2 teaspoons of frosting for each pastry.

CHAPTER 3

Northeastern Interior Spain

REGION OF THE PEPPERS

he cooking of my good friend
Pedro Narro at El Chorro res-
taurant in the hauntingly beautiful mountain village of Albarracín is amazingly straightforward and unstudied and yet the results are sophisticated
tastes that a schooled chef would find hard to match. I have often enjoyed the
company of Pedro, a heavyset man, with his hair somewhat out of control,
who is always ready to shoot the breeze over a glass of robust Aragonese
wine. He takes an irreverent, somewhat cynical attitude toward life in general and likes to belittle his simple cooking. But don't let that fool you: he is
plainly pleased and proud to receive compliments.

Pedro Narro personifies the easygoing approach to food in the Region
of the Peppers. In his closet-size kitchen equipped with nothing but the ba-
sics, and with the occasional assistance of his elderly mother, who taught
him how to cook, he effortlessly turns out wonderfully appetizing foods. His
lamb, for example, may be simply roasted in the oven, or left to stew for
hours in huge deep pots that dwarf his undersize stove burners, or cut into
chops that are grilled, then sprinkled with parsley, minced garlic, and a
squeeze of lemon juice.

Northeastern interior Spain, in which I have included the regions of
Navarra, Aragón, La Rioja, and the interior Basque province of Álava (for
culinary purposes Álava has much closer ties to the Region of the Peppers

than to the cooking of Spain's northern coast), is an area of extraordinary natural beauty and historical richness. It can be lushly green and crossed by rushing rivers, or majestic in its desolation. Aragón, important kingdom of the Middle Ages and birthplace of Catholic King Ferdinand, extends from the dazzling high peaks of the Pyrenees in the northern province of Huesca south to the unspoiled medieval villages that sit in isolated splendor in the awesome Maestrazgo mountains. Moorish influence was long-lasting here and is still apparent in Aragonese architecture and in its cooking. Simple pastries, like *almojábanas,* baked and bathed in honey, are Moorish even in name.

Ernest Hemingway extolled pastoral northern Navarra, where he loved to trout-fish and partake in the excitement of the Running of the Bulls in Pamplona, all of which he describes in *The Sun Also Rises.* The cultural wealth of Navarra is largely due to its location along the Way of Saint James, the route that led millions of pilgrims to the shrine of the apostle Saint James in Santiago de Compostela; magnificent Romanesque churches are everywhere to be seen. The passing of pilgrims through La Rioja—a region of gentle landscapes and benign climate—has likewise left exceptional churches and many tales of legendary saints who dedicated their lives to ailing pilgrims.

Despite their many physical differences, these regions of northeastern interior Spain all meet the mighty Ebro River, where a vast fertile valley produces some of Spain's best fruits and vegetables. It is here that culinary likenesses are most pronounced. Perhaps it seems odd to single out peppers to describe the gastronomy of this region, and yet so many traditional dishes rely on local peppers. More often than not the peppers are elongated and red—clearly favored over green—and include the exquisite *pimientos del piquillo* that have their own appellation of origin. Any dish designated "*chilindrón* style" or "a la riojana" is sure to have peppers as principal ingredients.

Early fall is my favorite time to visit the Region of the Peppers, for it is the season of the *vendimia,* when grapes are plucked from the vines and piled high in carts for their trip to the *bodegas,* and when red peppers are harvested. Village women sit at their doorsteps in the brilliant autumn light, charring the peppers over wood-burning fires. Freshly roasted, or preserved in jars, these thin delicate peppers are used in meat and poultry stews (chicken and lamb *chilindrón* style are typical dishes), stuffed with ground meat or fish, or simply sautéed with oil and garlic to serve as tapas or to accompany main courses. Many more red peppers are decoratively strung out to dry along whitewashed walls and balconies, adding a vivid note of color to village houses. Once the peppers are dried they may be pulverized for paprika (*pimentón*) or reconstituted to create wonderfully earthy sauces.

The agricultural richness of the Region of the Peppers of course goes far beyond peppers. Fine vegetables of intense flavors are principal ingredients in any number of dishes. There are delicate white asparagus (which also have their own appellation of origin), baby artichokes, tender peas, and beans, especially oversized kidney beans called *pochas,* which are dried and made into marvelous bean stews. Local potatoes, combined with chorizo and peppers, become a hearty soup, *patatas a la riojana,* good enough to make into a meal, and a wonderful medley of fresh baby vegetables flecked with mountain cured ham, *menestra de verduras a la riojana,* is one of my very favorite Spanish dishes. In the mountains of Aragón wild mushrooms grow in profusion (the mushroom and potato soup, *sopa de patata y rovellones* is splendid), and the region is a major source of truffles. Although commonly shipped off to France, truffles do appear in some time-honored dishes, like roast lamb Aragón style (*ternasco a la aragonesa*).

Breads from the Region of the Peppers can be seductive, like those of the bakery in El Arrabal (see p. 158) next to the village of Albarracín, but bread is often much more than a table loaf. It may be torn into pieces (*migas*), sautéed, then seasoned with chorizo and paprika and sometimes served with fried eggs. Rabbit with *migas,* a delicious mixture of rabbit with onion, garlic, and bread bits, is a traditional shepherd's dish, for it is based on ingredients readily available to those keeping a lonely vigil over their flocks.

Celebrated red wines of Rioja—smooth and complex—are produced in La Rioja and the southern Basque province of Álava, but wine is made throughout this northern interior region, from the light reds of Navarra to the robust reds of Aragón. There are marvelous cheeses as well. *Queso Roncal*—a somewhat piquant aged sheep's-milk cheese from the foothills of the Pyrenees in Navarra—and tangy white *queso Tronchón* from El Maestrazgo in Aragón are particularly distinctive. From the many streams that rush from the Pyrenees to feed the Ebro come an abundance of trout—they are usually sautéed with a slice of mountain cured ham (another noteworthy product of Aragón) or preserved in wine and vinegar (*trucha en escabeche*). Dried cod is also quite popular, especially *al ajo arriero* style—with peppers and tomatoes. Surely with so many fine ingredients and tasty preparations, the simple, unpretentious, unmannered cooking in the Region of the Peppers is every bit as good as the more schooled and sophisticated dishes of its Basque and Catalan neighbors.

Notes on Regional Wines and Liquors

The best-known wines of northeastern interior Spain are undoubtedly the smooth, well-balanced red wines of the Rioja appellation of origin. Some of my favorites (all the better if they are the longer-aged reservas of the same names) are Viña Monty and Montecillo from Bodegas Montecillo, Viña Tondonia (R. López Heredia), CUNE Imperial, and Viña Ardanza (La Rioja Alta).

Also gaining headway in the American market are the fresh light claretes of Navarra, made from the native garnacha grape, such as Agramont (Bodegas Cenalsa) and Las Campanas (Vinícola Navarra). Navarra is also noted for a typical liqueur, Pacharán, distilled from bilberries.

Although the wines of Aragón were once rough and unusually high in alcohol, today they have become somewhat more refined and are appreciated for their fruity aromas and intense flavors. They go well with red meats and game. There are three major production areas: Cariñena, Campo de Borja (which produces Don Ramón from Bodegas Aragonesas), and Somontano, a region in the foothills of the Spanish Pyrenees known for the high quality of its wines. Montesierra (Bodegas Pirineos) and Viñas del Vero (Compañía Vitivinícola Aragonesa) are fine examples.

The Elegant *Pimiento del Piquillo*

When Columbus reached the New World, he noted that the native food included something very spicy, and since he believed he had found a westerly route to the East, he assumed it was black pepper, already well known in Europe. He called it *pimienta*, the Spanish word for black pepper, and although he was completely mistaken, the word endured. Today the two distinct products, peppercorns and peppers, are distinguished in Spanish only by the last vowel: *pimienta* is black pepper and *pimiento* refers to fresh or jarred red or green peppers. Of similar origin is the word *pimentón*, which describes Spanish paprika made from dried and pulverized Spanish red peppers. It is somewhat sweeter and subtly different in taste from other paprikas.

Ever since then, peppers, which had been cultivated for thousands of years in the New World, were enthusiastically adopted in Spain. They have become an ingredient in countless dishes that are today considered traditional regional fare. But there is a very special variety of sweet red peppers, *pimientos del piquillo*, that are gastronomic stars.

Spain's finest restaurants deem preserved vegetables of any kind unfit for their tables, but are nevertheless among the biggest fans of jarred *pimientos del piquillo*—no other red pepper comes close to their flavor and versatility. Grown in La Rioja and Navarra around the Ebro River (the very best of the *piquillos* come from a small microclimate in Navarra and have the Lodosa appellation of origin), these delicate, wood-roasted, and just slightly piquant peppers, jarred without preservatives, are not more than four inches long and narrow to a "peak" (thus the name *piquillo*). Marvelous on their own, lightly sautéed with just a touch of garlic and extra virgin olive oil, they can also be stuffed with meat, in the Rioja style, or with fish, as chefs in Navarra and the Basque Country prefer. Sauces for stuffed red peppers range from flavorful broths to white sauce, ink sauce, or, as I like them best, with a puréed pimiento sauce.

Red bell peppers or jarred pimientos made from bell peppers are not acceptable alternatives for sautéing or stuffing in the Spanish

The Elegant *Pimiento del Piquillo* (continued)

style—they are much too large and fleshy and lack the delicacy of the *piquillos*. Imported *piquillos* can sometimes be found in gourmet shops; otherwise, look for elongated sweet red frying peppers, available in food markets at certain times of year, then roast, skin, and seed them, and proceed with any recipe that requires *piquillos*.

When using pimientos for other purposes (such as in marinades, as garnish, or as a puréed sauce for stuffed peppers), common pimientos will do, but buy them in jars rather than cans so you can choose those with the deepest red color. Drain and rinse them, pat dry with paper towels, then return to the jar and cover with olive oil. This will improve the flavor by removing the citric acid used as a preservative, and prevent an opened jar from spoiling rapidly.

Salads ❧ Soups ❧ Meals-in-a-Pot Vegetables

ENSALADA ARAGONESA DE ESCAROLA
(Escarole Salad)

This salad is specifically meant to accompany Roast Lamb, Aragón Style (p. 148), but is also excellent with other dishes.　　*Serves 4–5*

¼ cup extra virgin olive oil　　Freshly ground pepper
4 teaspoons red wine vinegar　　1½ tablespoons thyme leaves or
Salt　　　　　　　　　　　　　　¼ teaspoon dried

3 tablespoons pan drippings
 (when the salad accompa-
 nies roast lamb)
About 4 cups tender escarole
 leaves torn into pieces

4 radishes, very thinly sliced
1 small onion, preferably
 Vidalia or Spanish,
 very thinly sliced

In a small bowl, whisk together the oil, vinegar, salt, pepper, thyme, and pan drippings (if using), then toss in a salad bowl with the escarole, radishes, and onion.

ESPÁRRAGOS BLANCOS EN VINAGRETA DE PIQUILLOS
(White Asparagus in Pimiento Vinaigrette)

This delicate salad uses two of Navarra's celebrated crops: white asparagus and tiny sweet *piquillo* red peppers (see box, p. 127).   *Serves 4–6*

SALAD DRESSING

½ cup extra virgin olive oil
3 tablespoons white wine
 vinegar
1 teaspoon minced parsley
2 tablespoons minced pimiento,
 preferably Spanish *piquillo*
Salt

Freshly ground pepper
⅛ teaspoon Dijon-style
 mustard
1 small clove garlic, minced
¾ teaspoon thyme leaves or
 ⅛ teaspoon dried
Pinch of sugar

· · ·

Cooked large white asparagus
 spears, fresh or jarred,
 about 4 per person

In a processor, blend all the Salad Dressing ingredients until smooth. Arrange the asparagus on individual plates and pour on the dressing. Serve at room temperature.

SOPA DE BUNYOLETS MORELLENSE
(Thick Chicken Broth with Pastry Puffs)

This unusual soup, garnished with unsweetened pastry puffs that are seasoned with ham and parsley, is ideally made with the broth of the chickpea stew *cocido* (p. 242). Otherwise a chicken broth thickened and flavored with cooked potato and chickpeas approximates the broth necessary for this excellent first course, typically served in small squat bowls. The soup, as its name suggests, comes from the stunning walled town of Morella, built in tiers that rise steeply from its rocky base.   *Serves 4*

CHICKEN BROTH

½ pound chicken parts, including the neck and gizzard

A ¼-pound piece Spanish mountain cured ham or prosciutto, cut from the narrow end in 1 thick piece, or capicollo

1 small onion, peeled

1 clove garlic, peeled

½ cup mashed cooked chickpeas, freshly made or good-quality canned, rinsed and drained

¼ pound potatoes, peeled and cut in ½-inch cubes

2 sprigs parsley

1½ teaspoons thyme leaves or ¼ teaspoon dried

1 bay leaf

6 peppercorns

Salt

6½ cups water

BUNYOLETS

½ cup Chicken Broth

3 tablespoons olive oil

⅛ teaspoon salt

½ cup flour

2 eggs

Olive oil for frying

2 tablespoons minced parsley

2 tablespoons minced Spanish mountain cured ham, prosciutto, or capicollo

Put all the Chicken Broth ingredients in a soup pot and bring to a boil. Cover and simmer about 1½ hours. Remove the chicken pieces from the broth, then strain, pushing through as much solid matter as possible.

To make the Bunyolets, stir together in a saucepan ½ cup of the Chicken

Broth, 3 tablespoons oil, and the salt and bring to a boil. Lower the heat to medium, and add the flour all at once, stirring until the mixture leaves the sides of the pan and forms a ball. Cook, flattening and turning the dough with a wooden spoon, for 2 minutes. Remove from the heat and cool a minute. Transfer to a food processor, add the eggs, and beat for 15 seconds. Heat at least 1 inch of oil in a skillet (or better still, use a deep-fryer) until it quickly browns a cube of bread, then drop the dough in by ½ teaspoonfuls, lower the heat slightly, and fry until golden and puffed, turning once. Drain on paper towels (the recipe will probably make more than you need, but they are also very good eaten on their own).

Serve the soup in small bowls with several *bunyolets* floating on top.

SOPA DE PATATA Y ROVELLONES
(Potato and Wild Mushroom Soup)

A soup from the Maestrazgo, a stark and majestic mountain range of astonishing beauty, filled with awesome gorges and precipices. The terrain is ideal for wild mushrooms as well as truffles, both found in abundance in the area. Because truffle hunters are wary of others encroaching on their sources, the truffle market is a somewhat secretive affair that takes place under the cover of darkness in the town of Morella.

This exceptional soup is offered at Buj, a fine family restaurant in the quaint town of Cantavieja, which is run with obvious pride and joy by Doña Francisca and her two daughters. The potato should be grated finely enough so that it cooks away and thickens the broth. *Serves 4*

1 tablespoon olive oil
1 small onion, finely chopped
1 small tomato, peeled, seeded, and chopped
½ pound wild mushrooms, such as shitake, or a mix of wild and cultivated, stems trimmed, brushed clean, and finely chopped
¾ pound potatoes, peeled and grated

4 cups well-flavored chicken broth, preferably home-made (p. 298)
Salt
Freshly ground pepper
1 bay leaf
¾ teaspoon thyme leaves or ⅛ teaspoon dried

Potato and Wild Mushroom Soup (continued)

Heat the oil in a soup pot and sauté the onion until softened. Add the tomato, cook a minute, then add the mushrooms and potatoes. Stir in the broth and season with salt, pepper, bay leaf, and thyme. Bring to a boil, cover, and simmer about 1 hour.

PATATAS A LA RIOJANA
(Potato and Chorizo Stew)

Despite being little more than chorizo and potatoes, this appealing dish is a favorite in La Rioja and substantial enough to make a meal. Since chorizo is the only meat addition, it should be the best quality available. Note that the potatoes are broken rather than cut into pieces, a detail that may seem inconsequential but somehow really does make a difference in the final results.

Serves 4–6

3–4 pounds new potatoes, peeled

3 tablespoons olive oil

2 medium onions, finely chopped

2 red bell peppers, finely chopped

2 green bell peppers, finely chopped

6 cloves garlic, minced

Salt

2 bay leaves

1 pound sweet chorizo, in ¼-inch slices

1 teaspoon imported sweet paprika

3 cups chicken broth, preferably homemade (p. 298)

1½ cups water

A 2-inch piece dried red chile pepper, seeded

8 peppercorns

2 tablespoons minced parsley

Break the potatoes into pieces roughly 1½ inches in size by inserting a small knife and pulling apart.

Heat the oil in a large soup pot and sauté the onions, red and green peppers, and 2 cloves of minced garlic with the salt and bay leaves for 2 to 3 minutes. Cover and cook very slowly 15 minutes.

Turn up the flame to medium, add the potato pieces and chorizo, and sauté for 2 minutes. Stir in the paprika, pour in the broth and water, then add the chile pepper and peppercorns. Bring to a boil, lower the flame to medium, and cook, uncovered, for 20 minutes.

Meanwhile, in a mortar or mini processor mash to a paste the remaining 4 cloves minced garlic, the parsley, and a little salt. Add to the soup and continue cooking about 15 minutes more, or until the potatoes are just done. Cover and let sit 5 minutes before serving.

SOPA DE ALBONDIGUILLAS
(Meatball and Potato Soup)

Hearty enough to be a meal, this soup is thickened with grated potatoes and scattered with tiny lamb meatballs. It is somewhat like another soup from Andalucía (p. 345), and, like that one, is most probably a legacy of the important Jewish presence in Spain, even though ham, which was prohibited, is now one of the soup ingredients. *Serves 4*

BROTH

½ pound lamb meat with some bone
½ pound chicken backs
1 ham or beef bone (optional)
1 pig's foot (optional)
8 cups water
Salt

10 peppercorns
1 tablespoon thyme leaves or ½ teaspoon dried
Few sprigs parsley
1 small leek, well washed, or 2 large scallions

MEATBALLS

4 tablespoons (¼ cup) bread crumbs
¼ cup chicken broth
1 pound lean ground lamb
1 egg, lightly beaten

2 tablespoons minced parsley
2 cloves garlic, minced
½ teaspoon salt
Freshly ground pepper
Dash of cinnamon

Meatball and Potato Soup (continued)

. . .

2 tablespoons olive oil	mountain cured ham or
4 medium potatoes	prosciutto
6 tablespoons minced Spanish	2 hard-boiled eggs, minced

To make the Broth, combine in a soup pot all the broth ingredients. Bring to a boil, cover, and simmer 1 hour. Strain out 6 cups (if there is more, boil down). Taste for salt.

Meanwhile, make the Meatballs. In a bowl soak the bread crumbs in the chicken broth, then mix in all other meatball ingredients. Shape into balls the size of marbles.

Heat the oil in a skillet until very hot, add the meatballs, and brown well on all sides, shaking the skillet and turning the meatballs with a metal spatula. Drain on paper towels.

Peel and coarsely grate the potatoes and add to the broth. Simmer until the potatoes are done, about 10 minutes. Stir in the minced ham and eggs and cook 3 minutes more. Add the meatballs, cook a minute or so until they are heated, and serve.

LENTEJAS ARAGONESAS
(Lentil Soup, Aragón Style)

A thick, silky lentil soup, distinctively flavored with leeks, mushrooms, and sausage.   *Serves 6–8*

1 pound lentils, washed	1 *morcilla* (Spanish-style black
9 cups water	sausage) or 1 large breakfast
Salt	sausage, about 2 ounces, in
1 ham bone, or a ¼-pound piece	thick slices
Spanish mountain cured	2 small leeks, well washed,
ham or prosciutto, cut from	white part only, finely
the narrow end in 1 thick	chopped
piece, or capicollo	1 medium onion, finely
2 tablespoons olive oil	chopped

8 medium wild mushrooms
(about 2 ounces), such as
shitake, brushed clean and
chopped

½ pound tomatoes, skinned,
seeded, and chopped

Put the lentils, water, salt, and ham bone (or ham) in a soup pot, bring to a boil, cover, and simmer about 1¼ hours, or until the lentils are almost done.

Meanwhile, in a skillet, heat 1 tablespoon of the oil and brown the sausage. Drain on paper towels and add to the lentils. Wipe out the skillet, add the remaining oil, and sauté the leeks, onion, and mushrooms until the onion is softened. Stir in the tomatoes and cook 10 minutes more. Add this mixture to the soup pot and continue to cook 30 minutes more, or until the lentils are done.

CAPARRONES CON GUINDILLAS Y PAN DE AJO
(Red Bean Stew with Hot Peppers and Garlic Bread)

START PREPARATION 1 DAY IN ADVANCE

Here is a wonderfully tasty and appealing meal in a pot, made with the red beans of La Rioja, often referred to as *caparrones,* with the added attraction of garlic bread, lightly spread with the stewed slab bacon or salt pork (similar to the way you would serve bone marrow), and the contrasting flavor of pickled hot red peppers.   *Serves 4*

1 pound dried deep-red beans
6 cups water
¼ pound slab bacon or salt
   pork
1 sweet chorizo (about
   2 ounces)
1 pig's foot, split (optional)
½ head garlic in 1 piece, unpeeled, loose skin removed
1 tablespoon olive oil
1 onion, finely chopped

2 teaspoons imported sweet
   paprika
Salt
Eight ½-inch bread slices cut
   from a long narrow loaf
2 cloves garlic, peeled, cut in
   halves crosswise
Hot red peppers, preferably the
   elongated variety, preserved
   in water and vinegar

Red Bean Stew (continued)

Soak the beans in water to cover overnight. Drain and transfer to a deep pot. Add the 6 cups water, slab bacon, chorizo, optional pig's foot, and the half head of garlic. Bring to a boil, cover, and simmer 1½ hours.

Meanwhile, heat the oil and sauté the onion until it has wilted. Stir in the paprika. Add to the beans and salt to taste. Cover and continue cooking until the beans are done, about 30 minutes more. Toast the bread in a 350°F oven until golden on both sides, about 10 minutes, turning once.

If you have used the pig's foot, extract it from the pot, scrape the meat from it, and chop. Add to the beans. Fish out the chorizo, cut in thick slices, and return to the pot. Press the half head of garlic with the back of a wooden spoon to extract the garlic and mix with the beans. Discard the skin.

Rub the toast with the cut garlic cloves. Mash the slab bacon and spread thinly on the toast and reheat. Serve the beans accompanied by the garlic toast and the hot peppers.

COC EN PRIMENTÓ
(Pepper and Eggplant Pie)

Coc, coca, coque, all refer to a large single-crust savory pie found in Catalunya, the Levante, and in the mountains of the Maestrazgo in Aragón. In this case the base is a bread dough, covered with a delicious topping of eggplant, peppers, egg, tomato, tuna, anchovy, and black olives to form a pie considered an appropriate Lenten dish. I have found that pizza dough from my local pizzeria works perfectly and saves me the trouble of making my own bread dough. I have reduced the size of the *coc* to create individual portions, appropriate for a light meal, or to make it more manageable as a tapa.

Giorgio della Rocca, an Italian Hispanophile, has written an interesting book on the Maestrazgo in which he colorfully describes the tradition of the *coc* in the lovely mountain village of Calaceite:

"During Holy Week all the women—widows in black, matrons in quilted bathrobes—parade with their trays to the ovens so that one of the four village bakeries can cook [the *coc*] right next to the bread. It's a comforting and multicolored spectacle . . . in which the red of the peppers contrasts with the black of Lower Aragón's olives. . . . [The women] stop along the way, form circles, chat and look out of the corners of their eyes. . . . In villages, pleasures are few and down-to-earth. And among them the peaceful and healthy pleasure of conversation."   *Makes three 7-inch pies*

½ pound baby eggplant	15 cured black olives, pitted
2 red bell peppers	and halved
1 green bell pepper	12 anchovy fillets
¾ pound pizza dough (about	¼ pound tomato, skinned,
half of a large pizza dough),	seeded, and chopped
purchased or homemade	Salt
1 hard-boiled egg, in thin slices	Freshly ground pepper
3 tablespoons flaked tuna, pref-	Extra virgin olive oil
erably light or dark meat	

Place the eggplant and peppers in a roasting pan and roast in a 500°F oven 20 minutes, turning once. Skin, core, and seed the peppers. Skin, cut open lengthwise, and remove some of the seeds from the eggplant. Slice the peppers and eggplant into thin strips.

Divide the dough into three balls. Roll each to a 7-inch circle, making the dough slightly thicker around the edge, as you would a pizza. Place on a cookie tray sprinkled with cornmeal or flour (or better still, on a preheated baking stone), and bake the dough at 500°F for 5 minutes. Pull the oven rack out and arrange the pepper and eggplant slices over the dough, scatter on the egg, tuna, and olives, then garnish with the anchovy. Sprinkle on the tomato, salt and pepper to taste, and drizzle with olive oil. Reduce the heat to 400°F and continue baking until the crust is golden, about 15 minutes more.

MENESTRA DE VERDURAS A LA RIOJANA
(Mixed Vegetables, Rioja Style)

The vegetables that enter into this marvelous casserole from La Rioja—part of the vast Ebro River valley, where some of Spain's finest vegetables are grown—vary according to season and availability, ensuring that the *menestra* is always at its best. You, too, should choose your vegetables according to what is freshest and in season at your market. The vegetables used here, however, are those typical of La Rioja and most often found in this dish. I have microwaved the vegetables because by this method they retain their bright colors and the cooking time is reduced. You can of course boil the vegetables if you prefer.

Menestra is more than a simple vegetable medley. The added flavor provided by bits of ham, the contrasting texture of vegetables that are fried after they are boiled, and the addition of hard-boiled egg all contribute to making this a lovely light supper.   *Serves 4–6*

2 pounds Swiss chard, thick stems trimmed	2 cloves garlic, sliced
8 artichoke hearts, halved	¼ pound Spanish mountain cured ham, prosciutto, or capicollo, sliced ⅛ inch thick, then diced
1 pound snap peas or broad green beans	
½ pound peas, fresh or frozen	2 teaspoons flour plus flour for dusting
½ pound cauliflower, in small flowerets	Oil for frying
12 white asparagus, fresh or jarred, or 12 fresh green asparagus, ends snapped off	2 eggs, lightly beaten with 2 teaspoons water
1 tablespoon olive oil	2 hard-boiled eggs, cut in wedges

Cut the white portion of the Swiss chard into 2-inch pieces. Cut up the rest into similar size pieces, and place all of the Swiss chard in a large microwave-safe dish with salted water to cover. Cover tightly and cook on high about 4 minutes. Stir and continue cooking another 5 minutes, or until done to taste. Remove to a warm platter with a slotted spoon and pour off some of the liquid from the cooking dish, leaving just enough to cover the remaining vegetables. Add to microwave dish the artichokes, and cook, covered, on high, about 5 minutes, or to taste, then remove them to the platter. Continue cooking the remaining vegetables in the same liquid, transferring them to the platter as they are done (keep each vegetable separate). Cook the snap peas, peas, and cauliflower each about 4 minutes, or to taste. If using green asparagus, cook it also about 4 minutes. Reserve the cooking liquid—you will need ⅔ cup.

Set aside the cauliflower, artichokes, and the white portions of the Swiss chard for frying. Coarsely chop the green portions of the Swiss chard.

In a skillet, heat the olive oil and lightly sauté the garlic and ham. Stir in the 2 teaspoons flour, then add the reserved ⅔ cup vegetable broth and cook a minute until slightly thickened.

Heat the frying oil in a separate skillet, at least 1 inch deep (or better still, use a deep-fryer). Dust the artichokes, white Swiss chard pieces, and the cauliflower with flour, then coat with the beaten egg and drop them immediately into the hot oil. Brown lightly and drain on paper towels.

In a shallow casserole, preferably earthenware, arrange in layers the snap peas, then the peas, and chopped Swiss chard. Over this place the fried artichokes, fried Swiss chard, and cauliflower. Pour on the sauce and add salt to taste. Garnish with the egg wedges and the asparagus, gently simmer 5 minutes without stirring, then serve.

PIMIENTOS MORRONES SALTEADOS
(Sautéed Red Peppers)

This is the simple recipe I often turn to as an accompaniment to grilled or sautéed meat and chicken, guaranteed to add the taste of Spain to any meal. If you are fortunate enough to find jarred *piquillo* peppers (see box, p. 127), the preparation is still better and even easier. Just slice the *piquillo* peppers in strips. Heat the oil, add the garlic and peppers, and stir-fry briefly—they need only a minute or so. Omit the salt and chicken broth.   *Serves 4*

2 tablespoons olive oil
1½ pounds fresh red peppers, cored and seeded (or ¾ pound jarred *piquillo* peppers, cut in long narrow strips—see preparation note above)

Salt
2 cloves garlic, thinly sliced
Chicken broth or water

Heat the oil in a skillet until very hot. Add the peppers and stir-fry about 5 minutes. Sprinkle with salt, stir in the garlic, and add a tablespoon or so of broth. Lower the heat, cover, and cook about 20 minutes, or until the peppers are softened, stirring occasionally and adding a little more broth if the pan dries out.

Fish

TRUCHA A LA NAVARRA
(Marinated Pan-Fried Trout with Ham)

BEGIN PREPARATION 2–3 HOURS IN ADVANCE

Food writer Luis Antonio de Vega declares, "Navarra has taught the world how to eat trout." An overstatement, perhaps, but nevertheless this is surely a delicious way to prepare trout—marinated in wine (this part is optional in the traditional preparations) and stuffed with slices of cured ham.

Serves 4

4 freshwater trout, about
    ¾ pound each, cleaned,
    heads on

MARINADE

1 cup dry white wine	1 tablespoon olive oil
1 tablespoon mint leaves or	1 bay leaf, crumbled
½ teaspoon dried	1 tablespoon minced parsley
2 tablespoons thyme leaves or	1 tablespoon lemon juice
1 teaspoon dried	1 clove garlic, lightly smashed
Freshly ground pepper	and peeled

· · ·

Salt	tain cured ham or
Freshly ground pepper	prosciutto, thinly sliced
Flour for dusting	2 tablespooons olive oil
About ¼ pound Spanish moun-	Lemon juice

In a shallow bowl large enough to hold the trout in one layer, mix the marinade ingredients. Add the trout and turn to coat. Cover and marinate in the refrigerator 2 to 3 hours, turning occasionally. Dry the trout on paper towels and sprinkle inside and out with salt and pepper. Dust with flour.

Coat a skillet with oil and when it is very hot, give the ham slices a quick turn in the pan, then place them in the trout cavities. Heat the 2 tablespoons of oil in the skillet to the smoking point, add the trout, reduce the flame to medium-high, and brown. Turn and continue cooking until the trout is done, about 10 minutes to each inch of thickness, or until it reaches an internal temperature of 140°F. Sprinkle with salt, pepper, and lemon juice.

TRUCHA EN ESCABECHE
(Marinated Trout)

START PREPARATION I DAY IN ADVANCE

Escabeche is a blend of water or broth, wine, vinegar, herbs, and spices in which foods, particularly fish and game birds (see p. 266 for partridge), are cooked and then left to marinate. Besides adding wonderful flavor, the *escabeche* preserves the food for many days, and in its role as a preservative was a common and most practical preparation in the days before refrigeration. Trout is wonderful made this way; it is excellent as a first course, or cut into smaller pieces as a tapa.   *Serves 4*

2 pounds trout, cleaned, heads
    on or off
Flour for dusting
6 tablespoons extra virgin olive
    oil
1 small head garlic, separated
    into cloves and peeled
2 tablespoons chopped onion
1 teaspoon imported sweet
    paprika
3 bay leaves
1 teaspoon salt
4 sprigs thyme or ½ teaspoon
    dried
2 sprigs rosemary or
    ¼ teaspoon dried

1½ teaspoons minced oregano
    leaves or ¼ teaspoon dried
10 peppercorns
1 medium carrot, trimmed,
    scraped, and cut in ¼-inch
    crosswise slices
1 cup Fish Broth (p. 175) or
    ¾ cup clam juice diluted
    with ¼ cup water
1 cup water
1 cup dry white wine
1 cup white wine vinegar
Two 2-inch pieces leek (white
    portion only), well washed
    and cut in julienne strips

Marinated Trout (continued)

Sprinkle the trout inside and out with salt. Dust with flour. Heat 4 table-spoons of the oil in a shallow casserole, and brown the trout over medium heat until it is done, about 10 minutes to each inch of thickness. Remove the trout to a platter.

Add the garlic and onion to the casserole, sauté a minute, then stir in the paprika. Add the bay leaves, salt, thyme, rosemary, oregano, peppercorns, carrot, broth, water, wine, and vinegar. Bring to a boil and boil down by half. Stir in the leek and the remaining 2 tablespoons oil. Cool. Return the trout to the casserole, cover, and refrigerate overnight, spooning the sauce over the trout occasionally (you can keep the trout for several days). To serve, fil-let the trout, leaving the skin on, arrange on plates, spoon on some of the marinade, and garnish with the leek, carrot, and garlic.

BACALAO AL AJO ARRIERO
(Dried Cod with Tomatoes and Peppers)

START PREPARATION SEVERAL DAYS IN ADVANCE

There are many dishes, both fish and meat, that are described as *al ajo arriero*; what they all have in common are vinegar, garlic, and paprika. Naturally this version from Navarra, in a region known for its peppers and other fine veg-etables, includes red and green peppers, as well as tomato and potato. The contrasting tastes of the sweet vegetables and the somewhat strong-flavored dried cod are winning. Although this dish, which makes a complete meal, often calls for shredded cod, I prefer to leave it whole. It will, however, break into large pieces as it cooks.   *Serves 4–6*

2 pounds dried boneless salt cod	2 green bell peppers
3 medium-large potatoes, peeled, and cut in ¾-inch cubes	3 tablespoons olive oil
	6 cloves garlic, peeled
	6 sprigs parsley, stems trimmed
Olive oil to sprinkle on the potatoes	Flour for dusting
2 red bell peppers	6 cloves garlic, in thin slices

2 teaspoons imported sweet
  paprika
4 medium tomatoes, skinned,
  seeded, and finely chopped

1 bay leaf
5 tablespoons wine vinegar
Salt to taste

Soak the cod in cold water to cover in the refrigerator for 2 to 3 days, changing water once or twice daily, until desalted to taste. Drain and dry on paper
towels.

Arrange the cubed potatoes in a greased roasting pan, and drizzle with
olive oil. Put the peppers in another pan and place both in a 375°F oven.
Cook the peppers for about 35 minutes, turning once, or until the skin separates from the peppers, and the potatoes about 50 minutes, turning occasionally. Cool the peppers, then peel, core, seed, and cut into long strips.

In the meantime, heat 2 tablespoons of the oil in a large shallow casserole and sauté the whole garlic until lightly golden. Add the parsley sprigs
and sauté a second to soften. Transfer the garlic and parsley to a mortar or
mini processor and reserve.

Dust the cod with flour and quickly sauté on both sides in the casserole.
Add the sliced garlic and cook until it begins to turn golden. Stir in the paprika, then add the tomatoes, peppers, and bay leaf. Cook over a medium-
low flame for 5 minutes.

Mash the reserved garlic and parsley to a paste, stir in the vinegar, and
add this mixture to the casserole. Add the potatoes, cover, and cook slowly
10 minutes. Taste for salt.

Poultry ❀ Game ❀ Meats

POLLO AL CHILINDRÓN
(Chicken Braised with Red Peppers)

One of the great dishes of Aragón, here in one of the best versions I have
ever tasted.   *Serves 4*

Chicken Braised with Red Peppers (continued)

A 3–3½-pound chicken
Salt
2 tablespoons olive oil
½ medium onion, chopped
2 cloves garlic, minced
2 tablespoons coarsely
    chopped Spanish mountain
    cured ham, prosciutto, or
    capicollo
½ teaspoon imported sweet
    paprika

½ pound tomatoes, skinned,
    seeded, and chopped
4 pimientos, homemade (p.
    178) or imported, cut in
    ½-inch strips
A 1-inch piece, or to taste,
    dried red chile pepper,
    seeded
Freshly ground pepper

Cut the chicken into small serving pieces, detaching the wings and legs and dividing the breast into 4 pieces and each thigh in half crosswise. Sprinkle the chicken pieces with salt.

Heat the oil in a shallow casserole and brown the chicken on all sides. Add the onion and garlic and cook until the onion has wilted. Add the ham, cook a minute, then stir in the paprika. Add the tomatoes, cook a minute, then mix in the pimientos, chile pepper, salt, and pepper. Cover and simmer 45 minutes (the tomatoes should provide enough liquid for cooking—if not, add a little chicken broth or water).

PATO CON MEMBRILLO
A LA ARAGONESA
(Roasted Duck in Quince Sauce)

Almost all Spanish recipes for duck come from Catalunya, but here is one from the neighboring region of Aragón. It is made with quince, an ancient Mediterranean fruit closely related to the apple. Quince, which holds up better than the apple in cooking, is typically used in Spain to make a sweet paste that pairs beautifully with cured Manchego cheese. In this case, it is part of a sweet-sour sauce that is distinctive with duck.   *Serves 4*

2 ducks, about 4½ pounds each,
    trussed

2 duck necks (if available)
Salt

Freshly ground pepper

1½ cups chicken broth

2 tablespoons olive oil

1 medium onion, finely
　chopped

3 cloves garlic, finely chopped

1 medium carrot, trimmed,
　scraped, and finely chopped

1 bay leaf

1½ teaspoons thyme leaves or
　¼ teaspoon dried

Dash of cinnamon

Grating of nutmeg

1 clove

¾ pound quince or firm Golden
　Delicious apples, peeled,
　cored, and cut in ½-inch
　wedges

1 tablespoon honey

¾ cup dry white wine

½ cup orange juice, or other
　fruit juice

Prick the ducks all over with a fork. Place them with the optional necks in a shallow casserole, sprinkle with salt and pepper, and roast at 350°F for 1½ hours, spooning off the fat occasionally.

Remove the ducks and necks from the pan and cool. Quarter the ducks, remove the small rib bones from the breast, and remove the backbone, reserving the bones and neck. Transfer the ducks to a roasting pan.

Pour off any remaining fat from the casserole. Deglaze with the chicken broth, add the necks and bones, bring to a boil, cover, and simmer 30 minutes. Strain into a bowl (there should be about 1 cup) and wipe out the casserole.

Heat the oil in the casserole and sauté the onion, garlic, and carrot for 2 to 3 minutes. Add the bay leaf, thyme, cinnamon, nutmeg, and clove. Lower the heat, cover, and continue cooking about 15 minutes, or until the onion is tender but not browned. Add the quince, honey, wine, and salt and pepper to taste. Cover and simmer 45 minutes more.

Preheat the oven to 550°F. Pour the orange juice over the duck pieces and roast, skin side up, 10 minutes. Serve, spooning the sauce over the duck.

CODORNIZ A LA PARRILLA CON AJO Y PEREJIL
(Grilled Quail with Garlic and Parsley)

This dish is so simple, and yet my mind often wanders back to a summer stay in the Maestrazgo mountains of Teruel, where the quail were cooked in this way at the pleasant Hostal de la Trucha on the banks of a trout-fishing river. There are endless ways to prepare quail, but this is probably my favorite— quickly grilled, then coated with a mixture of olive oil, garlic, and parsley.

Serves 4

4 cloves garlic, minced
4 tablespoons (¼ cup) minced
    parsley
Salt

3 tablespoons extra virgin olive
    oil, plus oil for brushing
8 quail
Freshly ground pepper

Mash to a paste in a mortar or mini processor the garlic, parsley, and ⅛ teaspoon salt. Stir in the oil.

Butterfly the quail by splitting the breasts down the center to open. Pound lightly to flatten. Brush the quail on both sides with olive oil and sprinkle with salt and pepper. Broil on a tray 2 inches from the flame, until browned and cooked through, about 5 minutes to each side. Spoon the garlic sauce over the quail and serve.

Rabbit: The Other White Meat

When the ancient Romans reached the Iberian Peninsula in the third century B.C., they found a densely green virgin land overrun with rabbits, and for this reason, it is said, they named the peninsula Hispania, or "land of the rabbits." Indeed, the rabbit is thought to have originated in Spain (or in North Africa, before crossing into Spain); with its extraordinary ability to reproduce, it rapidly spread east through Europe and Asia, then crossed the frozen Bering Strait to America, where it was found by early explorers.

Most Americans, I have found, are appalled at the idea of eating rabbit, since it is so closely associated with cuddly Easter bunnies and with captivating cartoon characters. I remember a wonderful meal I once arranged for a group of Americans at one of Barcelona's most elegant restaurants, Vía Veneto, and it included an exquisite Catalan dish of rabbit sautéed with prunes. To my dismay and embarrassment most members of my party refused to taste it, and I was obliged to consult with the chef and select an alternate menu. Since then I have hesitated to request rabbit when preparing a menu for others, even though it is among my very favorite foods.

Spain, an often arid land covered with scrub bushes, is ideal terrain for rabbits and their larger relatives, hares, and both proliferate. Foods so readily available naturally become part of a country's cuisine, and in every region of Spain, rabbit is very much a part of traditional cooking—much more likely to be found on a restaurant menu than chicken. What's more, in a society as health conscious as ours, rabbit is far superior to chicken: its skin is never eaten and its meat—all white—is virtually fat-free. And rabbit is as versatile as chicken; it goes admirably well with fruits, all kinds of sauces, from sweet-sour to almond sauces, and is often included in paella.

Over the past decade America's culinary tastes have changed dramatically and today we embrace foods that were once unthinkable. Rabbit, surely, is headed for stardom and must already have many fans, for it is commonly found, albeit frozen, in local supermarkets. I leave you with Waverly Root's astute observation concerning rabbit: "It can serve as a touchstone to separate food snobs from those earthy characters who really like to eat."

CONEJO CON MIGAS
(Rabbit with Crisp Bread Bits)

A real country meal—and most enjoyable, as simple peasant food tends to be—prepared by shepherds watching over their flocks in Las Bárdenas Reales, an arid, uninhabited region of desolate, surreal beauty east of the city of Tudela. The dish consists of rabbit (which thrive in this region), sautéed, then combined with bread pieces and some liquid—the bread soaks up the sauce and becomes crisp as it cooks. And since rabbit has little fat (you can substitute skinless chicken, if you wish), there's no need to be concerned that the bread will become greasy.   *Serves 4*

A 2½–3-pound rabbit, or skinless chicken, all fat removed, cut in serving pieces	A 1-inch piece dried red chile pepper, seeded and crumbled
Salt	¼ cup chicken broth
2 tablespoons olive oil	¼ cup water
1 clove garlic, minced	2 cups good-quality, day-old bread torn into ½-inch pieces
⅓ cup finely chopped onion	

Sprinkle the rabbit pieces on all sides with salt. Heat the oil in a skillet and sauté the rabbit 20 minutes over a medium flame, turning once. Add the garlic, onion, and chile pepper and cook very slowly for 15 minutes more, stirring occasionally.

Pour in the chicken broth and water, bring to a boil, and add the bread. Continue cooking over a medium flame until the liquid is absorbed and the bread crisp, about 10 minutes more.

TERNASCO A LA ARAGONESA
(Roast Lamb, Aragón Style)

The lamb eaten in Aragón tends to be slightly older (but still much younger than what is available to us) than the baby lambs of Castilla that are only weeks old. Thus the name *ternasco*, which refers to young lamb. While in Castilla the baby lamb is simply roasted in a wood-burning oven, the lamb of Aragón admits more seasoning, as is the case in this recipe, which calls for herbs, garlic, wine, and a bed of potatoes. The optional truffle is not as exotic as it may sound, for although this is a rugged region of the country, where the food is always down-to-earth, truffles are found in abundance.

Any leg of lamb that your butcher has to offer will be far too large to reproduce this dish, so I have chosen instead to make it with a small rack of lamb which I think comes closer to the tenderness and quality of very young lamb. Keep any meaty scraps that you or your butcher trim and add them to the roasting pan for more flavorful drippings.

A traditional accompaniment is Escarole Salad (p. 128), with a dressing that includes some of the pan drippings.

2 pounds new potatoes, peeled and cut in ¼-inch slices

Salt

Olive oil

Two 1½-pound racks of lamb, well trimmed of fat (reserve any meaty scraps)

2 cloves garlic, mashed to a paste

Freshly ground pepper

1 tablespoon thyme leaves or ½ teaspoon dried

1 tablespoon minced rosemary leaves or ½ teaspoon dried

¼ cup chicken broth

4 cloves garlic, peeled

4 tablespoons (¼ cup) minced parsley

6 tablespoons dry white wine

2 tablespoons brandy

1 teaspoon minced black truffle or truffle skin (optional)

Arrange the potato slices in a well-greased roasting pan, sprinkling each layer with salt and a drizzling of olive oil. Sprinkle on 2 teaspoons water, and roast in a 400°F oven for 25 minutes.

Meanwhile, arrange the racks of lamb, meaty side up, in another roasting pan (with the lamb scraps, if available). Rub with the mashed garlic, brush with 1 tablespoon olive oil, and sprinkle with salt, pepper, thyme, and rosemary. Pour the chicken broth into the pan. Once the potatoes have roasted for 25 minutes, place the lamb in the same oven with the potatoes, turn the potatoes, and continue cooking another 15 minutes.

While the meat roasts, in a mortar or mini processor mash to a paste the 4 peeled garlic cloves with the parsley and ¼ teaspoon salt. Stir in 2 tablespoons oil, the wine, brandy, and optional truffle. Pour the mortar mixture over the meat and continue roasting, adding more chicken broth or water if necessary to keep some liquid in the pan, about 10 to 15 minutes more, or until the meat registers 145°F on a meat thermometer for medium-rare.

Remove the meat from the oven and let sit on top of the stove 10 min-

Roast Lamb (continued)

utes (you can leave the potatoes in the oven if they are not overly browned). Slice the meat into chops and serve with the potatoes, spooning the pan juices over the chops and potatoes. Serve with Escarole Salad.

CALDERETA DE CORDERO EL CHORRO
(Lamb Stew, El Chorro Style)

I am so partial to the grilled baby lamb chops that Pedro Narro (see p. 123) turns out in his unpretentious restaurant in the village of Albarracín that it was not until a reader of my guidebook to Spain who visited El Chorro restaurant alerted me to Pedro's sensational lamb stew that I tried it. And it was indeed outstanding. Pedro's cooking procedure is a bit unorthodox (slow-cooking the meat to brown, then boiling it until done), but it works. The sauce is magnificent, and the recipe couldn't be easier to prepare.

Serves 4

About 3–3½ pounds lamb
    stew meat with some bone,
    in 1½–2-inch pieces
Salt
2 tablespoons olive oil
1 bay leaf

6 peppercorns
¼ teaspoon imported sweet
    paprika
4 dried juniper berries
1 medium onion, chopped
¼ cup brandy

Put all ingredients in an open stewpot and cook over a medium flame at a low sizzle until the meat is browned and the liquid evaporated, about 45 minutes. Add 2 cups water, bring to a boil, cover, and boil over a medium-high flame until most of the liquid has evaporated, about 45 minutes. The sauce should be slightly thickened.

CORDERO EN CHILINDRÓN
(Lamb and Red Pepper Stew)

This lamb dish and Pollo al Chilindrón (p. 143) are two of the most traditional and well-known stews from the Region of the Peppers. The following version was given to me by one of the finest Spanish chefs in the United States, Antonio Buendía, who first marinates the lamb in white wine, then cooks it in red wine, which typically would be the robust red Cariñena wines of Aragón.

Serves 4

3½ pounds lamb stew meat
   with some bone, cut in
   1½–2-inch pieces
½ cup dry white wine
3 cloves garlic, peeled and
   crushed with the side of a
   knife
1 sprig rosemary or ¼ teaspoon
   dried
2 tablespoons olive oil
Salt
Freshly ground pepper
1 large onion, chopped

3 cloves garlic, minced
2 teaspoons imported sweet
   paprika
3 pimientos, imported or
   homemade (p. 178), cut in
   ½-inch strips
½ pound tomatoes, peeled,
   seeded, and chopped
1 tablespoon minced parsley
1 bay leaf
½ cup dry full-bodied red wine
½ cup veal or chicken broth

Place the lamb pieces in a bowl and stir in the white wine, crushed garlic, and rosemary and marinate 2 to 3 hours. Drain and dry the meat well on paper towels, discarding the marinade.

In a deep stewpot, heat the oil and sauté the meat until it is browned on all sides. Sprinkle with salt and pepper, then add the onion and minced garlic and continue cooking until the onion is softened. Stir in the paprika, then add the pimientos, tomatoes, parsley, bay leaf, and red wine. Bring to a boil, then cook at a high simmer, uncovered, for 10 minutes. Add the broth, more salt and pepper, if needed, cover, and simmer 1½ to 2 hours, or until the meat is tender.

PIMIENTOS DEL PIQUILLO RELLENOS DE CARNE EN SALSA DE PIMIENTOS
(Meat-Filled Red Peppers in Red Pepper Sauce)

In La Rioja meat is the traditional filling for the exquisite red peppers called *pimientos del piquillo* (see box, p. 127), here served in a puréed red pepper sauce and given a special flavor by the addition of a small amount of liverwurst to the meat filling. The peppers must be imported *piquillos* or roasted elongated sweet red peppers, sometimes available in food markets. Good-quality, deep-red jarred pimientos can be used to make the sauce but are not suitable for stuffing.

Serves 4

8 very small elongated fresh
    sweet red peppers or 16
    jarred imported *pimientos*
    del piquillo

½ pound mixture ground veal,
    beef, and pork in equal parts
1 clove garlic, minced
2 tablespoons minced parsley

PIMIENTO SAUCE

1 tablespoon olive oil
1 small onion, chopped
1 clove garlic, chopped
½ pound fresh red peppers,
    roasted and chopped, or
    a 7-ounce jar imported

    pimientos, drained and
    chopped
2 teaspoons brandy
½ cup chicken broth
Salt

. . .

1 tablespoon olive oil
Salt
1 clove garlic, mashed to a
    paste

A generous grating of nutmeg
2 tablespoons liverwurst or
    other liver pâté
2 tablespoons chicken broth

If you are stuffing fresh red peppers or using them for the Pimiento Sauce, roast them according to directions on page 96.

In a bowl, mix together the ground meats, the minced garlic, and the parsley. Let sit 10 minutes.

To make the Pimiento Sauce, heat the oil in a skillet and sauté the onion and garlic until the onion is softened. Add the peppers, then the brandy, and set aflame. Stir in the broth and add salt to taste. Simmer 10 minutes, cool, and transfer to a food processor. Beat to a smooth purée. The sauce should be of a medium thickness; if too thick, add more chicken broth or water.

Heat 1 tablespoon oil in a skillet, add the meat mixture, and sauté until the meat loses its color. Salt to taste. Turn off the heat and stir in the mashed garlic, nutmeg, liverwurst, and broth.

Stuff each *piquillo* pepper with 1 tablespoon of the meat mixture (stuff the larger homemade pimientos with 2 tablespoons) and place in a shallow casserole. Pour on the sauce and bake at 400°F for about 15 minutes.

RABO DE TORO PEDRO
(Pedro's Oxtail Stew with Juniper Berries)

Although Andalucía is the region that traditionally takes credit for its oxtail stew, this version from Pedro Narro (see p. 123) at El Chorro in Albarracín is the best I have ever tasted, in part because he adds juniper berries from the forestlands of Aragón. The preparation is effortless.   *Serves 4*

2 tablespoons olive oil	1½ teaspoons thyme leaves or
3½–4 pounds oxtail, cut in	¼ teaspoon dried
1½–2-inch-thick rounds,	1½ teaspoons oregano leaves or
fat trimmed	¼ teaspoon dried
1 medium onion, chopped	5 dried juniper berries
1 medium carrot, trimmed,	6 peppercorns
scraped, and cut in ¼-inch	1 small (¼-pound) tomato,
slices	skinned, seeded, and
Salt	chopped
¼ teaspoon paprika	2 cups dry white wine

Heat the oil in a deep pot and add all ingredients except the tomato and wine. Cook over a medium-high flame until the meat is lightly browned and the onion wilted, stirring frequently. Add the tomato and cook about 3 minutes more, then add the wine. Bring to a boil, reduce the heat, and simmer, un-covered, until most of the liquid is consumed, leaving a thick gravy. The meat needs about 3 hours to become tender; if the liquid is consumed sooner than this, cover the pot, and continue cooking.

ESTOFADO DE VACA ARAGONÉS
(Old-Fashioned Beef Stew)

Aragonese beef stew as it is made today is almost identical to a recipe called Dobladura de Ternera found in the sixteenth-century Catalan cookbook *El LLibre del Cuiner,* by Ruperto de Nola, chef to Spanish king Ferdinand of Naples. Naples was at that time a Spanish possession and Aragón and Catalunya formed one kingdom. This slow-cooking stew is fragrant with spices, as was common in medieval cooking.   *Serves 4*

2 pounds boneless stewing beef, such as chuck, in 1½-inch cubes
Salt
Freshly ground pepper
2 cloves garlic, mashed to a paste
1½ teaspoons pickled capers
1 tablespoon olive oil
2 tablespoons finely chopped bacon
1 medium onion, finely chopped

⅛ teaspoon cinnamon
⅛ teaspoon ground nutmeg
⅛ teaspoon ground ginger
1 clove
1 bay leaf
¼ cup chicken broth
½ cup dry white wine
1 teaspoon wine vinegar
Pinch of sugar
1 tablespoon pine nuts
2 tablespoons minced parsley
1 hard-boiled egg, finely chopped (optional)

Season the beef with salt, pepper, and garlic. Place the capers in a small bowl with water to cover and let sit.

Heat the oil in a deep casserole and brown the meat well on all sides. Add the bacon and cook until translucent, then stir in the onion and cook until it is softened. Add the cinnamon, nutmeg, ginger, clove, bay leaf, chicken broth, wine, vinegar, and sugar. Cover and cook slowly until the meat is tender, about 1½ to 2 hours, adding some water occasionally if necessary.

In a mortar or mini processor, mash to a paste the pine nuts with 1 tablespoon of the parsley and a little salt and add to the stew. Drain the capers and add. Cook 5 minutes more.

Serve, sprinkled with the optional chopped egg and the remaining tablespoon parsley. Although this dish probably predates the arrival of the potato from the New World, boiled or microwaved potatoes (p. 178) are a good accompaniment.

Desserts

MELOCOTÓN CON VINO
(Peaches Steeped in Red Wine)

START PREPARATION SEVERAL DAYS IN ADVANCE

So common is this dessert in Aragón, a region famed for the exceptional quality of its peaches, that a local refrain quips:

> The housewife in her house,
> priests in the pulpit
> soldiers in war
> and the peach . . . in wine.

Everywhere in Aragón and La Rioja food store displays feature the region's sweet peaches, presented in enormous jars, skinned and preserved whole in sugar syrup. A day or two before eating them, the wine is added. Of course, if it is the season for fresh peaches, and the fruit will be eaten within a couple of days, the peaches can be placed directly in the syrup and wine mixture. Increase the amount of syrup and wine according to the number of peaches you are using—they should be immersed—but always use equal amounts of syrup and wine.

4 cups sugar
4 cups water
1 stick cinnamon
2 slices lemon

⅛ teaspoon salt
About 4 large, very firm, but
　　flavorful peaches, skinned
2 cups full-bodied dry red wine

Peaches in Red Wine (continued)

In a saucepan combine the sugar, water, cinnamon, lemon, and salt. Bring to a boil and simmer 15 minutes. Cool. Place the peaches in a bowl or jar in which they fit fairly closely, then pour the syrup over the peaches (it should cover them). Cover and refrigerate for several days or more.

Pour off 2 cups of the syrup (you can reserve it for making more peaches or for other preserved fruits) and replace it with the 2 cups wine. Mix well. Refrigerate for a day or two. In Aragón the peaches are served whole in small bowls with some of the wine syrup, but for a more elegant presentation, cut the peaches in wedges, arrange attractively on dessert plates, and pour a small amount of the syrup over them.

MELOCOTÓN AL HORNO EN JARABE DE VINO
(Baked Peach in Wine Syrup)

Peaches in local wine is a ubiquitous dessert in Aragón and never seems to vary in its preparation. So when I ordered peaches in wine in the city of Jaca at La Cocina Aragonesa, a restaurant centering on an old kitchen that preserves its hearth and is decorated with old jugs and other antiques, I was pleasantly surprised to find this dessert refashioned into something unusual and elegant, although still quite simple. The peaches were baked and served warm in a syrup made with *vino rancio*—literally "rancid" wine, which is exposed to light and air to give it a sherry-like flavor. Such wines are sometimes available here, but a Spanish *amontillado* semi-dry sherry produces a similarly special flavor. "Don't use a regular table wine," advises spirited owner Merche Aldonondo; "it's not at all the same."   *Serves 4*

> 4 ripe but firm peaches
> ¼ cup water
> 1 cup sugar
>
> 1 cup *vino rancio* or semi-dry Spanish *amontillado* sherry

Place the peaches in a small baking pan, add the water, and bake at 350°F for about 45 minutes, or until the peaches are tender (the skin will be firm). Be sure there is always a little water in the pan. Cool the peaches slightly and peel.

While the peaches are baking, in a saucepan bring the sugar and wine to a boil, then simmer 10 to 15 minutes, or until the mixture is syrupy. Spoon over the peaches and serve warm.

MOSTILLO
(Autumn Fruits in Grape Syrup)

A wonderfully soothing and satisfying dessert—a fall dessert because of the fruits (this is an interesting mix that includes pears, figs, melon, and spaghetti squash) and because of the grape must (or juice, as I have used here), which gives the dessert its name, *mostillo*. The must, of course, is available in the fall when the grapes of La Rioja and of Aragón are pressed to make the region's outstanding wines.   *Serves 6*

5 cups white grape juice
½ pound firm but sweet green
   or orange melon, in 1-inch
   cubes
½ pound spaghetti squash,
   peeled and cut in 1-inch
   cubes
½ pound firm but sweet pears
   (seckel if available), peeled,
   cored, and cut in 1½-inch
   pieces

12 very small fresh or dried figs
Peel of ½ orange
1 stick cinnamon
2 tablespoons walnut pieces
2 tablespoons raisins

In a saucepan, bring the grape juice to a boil. Simmer 1 hour, uncovered. Add all the remaining ingredients, raise the heat, and cook at a high simmer for about 1 hour, or until the grape juice becomes a thick syrup. Store in the refrigerator, but serve at room temperature.

OREJONES AL VINO TINTO
(Dried Apricots in Red Wine Syrup)

Dried apricots are called *orejones*—big ears—because of their shape. When simmered in sugar and red wine they make a nice fruit dessert that is convenient to keep on hand in the refrigerator, where it will keep for weeks. I first enjoyed these apricots when dining on the simple Aragonese dishes at the Meseguer restaurant in the town of Alcañiz. The Old Quarter of Alcañiz is a national monument and its outstanding parador (government-sponsored hotel) set in the town's twelfth-century castle is one reason we pass this way so often. *Serves 4*

1 cup water	½ pound dried apricots or a
¼ cup sugar	mixture of dried apricots
1 slice lemon	and prunes
1 stick cinnamon	½ cup dry red wine

In a saucepan, bring the water and sugar to a boil. Add the lemon, cinnamon, and apricots, cover, and simmer 10 minutes. Add the wine and simmer 10 minutes more, or until the apricots are tender.

Remove the apricots to a glass jar and boil down the liquid until syrupy. Cool and pour over the apricots. Cover and keep at room temperature overnight, then refrigerate.

MANTECADOS DE ALMENDRA DE ALBARRACÍN
(Albarracín Almond Cookies)

The bakery just across the river from the magnificent walled village of Albarracín is known far and wide for its incredibly good bread, especially its large round country loaf and its flat torte brushed with olive oil (see p. 254 for a similar bread recipe). A line forms well before the morning opening (not really a line—more of a gathering of customers chatting with one another; they know perfectly well, however, where their place will be when the line takes shape).

(continued on page 160)

The Rehabilitation of Lard

Lard has become an evil word in our cholesterol-obsessed world. By virtually eliminating it from our diets, we have given up wonderfully flaky and flavorful pastry crusts and cookies as well as the special taste it imparts to foods when used in place of olive or other vegetable oils in cooking. In Spain lard has been overshadowed by olive oil, but it is still a necessity if you want your cookies and pastries to have the special taste of Spain.

In centuries past the use of lard in Spain had religious overtones. One way the Inquisition could determine if Jews and Arabs, whose religious beliefs did not allow the consumption of pork products, were true converts to Christianity was to find out if they cooked with lard or olive oil. If it was olive oil, that was one sure sign that they were secretly still following their former religions. It was not until the seventeenth century that one could safely cook with olive oil without being accused of heresy.

The good news is that recent studies show pork fat to have many of the healthful qualities of olive oil; it is much lower in saturated fats than butter or other beef fats and like olive oil has the acids that seem to have the ability to reduce cholesterol levels. Unfortunately the packaged lard commonly available today has been submitted to chemical processing and lacks the pure taste of freshly rendered lard, although I find it adequate for most recipes. Even in its processed form, it does give a very special taste to a variety of Spanish desserts, a taste that is completely absent when lard is replaced by butter (vegetable shortening is a better substitute).

To make your own lard, use pork fat scraps (or better still, use the superior fat from around the kidneys that becomes leaf lard). Render the fat and store in the refrigerator.

On a recent visit I also tried their almond cookies, which were so exceptional that they have been added to my list of reasons for returning to Albarracín. You may substitute vegetable shortening for the lard, but the lard makes a much better cookie.   *Makes 8–10 large cookies*

2 ounces blanched almonds
1 cup flour
4 tablespoons (¼ cup) lard or
    vegetable shortening
¼ cup sugar

1 egg yolk
⅛ teaspoon grated lemon peel
8–10 whole almonds, skin on
1 egg, lightly beaten

Place the blanched almonds in the bowl of a processor with 2 tablespoons of the flour and chop them as finely as possible.

With an electric mixer, beat the lard until light and fluffy, then beat in the sugar, egg yolk, lemon, and the chopped almonds. Stir in the remaining flour. Roll the dough on a floured board ⅜ inch thick, cut with a 2-inch heart-shaped cookie cutter, and place on a lightly greased cookie sheet. Press a whole almond into the center of each cookie and brush with the beaten egg. Bake at 350°F until well browned, about 15 to 17 minutes.

MANTECADOS UNCASTILLO
(Sugar Cookies Uncastillo)

I was with my tour group in the lovely town of Uncastillo (named after its castle crowning a hilltop), where quaint bridges cross the Riguel River to the houses on the other side. Having admired the exceptionally carved portal of the Romanesque Santa María church, we returned to our bus, to find that our driver and friend of many years, Trinidad Villamuelas, was nowhere about. We finally found him in the local bakery, taking freshly baked loaves from the oven with a long wooden paddle, the baker's being one of the many hats he has worn over the years. We bought some of the bakery's crunchy sugar cookies, cut in a variety of shapes (the star-shaped ones were the crispiest) to munch on the road, and they disappeared instantly. On a subsequent trip I succeeded in obtaining the recipe, but only after the chief baker had recovered from his surprise at having someone from New York come here specifically for his recipe.   *Makes about 14*

1½ cups flour

⅓ cup sugar

1½ tablespoons lightly beaten
   egg

¼ pound lard, vegetable shortening, or butter, softened

With your hands, work together all ingredients until a dough forms. Roll out on a floured surface to a ½-inch thickness. Cut into shapes about 2½ inches in size. Place on a cookie sheet covered with a greased sheet of foil and bake at 350°F for 15 minutes, or until well browned.

RUSOS DE ALFARO
(Almond Cookie "Sandwiches")

At roadside stops along the main routes in La Rioja, you are bound to see signs announcing the sale of these popular cookies that made the town of Alfaro famous. They are wafer-thin, made only with almonds, sugar, and egg white—and spread with an almond and egg cream.

Makes about 24 "sandwiches"

½ pound blanched almonds

1½ cups confectioners' sugar,
   plus more for dusting

4 eggs, separated

2 tablespoons granulated sugar

2 tablespoons water

2 tablespoons butter

Line a 10- by 15-inch rimmed cookie tray with foil and grease the foil with butter. Dust with flour. In a food processor, beat together the blanched almonds and the 1½ cups confectioners' sugar until the almonds are as finely ground as possible. Set aside 2 tablespoons. In a bowl, beat the egg whites until stiff but not dry. Fold in the remaining almond mixture.

Spread evenly with a rubber spatula over the cookie tray and bake at 350°F for about 12 minutes, or until lightly browned. Cool, trim off any edges that are irregular or too brown, and cut into 2½- by 1½-inch rectangles.

To make the sugar syrup, in a very small saucepan bring the granulated sugar and water to a boil and simmer for about 5 minutes, stirring occasionally, to make a thin syrup. In a larger saucepan, whisk the egg yolks and

Almond Cookie "Sandwiches" (continued)

slowly whisk in the syrup. Cook very slowly for 5 minutes, then raise the flame and cook, stirring constantly until thickened. Add the reserved almond mixture, cool briefly, then stir in the butter.

Spread the egg and almond mixture over half of the cookies. Fit a second cookie on top. Sprinkle with confectioners' sugar.

ALMOJÁBANAS
(Baked Doughnuts Bathed in Honey)

The name of these doughnuts clearly shows their Moorish origins (*al* is the article "the" in Arabic; therefore, just about every Spanish word that begins with these two letters comes from the Moors). The doughnuts remain the typical pastry of Albarracín—without doubt one of my favorite villages in Spain—where the Moorish presence is still palpable.

Makes about 40

Bunyolets (p. 130)   Confectioners' sugar
½ cup honey

Prepare the *bunyolets* according to instructions, substituting water for the chicken broth, eliminating the ham and parsley, and adding 1 teaspoon sugar. Instead of frying them, drop by the teaspoon onto a greased cookie sheet. Dip a finger in oil and press a hole into the center of each pastry, then bake at 350°F for about 25 minutes, or until puffed and lightly browned.

Liquefy the honey by warming it in a small saucepan. Coat each pastry with the honey, and place on a cake rack to drain. Sprinkle with confectioners' sugar.

FARINOSOS
(Spaghetti Squash Turnovers)

On a recent trip to Spain with a group of Americans, we sampled a variety of regional pastries with toppings or fillings that intrigued everyone; even the food buffs among us could not identify the mystery ingredient—candied spaghetti squash, or *cabello de ángel* (angel's hair), as it is called in Spain. Relatively new to most Americans, spaghetti squash has been a staple in Spanish dessert-making for centuries. Candied spaghetti squash works especially well as a filling for these turnovers, although if you do not wish to make it (easy as it is) you could substitute your choice of marmalade.

Makes 12 small turnovers

1¼ cups flour
2 tablespoons mild-flavored
    olive oil
1 tablespoon sugar
⅛ teaspoon salt
4 tablespoons (¼ cup) lard or
    vegetable shortening

1 tablespoon beaten egg
1 tablespoon honey
Spaghetti Squash Marmalade
    (p. 388)
Oil for brushing
Sugar for sprinkling

In a bowl combine the flour, oil, sugar, salt, lard, egg, and honey and work with your hands to form a dough. Wrap it in plastic and let sit at room temperature 30 minutes. Meanwhile, prepare the Spaghetti Squash Marmalade according to instructions and cool.

Roll the dough on a floured surface to a scant ⅛-inch thickness, cut into 3½-inch circles, and place about 2 teaspoons of candied spaghetti squash in the center of each. Fold in half, press the edges together, then seal with the tines of a fork and arrange on a greased cookie tray. Let sit for 1 hour. Brush with oil, sprinkle with sugar, and bake at 350°F for about 10 minutes, or until golden.

CHAPTER 4

Catalunya and the Baleares:

REGION OF THE CASSEROLES

If you visit Barcelona's legendary La Boquería market, which has been around more than six hundred years, you will be treated to an extraordinary display of the culinary richness of Catalunya. First a bounty of green vegetables, brought fresh from the farms and displayed at outdoor stands, greets the eye. Inside, the fruit and vegetable stands are a riot of brilliant colors, their produce arranged with the extreme care that comes from a deep-seated love and respect for food. In early spring, white asparagus and morels are the stars, and toward summer's end an astonishing selection of wild mushrooms appear, as well as fresh Spanish truffles. There is Mediterranean seafood of every imaginable description, including *pulpitos* (thumb-size octopus), and *espardenyes* (sea cucumbers), both peculiar to the Catalan coast, and special attention is bestowed upon fine-quality salt cod. At other stands dried sausages hang. Skinny or plump, long or stubby, they include Catalan specialties like *butifarra blanca* and *butifarra negra* (cooked white and black sausages), and two salami-style sausages, *fuet* and *salchichón de Vic*. There is rabbit, uncommonly popular in Catalunya, as well as game birds of every description and marvelous free-range chickens.

Catalunya from north to south runs a full gamut of climates and terrains. The grand heights of the Pyrenees enclose lushly green pastoral valleys, where cows peacefully graze and melting winter snows swell the trout-filled rivers that rush to the sea. The abrupt Costa Brava is spectacularly craggy, and its cliffs drop precipitously to the Mediterranean. Up and down the Catalan coast, seafood is extraordinary, and just a short distance from the sea many of Catalunya's highly esteemed wines, especially its fruity whites and world-class sparkling wines (*cavas*), are produced. The fertile agricultural enclaves of La Cerdanya and L'Empordà yield exceptional fruits and vegetables. L'Empordà, a name meaning marketplace, bestowed on this productive land by the ancient Greeks, gave birth to Catalan dishes that characteristically pair meat with fruits (duck with prunes and pork-stuffed baked apples are two noteworthy examples). But Girona province, of which L'Empordà is a part, also includes a long coastline, and creative combinations of ingredients of L'Empordà with products of the sea result in such splendid dishes as chicken and shrimp in almond and hazelnut sauce and cod with apples and honey.

Catalunya, indeed, is a privileged region, and food is just one manifestation of the Catalan pride that makes Catalunya culturally and gastronomically unique. Catalans strive to preserve the past—you can see this clearly in Barcelona, where historic buildings are lovingly preserved, where the traditional dance, *la sardana,* is performed in public squares by local folk at the drop of a hat, where the arts are revered (Catalunya has produced more than its share of world-class artists and musical performers), and where the Catalan language has been preserved (it is generally spoken instead of Spanish).

Catalunya traces its culinary roots to the Romans, who established one of their most important Mediterranean outposts in the Catalan province of Tarragona. From the Romans Catalunya received wheat, almonds, olive oil, and grape vines, and the Romans gave their name to Tarragona's supreme dish, *romesco de peix*—a fish casserole enriched with a mortar mixture of olive oil, garlic, nuts, and dried red peppers. This dish is the particular pride of my good friends chefs Simón and Antonio Tomás of Sol-Ric restaurant, who prepare it to perfection. A similar mortar mash results in the typical Catalan *picada,* made from nuts (almonds, hazelnuts, and/or pine nuts), garlic, and parsley, and it is truly the backbone of Catalan cooking, adding zest to so many casserole dishes, cooked in Spanish earthenware *cazuelas.* Although earthenware casseroles are common cooking utensils throughout Spain, they are absolutely essential to the preparation of countless traditional dishes in Catalunya and the Baleares. For this reason, Region of the Casseroles is certainly an appropriate title for this chapter.

Alioli (*allioli* in Catalan), a garlic mayonnaise which most likely originated with the Romans, is yet another Catalan way to give a final jolt of flavor to many foods, from simple grilled meats, poultry, and vegetables to seafood. *Bacalao con crema de ajos*, an extraordinary dish of fresh cod coated with *alioli* to which ground almonds have been added, that rests on a bed of herb-scented fresh tomatoes, was created by our wonderful friend Irene, the most gracious woman alive. She presides over Casa Irene, a charming country restaurant that counts King Juan Carlos among its ardent fans. Irene is a most persuasive spokesperson for Catalunya, for she virtually bursts with pride when she talks about the foods of the region and of her beloved Pyrenees village of Artiés.

The basic foods brought by the Romans to Catalunya were enhanced by ingredients introduced by the Moors, such as rice, eggplant, spinach, hazelnuts, and Eastern spices. With the Moors came a taste for sweet-sour foods, which disappeared elsewhere in Spain but to this day is characteristic of Catalan cooking. The creations of innovative Catalan chefs are in fact an extension of a long tradition in Catalunya of combining seemingly disparate ingredients. *El Llibre del Cuiner*, an important cookbook written in 1520 by Ruperto de Nola, Catalan chef to Aragonese King Ferdinand of Naples, contains many recipes which are the foundations of Catalan cooking today and indicate that even several centuries ago Catalans had an interest in food far beyond the simple subsistence cooking that prevailed in medieval times.

There was yet another culinary influence in Catalunya absent from the rest of Spain. In the sixteenth and seventeenth centuries Naples and Sicily were Spanish kingdoms, and Barcelona became the port of entry for European products. Thus, pasta, which rarely goes beyond a soup noodle in Spanish cooking, makes a strong showing in Catalunya. Cannellonis may be somewhat marginal in Italian cooking, but they are enormously popular in Catalunya, and *rossejat de fideus*, an oven-crisped seafood pasta baked in a *cazuela*, could not be more typically Catalan.

The Balearic Islands are perhaps best known today for their spectacular coastlines, fine beaches, and moderate climate, but their historical and culinary past was closely tied to Catalunya, both having been part of the medieval kingdom of Aragón. The islands, however, do not have the natural resources of Catalunya, and a limited water supply makes the land unsuitable for many crops. There is little livestock (except on the island of Menorca), and pigs are a major source of meat. The damp sea air is unfavorable for aging ham and sausage, and that is why *sobrasada*, a soft, semicured sausage spiced like chorizo, is very popular here. It is a favorite of mine, mixed into omelets, in a grilled sandwich, or simply spread on bread as a canapé (you can buy it from La Española—see Marketing Sources). Pork also provides the lard that is the secret to wonderfully flaky sweet and savory pastries called *cocarrons* and *rubiols,* tempting savory pies (*coques*), and sweet breads (especially the airy, spiraled *ensaimada*) at which the islands excel. Balearic seafood casseroles are splendid, none more so than *caldereta de langosta,* a lobster stew flavored with almonds, garlic, peppers, and tomatoes. And *tumbet,* a vegetable casserole combining zucchini, eggplant, peppers, potatoes, and tomatoes, is another outstanding example of *cazuela* cooking in the Baleares.

Eating in the Region of the Casseroles is indeed a journey through Spain's gastronomic history, as fascinating for the mind to contemplate as it is for the senses to enjoy.

Notes on Regional Wines and Liquors

Wines from the Penedès region of Catalunya have gained wide acceptance in America, especially the fruity whites like Ermita D'Espiells (Juvé y Camps) and Gran Viña Sol (Miguel Torres). World-class sparkling wines made by the méthode champenoise are produced in the area of Sant Sadurní d'Anoia, and among the best available in America are Gran Codorníu, Gran Cru (Juvé y Camps), and Reserva Heredad (Segura Viudas). Full-bodied red wines from Penedès also have their admirers, particularly the reds of René Barbier, Jean León, and Gran Coronas from Miguel Torres.

There are several other distinguished wine regions in Catalunya, but few of their wines have as yet reached us. One recent arrival is the elegant white wine Marqués de Alella (Parxet) from the Alella appellation of origin.

Cooking with Spanish Earthenware: An Age-Old Tradition

Spanish chefs prefer cooking with earthenware, the most ancient kind of cooking utensil known to man, but they have a hard time explaining why. "The food just tastes better," they are likely to say. Emeterio, owner and cook of Tres Coronas de Silos restaurant across from the Santo Domingo de Silos monastery (an architectural gem of the Romanesque period), who serves his outstanding garlic soup in earthenware bowls, gave me an equally vague explanation: "A bowl made of earthenware is essential to this soup; earthenware gives flavor."

Tradition and low cost account in part for finding earthenware in all sizes and shapes in every Spanish home and in every restaurant kitchen, no matter how trendy it may be (a famous Velázquez painting, *Old Woman Frying an Egg,* shows an egg being cooked over an open fire in an earthenware bowl). But there are other somewhat ineffable reasons why chefs will not part with their *cazuelas*—wide, shallow, primitively made casseroles that are the most common shape for cooking. Perhaps the food really does taste better, if only in a Proustian sense, for the cooking vessel recalls home, hearth, and mother in the kitchen. I learned long ago, however, that earthenware also has practical properties that make it exceptional.

Earthenware heats slowly, cooks evenly, and lends itself to a style of cooking that is neither a quick sauté (the casserole does not provide the intense heat of a metal skillet) nor a lengthy stew (*cazuelas* do not generally have lids for slow moist-heat cooking); typically, foods simmer, bake, or roast in a casserole. It is a most attractive dish to bring to the table, and it's versatile, made in every imaginable size and shape. Individual *cazuelitas* hold tapas, hot or cold. Gazpacho in earthenware bowls will keep its chill longer and hot soups will stay hotter. Stews and other dishes with sauce, as well as oven-roasted meats, are cooked and served in earthenware because they can go from stove to table bubbling hot. And perhaps earthenware really does add subtle overtones to foods, having absorbed so many complex flavors over the course of its lifetime.

Spanish earthenware can be found in some cookware shops and cooks' catalogs. Or bring some *cazuelas* home with you from Spain as I have done. Over the years I have amassed quite a collection: single-portion tapas dishes; several large round *cazuelas;* and oval, rectangular, and square baking and serving dishes. Also in my kitchen are earthenware tumblers, mugs, plates, and soup bowls; I always seem to reach for my earthenware first, although I really can't explain why.

For longer life, earthenware should be treated before using it over direct heat for the first time. To do this, immerse it in cold water for at least 1 hour. Drain and dry well. Always heat earthenware gradually and never subject it to sudden temperature changes that could cause cracking. If properly handled, *cazuelas* will last for years—and perhaps impart to your food certain inexplicable attributes that Spaniards swear really exist.

Dipping Sauces ❧ Salads ❧ Soups
Meals-in-a-Pot ❧ Vegetables
Egg Dishes ❧ Accompaniments

SALSA ROMESCO
(Red Pepper Sauce)

START PREPARATION 1 HOUR IN ADVANCE

Romesco is peculiar to the province of Tarragona (in its more elaborate version, *Romesco de Peix,* on p. 189, it is an extraordinary casserole dish). Here it becomes a dipping sauce to accompany simple grilled, baked, and fried seafood and seafood tapas (try it with Fish Baked in Salt, p. 360, and with Cod and Potato Fritters, p. 52). *Makes about ½ cup*

1 medium-large sweet dried red pepper or mild New Mexico style, or 1 minced pimiento plus 1 teaspoon paprika	4 cloves garlic, peeled
	A 1-inch piece dried red chile pepper, seeded and crumbled
5 blanched almonds	2 tablespoons minced parsley
5 hazelnuts	5 tablespoons olive oil
⅛ teaspoon salt	1 tablespoon vinegar
Freshly ground pepper	3 tablespoons warm water

Remove the stem from the dried red pepper and shake out the seeds. Soak for 1 hour in warm water to cover. Scrape off the flesh and discard the skin.

Toast the almonds and hazelnuts on a cookie sheet in a 350°F oven for about 5 minutes, or until the almonds are lightly browned. In a food processor, chop the almonds and hazelnuts as finely as possible. Mix in the salt, pepper, garlic, and chile pepper, then the flesh of the pepper (or the pimiento and paprika), and parsley. With the motor running, gradually add the oil and vinegar, and finally the warm water. Transfer to a serving bowl.

XATÓ
(Escarole Salad with Cod, Tuna, and Anchovy)

START PREPARATION 2–3 DAYS IN ADVANCE

An outstanding salad, full of flavor—from the cod that combines with the greens to the spicy red pepper and hazelnut salad dressing. *Serves 6*

¼ pound dried cod

DRESSING

1 medium dried sweet red pepper or mild New Mexico style, or 1 pimiento, finely chopped, plus 1 teaspoon paprika

10 hazelnuts

⅛ teaspoon salt

Freshly ground pepper

4 cloves garlic, peeled

2 tablespoons minced parsley

A 1-inch piece, or to taste, dried red chile pepper, seeded and crumbled

6 tablespoons extra virgin olive oil

2 tablespoons wine vinegar

. . .

1 medium head escarole, finely chopped

⅓–½ cup canned light-meat tuna, in chunks

6 anchovy fillets, chopped

18 cured black olives

6 radishes, in thin slices

Soak the cod in cold water to cover in the refrigerator for 2 to 3 days, changing the water once or twice daily, until desalted to taste. Drain and shred. Soak the dried red pepper in hot water for 1 hour. Toast the hazelnuts on a cookie sheet in a 350°F oven for 5 minutes.

To make the Dressing, scrape the flesh from the soaked pepper and discard the skin. In a mortar or mini processor, mash to a paste the hazelnuts, salt, pepper, garlic, parsley, and chile pepper. Add the flesh of the red pepper (or pimiento and paprika), then add 2 tablespoons of the oil and continue mashing. Whisk in the remaining oil and the vinegar.

In a salad bowl mix the shredded cod with the escarole, tuna, anchovy, olives, and radishes. Serve, spooning the Dressing over the salad.

ENSALADA DE HABAS
A LA CATALANA
(Fresh Bean Salad, Catalan Style)

The traditional Catalan combination of mint with young fresh beans similar
to limas makes a lovely dish.   *Serves 5–6*

1¼ pounds lima beans, fresh or
   frozen

2 sprigs fresh mint
½ cup water

DRESSING

1 teaspoon Dijon-style mustard
1 tablespoon sherry vinegar
2 tablespoons fruity extra
   virgin olive oil

Salt
Freshly ground black pepper
2 teaspoons finely chopped
   mint leaves

· · ·

2 ounces Spanish mountain
   cured ham, prosciutto, or
   capicollo, sliced ⅛ inch
   thick, then cut into matchsticks

½ small head Boston lettuce
   (about ¼ pound), shredded
Fresh mint leaves for garnish

Place the lima beans in a microwave-safe dish with the mint sprigs and the
water. Cover and cook on medium-high about 5 minutes, or until the limas
are cooked but still firm (or boil in a saucepan about 10 minutes). Cool the
limas in the cooking liquid.

Meanwhile, make the Dressing, whisking together all the ingredients.
Drain the limas well and discard the mint sprigs. Transfer to a bowl and
gently fold in the dressing, the ham, and the shredded lettuce. Garnish with
mint leaves and serve at room temperature.

Shellfish showcase, El Pescador, Madrid

Sampling tapas at Posada de la Villa, Madrid

Cigalas *(langoustines) and other seafood at the bountiful La Brecha market of San Sebastián*

Angulas a la bilbaína *(baby eels in garlic and olive oil), a delicacy of the Basque Country*

Galician cheese store, Santiago de Compostela

Hórreos *(Galician structures for food storage)*, Combarro

Asturian bean stew,
Casa Fermín,
Oviedo

Peppers from the Ebro Valley drying in the bright autumn sunlight of La Rioja

The grand Mercado Central of Valencia

Chorizo sausage and lamb chops grilling at Bodegón Tío Faustino, Zaragoza

ENSALADA A LA MALLORQUINA
(Mixed Salad with Anchovy Dressing)

The ingredients in this salad are not unusual, but the mixture is extremely tasty, especially with the added punch of an anchovy dressing.

Serves 4

1 cup torn escarole leaves
½ cup torn watercress, thick
    stems trimmed
1 cup torn chicory leaves
6 endive leaves, in ½-inch-wide
    lengthwise strips
1 carrot, trimmed, scraped, and
    cut into a 2-inch julienne

1 medium scallion, cut into a
    2-inch julienne
1 medium tomato, in thick
    slices, then cut in halves
Salt
Freshly ground pepper
2 radishes, thinly sliced
1 hard-boiled egg, minced

SALAD DRESSING

2 tablespoons extra virgin olive
    oil
2 teaspoons wine vinegar
¼ teaspoon Dijon-style
    mustard
1 clove garlic, mashed to a
    paste

2 anchovy fillets, minced
Salt
Freshly ground pepper
⅛ teaspoon sugar

In a salad bowl, mix the escarole, watercress, chicory, endive, carrot, scallion, and tomato. Season with salt and pepper to taste. Shower on the radishes and sprinkle with the egg.

    Whisk together the Salad Dressing ingredients and drizzle over the salad just before serving.

SUQUET DE PEIX
(Saffron-Scented Fish Soup)

START PREPARATION 2 HOURS IN ADVANCE

Our good friend Pepe González, a *madrileño* and chemist by trade (which in fact is not far removed from the alchemy of cooking), loves to get into the kitchen and prepare the Sunday midday meal, with the help of his wife, Carmen, and the able serving assistance of their three now-grown children, José Enrique, Luis, and Matilde. My husband, Luis (after whom Pepe's son was named), and I have often enjoyed fine meals and good company in their home.

Pepe's culinary background is somewhat bizarre, to say the least. His eccentric father, who spent a lifetime reading the seventy-volume Spanish *Espasa* encyclopedia (he had reached the R's at the time of his death), taught his son never to waste food, no matter what its source. So when an owl that had joined the household years before finally died, his father created a new kind of paella. In any case, Pepe developed a well-tuned palate, an example of which is his version of this beautifully flavored fish soup that comes from Catalunya.   *Serves 4*

½ cup dry white wine
1 dozen medium-size mussels, thoroughly cleansed (see box, p. 33)
½ pound hake or scrod steaks
½ pound monkfish
¼ pound medium shrimp in their shells
¼ pound bay scallops, or sea scallops cut in halves
Salt

Freshly ground pepper
Several strands of saffron, crumbled
1½ teaspoons thyme leaves or ¼ teaspoon dried
1 bay leaf
2 cloves garlic, mashed to a paste
2 tablespoons lemon juice

FISH BROTH

1 medium onion
1 small whiting (about
　¾ pound), cleaned
Few sprigs parsley
1 carrot, trimmed and scraped
½ stalk celery
1 small leek or 3 large scallions,
　well washed

1 bay leaf
Salt
6 peppercorns
1 cup clam juice
6½ cups water

. . .

2 tablespoons olive oil
Ten ¼-inch slices good-quality
　bread cut from a long
　narrow loaf
1 small onion, slivered
¼ pound leeks, well washed,

　tough outer leaves removed,
　in a fine julienne
1 clove garlic, minced
¾ pound tomatoes, skinned,
　seeded, and finely chopped
1 tablespoon minced parsley

Pour the wine into a skillet, add the mussels, cover, and boil, removing the mussels as they open. Reserve and strain the cooking liquid (there should be about ½ cup—add some water if necessary). Cool the broth. Remove the mussels from their shells.

Cut the hake and monkfish in ¾-inch pieces; shell the shrimp. (Save all bones, scraps, and shells for the Fish Broth.) In a bowl combine the mussel meat, shrimp, hake, monkfish, and scallops. Add the reserved mussel broth, salt, pepper, saffron, thyme, bay leaf, 1 mashed garlic clove, and the lemon juice. Marinate the fish in the refrigerator for 2 hours.

While the fish is marinating, make the Fish Broth, combining all ingredients, plus the reserved fish scraps, shells, and bones, in a large pot. Bring to a boil, cover, and simmer 1 hour. Strain the broth and reserve 6 cups.

Combine in a cup 1 tablespoon of the oil with the remaining mashed garlic clove. Brush the mixture on both sides of the bread slices and toast in a 350°F oven about 8 minutes, turning once, until lightly golden. Reserve.

Heat the remaining tablespoon oil in a shallow casserole and slowly sauté the onion, leek, and minced garlic until the onion has softened. Turn up the flame, add the tomatoes, and cook 5 minutes. Pour in the Fish Broth

Saffron-Scented Fish Soup (continued)

and simmer, uncovered, 30 minutes. Add the marinated fish with its liquid, bring to a boil, then simmer 5 minutes. Cover and let sit 10 minutes. Serve, floating the bread in the soup and sprinkling with the parsley.

SOPAS MALLORQUINAS
(Thick Vegetable Soup, Mallorcan Style)

The plural word *sopas* in this recipe title refers to the bread that is soaked in this soup, which in fact is not very soupy. It's somewhere between a soup and a vegetable stew—very flavorful and satisfying as a light meal. *Sopas* are sometimes accompanied by crudités like carrot sticks, strips of green pepper, radishes, and black olive.   *Serves 4*

2 tablespoons olive oil
4 scallions, green shoots
　　trimmed
¼ cup finely chopped onion
4 cloves garlic, minced
2 green bell peppers, cored,
　　seeded, and finely chopped
2 tablespoons minced parsley
½ pound tomatoes, skinned,
　　seeded, and chopped

¾ pound cabbage, coarsely
　　chopped
3 artichoke hearts, quartered
Salt
Freshly ground pepper
4½ cups chicken broth, prefer-
　　ably homemade (p. 298)
8–12 very thin slices day-old
　　country bread

In a shallow casserole, heat the oil and sauté for a minute or two the scallions, onion, garlic, peppers, and parsley. Cover and cook very slowly for 15 minutes. Turn up the heat, stir in the tomatoes, and cook 5 minutes. Add the cabbage and artichokes, season with salt and pepper, cover, and cook slowly 15 minutes more. Stir in the broth, cover, and cook for 20 minutes (the soup will be quite thick).

Slide half of the bread slices under the vegetables and arrange the rest on the top. Drizzle the bread that is over the vegetables with olive oil, transfer the casserole to a 450°F oven, and bake 10 minutes.

ACELGAS REHOGADAS
(Sautéed Swiss Chard)

Acelgas is a general term for greens, but the green generally used in Spain is quite similar to Swiss chard. For those unfamiliar with this vegetable, its large leaves are a deep silky green in contrast to its stark white stems, and the leaves and stems each have their own taste and texture. Without doubt it is the favorite green vegetable in our household—in fact there are few others that my husband will eat. I think you will find it has a magnificent flavor and a certain refinement, even though the preparation is perfectly straightforward.

Generally I prepare *acelgas* simply boiled with a drizzle of good olive oil, or boiled, then briefly sautéed. In Catalunya, pine nuts and raisins are a delicious addition. All three methods are given below.   *Serves 3–4*

2 tablespoons extra virgin olive oil	1 pound (weight after trimming) Swiss chard, thickest stems trimmed
Salt	

Bring a large pot of water to a boil with 1 tablespoon of the olive oil and salt. Add the greens and boil 15 minutes, or until done to taste. Drain and chop coarsely. Drizzle with the remaining oil, sprinkle with salt, and serve.

Variations

To sauté the greens: boil, drain, and chop, then heat the second tablespoon of oil in a skillet with a peeled garlic clove, lightly smashed, pressing the garlic with the back of a wooden spoon until it is browned on all sides. Discard. Add the greens, salt to taste, and sauté, stirring, about 5 minutes

To make the greens Catalan style: soak 2 tablespoons raisins in warm water for 10 minutes. Boil, drain, and chop the greens as directed above. Heat the remaining tablespoon oil in a skillet with the garlic, as described in the preceding variation. Discard the browned garlic and add the pine nuts. Sauté until they are very lightly golden. Add the greens, raisins (drained), and salt and continue to sauté and stir for about 5 minutes.

TUMBET MALLORQUÍN
(Mallorcan Potato and Vegetable Casserole)

Tumbet is a well-known Mallorcan vegetable dish, rich in flavor, that includes red and green peppers, potatoes, zucchini, eggplant, and tomato. It easily becomes a delicious meatless meal (as a full meal, figure that this recipe would serve 2 or 3). As traditionally prepared, however, most of the vegetables are fried, making the dish excessively greasy, so I have cut down on the calories (and on the work) by microwaving the potatoes and roasting the eggplant and peppers. The dish may be assembled in advance, then baked right before serving.   *Serves 4–5*

1¼ pounds eggplant, in ¼-inch crosswise slices

Kosher or sea salt

2 tablespoons olive oil, plus oil for brushing

Freshly ground pepper

2 green bell peppers

1 red bell pepper

½ pound zucchini, in ¼-inch crosswise slices

4 cloves garlic, minced

½ teaspoon imported sweet paprika

1 cup canned stewed tomatoes, finely chopped

2 tablespoons minced parsley

2 medium potatoes, peeled and cut in ⅛-inch slices

Sprinkle the eggplant slices on both sides with salt and place in a colander to drain for 1 hour. Dry between paper towels. Arrange the slices on a cookie tray, brush on both sides with olive oil, sprinkle with salt and pepper, and bake at 400°F about 10 minutes, turning once.

Place the green and red peppers in a roasting pan and bake at 500°F for about 20 minutes, turning once. Cool, core, seed, and cut in ½-inch strips.

In a skillet, heat 1 tablespoon of the oil and sauté the zucchini a minute, then add the peppers, salt, pepper, and 1 of the minced garlic cloves, and sauté another minute. Remove to a warm platter. Heat the remaining tablespoon oil, sauté the remaining minced garlic a few seconds, then add the paprika, tomatoes, and 1 tablespoon of the parsley. Simmer 5 minutes.

Grease a microwave-safe dish and arrange the potato slices in layers (you can save on clean-up if the shallow casserole in which the vegetables will later bake—preferably oval, about 13 by 7 inches—can double as the one in which the potatoes will cook). Drizzle each layer with olive oil and season with salt. Sprinkle 2 tablespoons water over the potatoes, cover, and microwave on high 8 minutes. Turn the potatoes, cover, and continue cooking in the microwave another 8 minutes, or until the potatoes are tender. Alternately, the sliced potatoes can be drizzled with oil (eliminate the water) and cooked in a greased roasting pan, tightly covered with foil, in a 350°F oven for about 1 hour, or until tender.

Arrange the zucchini and peppers over the potatoes in a shallow casserole, then cover with the eggplant slices. Pour on the tomato sauce and bake at 400°F about 15 minutes. Sprinkle with the remaining parsley and serve.

PA AMB TOMÀQUET
(Catalan Bread Seasoned with Tomato, Garlic, and Olive Oil)

In country restaurants all over Catalunya, you are likely to be served this deliciously seasoned bread in place of a plain loaf. Pa amb Tomàquet is so much a part of Catalan cooking that an entire book has been written on the subject, albeit somewhat tongue in cheek. It details with the aid of colorful drawings the precise method of preparation and even includes bread slice measurements, olive oil brands, and ideal acidity, as well as the optimum distance from which the oil should be drizzled on the bread (for your information, it is 10 centimeters).

You need not bother with such minutiae, but because the recipe is so simple, proper preparation and the finest ingredients are essential: the tomatoes should be juicy and flavorful (vine ripened, if possible) and the olive oil extra virgin, fruity, and assertive.   *Serves 4–6*

Six ½-inch-thick slices coarse-textured country bread, cut from a large round loaf
2 large cloves garlic, peeled and cut in halves crosswise
2 medium-size ripe and flavorful tomatoes, cut in halves crosswise and gently squeezed to extract the seeds
Extra virgin olive oil
Kosher or sea salt

Catalan Bread (continued)

Cut the bread slices in half crosswise and place on a cookie sheet. Bake in a 350°F oven about 3 minutes to each side, or until the bread is crisp but not browned. Cool.

Rub the bread slices on both sides with the cut edge of the garlic cloves. While gently squeezing the tomato, rub it on both sides of the bread, leaving a light coating of tomato juice and pulp. Drizzle with olive oil and sprinkle with salt.

COQUE DE ARENQUE
(Herring and Onion Pie)

This pizza-like pie called a *coque*, common in both Catalunya and Valencia, has one of the best toppings ever, made with lots of slowly sautéed onions and peppers and garnished with herring (although sliced sausage is another possibility). Unbaked pizza dough from your local pizzeria makes a perfect crust, but you can of course make your own if you prefer.

Coque will make a light meal or can be cut into smaller portions for tapas.

Serves 4

2 tablespoons olive oil
2 medium onions, preferably Vidalia or Spanish
3–4 medium green frying peppers (about ½ pound), cored, seeded, and cut in ½-inch strips
1 tablespoon pine nuts
¼ teaspoon imported sweet paprika

Salt
Freshly ground pepper
1 tablespoon minced parsley
¾ pound pizza dough (about half of a large pizza dough)
A 3-ounce can herring fillets (kipper snacks)

Heat the oil in a shallow casserole and sauté the onions and peppers for a minute or two. Cover and cook very slowly for 20 minutes, or until the onions and peppers are tender. Stir in the pine nuts, paprika, salt, pepper, and parsley.

Roll the dough into a ½-inch-thick oval, about 13 by 6 inches, making the dough slightly thicker around the edge, as you would a pizza. Place on a cookie sheet dusted with cornmeal or flour (or better still, on a baking stone preheated in a 500°F oven). Brush the dough with olive oil and bake at 400°F for 15 minutes. Pull the oven rack out and spread the onion and pepper mixture over the dough. Arrange the herring on top. Return to the oven and bake until the crust is golden and crisp, about 15 minutes more.

Rice Dishes ❧ Pasta Dishes

CANELONES DE ESPINACAS RACÓ DE'N JAUME
(Spinach-Filled Rolled Pasta)

This is a wonderful make-ahead company dish. Italian food lovers to whom I served it at a party were surprised to know that the dish is considered typically Spanish. The pasta squares are filled with a finely chopped mixture of onion, spinach, and cured ham and topped by a white sauce. If you can't find cannelloni pasta squares, cut them from a sheet of fresh pasta or use wonton skins. Smooth manicotti shells (not ribbed) can be used in a pinch, but are really too thick and will not give the delicacy the dish needs.

This recipe comes from the mother of the now-celebrated Jaume Bargués, owner of Jaume de Provença in Barcelona. At one time she had her own restaurant called Racó de 'n Jaume and it was she who instilled a love for fine food in her son, even though he eventually chose to follow a more "creative" and less traditional path.　　　　　　　　　　　　　　　　*Serves 6*

Spinach-Filled Rolled Pasta (continued)

24 dried cannelloni (about 2¾ inches square), fresh pasta cut in 4-inch squares, fresh wonton skins, or dried unridged manicotti

3 tablespoons olive oil

2 medium onions, finely chopped

2 cloves garlic, minced

¾ cup (about ½ pound) minced Spanish mountain cured ham, prosciutto, or capicollo

Freshly ground pepper

A generous grating of nutmeg

2 pounds washed spinach leaves, torn into pieces, left slightly damp

6 tablespoons grated cured Manchego or Parmesan cheese

Salt

1 recipe White Sauce (p. 322)

Butter

In a large pot of boiling salted water, to which a splash of olive oil has been added, cook the pasta squares until al dente, about 10 to 12 minutes for dried pasta and just a few seconds for fresh pasta and wonton skins. Drain, run under cold water, and dry on paper towels.

Heat 2 tablespoons of the oil in a skillet and sauté the onions and garlic a minute or two, then cover and cook very slowly for 10 minutes, until the onion has softened. Add the ham and cook 2 minutes more. Stir in the pepper and nutmeg and cool.

Place the spinach in a microwave-safe bowl and mix in the remaining tablespoon oil. Cover and cook on high 4 minutes (or simmer on the stove in a pot of water for about 10 minutes). Cool, chop finely, and squeeze dry between paper towels. Combine the spinach with the onion mixture, stir in 2 tablespoons of the grated cheese, and taste for salt. Place about 1½ tablespoons of filling along the length of each pasta square (you will need more if using manicotti). Roll up and arrange seam side down in a greased baking dish.

Make the White Sauce according to instructions and spoon over the *canelones*. Sprinkle with the remaining 4 tablespoons grated cheese, dot with butter, and heat in a 450°F oven about 10 minutes, or until bubbly and lightly browned. Run under the broiler if further browning is necessary.

CANELONES DE SETAS
(Rolled Pasta Filled with Wild Mushrooms)

Barcelona's central market, La Boquería, is a wonder in the fall when so many kinds of wild mushrooms make their appearance. For this dish you may use whatever varieties of wild mushrooms are available in your local market—and mix them if you wish with cultivated mushrooms to cut down on cost. I would not, however, use portobellos to make these outstanding *canelones*—they are too meaty and tend to discolor the filling and the sauce. Like the previous recipe for *canelones,* this is a wonderful make-ahead party dish. *Serves 4–5*

24 dried cannelloni, about 2¾ inches square, fresh pasta cut in 4-inch squares, fresh wonton skins, or dried un-ridged manicotti

Salt

2 tablespoons olive oil

2 medium onions, finely chopped

¾ pound wild mushrooms, such as cepes or shitake, or a mixture of wild and culti-vated mushrooms, brushed clean, stems trimmed, and chopped

¼ pound Spanish mountain cured ham, prosciutto, or capicollo, in ⅛-inch slices, then finely chopped

2 tablespoons heavy cream

1 egg yolk

7 tablespoons grated cured Manchego or Parmesan cheese

Freshly ground pepper

A generous grating of nutmeg

1 recipe White Sauce (p. 322)

Butter

In a large pot of boiling salted water, to which a splash of olive oil has been added, cook the pasta until al dente, about 10 to 12 minutes for dried pasta and just a few seconds for fresh pasta and wonton skins. Drain, run under cold water, and dry on paper towels.

Heat the oil in a skillet and sauté the onions a minute or two. Cover and continue cooking slowly for 20 minutes. Uncover, add the mushrooms and ham, and sauté 2 minutes. Stir in the cream, egg yolk, 4 tablespoons of the cheese, salt, pepper, and nutmeg. Cook a few minutes more, then cool.

Place 1½ to 2 tablespoons of filling along the length of each pasta square

Rolled Pasta Filled with Wild Mushrooms (continued)

(you will need more if using manicotti). Roll and arrange seam side down in a greased baking dish.

Make the White Sauce according to instructions and spoon over the *canelones*. Sprinkle with the remaining 3 tablespoons grated cheese, dot with butter, and heat in a 450°F oven about 15 minutes, or until bubbly and lightly browned. Run under the broiler if further browning is necessary.

ROSSEJAT DE FIDEUS
(Crisp Pasta with Allioli)

The Catalunya-based restaurant Eldorado Petit enriched the Spanish restaurant scene in New York City for all too brief a time and introduced New Yorkers to one of the finest Spanish chefs working in the United States today, Antonio Buendía. Although the New York offshoot of Eldorado Petit has closed its doors (and Chef Antonio has moved to Florida), Eldorado Petit is alive and well in Barcelona and in Sant Feliu de Guíxols. Under the watchful eye of owner Lluis Cruanyas, both remaining restaurants serve, as always, the finest Catalan cuisine.

In this unusual dish—a favorite of mine at Eldorado Petit—very fine dried pasta is fried until golden, cooked in a fish broth, mixed with shrimp, and served with garlic mayonnaise.   *Serves 4*

1 pound small-medium shrimp in their shells	2 medium onions, finely chopped
Kosher or sea salt	6 cloves garlic, minced
Fish Broth (p. 175)	1 pound plum tomatoes, finely chopped
Mild olive oil for frying	
4 cups capellini #9, broken into 2-inch pieces	Few sprigs parsley
3 tablespoons olive oil	1 recipe *Allioli* (p. 196)

Shell the shrimp and sprinkle with salt. Make the Fish Broth, adding the shrimp shells for more flavor. Strain and measure out 5 cups—if there is more, boil down.

In a large shallow casserole pour the frying oil to a depth of ¼ inch and heat until it slowly browns a cube of bread. Add the pasta, in several batches if necessary, and stir until it just turns golden (watch closely—it overcooks in a flash). Remove and drain on paper towels. Wipe out the casserole. Heat the 3 tablespoons olive oil in the casserole and quickly sauté the shrimp. Remove the shrimp to a warm platter. Add the onions and garlic to the casserole and sauté until the onions have wilted. Stir in the tomatoes and parsley and cook a minute, then pour in the Fish Broth and cook at a high simmer for 20 minutes.

Strain, measure out 4 cups, and return to the casserole. Bring to a boil and add the fried pasta. Cook at a slow boil for 4 minutes. Stir in 2 tablespoons of the *Allioli*, the shrimp, and salt to taste. Divide the pasta and shrimp among 4 shallow individual casseroles (preferably Spanish earthenware). Bake in a 400°F oven about 10 minutes, until the liquid is absorbed and the surface of the pasta crisps. Serve in the casserole dishes and pass a bowl with the remaining *Allioli*.

ARROZ CON GAMBAS A LA CATALANA
(Rice with Shrimp, Catalan Style)

Antonio Buendía, who provided this recipe, is among the most talented Spanish chefs in America. It was he whom the Culinary Institute of America called upon when they decided to teach their aspiring chefs the beauty of Spanish cuisine. The response was enthusiastic and I can only hope that Antonio has inspired others to follow in his footsteps.

Catalunya is adjacent to the rice-producing provinces of the Levante and includes an important rice region of its own in the delta of the Ebro River. This is a rice dish done in Catalan style—that is, in a shallow earthenware casserole. The result is a rice with great flavor—enhanced by the last-minute addition of anchovy, garlic, saffron, and parsley—and somewhat chewier than what a paella pan would produce.

Serves 6

Rice with Shrimp (continued)

½ pound tomatoes

3 tablespoons olive oil

18 large or extra-large shrimp,
    in their shells

2 medium onions, finely
    chopped

1 bay leaf

1 pound cleaned squid, cut in
    small pieces

1 medium red bell pepper,
    cored, seeded, and finely
    diced

3 cups short-grain rice

6 cups plus 2 tablespoons Fish
    Broth (p. 175) or 4½ cups
    clam juice diluted with 1½
    cups water, plus 2 table-
    spoons clam juice

Salt

4 anchovy fillets, chopped

2 cloves garlic, peeled

Few strands of saffron

4 tablespoons (¼ cup) minced
    parsley

Cut the tomatoes in halves crosswise and gently squeeze to extract the seeds. With a coarse grater, grate down to the skin, pouring off any excess liquid.

Heat 2 tablespoons of the oil in an 11- or 12-inch shallow casserole, preferably earthenware, and sauté the shrimp until they turn opaque. Remove to a warm platter. Add the remaining tablespoon oil to the casserole and sauté the onions until wilted, then add the tomatoes, bay leaf, squid, and red pepper. Cook slowly 15 minutes.

Stir the rice into the casserole, coating it well with the mixture. Add 6 cups of the Fish Broth and salt to taste, bring to a boil, and cook over medium heat about 8 minutes. Meanwhile in a mortar or mini processor, mash to a paste the anchovy, garlic, saffron, and parsley. Stir in the remaining 2 tablespoons Fish Broth. Add the mortar mixture to the rice and continue cooking 2 minutes, or until the rice is tender but firm. Arrange the shrimp over the rice and transfer to a 375°F oven for 5 minutes. Cover loosely with foil and let sit on top of the stove for 5 minutes before serving.

ARROZ A LA MALLORQUINA
(Rice with Pork, Sausage, and Vegetables)

Here is a rice dish good enough to be a main course but plain enough to accompany any simple meat preparation.

Serves 4–6 as a main course, 8–12 as a side dish

3½ cups chicken broth, preferably homemade (p. 298)

Few strands of saffron

2 tablespoons olive oil

½ pound lean boneless pork, in a ½-inch dice

2 tablespoons finely chopped Spanish mountain cured ham, prosciutto, or capicollo

1 medium onion, chopped

¼ pound green frying peppers, cored, seeded, and chopped

¼ pound chicken livers, chopped (optional)

3 tablespoons finely chopped chorizo

1 pound tomatoes, skinned, seeded, and chopped

Salt

Freshly ground pepper

Dash of cinnamon

1 clove, crushed

2 cups short-grain rice

3 cloves garlic, minced

2 tablespoons minced parsley

½ cup dry white wine

¼ cup peas, fresh or frozen

2 pimientos, cut in strips

Heat the chicken broth with the saffron slowly on a back burner. In an 11- or 12-inch shallow casserole, preferably earthenware, heat the oil and sauté the pork until it loses its color. Add the ham, onion, and green peppers and cook until the vegetables have softened, about 10 minutes.

Add the livers and chorizo and cook a minute, then stir in the tomatoes and cook 5 minutes. Season with salt, pepper, cinnamon, and clove. Stir the rice into the casserole, then add the garlic, parsley, broth, wine, and peas and boil 10 minutes, or until the rice is no longer soupy but some liquid remains to continue cooking the rice. Taste for salt, garnish with the pimiento strips, and transfer to a 375°F oven for 10 minutes. Remove from the oven, cover with foil, and let sit 5 minutes before serving.

The Magic of the Mortar

The mortar, a throwback to prehistoric times, was once used to grind wheat and pulverize seeds, herbs, and rice, and was, of course, essential to the apothecary. Although its utility today is greatly diminished, I would be lost without it in the kitchen.

I admit it gives me enormous pleasure to imagine the powers of alchemy and sorcery that the mortar suggests—it's as if I have the ability to transform matter and mix magic potions. But it is for more practical purposes that I turn time and time again to one of the many mortars in my kitchen. The food processor is, of course, indispensable in a modern kitchen, but when ingredients in small amounts are to be ground or mashed, the mortar and its accompanying pestle are easier to clean and in fact do a much better job, as any cook in Spain can tell you. The mortar occupies a place of honor in the Spanish kitchen, for mortar mashes redolent of garlic, parsley, saffron, herbs, spices, and nuts are the secret to so much of Spanish cooking.

The goal, you see, is not merely to mince such ingredients but to mash them to a paste. When this paste is added to any number of traditional sauces, or when it is brushed over foods, its flavor infuses the dish as mixtures merely chopped cannot. Take the example of quail (p. 145), grilled, then coated with a mortar blend of garlic, parsley, and olive oil—so simple and yet so appealing. You can do the same with meats and fish, vegetables and salads, transforming plain foods into extraordinarily tasty preparations.

Over the years I have assembled quite a collection of mortars and pestles, some for decorative purposes—they can be objects of great beauty and value—and others for use in the kitchen. Mortars may be made from wood, ceramic, metal, marble, and other less refined stone. My metal mortars are mainly ornamental because the food can't cling to them and thus they are less effective. But my Spanish yellow ceramic mortars, in three sizes with wooden pestles—the ones found in just about every Spanish household—are those that I reach for most frequently to accomplish my most common tasks of mashing garlic and parsley, although I prefer my marble mortar and pestle for pulverizing hard seeds like anise and cumin.

Give the mortar and pestle a try, and surely you too will be impressed by their culinary powers.

Shellfish ✿ Fish

ROMESCO DE PEIX
(Seafood Casserole in Romesco Sauce)

Romesco de Peix is the supreme creation of the ancient Roman city of Tarragona and as the name suggests, a dish, at least in part, of Roman origin. The ancient Romans called this region of Spain Tarraconensis, and if they in fact prepared *romesco* (some say it was a favorite of Tarragona's gladiators), the sauce would probably have been based on garlic, bread, olive oil, and perhaps nuts, although almonds and hazelnuts did not become common in Spain until the arrival of the Moors. Peppers, of course, were unknown until the discovery of America.

Chefs who are experts in the preparation of *romesco* are held in utmost esteem, and there are often contests to choose the grand masters of *romesco*, one of the highest honors in a region that prides itself on this dish. *Romesco* is the specialty of *romesco* masters Simón and Antonio Tomás, who feature it at their delightful restaurant, Sol-Ric, just outside the city of Tarragona. They seek out the finest seafood of Tarragona's coast, including prized tiny octopus (*pulpitos*) the size of a thumb joint.

Among the beauties of Romesco de Peix is that the sauce can be made hours in advance. Just 10 minutes are needed before serving time to simmer the seafood in the sauce. It is a superb special-occasion meal.

Serves 4

Seafood Casserole (continued)

2 sweet dried red peppers or mild New Mexico style, or 2 pimientos plus 2 teaspoons paprika

A 1¾-pound freshly killed lobster

¾ pound scrod, about 1 inch thick, cut in 4 serving pieces

¾ pound cleaned monkfish, about 1 inch thick, cut in 4 serving pieces

8 jumbo shrimp, in their shells

8 small cleaned (see p. 81) squid (about 3-inch body length), with their tentacles

Kosher or sea salt

6 tablespoons olive oil

4 cloves garlic, peeled

1 bread slice cut from a long narrow loaf, ½ inch thick, crusts removed, preferably 1 day old

20 blanched almonds

1 medium onion, finely chopped

4 cloves garlic, minced

½ pound tomatoes, finely chopped

½ pound very small shrimp, in their shells

½ cup dry white wine

4 cups water

2 dozen cockles or Manila clams, or 1 dozen very small littlenecks, thoroughly cleansed (see p. 33)

Remove the stems and shake out the seeds from the dried red peppers. Place in a bowl with hot water to cover and let soak 30 minutes. Split the lobster in half. Remove the large claws and cut each with kitchen shears into two sections. Crush lightly. Remove the tail and divide each piece in half crosswise. Reserve the head and small claws for the broth.

Sprinkle the lobster, scrod, monkfish, jumbo shrimp, and squid with salt and let sit at room temperature.

Heat the oil in a large shallow casserole, preferably earthenware, and sauté the peeled garlic, the bread slice, and the almonds, turning to brown evenly and removing to a mortar or mini processor as each turns lightly golden. Add ⅛ teaspoon salt to the mortar and reserve.

In the casserole sauté the onion and minced garlic, until the onion is translucent. Add the tomatoes, cook a minute or two, then add the small shrimp and the reserved lobster head and small claws and cook another minute. Stir in the wine and boil away, then pour in the water and salt lightly. Return to the boil and boil over high heat for 30 minutes.

Meanwhile, mash the mortar mixture until all ingredients are as finely chopped as possible. Drain, then finely chop the dried red pepper and add to the mortar. (If using pimiento and paprika, add here.) Mash to a paste.

Remove the small shrimp from the casserole (they will not be used further for this dish but are very tasty made into a chopped shrimp salad) and strain the remaining contents of the casserole, pressing with the back of a wooden spoon to extract as much liquid as possible. Taste for salt and reserve 2 cups of liquid.

Return the reserved liquid to the casserole and stir in the mortar mixture. Bring to a simmer, then add the lobster, scrod, monkfish, jumbo shrimp, and clams. Simmer 5 minutes. Add the squid and simmer 5 minutes more. Bring to the table in the casserole dish.

CALDERETA DE LANGOSTA CELLAR SA SINIA
(Lobster in Almond and Vegetable Broth)

While touring the scenically exciting island of Mallorca, we stopped to visit our cousins Pili and Rafa Salgado, whose splendid home overlooks the dazzling inlet of Cala d'Or. They insisted we pay a visit to Toni Ramón at Cellar Sa Sinia restaurant in nearby Porto Colom to taste his version of Mallorca's classic lobster *caldereta,* a dish that is somewhere between a stew and a soup. It was indeed magnificent—a bit messy to eat, perhaps, but that's all part of the fun.   *Serves 4*

Four 1¼–1½-pound freshly killed lobsters
Kosher or sea salt
4 ounces blanched almonds (about 1⅓ cups)
Eight ¼-inch bread slices cut from a long narrow loaf
8 cloves garlic, peeled
2 tablespoons minced parsley
¼ cup olive oil
2 medium onions, finely chopped

2 large green bell peppers, cored, seeded, and finely chopped
½ pound tomatoes, chopped
1 cup brandy
2 cups Fish Broth (p. 175) or 1½ cups clam juice diluted with ½ cup water
6 cups water
2 tablespoons thyme leaves or 1 teaspoon dried
Freshly ground pepper

Lobster in Almond and Vegetable Broth (continued)

Leaving the shell on, cut the tails from the lobsters and divide each tail in 2 or 3 rings. Open the heads, and remove and reserve the tomalley (the green matter). Divide each large claw into two pieces and lightly crush for easier removal of the meat. Leave the small claws whole. When cutting the lobsters, try to reserve as much of the liquid they give off as possible. Dry the lobster pieces on paper towels and sprinkle with salt.

Toast the almonds on a cookie tray in a 350°F oven for about 8 minutes, or until golden. Remove the almonds to a mortar or mini processor. Toast the bread in the oven about 5 minutes, turning once, until crisp on both sides but not browned. Reserve.

Mash to a paste in a mortar or mini processor the almonds, garlic, ¼ teaspoon salt, and the parsley. Gradually mash in the tomalley. Reserve.

In a shallow casserole, heat 2 tablespoons of the oil to the smoking point and quickly sauté the lobster pieces until the shells turn pink. Remove to a warm platter. Add the remaining 2 tablespoons of oil to the casserole and sauté the onions and peppers a minute or so. Cover and cook very slowly for 15 minutes. Turn up the flame, add the tomatoes, and sauté 5 minutes. Pour in the brandy and boil it away. Add the Fish Broth, water, the lobster heads, the small lobster claws, and the thyme. Stir in the mortar mixture, salt, and pepper and bring to a boil. Cook at a high simmer, uncovered, for 30 minutes. Strain, pushing through as much of the solid matter as possible with the back of a wooden spoon, and return to the casserole. Add the lobster pieces and cook, uncovered, at a high simmer for 10 minutes.

Bring the casserole to the table and place 2 bread slices on the bottom of each individual soup bowl. Serve some of the broth and a few pieces of lobster and let each diner help himself to more.

PESCADO AL HORNO ELS PESCADORS
(Fish Baked with Potatoes, Onions, and Wine)

Fish (whatever is freshest that day) baked over a bed of thin-sliced potatoes is one of the preferred ways to prepare fish in Catalunya. This version from Els Pescadors, a fine seafood restaurant commanding wonderful views of the sea and of the small port of L'Escala, is quite exceptional.

Serves 4

1 pound potatoes, in ⅛-inch slices

1 small–medium onion, slivered

About ¼ cup olive oil

Kosher or sea salt

Freshly ground pepper

¼ pound tomato, in very thin wedges

2 pounds turbot or other firm-flesh fish steaks like halibut, 1 inch thick

1½ teaspoons thyme leaves or ¼ teaspoon dried

1½ teaspoons minced rosemary leaves or ¼ teaspoon dried

1½ teaspoons minced marjoram leaves or ¼ teaspoon dried

2 tablespoons minced parsley

Freshly squeezed lemon juice

½ cup dry white wine

1 tablespoon dried bread crumbs

Arrange the potatoes and onion in layers in a greased baking pan, sprinkling each layer with oil (a total of 3 tablespoons), salt, and pepper (choose a pan in which you will have about 3 layers). Scatter the tomato wedges over the potatoes, cover tightly with foil, and bake in a 350°F oven about 45 minutes, or until the potatoes are almost tender. Meanwhile, sprinkle the fish steaks on both sides with salt and let sit.

Place the fish over the potatoes, brush the fish with about 1 tablespoon oil, then sprinkle the fish and potatoes with thyme, rosemary, marjoram, parsley, and lemon juice. Pour on the wine. Dust the fish with bread crumbs and cook until the fish is just done, about 15 minutes, basting several times.

MERO ESTILO MALLORQUÍN

(Grouper with Potatoes, Spinach, Raisins, and Pine Nuts)

The typically Catalan (and Mallorcan) mix of spinach, raisins, and pine nuts makes an attractive and flavorful topping for this fish that is baked over sliced potatoes.   *Serves 4*

2 pounds fish steaks, such as
   grouper, mullet, or scrod,
   about 1¼ inches thick
Kosher or sea salt
Flour for dusting
3 tablespoons olive oil
1 pound potatoes, in ⅛-inch
   slices
Freshly ground pepper
4 tablespoons (¼ cup) minced
   parsley
4 medium scallions, trimmed
   and chopped
3 cloves garlic, minced
6 ounces washed, dried, and
   chopped spinach leaves

(about 3 cups loosely
   packed)
⅓ cup skinned, seeded, finely
   diced tomato
⅛ teaspoon imported sweet
   paprika
A few strands of saffron,
   crumbled
1 tablespoon raisins
1 tablespoon pine nuts
Freshly squeezed lemon juice
8 thin tomato slices
2 teaspoons bread crumbs

Sprinkle the fish with salt and let sit 10 minutes. Dust with flour. Heat 1 tablespoon of the oil in a skillet and sear the fish on both sides. Remove to a warm platter and wipe out the pan.

Arrange the potato slices in layers in a greased microwave-safe dish, if possible a dish in which the fish will also fit in 1 layer. Sprinkle each layer of potato with salt, pepper, and a total of 1 tablespoon olive oil and 2 table-spoons water. Cover and cook on high for 8 minutes. Turn the potatoes, cover, and continue cooking for about 6 minutes. The potatoes should be almost tender. Alternately, the sliced potatoes can be drizzled with oil (elim-inate the water) and cooked in a greased roasting pan, tightly covered with foil, in a 350°F oven for about 45 minutes, or until almost tender.

In a skillet, heat the remaining tablespoon oil and slowly sauté the pars-ley, scallions, and garlic for 5 minutes. Stir in the spinach, diced tomato, salt, pepper, paprika, and saffron, cook a minute, then add the raisins and pine nuts.

Arrange the fish over the potatoes and sprinkle with lemon juice. Cover the fish with the spinach mixture, then place the slices of tomato over the spinach and sprinkle with the bread crumbs. Bake at 400°F for 10 minutes. Cover and continue cooking until the fish is done, about 5 to 10 minutes more.

RAPE EN SALSA DE ALMENDRAS Y AVELLANAS

(Monkfish in Almond and Hazelnut Sauce)

Not an overly saucy dish, this fish preparation owes its wonderful flavor to the typical Catalan *picada*—a mash, in this case, of garlic, almonds, hazelnuts, and parsley, which gives a more pronounced flavor.   *Serves 4*

2 pounds monkfish	12 cloves garlic, minced
Salt	6 tablespoons minced parsley
½ pound tomatoes	6 tablespoons dry white wine
16 blanched almonds	2 tablespoons olive oil
8 hazelnuts	Freshly ground pepper

Sprinkle the fish on both sides with salt and let sit. Cut the tomatoes in halves crosswise and gently squeeze to extract the seeds. With a coarse grater, grate down to the skin, draining off any excess liquid.

In a mortar or mini processor, mash to a paste the almonds, hazelnuts, 2 cloves of the garlic, 2 tablespoons of the parsley, and ⅛ teaspoon salt. Add 2 tablespoons of the wine and continue mashing until as fine as possible, then stir in the remaining 4 tablespoons wine.

Heat the oil in a shallow casserole and sauté the remaining 10 cloves garlic and the remaining 4 tablespoons parsley until the garlic just begins to color. Add the tomato and raise the heat to evaporate the liquid. Stir in the mortar mixture, taste for salt and pepper, and add the fish. Cover and cook over medium-low heat for about 15 minutes, or until the fish is done (about 10 minutes to each inch of thickness). Remove the fish to a warm platter and boil down the sauce a little if it has thinned.

RAPE ALLIOLI
(Monkfish Baked with Garlic Mayonnaise)

Allioli—garlic mayonnaise—is guaranteed to give a great taste to just about anything it accompanies, but it is particularly nice with fish. This is a dish quick to prepare, even when you make your own mayonnaise. Serve with boiled potatoes and put a dab of *allioli* on them also!

Serves 4

1¾–2 pounds monkfish, cut in 4 portions	Salt Freshly ground pepper

ALLIOLI (ALIOLI)

8 cloves garlic	1 teaspoon lemon juice
¼ teaspoon salt	1 cup olive oil
2 egg yolks or ¼ cup egg substitute made with egg white	

Arrange the fish pieces in a shallow, lightly greased baking dish, preferably earthenware. Sprinkle with salt and pepper.

Place the garlic and salt in a mortar and mash to a paste (or put the garlic through a garlic press, then mix in the salt). Transfer to a processor, add the egg yolks and lemon juice, and beat a few seconds. With the motor running, drizzle in the oil until a mayonnaise is formed.

Spoon some *allioli* over the fish (save the rest for some other purpose), place in a 450°F oven, and bake 10 minutes to each inch of thickness.

TRUCHAS AL VINO CON ALMENDRAS
(Trout with Onions and Almonds)

The bed of onions over which this trout is served has a wonderful flavor because it has absorbed the taste of the wine, garlic, and herbs. If you bone the fish before serving (leave the skin on), it is easier to appreciate the fish and the sauce as one.

Serves 4

2 tablespoons minced parsley

2 tablespoons dried bread
   crumbs

2 teaspoons freshly squeezed
   lemon juice

2 tablespoons blanched slivered
   almonds

2 cloves minced garlic

Kosher or sea salt

Four ¾-pound freshwater
   trout, cleaned, heads off

Flour for dusting

¼ cup olive oil

1 medium onion, slivered

1 tablespoon thyme leaves or ½
   teaspoon dried

2 bay leaves

A 1½-inch piece, or to taste,
   dried red chile pepper,
   seeded

½ cup dry white wine

1¼ cups Fish Broth (p. 175) or
   1 cup clam juice diluted
   with ¼ cup water

In a small bowl, combine the parsley, bread crumbs, and lemon juice. In a mortar or mini processor, mash to a paste the almonds, garlic, and ⅛ teaspoon salt.

Salt the trout in and out and dust with flour. Heat 2 tablespoons of the oil in a shallow casserole and brown the trout quickly on both sides. Remove to a warm platter and wipe out the casserole.

Heat the remaining 2 tablespoons oil in the casserole and sauté the onion until wilted. Add the thyme, bay leaves, and chile pepper and cook a minute. Stir in the wine and boil away. Add the Fish Broth, bring to a boil, then simmer 10 minutes. Salt to taste. Stir in the mortar mixture, return the trout to the casserole, cover, and cook until the trout is done, about 8 minutes to each inch of thickness. Sprinkle the bread-crumb mixture over the trout and run under the broiler to brown. Serve the trout over the onion mixture, preferably filleted.

MERLUZA CON CREMA DE AJOS
(Hake with Almond-Garlic Mayonnaise and Tomato)

This dish is a specialty at Casa Irene, a jewel of a restaurant high in the Pyrenees in the tiny village of Artiés. Owner and chef Irene España creates a warm, friendly atmosphere that is just as appealing to winter skiers as to summer vacationers.

This dish, which Irene once prepared with dried cod, is now made with fresh fish (improved transportation from the Spanish coasts to this isolated valley makes this possible). The flavors are refined and wonderfully complex; almond-garlic mayonnaise coats the fish, which rests on a bed of fresh tomato sauce seasoned with herbs.   *Serves 4*

ALMOND-GARLIC MAYONNAISE

1 clove garlic, minced
1 ounce slivered or chopped
    blanched almonds (about
    2 tablespoons)
½ teaspoon salt
1 small egg, or ¼ cup egg sub-
    stitute made with egg white
1 tablespoon freshly squeezed
    lemon juice

Freshly ground pepper,
    preferably white
¼ teaspoon Dijon-style
    mustard
⅔ cup mild-flavored extra
    virgin olive oil
2 tablespoons heavy cream

. . .

2 pounds ripe and flavorful
    tomatoes
2 tablespoons extra virgin olive
    oil
2 cloves garlic, minced
1½ teaspoons minced rosemary
    leaves or ¼ teaspoon dried
2 tablespoons minced parsley
1½ teaspoons minced oregano
    leaves or ¼ teaspoon dried

Salt
Freshly ground pepper
Fish Broth (p. 175) or clam
    juice diluted with ¼ part
    water
2 pounds hake or scrod, in
    4 portions (preferably cut
    from the thinner, tail end)

To make the Almond-Garlic Mayonnaise, in a mortar or mini processor mash the garlic, almonds, and ¼ teaspoon of the salt as fine as possible. Transfer to a large processor, then add the egg, lemon juice, another ¼ teaspoon salt, pepper, and mustard and beat until smooth. With the motor running, drizzle in the oil to form a mayonnaise. Pulse in the cream.

To make the tomato sauce, halve the tomatoes crosswise, squeeze out the seeds and excess liquid, and with a coarse grater, grate down to the skin. Place the tomato pulp in a saucepan, add the 2 tablespoons oil, the garlic, rosemary, parsley, and oregano and season with salt and pepper to taste. Simmer 10 minutes. Reserve.

Pour Fish Broth to a depth of 1 inch in a shallow pan in which the fish will comfortably fit, and bring to a boil. Add the fish, cover, and simmer for about 10 minutes to each inch of thickness of the fish.

Heat the tomato sauce and spoon into an ovenproof dish (if possible, one that can be brought to the table) and arrange the fish over it. Spoon the Almond-Garlic Mayonnaise over the fish and pass briefly under the broiler until golden.

BACALAO CON MANZANA Y ALLIOLI DE MIEL
(*Salt Cod with Apple Purée and Honey* Allioli)

START PREPARATION 2–3 DAYS IN ADVANCE

As unlikely as this recipe may sound, it works beautifully, using a Catalan blend of flavors typical of medieval times, although today the dish might be taken for a creation of some innovative chef. At the Can Ametller restaurant in the Catalan town of Sant Cugat del Vallés these seemingly conflicting ingredients are deliciously married in this dish.   *Serves 4*

1½ pounds dried boneless salt cod, cut in 4 portions
Fish Broth (p. 175) or clam juice diluted with ¼ part water
4 tablespoons butter
1½ teaspoons thyme leaves or ¼ teaspoon dried
10 peppercorns
1 bay leaf
2 Golden Delicious apples,

skinned, cored, and quartered
Allioli (p. 196), made with 1 clove garlic
2 teaspoons honey
4 scallions, white and pale green shoots only, finely chopped
½ cup milk
Salt
2 tablespoons minced parsley

Soak the cod in cold water to cover in the refrigerator for 2 to 3 days, changing the water once or twice daily, until desalted to taste. Drain.

Salt Cod with Apple Purée (continued)

Pour the Fish Broth into a shallow casserole to a depth of about 1½ inches, add 2 tablespoons of the butter, the thyme, peppercorns, and bay leaf and bring to a boil. Simmer 10 minutes, then add the cod and simmer 15 minutes more. Transfer the cod to a warm platter and lightly cover with foil. Reserve ½ cup of the Fish Broth. Wipe out the casserole.

Chop 1½ apples and cut the remaining ½ apple in paper-thin slices. In a small bowl combine the *Allioli* with the honey.

Melt the remaining 2 tablespoons butter in the casserole and sauté the scallions briefly until softened. Add the chopped apples, cover, and cook slowly until the apples are tender, 5 to 10 minutes. Add the ½ cup reserved broth and simmer, uncovered, 10 minutes, then add the milk, taste for salt, and boil down until most of the liquid has evaporated. Transfer the contents of the casserole to a processor and purée, then pour into a shallow baking dish in which the cod will fit snugly and sprinkle with the parsley. Place the cod over the purée, arrange the raw apple slices over the cod, and cover each piece of cod with *Allioli*. Run briefly under the broiler until well browned (watch carefully).

BACALAO A LA CATALANA
(Dried Cod with Spinach, Raisins, and Pine Nuts)

START PREPARATION 2–3 DAYS IN ADVANCE

The Catalan penchant for adding sweet ingredients to main courses works remarkably well in this salt cod preparation. It is a singular and most delicious dish, much too good to be merely a Lenten dish, as it traditionally is.

Serves 4

1½ pounds dried boneless salt cod	Salt
3 tablespoons raisins	3 tablespoons olive oil
3 tablespoons pine nuts	Flour for dusting
1 pound torn spinach leaves, well washed (about 8 cups loosely packed)	¼ cup minced onion
	2 cloves garlic, minced
	Freshly ground pepper

Soak the cod in cold water to cover in the refrigerator for 2 to 3 days, changing water once or twice daily, until desalted to taste. Soak the raisins and pine nuts in water to cover for 2 hours. Place the spinach in a colander and sprinkle with salt to release its liquid.

Drain and dry the cod and spinach on paper towels. Drain the raisins and pine nuts. Heat 2 tablespoons of the oil in a shallow casserole, dust the cod with flour, and sauté over a medium-high flame until golden on both sides. Remove, and wipe out the skillet.

Heat the remaining tablespoon oil and sauté the onion and garlic until the onion is softened. Add the spinach and season with salt and pepper. When the spinach has wilted, add the raisins and pine nuts. Place the cod over the spinach mixture, drizzle in 2 tablespoons water, cover, and simmer about 10 minutes.

Poultry ❧ Game ❧ Meats

POLLO A LA PARRILLA CON ALLIOLI
(Marinated Grilled Chicken with Garlic Mayonnaise)

START PREPARATION 2 HOURS IN ADVANCE

Garlic mayonnaise accompanies so many regional dishes—the truth is that it tastes great with just about anything, from meat, fish, and poultry to vegetables. I like it here as a complement to marinated chicken (and of course, rabbit would be excellent as well).

Serves 4

Marinated Grilled Chicken (continued)

A 3–3½-pound chicken, split in
half

MARINADE

¾ cup dry white wine
¾ cup extra virgin olive oil
2 bay leaves, crumbled
4½ teaspoons thyme leaves or
    ¾ teaspoon dried
3 cloves garlic, mashed to a
    paste

½ teaspoon ground cumin,
    preferably freshly ground in
    a mortar or spice mill
Salt
Freshly ground pepper

. . .

Garlic Mayonnaise (p. 196)

Gently pound the chicken to flatten it. Mix together the marinade ingredients
in a shallow bowl. Add the chicken to the marinade and turn to coat well.
Marinate, skin side down, 2 hours, basting occasionally.

    Remove the chicken from the marinade and place skin side down on a
broiler tray. Broil about 7 minutes to each side to brown the chicken, basting
occasionally with the marinade. Transfer to a 400°F oven and continue
cooking and basting skin side up about 15 minutes more. Serve with the Garlic Mayonnaise on the side.

POLLO AL VINO CON MELOCOTONES EN JARABE
(Chicken with Peaches in Syrup)

Here is another fine example of the Catalan tradition of combining fruit into
main-course dishes. In this case, peaches that have been cooked in a sugar
syrup are added to the chicken with some of their syrup.   *Serves 4*

1 cup water
⅓ cup sugar
½ cinnamon stick

1 slice lemon
3 medium peaches, skinned,
    pitted, and halved

A 3–3½-pound chicken, cut in
   serving pieces
Kosher or sea salt
1 tablespoon olive oil

1 clove garlic, minced
¼ cup dry white wine
¼ cup chicken broth

In a saucepan bring to a boil the water, sugar, cinnamon, and lemon. Simmer 5 minutes. Add the peaches, simmer a minute, turn off the flame, cover, and let steep.

Sprinkle the chicken pieces with salt. In a shallow casserole, heat the oil and brown the chicken well on all sides. Add the garlic, cook a minute, then pour in the wine and bring to a slow boil. Reduce the wine by half. Stir in the chicken broth, cover, and simmer 20 minutes. Add the peaches and 2 tablespoons of the peach syrup. Transfer to a 400°F oven and continue cooking, uncovered, for 15 minutes.

POLLO EN SALSA CARAMELIZADA CON SAMFAINA

(Chicken with Stewed Vegetables in Caramelized Sugar Sauce)

This is a sensational dish—the caramelized sugar coats the chicken as well as adding a slight sweetness to the *samfaina,* a traditional vegetable medley of eggplant, peppers, and tomatoes.   *Serves 4*

1 medium eggplant, partially
   skinned with a potato peeler
   and cut in ¾-inch cubes
Kosher or sea salt
3 tablespoons olive oil plus oil
   for brushing
Freshly ground pepper
1 medium onion, slivered
1 clove garlic, minced
1 red bell pepper, cored,

seeded, and cut in ½-inch
   dice
2 medium tomatoes, skinned,
   seeded, and chopped
1 tablespoon minced parsley
¼ cup chicken broth
A 3–3½-pound chicken
3 tablespoons sugar
¼ cup water

Place the eggplant cubes in a colander and sprinkle with salt on all sides. Leave to drain for 30 minutes. Dry on paper towels and place on a greased

Chicken with Stewed Vegetables (continued)

baking tray. Brush with oil, sprinkle with salt and pepper, and bake in a 400°F oven until tender, about 15 minutes.

In a shallow casserole, heat 1 tablespoon of the oil, and slowly sauté the onion, garlic, and red pepper until the vegetables have softened. Add the tomatoes, parsley, salt, and broth and cook, uncovered, over a medium flame about 15 minutes. Add the eggplant and cook 5 minutes to blend the flavors. Taste for salt and reserve.

Cut the chicken into small serving pieces, detaching the wings and legs and dividing the breast in 4 pieces and each thigh in half crosswise. Sprinkle the chicken pieces all over with salt. In a skillet, heat 2 tablespoons of the oil over a medium-high flame, and sauté the chicken until cooked through, about 20 minutes, turning occasionally. Drain off the oil.

Sprinkle the sugar in the skillet and pour in the water. Cook, spooning the liquid over the chicken, until the liquid is lightly caramelized. Transfer the chicken to a platter or to individual dinner plates and spoon half of the caramelized sugar over the chicken. Add the reserved vegetable mixture to the skillet, mixing with the caramelized sugar that remains in the pan. Heat, and serve the chicken over the vegetables.

POLLASTRE AMB GAMBES
(Chicken and Shrimp in Almond and Hazelnut Sauce)

In typical Catalan style, this unusual and uncommonly good regional specialty combines poultry, shellfish, and nuts. Yet contrary to what it might seem, this dish will not at all startle the taste buds. Any gap that exists between surf and turf is bridged by the almond and hazelnut wine sauce.

Serves 4

A 3–3½-pound chicken, cut in serving pieces	20 medium shrimp in their shells
Salt	3 tablespoons olive oil
Freshly ground pepper	1 medium onion, chopped
Flour for dusting	2 cloves garlic, minced

1 medium tomato, peeled,
　　seeded, and chopped
2 tablespoons minced parsley
1½ teaspoons minced oregano
　　or ¼ teaspoon dried
1½ teaspoons thyme leaves or
　　¼ teaspoon dried
1 bay leaf

A 3-inch piece of leek (white
　　part only), well washed, cut
　　lengthwise into 4 slices
½ cup chicken broth
¼ cup dry white wine
5 blanched almonds
5 hazelnuts
1 tablespoon brandy

Sprinkle the chicken pieces on all sides with salt and pepper. Dust with flour. Shell the shrimp, reserving the shells. Sprinkle the shrimp with salt and dust with flour.

Heat the oil in a shallow casserole and brown the chicken on all sides. Transfer to a warm platter. Briefly sauté the shrimp and remove to the same platter. Add to the casserole the onion and garlic and sauté until the onion has softened. Stir in the tomato, parsley, oregano, thyme, bay leaf, and leek, then add the chicken broth, the wine, and the shrimp shells. Add the chicken, cover, and cook 30 minutes.

In a mortar or mini processor mash to a paste the almonds, hazelnuts, and ⅛ teaspoon salt. Stir in the brandy. Add to the casserole and cook 5 minutes. Strain the sauce and return to the casserole. Add the shrimp and cook 5 minutes more.

PATO A LA CATALANA
(Duck with Prunes and Pine Nuts)

Catalan restaurateurs who venture to America tear their hair out trying to reproduce their traditional duck casserole dishes because our ducks have much more fat. The solution is to pre-roast the duck by the method I learned from a fine Hispanic Philadelphia chef, Alfred Stariko, whose duck is renowned there, then remove the fat and prepare the sauce with the pan drippings.

Prunes are often paired with duck, chicken, and rabbit in Catalan recipes, and certainly their sweetness and flavor are perfectly complementary.

Serves 4

Duck with Prunes and Pine Nuts (continued)

2 ducks, about 4 ½ pounds
    each, trussed
Salt
Freshly ground pepper
2 duck necks
1 ½ cups chicken broth
1 tablespoon olive oil
1 medium onion, chopped
4 cloves garlic, minced
1 medium carrot, trimmed,
    scraped, and thinly sliced

2 tablespoons pine nuts
1 bay leaf
1 ½ teaspoons thyme leaves or
    ¼ teaspoon dried
¾ cup dry white wine
1 tablespoon brandy
12 large pitted prunes
½ cup orange juice or other
    fruit juice

Prick the ducks all over with a fork, and sprinkle inside and out with salt and pepper. Place the ducks and duck necks in a shallow casserole and roast at 350°F for 1 ½ hours, spooning off the fat occasionally. Remove the ducks and necks from the pan and cool. Quarter the ducks, remove the small rib bones from the breast, and remove the backbone, reserving the bones and neck. Transfer the duck to a roasting pan.

Pour off any remaining fat from the cassserole. Deglaze the casserole with the chicken broth, add the necks and bones, bring to a boil, cover, and simmer 30 minutes. Strain, return the broth to the casserole, and reduce to ½ cup. Transfer the broth to a small bowl and wipe out the casserole.

In the casserole, heat the oil and add the onion, garlic, carrot, pine nuts, bay leaf, and thyme and sauté 2 to 3 minutes. Lower the heat, cover, and continue cooking about 15 minutes, or until the onion is tender but not brown. Pour in the wine, brandy, and the reserved broth. Cover and simmer 10 minutes. Add the prunes, cover, and simmer until the prunes are tender, about 15 minutes more (everything can be made in advance up to this point).

Heat the oven to 550°F. Pour the orange juice over the duck pieces and roast, skin side up, 10 minutes. Bring the sauce to a simmer. To serve the duck, spoon on the sauce and garnish with the prunes. Saffron Rice with Pine Nuts (p. 297, omitting the pine nuts) is a fine accompaniment.

CODORNIZ EN ESCABECHE CASA IRENE
(Marinated Quail)

PREPARE AT LEAST 1 DAY IN ADVANCE

Quail in *escabeche*—a sauce in which quail or other birds or fish cook, then marinate for several days—is found all over Spain, but our friend Irene at Casa Irene (see p. 197) in the Pyrenees knows how to give the dish a certain delicacy. *Serves 4*

8 quail

7 tablespoons extra virgin olive oil

6 cloves garlic, peeled and lightly smashed

2 bay leaves

¼ teaspoon freshly ground nutmeg

2 sprigs rosemary or ½ teaspoon dried

10 peppercorns

¼ cup wine vinegar

Salt

2 tablespoons chicken broth

Leave the quail whole, but gently pound the breast bone to flatten the birds slightly. Heat 1 tablespoon of the oil in a shallow casserole in which the quail will fit somewhat closely and sauté the quail until browned on all sides. Remove to a warm platter and wipe out the casserole.

Add the remaining 6 tablespoons oil and heat with the garlic, bay leaves, nutmeg, rosemary, peppercorns, vinegar, and a little salt until the mixture comes to a sizzle. Return the quail to the casserole, breast side down, cover, and simmer 45 minutes, turning once.

Remove the quail and quarter them. Add the broth to the casserole, bring to a boil, then turn off the flame. Return the quail to the casserole, spooning some of the sauce over them. Cool, cover, and marinate overnight in the refrigerator, turning occasionally. Bring to room temperature before serving.

CONILL AMB ALLIOLI GRATINAT
(Rabbit Coated with Honey-Garlic Mayonnaise)

Just a short walk from the magnificent Poblet monastery in the province of Tarragona is a hamlet known as Les Masies de Poblet. Here we discovered the small, immaculately kept Masía del Cadet, where Mercè Vidal, a veritable bundle of energy, is in command, taking care of everything from helping us with luggage to answering the phone. When the dinner hour arrived, she donned her chef's cap.

I thoroughly enjoyed this sensational dish she prepares, which consists of sautéed rabbit (you may substitute chicken but I much prefer it with rabbit) covered with a honey-garlic mayonnaise well seasoned with thyme and bay leaf and run under the broiler.

Homemade mayonnaise is always preferable to bottled, but if you don't make your own, omit the egg and salt, reduce the oil to 1 tablespoon, and combine the oil and all remaining Honey-Garlic Mayonnaise ingredients with 1 cup prepared mayonnaise.   *Serves 3–4*

HONEY-GARLIC MAYONNAISE

2 cloves garlic, mashed to a paste in a mortar or garlic press	1 tablespoon honey
	⅔ cup extra virgin olive oil
Salt	2 tablespoons minced thyme or 1 teaspoon dried
1 egg or ¼ cup egg substitute made with egg white	1 bay leaf, finely crumbled
1 teaspoon lemon juice	½ teaspoon freshly ground pepper
¼ teaspoon Dijon-style mustard	

. . .

A 2½–3-pound rabbit, or 3–4 skinless chicken breast halves	Kosher or sea salt
	1 tablespoon olive oil
	1 tablespoon butter

To make the Honey-Garlic Mayonnaise, combine in a food processor the garlic, salt, egg, lemon juice, mustard, and honey and blend a few seconds.

With the motor running, drizzle in the oil. Add the thyme, crumbled bay leaf, and pepper and pulse to blend. Transfer to a bowl and stir in enough hot water to give the mayonnaise the consistency of a thick sauce.

Cut the rabbit into pieces of about 1½ inches, eliminating any fat and as much of the bone as possible. Sprinkle with salt. Heat the oil and butter in a shallow casserole and sauté the rabbit over medium heat until cooked, about 15 minutes, turning once.

Spoon the mayonnaise over the rabbit pieces and run under the broiler until lightly browned.

LOMO DE CERDO RELLENO DE ESPINACAS, CIRUELAS, Y PIÑONES
(Pork Loin Stuffed with Spinach, Prunes, and Pine Nuts)

I love this exceptional pork preparation that uses many of the most characteristic ingredients of Mallorcan cooking, complemented by a light honey-mustard sauce. The dish comes from Es Menjador restaurant in Manacor.

Serves 4

8 prunes
¾ cup cranberry or apple juice
2 cups (packed) coarsely chopped washed spinach leaves, left slightly damp
Salt
4 teaspoons Dijon-style mustard
2 teaspoons honey

A 1½-pound boneless pork loin
Freshly ground pepper
¼ cup dry white wine
4 teaspoons chopped pine nuts
Flour for dusting
2 tablespoons olive oil
1 small onion, finely chopped
½ cup chicken broth

Place the prunes in a small saucepan with the cranberry or apple juice. Cover and simmer about 15 minutes, or until tender. Meanwhile, place the spinach in a microwave-safe dish, sprinkle with salt, cover, and microwave 4 minutes (or simmer on the stove in a pot of water for about 10 minutes). Drain and squeeze dry between paper towels.

In a small cup combine the mustard and honey. Butterfly the pork, splitting lengthwise just far enough so that the meat opens up into one flat piece.

Stuffed Pork Loin (continued)

Brush the cut sides with a light coating of the honey-mustard mixture, and sprinkle both cut sides with salt and pepper. Mix the wine with the remaining honey mustard and reserve.

Drain, pit, and coarsely chop the prunes. Arrange the spinach and prunes over one side of the pork, and sprinkle with the pine nuts. Reassemble the pork and tie securely. Sprinkle with salt and pepper and dust with flour. Heat the oil in a deep stewpot and brown the meat on all sides. Add the onion and sauté until wilted, then add the mustard mixture, the broth, salt, and pepper. Cover and simmer about 45 minutes, or until the meat is just cooked through or reaches 170°F at its center. Slice and serve with the sauce.

LOMO DE CERDO EN JARABE DE GRANADA
(Pork Loin Marinated in Pomegranate Syrup)

START PREPARATION 2 HOURS IN ADVANCE

Any dish made with pomegranate juice is surely of Moorish descent, and indeed, the Balearic Islands, from which this recipe comes, were of strategic importance to the Moors, who remained here for five hundred years. Pork with fruit is of course a well-known match, and pork flavored with pomegranates is one more example of that ideal pairing.   *Serves 4–6*

2 large pomegranates
½ medium onion, slivered
1 tablespoon thyme leaves or
    ½ teaspoon dried
2 bay leaves, crumbled
1 tablespoon rosemary leaves
    or ½ teaspoon dried

2 tablespoons minced parsley
¼ cup dry white wine
3 tablespoons extra virgin olive
    oil
Salt
Freshly ground pepper
A 2-pound boneless pork loin

Cut the pomegranates in quarters, remove the seeds, and place them in a food processor. Blend 2 or 3 seconds—just long enough to break the seeds and release the juice. Strain—there should be about 1½ cups juice. Place in a saucepan and boil down to reduce by half. Cool completely.

In a deep bowl combine the pomegranate juice and all other ingredients except the meat. Add the meat and marinate 2 hours, turning occasionally. Transfer the meat to a roasting pan, scatter the onion from the marinade around it, and add just enough of the marinade to moisten the pan. Place in a 375°F oven and roast until the meat is done, about 35 minutes to the pound, adding more marinade occasionally to keep the pan juices from burning. By the time the meat is done, you should have added all the marinade—if more liquid is necessary, use chicken broth or water. Slice the meat and spoon the sauce over it. Serve with Saffron Rice with Pine Nuts (page 297), omitting the saffron.

LOMO DE CERDO CON CIRUELAS Y PERAS
(Pork Loin with Prunes and Pears)

Many of the typical elements of Catalan and Balearic cooking are incorporated in this excellent pork casserole: the combination of fruits with meats and the addition of ground almonds and garlic. The recipe comes from the island of Mallorca.   *Serves 4*

½ pound ripe but firm pears, preferably small, like seckel pears
Lemon juice
About 1 cup dry red wine, to cook the pears, plus 5 tablespoons
1 cinnamon stick, broken in 3 pieces
A 1½-pound boneless pork loin
Salt
Freshly ground pepper
2 tablespoons olive oil
2 tablespoons brandy

1 small onion, finely chopped
1 bay leaf
¾ cup chicken broth
2 ounces blanched almonds (about ⅓ cup)
2 cloves garlic, minced
1½ teaspoons thyme leaves or ¼ teaspoon dried
1½ teaspoons oregano leaves or ¼ teaspoon dried
¼ pound mushrooms, brushed clean and quartered
12 medium prunes

Skin the pears (easy to do with a good potato peeler), rub with lemon juice, and place in a small saucepan. Add red wine to cover and the cinnamon stick.

Pork Loin with Prunes and Pears (continued)

Bring to a boil and simmer about 20 minutes, or until the pears are tender. Remove the saucepan from the heat and let the pears steep until ready to use.

Sprinkle the pork with salt and pepper. Heat the oil in a deep casserole and quickly brown the meat on all sides. Add the brandy and ignite, keeping well away from the pot. When the flames subside, add the onion and sauté until softened. Stir in the 5 tablespoons wine and reduce to less than half. Add the bay leaf and ½ cup of the broth. Cover and cook slowly 20 minutes.

Meanwhile, place the almonds on a cookie sheet in a 350°F oven and toast until lightly golden, about 5 minutes. Cool and transfer to a food processor with the garlic, thyme, and oregano; blend as smooth as possible. With the motor running, gradually pour in the remaining ¼ cup broth.

Add the mushrooms, the almond mixture, and the prunes to the casserole and taste for salt. Cook another 30 minutes, or until the meat is cooked through.

Cut the pears in quarters, core, and cut into ½-inch wedges. Gently mix the pear wedges into the casserole and turn off the heat. Remove the meat and slice. To serve, arrange the pears in overlapping rows around the meat, garnish with the prunes, and spoon on the sauce.

LOMO DE CERDO AL HORNO CON CEBOLLA Y PUERROS
(Roast Pork Loin with Onions and Leeks)

A complete meal—meat, vegetable, and potatoes, all roasted together.

Serves 4

A 1½-pound boneless pork loin
2 medium onions, slivered
2 carrots, trimmed and scraped, cut in julienne strips
½ pound leeks, well washed, white part and light green inner shoots only, cut in julienne strips
2 cloves garlic, peeled

2 medium potatoes, peeled and cut in 1-inch balls with a melon scoop
Salt
Freshly ground pepper
Olive oil
½ cup dry white wine
Chicken broth

Place the pork in the center of a roasting pan. Arrange the onions, carrots, leeks, garlic, and potatoes around the meat. Sprinkle the meat and vegetables with salt and pepper and drizzle with olive oil. Cook in a 400°F oven, and when the dish has baked 15 minutes, add the wine and continue cooking, stirring the vegetables occasionally. If the liquid evaporates, keep the pan moist with chicken broth. Continue cooking about 45 minutes more, or until the pork reaches an internal temperature of 170°F.

Slice the meat, spoon the vegetables over the meat slices, and arrange the potatoes around the meat. Deglaze the pan with more chicken broth and pour the pan juices over the meat.

MANZANAS RELLENAS DE CERDO
(Pork-Stuffed Baked Apples)

Although we tend to think of baked apples for dessert, here they are filled with ground pork to make a delicious and distinctive main course. Pork blends effortlessly with fruit flavors, and the addition of carrots and raisins to the meat filling echoes the sweetness of the apples. This is a centuries-old Catalan recipe that remains popular today.

Serves 4

2 tablespoons raisins	Salt
8 medium Golden Delicious apples, peeled	Dash of cinnamon
	½ teaspoon grated lemon peel
Lemon juice	¾ cup dry white wine
1 tablespoon olive oil	2 tablespoons coarsely chopped
1 large onion, finely chopped	pine nuts
2 medium carrots, trimmed,	½ cup chicken broth
scraped, and finely chopped	1 egg, lightly beaten
1½ pounds lean ground pork	½ teaspoon sugar

Soak the raisins in warm water for 10 minutes. Drain. Hollow out the apples leaving a ¼-inch shell. Sprinkle with lemon juice. Save several scraps of apple to cover the pork filling as it bakes.

In a skillet, heat the oil and sauté the onion and carrots for a minute or two. Cover and continue cooking very slowly 15 minutes. Add the meat,

Pork-Stuffed Baked Apples (continued)

turn up the flame, and cook until the meat loses its color. Stir in the salt, cinnamon, and grated lemon peel, then add ¼ cup of the wine and cook away. Add the pine nuts, raisins, and ¼ cup of the broth. Simmer 10 minutes. Turn off the flame, cool slightly, then stir in the egg.

In a shallow casserole, combine the remaining ¼ cup broth, the remaining ½ cup wine, and the sugar. Fill the apples with the pork mixture (about 5 tablespoons filling in each), and cover each with a scrap of apple. Bake at 350°F for about 50 minutes, or until the apples have softened.

PASTEL MALLORQUÍN DE CARNE
(Mallorcan Mini Meat Pies)

Remarkably similar to a British Mawbry pie, fragrant with spices and enclosed in a short crust, these savory pastries are commonly found in Palma de Mallorca's pastry shops. One of these pies, accompanied by a big salad, makes a nice supper.   *Makes 7–8 pies*

1¼ pounds boneless pork loin, including some of its fat, in a ¼-inch dice
2 tablespoons brandy
2 eggs
1 clove garlic, minced
2 tablespoons minced onion
1 teaspoon salt
½ teaspoon freshly ground pepper
1 clove, crushed
1½ teaspoons minced basil leaves or ¼ teaspoon dried

1½ teaspoons thyme leaves or ¼ teaspoon dried
1 small bay leaf, finely crumbled
⅛ teaspoon freshly ground nutmeg
1½ teaspoons minced sage leaves or ¼ teaspoon dried
1½ teaspoons minced marjoram leaves or ¼ teaspoon dried
1 egg, lightly beaten with 1 teaspoon water

PIE CRUST

3¼ cups flour

¾ cup chilled lard or vegetable
    shortening, cut in several
    pieces

8 tablespoons iced water

In a bowl mix the pork with all the other ingredients except the beaten egg. Let sit at room temperature while preparing the crust.

To make the Pie Crust, place the flour and lard in a food processor and pulse until the lard is incorporated into the flour. Pulse in the water.

Roll about ⅔ of the dough to a scant ⅛ inch thick and cut into seven or eight 8½-inch circles. Press the circles into 3¼-inch muffin tins, and fill with about 5 tablespoons of the meat mixture. Roll the remaining dough a scant ⅛ inch thick and cut into seven or eight 4-inch circles to cover each pie. Roll up the edges and seal with a fork. Make a small hole at the center. Brush with the beaten egg and bake at 350°F 45 to 60 minutes, or until the crust is lightly browned.

JARRETE DE TERNERA CON MANZANA Y PIÑONES
(Veal Shanks with Apples and Pine Nuts)

This recipe, from the fine restaurant Masía del Cadet (see p. 208) near the Poblet monastery in the province of Tarragona, makes an incredibly tender meat in an excellent sauce that contrasts beautifully with the sweetness of the apple garnish. A star company dish. *Serves 4*

Veal Shanks with Apples (continued)

3 tablespoons olive oil	2 bay leaves
2½ pounds veal shanks, cut about 1½ inches thick	1 tablespoon thyme leaves or ½ teaspoon dried
Salt	1¼ cups dry white wine
Freshly ground pepper	1¼ cups chicken broth
1 medium onion, chopped	2 Golden Delicious apples, peeled, cored, and cut in ¼-inch wedges
¼ pound green frying peppers, cored, seeded, and chopped	
16 cloves garlic, minced	2 tablespoons pine nuts
2 medium tomatoes, skinned, seeded, and chopped	2 tablespoons sugar
	¼ cup brandy

Heat 2 tablespoons of the oil in a shallow casserole. Sprinkle the shanks with salt and pepper and quickly brown. Remove to a warm platter. Add to the casserole the onion, peppers, and garlic and cook until the onion is wilted. Add the tomatoes, bay leaves, thyme, salt, and pepper and cook 2 minutes. Stir in the wine.

Return the shanks to the casserole. Cover and bake 30 minutes at 350°F. Add the chicken broth and bake 1 hour more.

When ready to serve, in a medium skillet heat the remaining tablespoon oil and sauté the apples and pine nuts until the nuts turn golden. Sprinkle with the sugar, add the brandy, and carefully ignite. When the flames die, cover the pan and simmer until the apples are softened.

Remove the shanks to a serving platter. Strain the sauce and pour over the shanks. Garnish with the apples arranged in overlapping rows.

Desserts

MERMELADA DE MELOCOTÓN
(Peach Marmalade)

This is a variation on Manzanas en Jarabe (p. 219), made with peaches, apricots, or pears instead of apples and eliminating the almonds. It has a consistency closer to marmalade, and you use it as you would any marmalade, or serve it, slightly thinned, as a sauce with simple custard desserts, such as Cottage Cheese Bread Pudding (p. 222).   *Makes about ½ cup*

½ cup dry white wine
½ cup orange juice
½ cup sugar
¼ teaspoon ground nutmeg
4 cloves
1 cinnamon stick
¼ teaspoon ground cardamom
Peel of ¼ of a small orange,
cut in julienne strips, then
minced
½ pound fresh peaches, apricots, or pears, skinned, pitted or cored, cut in ¼-inch wedges, then in ¾-inch pieces

In a small saucepan combine the wine, orange juice, sugar, nutmeg, cloves, cinnamon stick, cardamom, and orange peel. Bring to a boil, then cook at a slow boil until slightly thickened, about 10 minutes. Add the peaches and continue cooking at a high simmer until the peaches are tender and the syrup thick, about 30 minutes. To serve as a sauce rather than a jam, thin with a little water.

BUÑUELOS DE MANZANA
(Apple Fritters)

Apple fritters are especially popular in Catalunya and often served over a pool of sauce—among my favorites: honey and lemon (page 421), a light soft custard, or apricot sauce. The latter two recipes are given here.

Serves 4

Apple Fritters (continued)

BATTER

¾ cup flour
1½ teaspoons baking powder
⅛ teaspoon salt
¼ cup plus 1 tablespoon water

¼ cup milk
2 tablespoons mild olive oil
1 egg white

APRICOT SAUCE

½ cup apricot preserves
1 teaspoon medium-sweet
   Spanish sherry (*oloroso*)

4 teaspoons fruit juice, such as
   apple

LIGHT CUSTARD SAUCE

2 egg yolks
3 tablespoons sugar
1 tablespoon flour

⅛ teaspoon salt
2 cups milk

· · ·

4 tablespoons (¼ cup) sugar
¼ teaspoon cinnamon
¼ teaspoon lemon juice
A generous grating of nutmeg
1 apple, such as McIntosh or

Golden Delicious, peeled,
   cored, and cut in twelve
   ¼-inch rings or wedges
Oil for frying

To make the Batter, mix together in a bowl the flour, baking powder, and salt. Gradually add the water, milk, and oil and stir until smooth. In a separate bowl, beat the egg white until stiff but not dry. Gently stir into the batter.

If using the Apricot Sauce, combine all ingredients and set aside. If making the Light Custard Sauce, whisk the egg yolks with the sugar, flour, and salt in a saucepan or in the top of a double boiler until pale yellow. Gradually stir in the milk. Cook over boiling water, stirring constantly, until thickened to a soft custard consistency. Cool, stirring frequently.

Combine in a small shallow bowl the sugar, cinnamon, lemon juice, and nutmeg. Coat the apple slices with this mixture.

Pour the oil to a depth of 1 inch in a skillet (or better still, use a deep-fryer) and heat until it quickly browns a cube of bread. Coat the apple slices with the batter and drop into the oil. Fry until lightly golden, turning once. Drain on paper towels.

Spoon the sauce of your choice onto 4 dessert dishes and arrange 3 apple fritters over the sauce on each dish.

MANZANAS EN JARABE
(Apples in Spiced Wine Syrup)

There is an interesting subtle spiciness to these apples that comes from the Eastern touches of nutmeg, clove, cinnamon, and cardamom. This recipe is quite similar to one in Ruperto de Nola's sixteenth-century cookbook (see p. 166). It happens to be the book's last entry, and the recipe finishes by saying, ". . . sprinkle with sugar and cinnamon. And here this book comes to an end."

Serves 4

¼ cup slivered blanched
    almonds
1 cup dry white wine
¾ cup sugar
¼ teaspoon ground nutmeg
4 cloves
1 cinnamon stick

¼ teaspoon ground cardamom
Peel of ½ small orange, cut in
    julienne strips, then minced
2 large Golden Delicious
    apples, skinned, cored, and
    quartered

Spread the almonds on a cookie sheet and bake at 350°F about 5 minutes, or until golden.

Combine in a saucepan the wine, sugar, almonds, nutmeg, cloves, cinnamon stick, cardamom, and orange peel. Bring to a boil, then cook at a high simmer, about 10 minutes. Add the apples and continue cooking until the apples are tender, about 30 minutes. Turn off the heat, remove the apples, and continue to cook the syrup at a high simmer until it has thickened to a heavy syrup consistency and is slightly caramelized. Return the apples to the syrup and let steep until ready to serve.

To serve, slice the apples into thin wedges and arrange attractively on 4 dessert dishes. Spoon on the sauce and serve with a little cream or a scoop of ice cream, if so desired.

MANZANAS RELLENAS DE CREMA CATALANA QUATRE BARRES

(Baked Apples Filled with Catalan Custard)

Josep Lladonosa i Giró was the chef and founder of the Quatre Barres restaurant in Barcelona, and his mission was to recover and present on his menu traditional Catalan recipes from the past, as well as those that are perennially popular. Here is an exceptional rendition of apples filled with Catalan custard that comes from that restaurant. The caramelized sugar becomes a sauce in which to bathe the apples.   *Serves 8*

½ recipe Crema Catalana
    (p. 221), using ¼ cup sugar
    and omitting the
    caramelized coating
8 apples suitable for baking,
    such as Golden Delicious
Lemon juice

½ cup water
½ cup white wine
½ cinnamon stick
Peel of ½ lemon, in several
    pieces
4 tablespoons (¼ cup) sugar

CARAMELIZED SUGAR SYRUP

½ cup sugar
½ cup hot water

Prepare the Crema Catalana according to instructions, cooling the custard in the saucepan without stirring.

Peel the apples and rub with lemon juice to prevent discoloration. Hollow out enough of each apple, being sure to remove the core and seeds, so that there will be room for 2 tablespoons of custard filling. Place the apples in a shallow baking pan and add the water, wine, cinnamon stick, and lemon peel. Sprinkle the apples with the sugar and bake in a 350°F oven 30 to 40 minutes, or until the apples are softened, basting the apples occasionally and adding more water if the liquid evaporates. Cover with foil and bake 10 minutes more. Cool.

To prepare the Caramelized Sugar Syrup, combine in a very small saucepan the sugar and 3 tablespoons of the water. Cook over a high flame, stirring constantly, until the syrup is a light golden color. Very gradually and very carefully stir in the remaining 5 tablespoons hot water.

To serve the apples, spoon some of the liquid from the baking pan onto individual dessert dishes. Fill each apple with custard (about 2 tablespoons for each apple) and place one on each dish. Spoon the caramelized sugar over the apples.

CREMA CATALANA
(Sugar-Crusted Custard)

Catalan custard—an enriched soft custard covered with a crackling cara-melized sugar coating—has traveled the world; it is as well known today in New York as it has been for generations in Catalunya. Traditionally the sugar is caramelized with a salamander (an iron disk with a long handle, available in kitchenware shops), but many chefs today prefer a blow torch, sold specifically for that purpose; it does the job neatly and quickly. The bottom of a small saucepan can also be used. In any case, do not sprinkle on the sugar or caramelize it until ready to serve or the coating will soften.

Serves 6

2 tablespoons plus ½ teaspoon
  cornstarch
2⅔ cups plus 2 tablespoons
  milk
6 egg yolks

¾ cup plus 2 tablespoons sugar
Peel of ½ lemon, cut in several
  pieces
1 cinnamon stick

In a small bowl, dissolve the cornstarch in 2 tablespoons of the milk. Stir in the egg yolks and reserve.

In a saucepan, bring the remaining milk to a boil with ½ cup of the sugar, the lemon peel, and the cinnamon stick. Simmer 15 minutes. Gradu-ally stir the hot milk mixture into the cornstarch mixture. Return to the saucepan and cook over a medium flame, stirring constantly, until the cus-tard starts to bubble. Discard the lemon peel and cinnamon stick, and divide the mixture into 6 shallow dessert bowls, preferably Spanish earthenware. Cool without stirring.

Sprinkle the remaining 6 tablespoons sugar—1 tablespoon for each serv-ing—over the custards. To caramelize the sugar, heat a salamander over a

Sugar-Crusted Custard (continued)

high flame until very hot. Rest it over the sugar until the sugar is caramelized (do by sections if the salamander is not large enough to cover the whole surface). Wipe off the salamander, reheat, and repeat for the remaining custards. If a salamander is not available, place a few tablespoons of water in a saucepan the width of the custard dishes, and heat until very hot. Rest the bottom of the hot saucepan over the custard until the sugar is caramelized.

PASTEL DE GREIXONERA
(Cottage Cheese Bread Pudding)

Greixonera in Mallorcan cookery refers to the earthenware casserole in which many main-course and dessert dishes are prepared. Among them is a kind of bread pudding that uses either *ensaimada*—a popular Mallorcan sweet bread—or *bizcocho* (light sponge cake). In this version, cottage cheese is an added ingredient, and the result is a wonderfully pure-tasting cake-custard that I think is especially appealing with a fruit topping, like Peach Marmalade (page 217).   *Serves 8*

1 pound small-curd cottage cheese	1¼ cups milk
¼ cup heavy cream	3 ounces ladyfingers or light sponge cake, crumbled
¾ cup sugar	2 tablespoons unsalted butter, melted
4 eggs	Granulated sugar for dusting
⅛ teaspoon salt	Confectioners' sugar for sprinkling
¼ teaspoon grated lemon peel	
¼ teaspoon cinnamon plus some for sprinkling	

With an electric mixer, beat the cottage cheese until smooth, then beat in the cream and sugar. Add the eggs, salt, grated lemon peel, and cinnamon and beat until smooth. Stir in the milk and ladyfingers and let sit 10 minutes. Beat again until smooth.

Brush a mold (I use a shallow oval earthenware casserole, similar to what is typically used for this dessert) with the melted butter and dust with sugar. Pour in the batter and bake at 350°F about 50 minutes, or until the mixture is set. Cool, then chill.

Divide into dessert dishes or bowls and sprinkle with cinnamon and confectioners' sugar. This dessert is enhanced by serving it with fruit preserves or fresh berries.

PASTISSETS
(Powdered Sugar Cookies)

Wonderfully short cookies scented with cinnamon and lemon peel which are hard to resist. If you don't make them with lard, you will lose part of their exceptional flavor. These cookies keep well in a closed tin.

Makes about 30

⅔ cup lard, vegetable shortening, or unsalted butter, softened
⅓ cup unsalted butter, softened
½ cup sugar
1 egg yolk

½ teaspoon grated lemon peel
¼ teaspoon cinnamon
2 cups flour
Sifted confectioners' sugar for dusting

With a wooden spoon, beat together the lard and butter, then incorporate the sugar, egg yolk, and lemon peel. Combine the cinnamon and flour and stir in, working with your hands to form a smooth dough.

On a floured surface, roll the dough a scant ¼ inch thick, and cut with a 3-inch scalloped cookie cutter (other shapes can of course be used). Arrange the cookies on a greased cookie sheet and bake at 350°F about 10 minutes, or until golden. Cool, then coat with confectioners' sugar.

AMARGOS
(Almond Cookies)

Chewy macaroon-like cookies from the Balearic Islands that have no cholesterol—they are made without egg yolks or shortening.   *Makes 24*

1⅓ cups sugar	½ teaspoon grated lemon peel
10 ounces blanched almonds	¼ teaspoon cinnamon
2 egg whites	¼ teaspoon vanilla
2 teaspoons honey	

Place the sugar and almonds in a food processor and process until the almonds are finely ground.

Beat the egg whites until stiff but not dry. Fold in the almond and sugar mixture, the honey, grated lemon peel, cinnamon, and vanilla.

With wet hands, shape the mixture into 1¼-inch balls and place, well spaced, on a greased cookie sheet. Bake at 350°F until golden, about 8 minutes.

RUBIOLS DE REQUESÓN
(Cheese Turnovers)

These sweetened cheese pastries from the island of Mallorca are also excellent filled with apricot preserves (about 1½ cups); add to the preserves the same amount of grated lemon peel and cinnamon called for in this recipe. Or you can make your own fruit filling (see p. 217).   *Makes 12*

1 pound farmer or cottage cheese	1 recipe Mallorcan Orange-Flavored Turnover Dough (recipe follows)
½ teaspoon grated lemon peel	1 egg, lightly beaten with 1 teaspoon water
½ cup plus 2 tablespoons sugar	
½ teaspoon cinnamon	Sugar for dusting
⅛ teaspoon salt	

Prepare the turnover dough as directed. In a bowl combine the cheese, grated lemon peel, sugar, cinnamon, and salt.

Roll the dough on a floured surface to less than ⅛ inch and cut in 5- to 6-inch rounds. Place 2 tablespoons cheese mixture in the center of each, bring up the sides, and press together. Place the turnovers flat on the work surface and press the edges with a fork to seal. Brush with the egg and sprinkle well with sugar. Bake in a 350°F oven for about 20 minutes, until lightly browned.

MASA DE EMPANADILLA A LA MALLORQUINA
(Mallorcan Orange-Flavored Turnover Dough)

START PREPARATION 1 HOUR IN ADVANCE

You can use this wonderful short dough with any kind of sweetened filling, but it is especially good with cottage cheese (see Rubiols de Requesón, p. 224) or filled with Spaghetti Squash Marmalade (p. 388).

2 tablespoons orange juice	2 teaspoons sugar
3 tablespoons mild olive oil or	Pinch of salt
vegetable oil	2 tablespoons lard or vegetable
1 egg yolk	shortening
1 cup flour	

In a small bowl, whisk together the juice, oil, and egg yolk. Combine in a food processor the flour, sugar, and salt. Add the lard and pulse to evenly incorporate into the flour mixture. Pulse in the juice mixture. Wrap in plastic wrap and refrigerate 1 hour before using.

FORMETJADES RELLENOS DE MERMELADA Y ALMENDRA
(Pastries Filled with Marmalade and Almonds)

START PREPARATION 1 HOUR IN ADVANCE

Dainty deliciously short pastries, among the many kinds of filled pastries, both sweet and savory, that are special to the Balearic Islands. The secret to the unusually flaky pastry made in the islands is lard (see box, p. 159), although you may substitute other shortenings. I particularly like these pastries from Mallorca filled with peach or apricot marmalade mixed with ground almonds.   *Makes 12 small pastries*

2⅔ cups flour
1 egg yolk
1 tablespoon sugar
¼ pound lard or vegetable
    shortening
¼ cup water
¼ cup mild olive oil

1 ounce (about 18) blanched
    almonds
¾ cup peach or apricot mar-
    malade (page 217), or other
    fruit preserves
1 egg, lightly beaten with
    1 teaspoon water

Place the flour in a bowl and add the egg yolk, sugar, lard, water, and oil. Work lightly with your hands to form a smooth dough. Wrap in plastic wrap and let sit 1 hour. Meanwhile, toast the almonds on a cookie sheet at 350°F for 3 to 4 minutes. Cool, then grate or beat in a food processor until as finely ground as possible. Combine with the marmalade.

Roll the dough on a floured surface a scant ⅛ inch thick, and cut into 3½-inch circles. Place about 1 tablespoon of the marmalade mixture in the center of half of the circles, and cover each with another circle. Press the edges together with your fingers, then turn up the edges and press to seal. Brush with the beaten egg and bake on a greased cookie sheet at 325°F for 25 to 30 minutes, or until golden.

CHAPTER 5

The Central Plains

REGION OF THE ROASTS

The vast central plains of Spain, broadly comprising northern Castile, La Mancha, and Extremadura, is a land of austere grandeur, dotted with crumbling castles that remain as reminders of Christian-Moorish conflict and symbols of more illustrious times when Toledo was a world center of learning and León, Valladolid, and Burgos were important seats of royal government. Once covered by thick forestland and still embracing pockets of green, central Spain suffered defoliation by man that transformed the region into an arid windswept land, sometimes bitterly cold in winter and scorched by the summer sun. Wheat fields dominate the landscape, and shepherds tending to their flocks are a familiar sight. The importance of sheep in central Spain goes back centuries, to the days when lamb's wool from Spanish merino sheep was prized all over Europe.

The obsession with lamb for its culinary worth did not take hold until long after the once profitable wool market collapsed. Today, roast baby lamb, especially in northern Castile, is an object of passion among Spaniards. My husband and I have always gone out of our way to savor the best of the extraordinary lamb in the Region of the Roasts, but we never imagined that a Sunday outing from Madrid to eat roast baby lamb in Sepúlveda at our favorite village restaurant, Figón Zute El Mayor "Tinín," would turn into a full-day lamb bacchanalia.

Sepúlveda is a centuries-old town in the province of Segovia, set at the edge of the spectacular Duratón River gorge, and there our dear friend Pepe Sanz awaited us with two friends, Flavio and José Luis, affectionately known as Los Gordos (the fat ones), each of whom had paunches of enormous rotundity but bodies of otherwise normal proportions ("expensive stomachs," remarked Pepe, "nurtured on the finest Spanish shellfish"). They were as proverbially jolly—actually riotously funny—as their girth might suggest. Among us we polished off four quarters of exquisitely tender baby lamb with crackling skin—roasted, as is the custom, in a brick wood-burning oven—along with big bowls of salad, a large loaf of the wonderful round flat bread of lamb country, and a prodigious quantity of local wine served in earthenware jugs. After that came Manchego cheese and quince preserves for dessert, then coffee and Spanish brandy at a nearby bar. As far as we were concerned, there was no need to eat again in the foreseeable future, but our new friends Flavio and José Luis had other plans. They announced it was time to begin preparing a lamb chop barbecue. We were incredulous, but they assured us that it would be a special event and that hunger would return.

We drove to the town of Roa, where one of Los Gordos bought freshly baked country bread and found a butcher who provided baby lamb chops as well as black sausage. Thus stocked, we continued to Mambrilla de Castrejón, where José Luis picked up his motor scooter from his family's country home, gathered an armful of dried vine shoots, and led us to the outskirts of town, where each villager has a wine cave to store his allotment of the local wine production. There we commenced to burn the vine shoots (the only fuel that gives the proper flavor to the chops, Los Gordos insisted), and there we spent the balance of the afternoon and early evening.

We consumed tiny chops by the dozens and thick slices of sausage as they came off the grill, using chunks of bread in lieu of plates to rest the meats and catch the drippings (our appetites did indeed return). Whenever the wine was depleted, we descended to the cave for a new supply, which we drank from *porrones* (glass spouted jugs) instead of glasses. The local undertaker joined in the festivities and introduced us to a primitive village game somewhat like bocce called *turusa*, which we played with child-like enthusiasm. The hours stretched on pleasurably under a warm summer sun, and it was 8:30 p.m. before we managed to say goodbye and continue to our destination for that evening, which we reached long after darkness had fallen.

Lamb is undeniably one of the sublime foods of central Spain, but the region can otherwise be somewhat Spartan when it comes to good eating, although there are many fine products besides baby lamb. Roast suckling pig, for example, is another great regional delicacy, also cooked in a wood-burning oven and meltingly delicious, and game birds like quail and partridge are found in abundance (partridge, slowly stewed in a rich wine sauce, is a favorite dish). There is inimitable Manchego sheep's-milk cheese and the fresh pure-tasting cheese of Burgos; Spain's best chorizo and sublime cured hams; and excellent beans and chickpeas (chickpeas are essential to the region's wonderful boiled pot, *cocido*). Quality wines from Ribera del Duero in northern Castile—crisp and well balanced—have received international acclaim.

Despite the austerity associated with central Spain, three monasteries in Extremadura were legendary for promoting The Good Life. Yuste Monastery, where Emperor Charles V, a renowned gourmand who suffered from gout, retired after passing the crown to his son Philip, was a haven of fine food. By order of Charles, oysters and other fresh shellfish were packed in snow and rushed here from the coasts of Spain. Many other delicacies were also available for the king's pleasure, including savory eel pies, all kinds of large and small game, fresh trout and salmon, and choice fruits and vegetables.

In another monastery at Alcántara the monks prepared such exquisite meals as pheasant with fois gras and truffles, a dish that later became associated with French cooking when Spain was invaded by Napoleon's troops and the monastery's cookbook was spirited off to France. And in the monastery of Guadalupe, where the monks supposedly led a life of utmost luxury (a Spanish refrain quips "better than count or duke, a monk in Guadalupe"), fine food was prepared not only for the monastic table, but for the monastery's hostel, where kings, *conquistadores*, and illustrious writers like Cervantes have stayed since the fifteenth century when they came to worship the venerated Virgin of Guadalupe. The hostel is still in operation today, and in fact several of my most prized recipes—among them, cumin-scented tomato soup with figs—come from Fray Juan Barrera, the monk currently in charge of the kitchen (for more on these monasteries and their environs, see my book *Discovering Spain: An Uncommon Guide*).

Madrid falls squarely at the center of the Region of the Roasts, but as an international hub it takes on culinary characteristics independent of the region. Here you will find restaurants serving all of Spain's regional cuisines as well as restaurants that prepare upscale creative cooking and international fare. What is most surprising about eating in landlocked Madrid is the predominance of seafood. Defying all sense of logic and practicality, Madrid is considered Spain's leading "seaport." Up and down the Spanish Mediterranean and Atlantic coasts, trucks and vans by the hundreds and fleets of private planes impatiently await the arrival of the local fishing boats to speed the day's catch to Madrid—so fast that the fish is sometimes still twitching when it reaches its destination. The variety of sea creatures available to diners in Madrid is truly remarkable: baby eels, hake, and porgy (a fish that Madrid has adopted as its own) from the Basque Country; scallops, lobster, and goose barnacles from Galicia; and prawns, tiny *chanquetes* (gobies), and white anchovies from the Mediterranean are but a sampling of the wonderful seafood that *madrileños* enjoy.

Madrid, indeed, is a world unto itself, but it is the stern countryside of the central plains—the cradle of the Spanish nation—that best represents the timeless character of the people and the foods of this region.

Notes on Regional Wines

The Ribera del Duero region in northern Castile has become in recent years a preeminent wine region, producing crisp and exceedingly elegant red wines of international renown. Topping the list are the legendary wines of Vega Sicilia—Valbuena, produced yearly, and Único Reserva, made only from superior vintages. But there are many other bodegas in this region that are making their mark, producing exceptional wines made predominantly with the native garnacha and tempranillo grapes. Among my favorites are Yllera, Pesquera (Bodegas Alejandro Fernández), and Torremilanos (Bodegas Peñalba López).

The fine reputation of the Rueda region in Valladolid is relatively recent and is based principally on its white wines, both young and slightly aged, made mainly from the white verdejo grape. I have always enjoyed the white wines of Marqués de Riscal, which are the ones you are most likely to find in America.

Toro, yet another Castilian appellation of origin, has in recent years produced very well received red wines, in particular the Gran Colegiata of Bodegas Fariña and Señorío de Toro from Bodegas Fermoselle.

Venturing into the Badajoz province of Extremadura and its wine region of Tierra de Barros, we find few quality wines except for those of Lar de Barros (INVIOSA) that have sparked interest internationally.

Glory of La Mancha: Manchego Cheese

Manchego, a cured sheep's-milk cheese, surely has its counterparts in other cheese-producing countries, and yet I have never found a substitute for this extraordinary cheese from the central plains of La Mancha. Perhaps it is the climate of La Mancha, or the special taste of the milk from its hardy breed of sheep. Whatever the reason, Manchego cheese tastes like no other.

When Don Quixote roamed La Mancha in search of adventure he undoubtedly met up with Manchegan sheep, and his austere diet most likely included Manchego cheese. After all, in this poor arid area of Spain cheese was always available regardless of crop yields. Certainly in the sixteenth century, when Cervantes conceived his novel, *Don Quijote de la Mancha*, sheep herding was at its height in Spain, not principally for cheese production but because Spanish merino wool was prized all over Europe. As the wool industry declined, cheese production gained in importance.

La Mancha, high above sea level on Spain's central *meseta*, is subjected to harsh climate conditions—biting cold in winter and fiery heat during the summer months. The sheep of La Mancha have adapted admirably to these extremes, eking nourishment from an often barren land. They feed on parched grass and aromatic plants of concentrated

Glory of La Mancha: Manchego Cheese (continued)

essences, and transfer all the subtle flavors of the countryside to their rich milk.

Manchego cheese is the result of a process virtually unchanged for centuries. Today much of the region's cheese is made commercially, but artisan methods persist and without doubt achieve the finest product. A compact cheese even when young, Manchego ages beautifully and is at its best when well cured. It is characterized by an earth-tone rind imprinted with geometric designs transferred from special wood molds.

Although most popular as a tapa, sliced or cut in cubes, Manchego becomes a typical Spanish dessert when served with quince preserves. When very well cured, Manchego can be grated and used in cooking. Beware of imitations spawned by the great popularity of this cheese. Always look for the appellation of origin seal to insure that a cheese is in fact from La Mancha and made exclusively with sheep's milk.

Salads ❀ Soups ❀ Meals-in-a-Pot Vegetables ❀ Egg Dishes Accompaniments

ENSALADA DE LECHUGA CON GRANADAS
(Mixed Salad Greens with Pomegranate Seeds)

Although this marvelous salad is specifically meant to accompany *cocido* (see p. 244) I think you will find its slightly sweet taste appropriate and unusual with many other dishes.　　　　　　　　　　　　　*Serves 6*

1 pomegranate

SALAD DRESSING

6 tablespoons extra virgin olive oil	1 tablespoon pomegranate juice
2 teaspoons sherry vinegar	Salt
4 teaspoons red wine vinegar	Freshly ground pepper

· · ·

Mixed salad greens	2 scallions, chopped
½ small onion, slivered	

Slice the pomegranate into 4 wedges and separate the seeds. Reserve about ¾ cup for the salad and mash some of those that remain to make 1 tablespoon juice for the salad dressing.

In a small bowl, whisk together the Salad Dressing ingredients. In a large bowl toss the salad greens with the onion, scallions, and salad dressing. Sprinkle the pomegranate seeds over the salad.

SOPA DE TOMATE AL COMINO CON HIGOS
(Cumin-Scented Tomato Soup with Fresh Figs)

Among the outstanding recipes forwarded to me by Brother Juan Barrera at the Guadalupe Monastery (see page 229) was this tomato soup, which caught my attention because of its seasoning of cumin and because I was intrigued by his suggestion to serve it with fresh figs. I discovered to my surprise that tomato, cumin, and figs provide a sensational blend of flavors perfectly matched to one another. Only someone like Fray Juan with his extraordinary culinary sensibility could have come up with a dish this simple and yet inspired.   *Serves 4*

1 tablespoon olive oil	1½ cups imported canned
1 clove garlic, peeled	crushed tomatoes
1 small onion, finely chopped	Salt
4 cloves garlic, minced	1 bay leaf
¼ pound green frying peppers,	2 sprigs parsley
lightly colored red if possi-	¾ teaspoon ground cumin,
ble, cored, seeded, and	preferably freshly ground in
finely chopped	a mortar or spice mill
1 pound ripe and flavorful	2 cups water
tomatoes, skinned, seeded,	1 cup of ½-inch bread cubes,
and chopped	crusts removed
¼ teaspoon imported sweet	4 figs, preferably purple
paprika	

In a soup pot, heat the oil and lightly brown the whole garlic on all sides. Remove and reserve. Add to the pot the onion, minced garlic, and peppers and sauté a minute or two. Cover and cook very slowly for 20 minutes. Add the fresh tomatoes, turn up the heat, and cook 5 minutes. Stir in the paprika, the canned tomatoes, salt, bay leaf, parsley, ½ teaspoon of the cumin, the reserved garlic clove, and the water. Bring to a boil, cover, and simmer 1 hour.

Meanwhile, arrange the bread cubes on a cookie sheet and bake at 350°F about 5 to 10 minutes, or until crisp and browned on all sides.

Remove the soup from the heat and add the remaining ¼ teaspoon cumin. Adjust the salt (it should be well seasoned). Cut the figs in quarters, lengthwise, without slicing all the way through. Divide the bread cubes into 4 soup bowls (preferably earthenware) and pour in the soup. Place a fig in the center of each bowl and open the fig into the shape of a star.

SOPA DE LENTEJAS DEL HERMANO PEDRO
(Brother Peter's Lentil Soup)

Monasteries and convents in Spain have long been appreciated for the quality of the liqueurs, cheeses, and sweets they make as a means of raising funds for their orders. But within these communities there are many fine cooks who prepare the daily meals, always based on simple, inexpensive, and easy-to-obtain ingredients. Such is this lentil soup, adapted from a recipe by Brother Peter of the Paúles order in Burgos. *Serves 4–6*

1 pound lentils	1 medium tomato, skinned,
1 medium onion, peeled	seeded, and chopped
1 head garlic, unpeeled, loose	½ teaspoon paprika
skin removed	1½ teaspoons minced thyme
1 bay leaf	leaves or ¼ teaspoon dried
2 parsley sprigs	1½ teaspoons minced rosemary
¼ pound salt pork	leaves or ¼ teaspoon dried
Freshly ground pepper	2 teaspoons vinegar
1 tablespoon olive oil	Salt
4 large sweet sausages	4 small potatoes (about 2 inches
1 medium onion, chopped	diameter), peeled

Wash the lentils and transfer to a soup pot. Add the whole onion, the head of garlic, bay leaf, parsley, salt pork, and pepper, and about 6 cups water. Bring to a boil, cover, and simmer for 45 minutes.

Meanwhile, heat the oil in a skillet and brown the sausages until they give off their fat. Add the sausages to the lentils and drain all but 1 tablespoon of the fat in the skillet. Add the chopped onion and sauté until wilted. Stir in the tomato, cook a minute, turn off the flame, and add the paprika, thyme, and rosemary and transfer this mixture to the lentils, along with the vinegar, salt, and the potatoes, if using. Cover and cook 45 minutes more, or until the lentils and potatoes are tender. The soup should be thick—boil down or add more water as necessary.

SOPA DE AJO A LA CASTELLANA
(Castilian-Style Garlic Soup)

Emeterio Martín and his wife, Pilar, are the proud owners of a lovely little hotel in an eighteenth-century noble home in Santo Domingo de Silos, province of Burgos. The town's claim to fame is its monastery, in particular the monastery's cloister—a jewel of medieval Romanesque art. Emeterio and Pilar also take charge of the hotel's small Castilian-style restaurant, and there I enjoyed the best *sopa de ajo* I have ever tasted. The utter simplicity of this soup—nothing more than garlic, bread, and water (although admitting some limited embellishments)—makes it the quintessential poor man's soup. Why, then, do some versions taste like dishwater and others achieve perfection? In the opinion of Juan Gabriel Abad Zapatero, author of a monograph on Silos, "Garlic soup has . . . something macho, uncomplicated, sober, primitive, that pairs well with the Iberian spirit . . . a miracle of alchemy not as easy to produce as its ingredients suggest."

With persistent prodding, the secrets of Emeterio and Pilar were gradually revealed, and they had more to do with the order in which ingredients were combined than departures from traditional ingredients. Emeterio also considers earthenware soup bowls to be essential. "They too give flavor," he affirms—and he is not the first Spanish cook who has told me so.

Serves 6

6 tablespoons olive oil	4½ cups water
4 cloves garlic, minced	Salt
4½ cups day-old country	Freshly ground pepper
bread, crusts removed,	4 cups beef broth or beef
cut in ½-inch slices	consommé
then torn roughly	6 eggs (optional)
into crouton-size pieces	6 tablespoons chopped Spanish
2 teaspoons imported sweet	mountain cured ham,
paprika	prosciutto, or capicollo,
4 cloves garlic, lightly crushed	in a ¼-inch dice
and peeled	

Place 5 tablespoons of the oil and the minced garlic in a skillet and slowly heat until the garlic begins to color. Add the bread pieces and sauté slowly until they are crisp and golden, about 15 minutes. Sprinkle in 1 teaspoon of the paprika and stir to coat the bread. Reserve.

To make the garlic broth, in a soup pot heat the remaining tablespoon of oil and lightly sauté the peeled, crushed garlic cloves. Stir in the remaining teaspoon paprika, the water, salt, and pepper. Bring to a boil, cover, and simmer 45 minutes—you should have about 4 cups (these first two steps may be done in advance).

Bring the beef broth to a boil. Arrange 6 ovenproof soup bowls on a baking tray and add 1 tablespoon of the beef broth to each. If you are using eggs, slip one into each bowl, scatter in the ham, and pour in more beef broth (the bowls should be half full). Place the tray with the bowls in a 450°F oven until the eggs are set, about 4 minutes. Fill the bowls with the reserved garlic broth, boiling hot, and scatter in the bread pieces. Serve immediately.

Chorizo: Unique Iberian Sausage

Pork products, prohibited for religious reasons in Spain's large Moorish and Jewish communities of centuries past, were embraced with a vengeance by the end of the fifteenth century, when the Catholic Kings and Spain's Christian population sought to erase most reminders of "foreign" cultures and religions that had once dominated the country. Thus, converted Jews and Moors who remained in Spain were especially obliged to eat pork products, if for no other reason than to show they had sincerely converted to Christianity.

Ever since then, Spaniards have been hearty and enthusiastic consumers of pork and especially of pork sausage. Chorizo, a wonderfully flavorful cured sausage seasoned with paprika and garlic, and sometimes with nutmeg, oregano, and pepper, is Spain's contribution to the enormous diversity of sausage products found throughout the world.

Just about every region of Spain has its own interpretation of chorizo. Asturians, for example, like their chorizo spicy and heavily seasoned to simmer in *fabada* bean stew, and in Castilla, where some of the best chorizo is produced (and where chorizo most likely originated,

Chorizo: Unique Iberian Sausage (continued)

since the word was first used there), chorizo may have the texture of a coarse dried salami when used as a tapa, but is generally softer and less cured when used for cooking. In my experience, some of the best chorizo is homemade and naturally aged in remote villages, sometimes in rustic kitchens with dirt floors and wood-burning fires, where the chorizo acquires wonderfully earthy flavors.

Chorizo was adopted by Spain's former colonies in the New World, and is therefore not hard to find in the United States, although what is made here cannot match Spain's finest (the many varieties of chorizo from La Española—see Marketing Sources—are, however, exceptionally good). Chorizo may be hot or mild—mild is generally the one you will want for Spanish cooking. When chorizo is purchased, it is often soft and more suitable for cooking. To enjoy as a cold cut, hang the chorizo in your kitchen until it reaches the desired firmness (it needs no cooking).

As a tapa, chorizo may be simply sliced, sautéed, or simmered in wine. It is essential in so many Spanish bean, chickpea, and potato stews and combines with any number of rice and egg dishes as well. Chorizo has the ability to transform whatever dish it joins and give a flavor that is uniquely Spanish.

JUDÍAS CON CHORIZO
(Beans with Chorizo)

START PREPARATION 1 DAY IN ADVANCE

I have never tasted a version of beans and chorizo anywhere in central Spain that did not live up to expectations. You can count on this bean dish to be hearty, satisfying, and well seasoned no matter where you eat it, and there are surprisingly few variations from one chef or one province to the next—the scallions in this recipe are one of those rare deviations.   *Serves 6*

¾ pound large dried white
   beans
4½–5 cups water
½ pound sweet chorizo
½ onion, peeled
1 pig's foot (optional)
6 cloves garlic, peeled
2 sprigs parsley
Freshly ground pepper

1 bay leaf
1 tablespoon olive oil
3 large scallions, chopped
2 tablespoons chopped
   pimiento, homemade
   (p. 178) or imported
1 teaspoon paprika
1 teaspoon vinegar
Salt

Soak the beans overnight in cold water to cover. Drain.

Combine in a soup pot the beans, the water, chorizo, onion, pig's foot (if using), garlic, parsley, pepper, and bay leaf. Bring to a boil, cover, and simmer 2 hours, or until the beans are almost tender.

Meanwhile, heat the oil in a small skillet and slowly sauté the scallions for a minute. Add the pimiento, sauté a minute, then remove the skillet from the heat and stir in the paprika and vinegar. Add the mixture to the beans. Salt to taste and cook 30 minutes more, or until the beans are done.

To serve, chop the pig's foot meat and discard the bone. Cut the chorizo into several pieces and include some in each portion.

JUDIONES DE EL BARCO DE ÁVILA
(Broad Bean Stew)

START PREPARATION I DAY IN ADVANCE

Judiones, oversize dried beans, similar to but much larger than dried kidney beans, are grown and highly prized in Castilla—especially Segovia and Ávila provinces—and in neighboring La Rioja, where they are called *pochas*.

This tasty preparation, accented by the flavor of chorizo and black sausage (*morcilla*), is also appropriate for other varieties of dried white beans.

Serves 4–6

1 pound very large dried white
    beans, such as large lima
    beans
7 cups water
10 cloves garlic, peeled
2 bay leaves
1 pig's foot, split in half
A ¼-pound piece Spanish
    mountain cured ham or
    prosciutto, cut in 1 thick
    piece from the narrow end,
    or capicollo
¼ pound sweet chorizo
1 black sausage, preferably
    Spanish-style *morcilla*
1 tablespoon olive oil
1 medium onion, finely
    chopped

1 teaspoon imported sweet
    paprika
¼ pound tomato, peeled,
    seeded, and chopped
2 tablespoons finely chopped
    pimiento, homemade
    (p. 178) or imported
A 1-inch piece, or to taste,
    dried red chile pepper,
    seeded
2 tablespoons minced parsley
½ pound very small new or red
    waxy potatoes (about 2
    inches diameter), peeled
Salt

Soak the beans overnight in cold water. Drain and place in a deep soup pot with 7 cups of water, the garlic, and the bay leaves. Bring to a boil, cover, and simmer 30 minutes. Add the pig's foot, ham, chorizo, and black sausage. Cover and cook 30 minutes more.

Meanwhile, in a skillet, heat the oil and slowly sauté the onion until wilted. Stir in the paprika, tomato, pimiento, dried chile, and parsley and cook 5 minutes more.

Add the skillet mixture to the beans with the potatoes. Salt to taste, cover, and cook another 30 minutes, or until the beans and potatoes are tender. Turn off the flame and let sit, covered, 30 minutes. Reheat and serve.

POTAJE DE GARBANZOS LERRANZ
(Chickpea, Spinach, and Cod Potage Lerranz)

START PREPARATION SEVERAL DAYS IN ADVANCE

Our old friend Tomás Herranz, tall, reed thin, and charmingly boyish, is one of Madrid's star chefs; he divides his attention between his elegant restaurant, El Cenador del Prado, and his upscale tapas bar, Lerranz, just around the corner (they share a common kitchen). The first turns out the innovative fare for which Tomás has achieved fame; the latter, although decorated in high-tech style, concentrates on the down-to-earth country cooking that remains close to his heart. This splendid potage is a traditional Spanish Lenten dish.

Serves 6

½ pound boneless dried salt cod
1 pound dried chickpeas
2 tablespoons olive oil
4 cloves garlic, minced
1 medium onion, finely
    chopped
2 tablespoons minced parsley
2 teaspoons flour
2 teaspoons imported sweet
    paprika
¼ teaspoon crumbled saffron
    strands
10 cups water
½ head garlic, in one piece,
    loose outer skin removed
1 medium onion, peeled and
    halved

1 small leek, well washed
1 bay leaf
Salt
Freshly ground pepper
½ teaspoon ground cumin,
    preferably freshly ground in
    a mortar or spice mill
½ pound new or red waxy
    potatoes, peeled and cut in
    ½-inch cubes
½ pound washed spinach
    leaves, coarsely chopped
    (about 4 cups, loosely
    packed)
1 hard-boiled egg, minced

Soak the cod in cold water to cover in the refrigerator for 2 to 3 days, changing the water once or twice daily until desalted to taste. Cover the chickpeas with water and soak overnight. Drain the cod and the chickpeas.

In a large soup pot, heat the oil and sauté the minced garlic, chopped onion, and the parsley slowly until the onion is translucent. Stir in the flour,

Chickpea, Spinach, and Cod Potage (continued)

paprika, and saffron. Pour in the water, then add the ½ head garlic, the halved onion, leek, bay leaf, and cod. Bring to a boil, removing the cod as soon as the boil is reached. Shred the cod with your fingers and reserve. Add the chickpeas to the pot, cover, and simmer 1 hour. Season with salt, pepper, and cumin and continue cooking 1 hour more, or until the chickpeas are almost tender.

Add the potatoes to the soup pot, cover, and continue cooking until the potatoes are almost tender. Discard the leek, the half head of garlic, and the bay leaf. Add the shredded cod and the spinach, cover, and cook 5 minutes more. Let sit for 1 hour, covered, to thicken and let the flavors blend. Adjust the seasonings, adding more salt, pepper, and cumin to taste. Reheat and serve, sprinkled with the minced egg.

"Mother" Cocido: The National Dish of Spain

Without a doubt, *cocido*, a meal-in-a-pot based on chickpeas, vegetables, and meats that has been praised in poetry and lauded in popular song, is Spain's ultimate comfort food.

Cocido is said to have originated among the Spanish Sephardic Jewish community because it could be started the day before the Sabbath, then simmered all that day, untouched by human hands (*cocido* derives from *cocer*, which means to cook or boil). Chickpeas, however, came to Spain by way of the Moors, and through the centuries have been disdained as lowly peasant food. Nevertheless, writers who wax rhapsodic over *cocido* sometimes attribute Spain's supreme accomplishments to the chickpea. "Thanks to our chickpeas," says José Estéban, writer of a veritable treatise on the subject of *cocido*, "we have achieved our greatest triumphs, from *Don Quijote* . . . to our victories over Napoleon." French writer Alexander Dumas, however, had a radically different opinion of the chickpeas he ate in Spain, comparing them to high-caliber bullets, practically impossible to digest. Today, of course, the chickpea is hailed as an exceptional health food.

Undeniably of peasant origin, *cocido* eventually moved up the social ladder and became as popular with the aristocracy as with the poor (in this century King Alfonso XIII was a great fan, and one of the most refined recipes for *cocido* comes from the king's aunt, the Infanta Isabel). Indeed, in the past few decades the high cost of *cocido* ingredients has made it a luxury dish, reserved for special occasions. Even the most sophisticated gastronomes keep a warm spot in their hearts and on their tables for this meal that is tradition itself.

The basic ingredients of *cocido* are meats and sausage products, vegetables, such as potatoes, carrots, and cabbage, and, of course, chickpeas, but Spaniards from Catalunya to Andalucía cherish their regional variations. Some *cocidos* in central Spain include a kind of meatball made with chopped ingredients from the stewpot (a distant reminder of the whole eggs that the Jews added to their porkless version called *adafina*); in Catalunya there are beans as well as chickpeas in their *cocido* called *escudella*, and chorizo sausage is replaced by *butifarra*, a white Catalan sausage. The *cocidos* of Andalucía and the Canary Islands can be somewhat more exotic, including such varied ingredients as squash, pears, and corncobs. In fact, exploring the diversity of this grand dish, region by region, can yield a wealth of information related to Spain's culinary history and development.

COCIDO CASTELLANO
(Castilian Chickpea Stew)

START PREPARATION 1 DAY IN ADVANCE

I have chosen a *cocido* from central Spain for this recipe because I think it is most representative of the *cocidos*—long-simmering meat and vegetable stews—found in every region of the country. I have included the *pelota*, or *bola*—a meatball similar to a quenelle—which, although not found in all *cocidos*, brings an added element to the stew (according to one writer, "*Cocido* without *pelotas* is like youth without love"). I also highly recommend serving the *cocido* with a pomegranate salad, an ideal complement that our good friend Charito (who was raised in Córdoba, lived in Madrid, and had a ranch in Extremadura) assures me is authentic and acts as a perfect digestif. A full-bodied red wine is also undoubtedly an essential accompaniment to a *cocido*.

Although the list of ingredients and hours of cooking make the recipe look daunting, don't be put off. There is nothing difficult about this dish. It is a rewarding meal, albeit time-consuming, and that's why Spaniards today reserve it for special occasions.

You will need a small cheesecloth or cotton net sack to keep the chickpeas together so they can easily be removed from the *cocido* for serving.

I like to serve the soup and then bring the meat and vegetable platters to the table without retiring the soup bowls; that way you can continue to sip the soup, then add some of the meats and vegetables to the remaining broth, and refill from the platters as needed. *Serves 6–8*

1 pound dried chickpeas	¼ pound meaty slab bacon, some of the fat trimmed
18 cups water	2 beef or ham soup bones
2½ pounds lean beef chuck	1 onion, studded with a clove
4 chicken thighs, skinned and trimmed of all fat	1 bay leaf
A ¼-pound piece of Spanish mountain cured ham or prosciutto, cut in 1 thick slice from the narrow end, or capicollo	3 sprigs parsley
	1 leek, well washed
	¼ pound turnips, peeled
	2 large carrots, trimmed and scraped

½ pound sweet chorizo

1 pound red waxy potatoes
(about 3-inch diameter),
peeled

¼ pound black sausage
(*morcilla*)

Salt

Freshly ground pepper

PELOTAS (MEATBALLS)

2 eggs

6 tablespoons bread crumbs

1 clove garlic, minced

2 tablespoons minced parsley

⅛ teaspoon ground nutmeg

¼ teaspoon imported sweet
paprika

1 tablespoon olive oil

. . .

2 cloves garlic, peeled

4 peppercorns

Several strands of saffron

SAUTÉED CABBAGE

1 tablespoon olive oil

1 small onion, chopped

2 cloves garlic, minced

¼ teaspoon paprika

2 pounds cabbage, chopped

Salt

Freshly ground pepper

. . .

1 cup cooked thin noodles

Soak the chickpeas overnight in cold water to cover. Drain. Pour the 18 cups water into a very large soup pot and add the beef, chicken, ham, bacon, soup bones, onion, bay leaf, parsley, leek, turnips, and carrots. Bring to a boil and cook 10 minutes. Skim off the foam, then add the chickpeas, loosely enclosed in a cheesecloth or cotton net sack, cover, and simmer 2 hours. Add the chorizo, potatoes, black sausage, salt, and pepper and cook 1 hour more.

To make the *Pelotas*, remove from the pot a piece of beef, some of the chorizo, ham, slab bacon, and chicken and chop for a total of 1½ cups (about 1 cup should be beef). Place in a food processor with the eggs, bread crumbs, garlic, parsley, nutmeg, paprika, and 2 tablespoons water. Pulse until the meats are finely chopped. Shape into 2½-inch elongated balls. Heat the oil in a skillet and lightly brown the meatballs. Drain, then put into the soup.

Castilian Chickpea Stew (continued)

In a mortar mash the garlic, ⅛ teaspoon salt, peppercorns, and saffron. Stir into the soup and cook 1 hour more. Turn off heat and let sit 30 minutes.

Meanwhile, prepare the cabbage. Heat the oil in a skillet and sauté the onion and garlic until the onion is translucent. Stir in the paprika, then the cabbage, salt, and pepper (it should be well seasoned), and sauté 10 minutes. Cover and continue cooking until done to taste. Set aside.

When you are ready to serve the *cocido*, remove all the meats and vegetables to a warm platter. Discard the bones and strain the broth (it should be slightly thickened; if not, boil down). Stir in the cooked noodles and reheat.

Cut the meats in serving pieces and arrange on a platter with the chickpeas in the center. Reheat the cabbage and arrange on another platter with the potatoes, carrots, and leek, all cut in serving pieces.

SETAS CON MIGAS
(Wild Mushrooms with Garlic Bread Bits)

Here is a great mixture of tastes and textures; the garlic flavor is in the croutons as well as the mushrooms and the dish is perfect with simple meats or poultry.   *Serves 4*

2 tablespoons fruity extra
   virgin olive oil
1 clove garlic, mashed in a garlic press or mortar
1½ cups crustless bread in
   ½-inch cubes, cut from a
   country loaf
1 pound wild mushrooms, such

as shitake, brushed clean,
   stems trimmed, cut in halves
   or quarters
Salt
Freshly ground pepper
1 clove garlic, minced
1 tablespoon minced parsley
Lemon juice

In a cup, combine 1 tablespoon of the oil with the mashed garlic. Arrange the bread cubes on a cookie tray and bake in a 350°F oven for about 8 minutes, turning once, or until golden and crisp. Drizzle with the oil-garlic mixture and reserve.

Heat the remaining tablespoon oil until very hot and quickly stir-fry the mushrooms. Sprinkle with salt, pepper, the minced garlic, the parsley, and a squeeze of lemon juice. Cook until the mushrooms are softened to taste, remove from the flame, and stir in the bread cubes.

TRIGUEROS ALMENDRADOS
(Green Asparagus in Almond Sauce)

This is a wonderful sauce for asparagus that is distinctively flavored with tomato, toasted almonds, and lots of roasted garlic. Its ingredients are beaten together to form what resembles a mayonnaise, but it is made without egg.

Serves 4

1 small tomato
½ small head garlic, unpeeled
¼ cup slivered blanched
    almonds
½ teaspoon sherry vinegar

Salt
¼ cup extra virgin olive oil
¾ pound green asparagus, ends
    snapped off

Roast the tomato and garlic in a 350°F oven for 15 minutes. Peel the tomato and the garlic cloves. Cut the tomato in half crosswise and gently squeeze out the seeds. Place the almonds on a cookie sheet and toast in the oven about 4 minutes, or until golden.

Beat together in a food processor the tomato, garlic, almonds, vinegar, and salt, until as smooth as possible. With the motor running, drizzle in the oil to form a mayonnaise-like emulsion. Taste for salt.

Heat a greased griddle or skillet and grill the asparagus, turning occasionally, until done to taste about 10 to 15 minutes. Serve with the sauce.

PATATAS PANADERAS
(Oven-Roasted Potatoes)

These are my favorite potatoes, and I make them all the time. They have only a drizzle of oil and are effortless to prepare. They are the perfect complement to any simple meat, poultry, or fish dish. *Serves 4*

Oven-Roasted Potatoes (continued)

Olive oil

3 medium baking potatoes,
    peeled and cut in ⅛-inch
    slices

1 clove garlic, unpeeled and
    lightly crushed

1 bay leaf

Salt

Freshly ground pepper

Grease with olive oil a roasting pan or shallow casserole in which the potatoes will fit in two layers. Arrange one layer of potato slices, bury the garlic
and bay leaf between the slices, and sprinkle with salt and pepper. Drizzle
with olive oil. Add the second layer and again sprinkle with salt and pepper
and drizzle with oil. Bake uncovered in a 350°F oven for about 1 hour, or
until the potatoes are tender (some of them should be browned and crisp),
turning once with a metal spatula.

PATATAS MAJAELRAYO
(Potatoes with Sautéed Peppers)

We had just traveled 20 kilometers through the mountains on a dirt road
from the so-called Sierra Pobre ("Poor Mountains") in the province of
Madrid to Guadalajara. We emerged at the foot of the Ocejón peak in the
village of Majaelrayo, one of the "Black Villages," named for their dark
stone construction and the beautiful black slate roofs of the houses.

Wouldn't you know that even in this isolated town there is a bar—and a
modern one at that—presided over by an energetic young blond woman
who brought us the *bocadillos* (hero-style sandwiches) of ham and chorizo
(each a full foot long) we had requested. She also brought us this simple tapa
that was uncommonly good; when we praised it she somewhat shyly but
proudly told us of her reputation as the best cook around. The mixture of
potatoes, peppers, and chorizo also makes an excellent accompaniment to
any simple meat or poultry dish.   *Serves 3–4*

2 medium potatoes, in ½-inch
    cubes

Salt

Freshly ground pepper

2 tablespoons olive oil
2 medium Italian green frying
    peppers, cored, seeded, and
    cut in 1-inch pieces

1 tablespoon finely chopped
    chorizo (optional)

Grease a microwave-safe dish, add the potatoes, and mix in the salt, pepper, 1 tablespoon of the olive oil, and 1 tablespoon water. Cover and cook on high for 5 minutes. Stir the potatoes and continue cooking 5 minutes more, or until tender. Alternatively you can oven-roast the potatoes, omitting the water.

Meanwhile, in a skillet heat the remaining tablespoon of oil, add the peppers, sprinkle with salt, and stir-fry a minute or two. Lower the heat, cover, and continue cooking until tender. Add the chorizo, if using, cook a minute, then mix in the potatoes, cooking briefly to brown them lightly.

PATATAS VIUDAS
("Widowed" Potatoes)

This simple potato potage is a favorite of Castilian convent nuns and is popular in Asturias as well. It is meant to be a meal, and has no other major ingredients except the potatoes (thus its name). In this rendition, however, I have reduced the liquid and serve the potatoes as a side course.

Serves 4

4 medium potatoes, peeled and
    cut in ¾-inch cubes
Salt
2 tablespoons olive oil
¾ cup finely chopped onions
2 cloves garlic, minced
2 tablespoons minced parsley

1 bay leaf
½ teaspoon sweet or hot
    paprika

Bring the potatoes to a boil in salted water, cover, and simmer until just tender.

Meanwhile, in a skillet heat the oil and sauté the onions, garlic, parsley,

"Widowed" Potatoes (continued)

and bay leaf about 2 minutes. Cover and continue cooking very slowly until the onions have softened, about 10 minutes. Stir in the paprika.

Drain the potatoes, reserving 4 tablespoons of the cooking liquid. Add the potatoes and the reserved liquid to the skillet and cook briefly to blend all ingredients.

REVUELTO DE LANGOSTINOS Y ESPINACAS CASA LUCIO
(Gently Scrambled Eggs with Shrimp and Spinach)

Casa Lucio, a centuries-old restaurant in Old Madrid, attracts royalty (including Spain's king), celebrities, and Madrid's movers and shakers, not to mention every visiting dignitary and movie star who passes through Madrid. Its extraordinary and long-lasting popularity is due as much to the charm of owner Lucio Blázquez as to the high quality of the simple dishes that are prepared here.

The success of this egg dish depends on the very best ingredients and the speed of preparation. I watched it being made in the tiny kitchen of Casa Lucio on a Saturday night, when the pace was feverish, and the dish was completed in the blink of an eye. The eggs should be very softly set; otherwise the delicacy of the dish is lost.

Serves 1

4 medium shrimp, shelled and each cut in 3 pieces	¼ cup torn and lightly cooked spinach leaves (about 2 cups uncooked), well drained
Kosher or sea salt	
2 teaspoons olive oil	2 eggs

Sprinkle the shrimp pieces with salt and let sit at room temperature 15 minutes.

Heat the oil in a small skillet over medium-high heat. Add the shrimp and sauté quickly (a few seconds will do) until they just begin to turn opaque. Stir in the spinach. Break the eggs into the skillet and stir rapidly, removing the skillet from the flame almost immediately. Sprinkle with salt and continue stirring until the eggs are no longer liquid and have just begun to set. Transfer immediately to a plate to prevent further cooking.

HUEVOS ESTRELLADOS LUCIO
("Crashed" Fried Eggs and Potatoes)

This dish is nothing but a different form of the dish that Spaniards love most: fried eggs with fried potatoes. And yet by cutting up the egg after it is cooked and blending it with the potatoes, it somehow becomes an exciting new dish. Almost everyone at Casa Lucio (see p. 250) orders Huevos Estrellados as a shared first course, and it's one of those dishes that for me say "Spain." I can of course make these eggs at home, but I prefer the anticipation of ordering them at Lucio's as soon as I arrive in Madrid.

The secret of this dish (besides best-quality potatoes and eggs) is timing; the eggs and potatoes should be just done but not browned.   *Serves 1*

1 medium potato, peeled and cut lengthwise into ½-inch fries	Salt
	2 tablespoons olive oil
Olive oil for frying	2 eggs

Deep-fry the potatoes (preferably in the basket of a deep-fryer; otherwise in a skillet in at least 1 inch of oil) in two stages—first at a low simmer (300°F) until softened but not browned. Drain in the frying basket or on paper towels. At serving time return the potatoes to the oil, now heated to 350°F (medium-high) for a few seconds to crisp, but not to brown. Drain once again. Sprinkle with salt, arrange in a shallow individual casserole, and keep warm in a 200°F oven.

Heat the 2 tablespoons oil in a medium skillet, preferably one that is well seasoned or nonstick, until it reaches the smoking point. Break in the eggs and cook very briefly until just set underneath. Rather than flipping, carefully roll them over with the aid of a pancake turner (they should not brown). Sprinkle with salt and place over the potatoes. Cut up the eggs and potatoes so that the yolks blend with the potatoes, and serve immediately.

TORTILLA A LA SEGOVIANA
(Potato and Vegetable Omelet)

Here is a variation on the typical Spanish potato omelet that incorporates several vegetables, ham, and chorizo. It makes a satisfying supper.

Serves 4–6

½ cup olive oil for frying
2 medium baking potatoes,
    peeled, in ⅛-inch slices
1 small onion, in thin slices
Salt
4 eggs
1 tablespoon minced parsley
3 tablespoons diced Spanish
    mountain cured ham or
    prosciutto

3 tablespoons diced sweet
    chorizo
1 tablespoon chopped pimiento
1 small carrot, scraped, cooked,
    and diced
⅓ cup cooked peas
½ cup cooked cut green beans
Eight 4-inch cooked asparagus
    tips, cut in 1-inch pieces

Heat the oil in an 8- or 9-inch skillet until it sizzles a potato. Add the potato and onion slices one at a time to prevent sticking. Salt lightly. Cook slowly (in effect "simmering" the potatoes and onions in the oil) until they are tender but not browned (this may also be done in the basket of a deep-fryer; or see Patatas Panaderas, page 247, for an oven-roasting alternative that uses a minimum of oil). Reserve about 2 tablespoons of the oil, then drain the potatoes and onions in a colander and pat with paper towels. Wipe out the skillet, scraping off any stuck particles.

In a large bowl, lightly beat with a fork the eggs and a little salt. Add the potatoes and onions, parsley, ham, chorizo, pimiento, carrot, peas, green beans, and asparagus. Let sit 5 minutes.

In the skillet, heat 1 tablespoon of the reserved oil to the smoking point. Add the egg mixture, rapidly spreading it out in the skillet with the aid of a pancake turner. Lower the heat to medium-high and shake the pan continuously to prevent sticking. When the omelet begins to brown underneath, slide it onto a plate. Place another plate over it and invert. Lightly coat the skillet with more oil, slide the *tortilla* back into the pan, and brown on the other side, shaking all the while. Lower the heat to medium. Turn the *tortilla* 2 or 3 more times (this helps to give it a good shape), cooking briefly on each side. It should be a little juicy within. Serve warm or at room temperature (it can be made several hours in advance).

MIGAS EXTREMEÑAS, FRAY JUAN
(*Sautéed Bread Bits with Peppers and Chorizo*)

I always enjoy returning to the town of Guadalupe—not only to visit the town's wonderful monastery with its venerated black virgin and impressive art treasures, but to dine in the monastery's restaurant, where Brother Juan Barrera is in charge of the kitchen. His dishes are traditional and uncomplicated, but when I first tasted his food I knew right away that here was a man with an uncommon palate, genuine culinary talent, and a real love for good food.

You can find peasant dishes similar to this one throughout central Spain (see another excellent version from Andalucía, on p. 356), but nowhere as exceptional as at the Guadalupe Monastery. I love *migas* (crisp bread bits) on their own, but like them even more with Spanish-style fried eggs. Be sure that the bread you use is good quality and a day or two old.   *Serves 2*

1 tablespoon olive oil

¼ cup cored, seeded, and finely chopped green frying peppers

1 tablespoon fresh or cured slab bacon, or pancetta, in a ¼-inch dice

¼ cup lean pork in a ¼-inch dice

3 tablespoons sweet chorizo in a ¼-inch dice

2 cloves garlic, lightly smashed and peeled

4 cups day-old country bread, crusts removed, in ½-inch cubes

Salt

4 eggs (optional), at room temperature

Mild olive oil for frying eggs

Heat the 1 tablespoon oil in a skillet and sauté the peppers very slowly until they are softened, about 10 minutes. Turn up the heat to medium, add the bacon, pork, and chorizo, and cook until the pork loses its color and the meats have given off their oils. Remove the meats and reserve.

Add the garlic to the skillet (adding a little more oil if necessary) and sauté, pressing with the back of a wooden spoon, until it is lightly browned

Sautéed Bread Bits (continued)

on both sides. Discard the garlic, then add the bread cubes and mix well. Dissolve ⅛ teaspoon salt in ¼ cup water and sprinkle over the bread. Continue cooking, stirring frequently, 10 minutes over a medium-low flame. Stir in the reserved meats and continue cooking until the bread is crisp and golden. Remove the skillet from the heat, cover and keep warm while preparing the eggs, if using.

To fry the eggs Spanish style, pour olive oil to a depth of ¼ inch in a 9-inch skillet. Heat to the smoking point. Break 1 egg into a cup, then slide into the hot oil. You must work very quickly, folding in the edges of the egg white with the aid of a wooden spoon. Then with a large metal spoon, pour the hot oil over the egg so that it puffs up and becomes crisp around the edges. All this must be done in a matter of seconds so that the yolk remains soft.

Remove the egg with a metal slotted pancake turner, rest the egg and the pancake turner briefly on paper towels to drain, and slide the egg onto one side of a dinner plate. Repeat for the remaining eggs, placing 2 eggs on each plate. Heat the bread mixture and pile in the center of the dish.

PAN DE ARANDA
(Aranda Bread Tortes)

Whenever I travel to Aranda de Duero in the Castilian province of Burgos it is for the purpose of eating the exceptional roast lamb at Mesón de la Villa. But I am so captivated by the restaurant's bread—somewhat flat and incredibly moist—that I long for an occasion when I can consume an entire loaf without the distraction of other foods. Unfortunately, that opportunity has never arisen, so I decided to reproduce the bread at home. Of course it can never be exactly the same, if for no other reason than not being in situ, but I am extremely pleased with the recipe I have devised.

You can make one large round loaf, if you have a baking sheet or a baking stone large enough to hold it; otherwise make two smaller loaves.

Makes 1 large or two 9-inch round loaves

1½ packages (1 tablespoon) dry yeast
1½ cups warm water
3 cups flour, preferably bread flour

1½ teaspoons salt
Cornmeal or flour
Extra virgin olive oil

Dissolve the yeast in ¾ cup of the warm water. Place 2 cups of the flour in a processor, add the dissolved yeast, and process for 1 minute. Transfer the dough to an oiled bowl, turn to coat, and let rise in a warm enclosed spot (like an unlit oven), covered with a damp towel, for 3 hours (both the mixing and rising can be done instead in a bread machine big enough for 1½-pound loaves).

Punch down the dough and return it to the processor or bread machine. Add the remaining cup of flour, the salt, and the remaining ¾ cup warm water. Process 1 minute. Remove with well-floured hands (it will be quite sticky) and knead briefly on a floured board. Return to the oiled bowl, covered as before, and let rise 3 hours more (or mix and let rise as before in the bread machine).

Heat the oven to 400°F and place a pan of water on the floor of the oven (if you have a baking stone, preheat it in the oven and omit the pan of water). Punch down the dough and roll into a circle about ½ inch thick and 18 inches across; or if making two loaves, divide the dough in half and roll each ½ inch thick and 9 inches across. Score with a sharp thin knife to within 1 inch of the edge. Transfer to a cookie sheet or to the preheated baking stone, either of which should first be sprinkled with cornmeal or flour. Bake in the 400°F oven for 10 minutes. Remove the pan of water (if using) and brush the bread with olive oil. Continue baking 5 to 10 minutes more, until lightly browned. Cool on a rack.

ZAPATILLA
(Flat Bread Loaf)

Zapatilla, also known as *chapata*, is a somewhat flattened bread (it is punched down after the second rising) that has become fashionable in Madrid and appears in gourmet shops cut in large squares with simple but irresistible fillings—my favorite is one with Spanish mountain cured ham, garlic, and a touch of tomato, drizzled with fruity olive oil (see p. 25). The dough is the same as for the preceding recipe, but the shape and thickness are different, and this one is not brushed with oil.

Makes 2 long flat loaves

1 recipe Pan de Aranda dough   Cornmeal or flour for dusting
   (p. 254)

Prepare the Pan de Aranda as described. After it has been punched down for the second time, heat the oven to 400°F and place a pan of water on the floor of the oven (if you have a baking stone, preheat it in the oven and omit the pan of water). Divide the dough in half and roll each piece into a rectangle 16 inches by 4½ inches. Score and dust with flour. Transfer to 2 cookie sheets or to the preheated baking stone, either of which should first be sprinkled with cornmeal or flour. Bake in a 400°F oven for 10 minutes. Remove the pan of water (if using) and continue baking 5 to 10 minutes more, until the bread is lightly browned. Cool on a rack.

Fish

BESUGO A LA MADRILEÑA
(Baked Porgy, Madrid Style)

For more than a century, *besugo*, rushed from the northern coast to Madrid—once by caravan, today by truck or plane—has been an indispensable part of the city's traditional Christmas Eve dinner. Despite Madrid's landlocked location, this dish is uniquely *madrileño*, adopted as the city's own (a well-known food writer, Julio Camba, once wrote, "I suspect that *besugo* doesn't feel at home until it reaches Madrid and is placed in the oven").

There is, however, one tenuous connection between this fish dish and Madrid's culinary heritage, and that is the wood-burning oven in which it ideally bakes, an oven essential for baking authentic Castilian bread and roasting baby lamb and suckling pig.   *Serves 4*

4 cloves garlic
2 tablespoons minced parsley
Salt
Freshly ground pepper
1½ teaspoons minced oregano
    leaves or ¼ teaspoon dried
1 bay leaf, crumbled
¼ cup freshly squeezed lemon
    juice

¼ cup olive oil
½ cup dry white wine
1 medium onion, thinly sliced
Two 1½-pound porgies or red
    snappers, cleaned, heads on
1 lemon, in thin slices
2 tablespoons bread crumbs

In a mortar or mini processor, mash to a paste the garlic, parsley, salt, pepper, oregano, and bay leaf. Stir in the lemon juice, 2 tablespoons of the oil, and the wine.

Brush a roasting pan with the remaining 2 tablespoons oil, scatter in the onion slices, and place the fish over the onion. Sprinkle with salt. Arrange the lemon slices over the fish and pour on the mortar mixture. Sprinkle the fish with bread crumbs and bake at 350°F for about 30 minutes, basting occasionally with the pan juices and adding some water, if necessary, to keep the pan moist.

Cut each fish into 2 portions and spoon the onion and the pan juices over the fish.

BESUGO A LA ESPALDA
(Butterflied Baked Porgy)

Besugo is generally translated as porgy and is indeed closely related to that fish. But I think red snapper, despite its different color, seems to have more of the refined taste of *besugo*. This simple preparation is one of the most popular way to serve *besugo* in Madrid, and it is very good, lightly seasoned with lemon, a small amount of fresh tomato, garlic, parsley, and a hint of chile pepper.

Cut down on work by having your fishmonger butterfly and bone the fish.   *Serves 4*

Two 1¾-pound red snappers or porgies, cleaned, heads on
Salt
Freshly ground pepper
5 tablespoons freshly squeezed lemon juice
¼ pound tomato, skinned, seeded, and coarsely chopped

2 tablespoons minced parsley
1 small bay leaf, broken into 4 pieces
¼ cup extra virgin olive oil
4 cloves garlic, thinly sliced
Four ½-inch pieces dried red chile pepper, seeded

Butterfly the fish, leaving the backbone joined and removing as much of the remaining bone as possible. Place the fish, skin side down, in a shallow casserole, preferably earthenware. Rub the fish with salt and pepper and sprinkle with the lemon juice. Scatter the tomato over the fish, sprinkle with parsley, and add the pieces of bay leaf.

In a small skillet, heat the oil. Sauté the garlic and chile slowly until the garlic is very lightly browned. Pour the contents of the skillet over the fish and bake in a 450°F oven until just done, about 14 minutes, or until a meat thermometer registers 145°F when placed in the thickest part of the fish. Separate each fish in half lengthwise and serve, spooning on the sauce.

RAPE CASTELLANO
(Monkfish in Almond and Pine Nut Sauce)

There are only a handful of fish dishes considered typical of the central plains of Spain, and for obvious reasons—the region is landlocked and far from the sea. Nevertheless, for at least the last century, a limited amount of fish has found its way to Castilla (in the last few decades, Madrid has become one of the seafood capitals of the world). This exceptional preparation of monkfish, in which the fish is coated with egg and quickly sautéed (which keeps the fish succulent), then baked in a flavorful sauce of almonds, pine nuts, and wine, is one of those rare fish creations of Castilian origin.   *Serves 4*

3 cloves garlic, peeled
1 tablespoon minced parsley
Salt
¼ cup chopped blanched
    almonds
1¾ cups Fish Broth (p. 175) or
    1¼ cups clam juice diluted
    with ½ cup water
1 medium-large tomato
2 pounds monkfish, about 1½
    inches thick
Flour for dusting
3 tablespoons olive oil
1 egg, lightly beaten with
    1 teaspoon water

1 medium onion, finely
    chopped
1 clove garlic, minced
¼ teaspoon imported sweet
    paprika
¼ cup dry white wine
1 tablespoon tomato sauce
    (optional)
2 tablespoons pine nuts
8 small littlenecks or 16 cockles
    or Manila clams, thoroughly
    cleansed (see p. 33)
    (optional)
2 tablespoons minced parsley
    for garnish

Mash to a paste in a mortar or mini processor the garlic cloves, the tablespoon of parsley, and ⅛ teaspoon salt. Add the almonds and continue mashing until as fine as possible, then add 2 teaspoons of the Fish Broth and mash still finer.

Cut the tomato in half crosswise. Squeeze gently to extract the seeds, and with a coarse grater, grate down to the skin, draining off any excess liquid.

Sprinkle the fish with salt and dust with flour. Heat 2 tablespoons of the oil in a shallow casserole. Coat the fish with the beaten egg and sauté over a medium-high flame until lightly browned, turning once (the fish will be only partially cooked). Transfer to a warm platter. Wipe out the pan, then add the remaining tablespoon oil, and sauté the onion and the minced garlic for a minute or two. Cover and continue cooking slowly until the onion has softened. Stir in the paprika, then pour in the remaining Fish Broth, wine, and the grated tomato, and add the mortar mixture. Bring to a boil and reduce by half. Stir in the optional tomato sauce and taste for salt.

Return the fish to the casserole, spooning some of the sauce over it.

Monkfish in Almond and Pine Nut Sauce (continued)

Sprinkle with pine nuts and place in a 400°F oven for about 15 minutes, or until the fish has reached an internal temperature of 145°F. Meanwhile, steam open the clams, if using, in a covered pan with a few tablespoons water. Arrange the clams in the casserole, sprinkle with parsley, and serve.

MERLUZA CASA LUCIO
(Hake with Tomatoes and Brandy)

This dish is typical of the down-to-earth cooking in Casa Lucio (see p. 250) and of the simple fish preparations found in Madrid that enhance rather than mask the natural flavor of the fish. The sauce ingredients are certainly not unusual, but somehow produce an exceptional medley of flavors.

Serves 4

¼ cup extra virgin olive oil
2 large onions, finely chopped
2 medium tomatoes, skinned, seeded, and chopped
2 cloves garlic, minced
A 2-inch piece dried red chile pepper, seeded
½ teaspoon paprika
Salt
Freshly ground pepper
¼ cup brandy
¼ cup Fish Broth (p. 175) or

3 tablespoons clam juice diluted with 1 tablespoon water
2 pounds scrod or hake, about 1 inch thick
12 medium-large shrimp, shelled
2 dozen cockles or Manila clams or 1 dozen very small littleneck clams, cleansed (see p. 33)

In a shallow casserole, preferably earthenware, heat 2 tablespoons of the oil and sauté the onions for a minute or two. Cover and cook very slowly for 15 minutes more (the onions should not brown). Turn up the heat, add the tomatoes, garlic, hot pepper, paprika, salt, and pepper, and cook a minute. Stir in the brandy and simmer 5 minutes, then add the Fish Broth and cook 2 minutes more.

Sprinkle the fish on both sides with salt. In a skillet, heat the remaining 2 tablespoons oil, quickly sear the fish, and remove to a warm platter. Add to the skillet the shrimp and sauté briefly, just until they are opaque, and remove to the platter. Then add the clams and ¼ cup water, cover, and cook over a medium-high flame, removing the clams to the platter as they open.

Add the fish to the casserole and bake in a 350°F oven for about 5 to 8 minutes, or until the fish is just cooked (about 145°F internal temperature). Arrange the clams and shrimp in the casserole and return to the oven just long enough to warm them.

Poultry ❦ Game ❦ Meats

POLLO AL AJILLO CASA LUCIO
(Garlic Chicken)

I have always maintained that Casa Lucio (see p. 250) has the best garlic chicken I have ever tasted, due in part to the free-range chickens that Lucio insists on using ("They are bred in Burgos," he boasts, "then walk all the way to Madrid"). Contrary to most garlic chicken recipes (you will find others in this and other chapters) Lucio's has no garlic sauce; it is a garlic-flavored chicken that is greaseless, crisp, and very quick to prepare (since the chicken is cut in very small pieces, it cooks, over a high flame, in the same time it takes to brown). Once the chicken is done, Lucio sometimes coats the chicken with extra garlic, and a little saffron, vinegar, and/or wine before serving, which add a last-minute punch of flavor.   *Serves 4*

A 3-pound chicken, preferably
   free-range
Kosher or sea salt
Olive oil for frying
1 head garlic, divided into
   cloves, unpeeled, lightly
   crushed

2 cloves garlic, minced
1 teaspoon wine vinegar
1 tablespoon dry white wine
1 tablespoon chicken broth
Several strands of saffron,
   crumbled

Cut the chicken wings in two parts, discarding the tips. Hack off the bony end of the legs. Divide the remainder of the chicken into quarters, then hack or cut with kitchen shears into 2-inch pieces. Sprinkle well with salt on both sides and let sit 10 minutes.

Garlic Chicken (continued)

Heat the olive oil (it should be ¼ to ½ inch deep) in a large skillet until very hot. Add the chicken and the garlic cloves and cook over a high flame, shaking and turning the pieces frequently for about 12 to 13 minutes, until the chicken is well browned and cooked through. Drain the chicken in a mesh strainer, discarding the oil.

In the skillet in which the chicken has cooked combine the minced garlic, vinegar, wine, chicken broth, saffron, and a pinch of salt. Bring to a boil, add the chicken pieces, and toss until the liquid is absorbed.

POLLO AL AJILLO CON LIMÓN
(Chicken with Garlic and Lemon)

START PREPARATION 2 HOURS IN ADVANCE

A lemon-marinated broiled chicken from the nuns of the Santa Clara Monastery in Burgos that is an extremely simple but most appealing preparation.   *Serves 4*

A 3–3½-pound chicken	2 tablespoons freshly squeezed
5 cloves garlic, peeled	lemon juice
1 tablespoon minced parsley	¼ cup extra virgin olive oil
1½ teaspoons thyme leaves or	¼ cup dry white wine
¼ teaspoon dried	Freshly ground pepper
Salt	

Cut the chicken into small serving pieces, detaching the wings and legs and dividing the breast in 4 pieces and each thigh in half crosswise.

In a mortar or mini processor, mash to a paste the garlic, parsley, thyme, and ¼ teaspoon salt. Stir in the lemon juice, oil, and wine. Arrange the chicken pieces in a shallow ovenproof casserole. Pour the mortar mixture over the chicken and marinate 2 hours.

Heat the broiler. Remove the chicken from the marinade (leave the marinade in the casserole) and place skin side down on a broiler tray about 3 inches from the flame. Broil 5 minutes, or until browned. Turn, baste with the marinade, and broil 5 minutes more.

Return the chicken, skin side up, to the marinade in the casserole. Season with salt and pepper and place in a 400°F oven for 15 minutes, basting occasionally.

POLLO AL AJILLO CON VINO
(Garlic Chicken with Wine)

This is how garlic chicken is made in the historic university town of Alcalá de Henares in the province of Madrid. *Serves 4*

A 3–3½-pound chicken
Kosher or sea salt
2 tablespoons olive oil
4 cloves garlic, sliced
1 tablespoon wine vinegar
1 bay leaf
¼ cup dry white wine
A 1-inch piece dried red chile
  pepper, seeded, or

¼ teaspoon crushed red
  pepper
¼ teaspoon paprika
Freshly ground pepper
Pinch of sugar
1 tablespoon minced parsley

Cut the chicken into small serving pieces, detaching the wings and legs and dividing the breast in 4 pieces and each thigh in half crosswise.

Sprinkle the chicken pieces with salt. Heat the oil in a large shallow casserole, add the chicken, and brown well on all sides. Add the garlic and cook until it just begins to color. Add the vinegar and boil it away, then mix in the bay leaf, wine, chile pepper, paprika, pepper, sugar, and parsley. Cover, simmer for 45 minutes, and serve.

POLLO AL VINO
(Roast Chicken in Wine Sauce)

In this chicken recipe the Paúles monks of Tardajos in Burgos province recombine familiar, everyday ingredients into a great dish with a delicious sauce, quite unlike others that may have similar ingredients. *Serves 4*

Roast Chicken in Wine Sauce (continued)

A 3–3½-pound chicken, cut in
   small serving pieces
Lemon juice
Kosher or sea salt
Freshly ground pepper
1 small–medium onion, in
   coarse slivers

2 cloves garlic, minced
2 tablespoons minced parsley
2 tablespoons olive oil
¼ cup dry white wine
Chicken broth

In a roasting pan, arrange the chicken pieces. Sprinkle with lemon juice, salt, and pepper. Scatter the slivered onion around the pan.

In a mortar or mini processor, mash to a paste the garlic, parsley, and a little salt and pepper. Stir in the oil and the wine. Pour over the chicken and roast at 350°F for about 50 minutes, adding some chicken broth if the liquid evaporates. Make sure there is always some liquid in the pan. Serve, spooning the sauce over the chicken.

POLLO ENCEBOLLADO
(Braised Chicken and Onion)

A down-to-earth chicken dish that owes its great taste to a goodly amount of onion and garlic.   *Serves 4*

A 3–3½-pound chicken
Kosher or sea salt
Freshly ground pepper
5 cloves garlic, minced

2 tablespoons minced parsley
½ cup dry white wine
3 tablespoons olive oil
2 medium onions, chopped

Cut the chicken into small serving pieces, detaching the wings and legs and dividing the breast in 4 pieces and each thigh in half crosswise. Sprinkle on both sides with salt and pepper.

In a mortar or mini processor, mash the garlic, parsley, and ⅛ teaspoon salt to a paste. Stir in the wine and reserve.

Heat the oil in a shallow casserole and brown the chicken on all sides. Add the onions and continue cooking until they have softened. Stir the mortar mixture into the casserole, cover, and simmer 45 minutes.

CONEJO MIRABEL
(Marinated Rabbit in Sherry Sauce)

START PREPARATION 3 DAYS IN ADVANCE

Another great dish from Fray Juan (see p. 229) of the Guadalupe Monastery, whose recipes always seem to bring out the best in foods. In this instance, rabbit (or chicken if you wish) is marinated for several days in sherry, garlic, and herbs, then simmered in the marinade, which becomes an outstanding sauce. Fray Juan recommends serving the rabbit with oven-roasted potatoes (such as those on p. 247) and a spicy escarole salad (use the recipe on p. 128, eliminating the pan juices and adding to the dressing 1 garlic clove, mashed to a paste, and several drops of Tabasco).

Serves 3–4

A 2½–3-pound rabbit, cut in
    serving pieces

MARINADE

2 cloves garlic, minced	1½ teaspoons minced rosemary
1 bay leaf	leaves or ¼ teaspoon dried
1½ teaspoons thyme leaves or	Freshly ground pepper
¼ teaspoon dried	½ cup dry Spanish sherry (*fino*)
1½ teaspoons minced marjoram	
leaves or ¼ teaspoon dried	

． ． ．

Salt	2 cloves garlic, minced
Freshly ground pepper	1 teaspoon flour
2 tablespoons olive oil	A 1-inch piece, or to taste,
1 small onion, cut in slivers	dried red chile pepper

Arrange the rabbit in a shallow bowl. Combine the marinade ingredients and pour over the rabbit. Cover and marinate 3 days in the refrigerator, turning the rabbit occasionally. Remove the rabbit (leaving the marinade in the bowl), drain, and dry on paper towels. Sprinkle with salt and pepper.

Heat 1 tablespoon of the oil in a shallow casserole and slowly sauté the

Marinated Rabbit in Sherry Sauce (continued)

onion and garlic until the onion is translucent. Stir in the flour and add this mixture to the marinade. Wipe out the casserole.

Heat the remaining tablespoon of oil in the casserole and sauté the rabbit pieces over a medium-high flame for 10 to 15 minutes, or until well browned. Pour in the marinade, add the chile pepper, cover, and simmer about 30 minutes, or until the rabbit is done.

PERDIZ EN ESCABECHE
(Marinated Partridge)

PREPARE SEVERAL DAYS IN ADVANCE

Spain is game country, and preserving the hunt in *escabeche* has long been a Spanish tradition. Partridge, in particular, marinated in vinegar, herbs, and garlic, is deliciously refreshing and particularly appealing in summer.

Some versions I find a bit heavy on vinegar, but never have I tasted a more delicate *escabeche* than this one, prepared by chef Fermín Merino Sánchez of the parador of Albacete in the region of La Mancha. A diminutive man, almost elf-like, with a deeply creased and weathered face that frequently crinkles up into a broad smile, Fermín has worked for the paradors most of his life, principally in this magnificent one—a grange that centers around a beautiful patio and hallways that overflow with the healthiest plants I have ever seen. Fermín proudly led me to his kitchen to better explain exactly how he makes the partridge. One of his secrets is the extravagant amount of saffron he uses.

This marinade serves equally well for quail, and Fermín also likes it with chicken. *Serves 4*

2 partridges, split, 8 quail, whole and trussed, or 2 Cornish hens, split	½ teaspoon salt
	3 bay leaves
	10 peppercorns
2 cups water	2 sprigs rosemary or
1 cup chicken broth	¼ teaspoon dried
1 head garlic, separated and peeled	4 springs thyme or
	¼ teaspoon dried

1 cup white or amber wine vinegar	½ teaspoon crumbled thread saffron

Place the birds breast down in a shallow casserole. Add all other ingredients except the saffron and bring to a boil. Cover and simmer 1 hour.

Transfer the birds to a bowl or other container in which they fit snugly. Remove the garlic from the casserole and transfer to a processor. Leave the bay leaves and cooking liquid in the casserole. Add the saffron and 3 tablespoons of the cooking liquid to the processor and blend. With the motor running, gradually add just enough more cooking liquid to form a purée. Combine this mixture with the cooking liquid remaining in the casserole and taste for salt.

Pour the marinade over the birds (it should cover them). Cover and refrigerate. The dish is ready to eat after several days, but will keep for several weeks. Bring to room temperature before serving. Good accompaniments are boiled and cooled small new or red potatoes and Sautéed Red Peppers (p. 139), also at room temperature.

PERDIZ A LA TOLEDANA
(Partridge in White Wine Sauce, Toledo Style)

Small game birds abound in Spain, where the climate and terrain are ideal for quail, partridge, and pheasant. Every fall hunters gather from around the globe, and they concentrate on the hilly land of eastern Andalucía and the area of La Mancha around Toledo, the province that is famous for the way it cooks partridge. There's not much to the recipe—this one, in fact, is slightly more elaborate than some—but the sauce has a wonderfully rich flavor.

Serves 4

Partridge Toledo Style (continued)

2 partridges, or other small
   game birds like pheasant
Salt
Freshly ground pepper
2 tablespoons olive oil
1 large onion, finely chopped
12 cloves garlic, lightly
   smashed and peeled
2 tablespoons chopped leek or
   scallion, white part only
2 tablespoons brandy

1 tablespoon wine vinegar
1 cup dry white wine
1 carrot, trimmed, scraped, and
   cut in 4 pieces
Few strands of saffron
1 bay leaf
4 peppercorns
1 tablespoon minced parsley
1½ teaspoons thyme leaves or
   ¼ teaspoon dried

Sprinkle the partridges inside and out with salt and pepper. Truss. Heat 1 tablespoon of the oil in a stewpot in which the birds will fit closely, and brown the partridges on all sides. Stir in the remaining tablespoon oil, the onion, garlic, and leek and sauté until the onion has wilted. Add the brandy and carefully ignite. When the flames die, mix in all the remaining ingredients. Salt to taste, cover, and simmer about 1½ hours, adding a little water or chicken broth if necessary and turning the partridge occasionally.

Remove the birds to a warm platter and strain the sauce, pushing with the back of a wooden spoon to extract as much of the solid material as possible. Serve a half partridge per person and spoon on the sauce.

CHULETAS DE CERDO AL HORNO CON AJO Y LIMÓN
(Baked Pork Chops with Garlic and Lemon)

Redolent with garlic, these pork chops will fill your kitchen with the most enticing aromas.   *Serves 4*

8 cloves garlic
4 tablespoons (¼ cup) minced
   parsley
Salt
¼ cup olive oil

¼ cup freshly squeezed lemon
   juice
3 medium baking potatoes, in
   ⅛-inch slices
Freshly ground pepper

4 pork chops, about 1¼–1½   ¼ cup chicken broth
    inches thick

Mash to a paste in a mortar or mini processor the garlic, parsley, and ¼ teaspoon salt. Stir in 3 tablespoons of the oil and the lemon juice. Spread 2 teaspoons of this mixture over the bottom of a shallow casserole and arrange
half of the potato slices in the casserole. Sprinkle with salt and pepper. Brush
with a little of the mortar mixture.

    In a skillet, heat the remaining tablespoon of oil and sear the chops on
both sides. Sprinkle with salt and pepper, brush with the mortar mixture, and
place the chops over the potatoes. Arrange the remaining potatoes over the
chops, sprinkle with salt and pepper, and spoon on the remaining garlic mixture. Add the chicken broth, cover, and bake at 350°F for 45 to 60 minutes,
or until the potatoes are tender.

Jamón Jamón:
The Cult of Mountain Cured Ham

A recent Spanish film with the odd title *Jamón Jamón* ("Ham, Ham")
was so named because its director believed that the passion for cured
ham in Spain—approaching cult status—was the perfect metaphor for
contemporary Spanish life. Indeed, *jamón* is eaten all over the country
with abandon, without a thought to its extraordinary price, somewhat
in the manner that Spaniards often like to live their lives—for the moment, with little regard to consequences and not much thought of the
future.

    Caviar, fois gras, truffles—nothing is quite so tempting to a
Spaniard as *jamón*. And although *jamón* is the generic word for any
kind of ham, be it baked, boiled, or cured, in practice the word by itself, without further qualifiers, is understood to mean Spain's exceptional cured ham. It may also be called *jamón serrano*, a general term for
mountain cured ham, or *jamón ibérico*, referring to the sublime, nutty,

Jamón Jamón (continued)

top-of-the-line ham from native black-hoofed Iberian pigs raised on a steady diet of acorns. *Ibérico* hams, it is generally agreed—even by Italians partial to prosciutto—surpass in flavor and texture any of the finest cured hams made elsewhere in the world.

Jamón is in great demand as a tapa, thinly sliced, and whole hams by the dozens hang from the rafters in most bars and taverns and in many restaurants. It is ordered as a matter of course by restaurant diners as a sensual and seductive nibble while awaiting other foods. But *jamón* is also a key ingredient in Spanish cooking. You will find countless recipes calling for a tablespoon or two of chopped *jamón*; indeed, it greatly enriches the flavor of so many dishes, from tapas and vegetables, to chicken, meat, and fish courses. Ham bones, once stripped of their exquisite meat, enhance soups and stews. *Jamón* is one of the secrets to the wonderful flavor of Spanish food, and a Spanish kitchen would never be without *jamón*, no matter what its price.

Since mountain cured ham imported from Spain is at present very difficult to find in this country (and "Spanish" or "Serrano" style hams made here at times do not taste at all like the real thing), prosciutto is a good substitute. Note that most recipes do not call for ham in thin slices, but diced, and to do this you will need a slice at least ⅛ inch thick. Some recipes for stews and soups may call for a chunk of ham, and your best bet is to buy the narrow end of the ham (I often purchase it at a substantial reduction in price since it is the least desirable part of the ham for slicing). Another possibility is capicollo—pork that is cured like ham but comes from the loin instead of the leg. It has a narrow shape like a salami and can easily be cut in thick slices.

LOMO DE CERDO EN ADOBO
(Marinated Pork Loin)

START PREPARATION 1 DAY IN ADVANCE

All over Spain, but especially in the central plains, pork loin marinated in garlic, herbs, and paprika is a staple. It is delicious sliced, sautéed, and served with oven-roasted potatoes (p. 247) or puréed potatoes (p. 72). And it also makes a great tapa (p. 57). *Serves 4*

MARINADE

5 cloves garlic, crushed to a paste in a mortar or garlic press
4 tablespoons (¼ cup) minced oregano leaves or 2 teaspoons dried
1½ teaspoons thyme leaves or ¼ teaspoon dried

1 tablespoon dry white wine
1 tablespoon imported sweet paprika
⅛ teaspoon salt
Freshly ground pepper
1 tablespoon minced parsley
5 tablespoons extra virgin olive oil

. . .

1¼ pounds lean boneless pork loin

Combine in a bowl the Marinade ingredients. Add the meat and turn to coat on all sides. Cover and refrigerate at least 24 hours, turning occasionally.

Cut the meat in ½-inch slices, allowing some of the marinade to cling to the meat. Coat a skillet or griddle with olive oil and heat to the smoking point. Brown the meat on both sides, reduce the flame to medium, and continue cooking until the meat is just done.

Roast Lamb and Suckling Pig: Gastronomic Stars of the Spanish Plains

When weekends and holidays come around, the roads from Madrid are choked with cars of city dwellers making their exodus to the countryside. Many are off to second homes, but just as many may be on their way to feast on the great delicacies of the Castilian heartland: roast baby lamb and suckling pig. Once the privilege of nobility, the satisfaction of savoring the succulent meat and crackling skin of these animals, as young as three weeks old, is now open to everyone. Neither the baby lambs nor the pigs have consumed anything but mother's milk, which, in the case of the lamb, imparts the flavors of the aromatic plants on which their mothers have grazed. Both lamb and pig are placed in oval earthenware casseroles and roasted in brick vaulted baker's ovens, heated by smoldering fragrant woods. The roasts need no condiment save a dash of salt and are so tender that they can be cut without the aid of a knife.

You may be surprised to find that I have not included recipes for either of these delectable roasts, simply because you just can't find animals this young and with similar flavor; anything older produces an entirely different dish. So I leave it to you when traveling in Spain to visit the province of Segovia in particular and perhaps stop at Casa Cándido in the city of Segovia for its suckling pig, which has been renowned for centuries. Then travel to Sepúlveda to our friend Tinín's rustic restaurant, Figón Zute El Mayor "Tinín," for the best roast baby lamb. You can find more information on this long and venerable Castilian tradition and more restaurant listings in my book *Discovering Spain: An Uncommon Guide*.

CHULETILLAS DE CORDERO A LA PARRILLA
(Grilled Baby Lamb Chops)

What pass for baby rib lamb chops in America are never quite as tiny as those in Spain, which are hardly a mouthful. The smallest I have been able to find are sold as rack of lamb and need only to be sliced into chops. They are best cooked over charcoal (with the sprigs of herbs, which give additional subtle flavor); otherwise use a stovetop griddle.   *Serves 4*

> Baby rib lamb chops, ¾–1-inch   Salt
>   thick (about 3 per portion)   1 clove garlic, minced
> Olive oil   1 tablespoon minced parsley
> A bunch of rosemary and/or
>   thyme sprigs, dampened
>   (optional)

Brush the chops on both sides with oil. Scatter the optional dampened rosemary and thyme sprigs over the hot coals, then place the chops on the barbecue grill. Cook until done to taste, turning once, and remove to a warm platter. Sprinkle with salt, then with the garlic and parsley. Serve with Patatas Panaderas (p. 247).

CALDERETA DE CORDERO EXTREMEÑO
(Lamb Stew, Extremeño Style)

This lamb stew from the restaurant of the Guadalupe Monastery (see p. 229) is a common country dish in Extremadura, but everyday dishes are sometimes the most difficult to find perfectly prepared. In this splendid version, it is the mortar mixture of garlic, onion, peppercorns, and red pepper that gives the dish an uncommon touch.   *Serves 4*

Lamb Stew (continued)

2 tablespoons olive oil
6 cloves garlic, peeled
1 small onion, slivered
About 3½ pounds lamb stew
    meat with bones, or
    2 pounds boneless, cut in
    1½–2-inch pieces
3 bay leaves
¾ teaspoon imported sweet
    paprika

Salt
¾ cup dry full-bodied red wine
1½ tablespoons wine vinegar
¾ cup chicken broth
6 peppercorns
2 tablespoons finely chopped
    fresh red pepper

Heat the oil in a stewpot and sauté the garlic and onion until the onion has softened. Remove the garlic and onion and reserve. Add the meat, bay leaves, and paprika to the pot and mix well. Brown the meat lightly and sprinkle with salt. Stir in the wine and vinegar, turn up the flame, and cook away the liquid. Stir in ½ cup of the broth, cover, and cook 1 hour, or until the meat is almost tender.

Meanwhile, in a mortar or mini processor mash to a paste the reserved garlic and onion, the peppercorns, and red pepper. Stir into the stew along with the remaining ¼ cup broth and cook about 30 minutes more, or until the meat is tender.

FRITE CACEREÑO
(Sautéed Marinated Lamb)

START PREPARATION 2 HOURS IN ADVANCE

A specialty of the province of Cáceres and in particular of the Restaurante Pizarro on the main square in historic Trujillo, a splendid town filled with noble homes and palaces from the times of the conquest of America. This spotless and beautifully appointed restaurant, lovingly cared for by Isabel Carrasco, has been in her family for more than sixty years, and looks out upon the magnificent palace of the brother of native son Francisco Pizarro, who left here a desperately poor man and returned from America with fabulous riches.   *Serves 4*

1¾–2 pounds boneless leg of
    lamb, in 1½-inch cubes
1 bay leaf, crumbled
4 cloves garlic, peeled
Salt
Freshly ground pepper

1 tablespoon paprika
1 tablespoon minced oregano
    leaves or ½ teaspoon dried
½ cup olive oil
2 cloves garlic, unpeeled and
    lightly smashed

Place the meat in a bowl. Mash to a paste in a mortar or mini processor the bay leaf, peeled garlic, ⅛ teaspoon salt, pepper, paprika, and oregano. Gradually stir in 6 tablespoons of the oil and pour the mixture over the meat, stirring to coat well. Cover and marinate 2 hours.

Heat the remaining 2 tablespoons oil in a skillet and sauté the unpeeled garlic until golden, pressing with the back of a wooden spoon to extract its flavor. Discard the garlic. Add the meat and cook over a medium flame until browned outside but still lightly pink within. Sprinkle with salt and serve.

SOLOMILLO AL AJO TOSTADO
(Filet Mignon with Toasted Garlic Mayonnaise)

Filet mignon lacks the robust flavor of other cuts of beef and can be bland, but not in this preparation from Tomás Herranz (see p. 241) of the Cenador del Prado restaurant in Madrid. He coats the meat with a garlicky mayonnaise, then runs it under the broiler.   *Serves 4*

4 filets mignons
6 tablespoons Garlic
    Mayonnaise (p. 196)

Parsley sprigs for garnish

Pan-fry or broil the filets mignons until done to taste. Coat each filet with about 1½ tablespoons of the Garlic Mayonnaise and quickly run under the broiler until the mayonnaise topping is lightly browned. Garnish with parsley sprigs.

Desserts

FRESONES AL VINAGRE
(Strawberries with Sugar and Vinegar)

An extremely simple fruit preparation that comes from an Augustinian monastery in Burgos: strawberries in a sugar syrup, given an interesting new twist by the addition of a little vinegar.   *Serves 4*

    1½ pounds medium-size straw-   6 tablespoons sugar
        berries, hulled and quar-   1 tablespoon red wine vinegar
        tered, or small whole
        strawberries

In a bowl mix the strawberries with the sugar. Cover and let sit at room temperature for 30 minutes. Stir in the vinegar and refrigerate 2 hours. Serve, if you wish, drizzled with heavy cream or topped with a dollop of whipped cream.

BAYAS CON CREMA DE YOGURT
(Summer Berries with Yogurt Cream)

Leave it to the frugal, practical, and inventive monks of Spain—in this case, the Claretians (Claretianos) from Aranda de Duero in Castile—to come up with a rich creamy dessert that is simplicity itself and can be put together in less than 5 minutes. The berries are my addition, being, I think, the perfect flavor complement.   *Serves 6*

    ¾ cup plain yogurt   3 cups berries (such as blueber-
    ¾ cup Dulce de Leche (p. 277)   ries, raspberries, and/or
        or sweetened condensed   blackberries)
        milk   6 mint leaves for garnish
    ¼ cup lemon juice   (optional)

In a bowl, lightly whisk together the yogurt, Dulce de Leche, and lemon juice. Chill well. Spoon the yogurt mixture in the center of 6 dessert dishes and arrange the berries around each dish. Garnish with mint leaves, if you like.

DULCE DE LECHE
(Sweet Cream of Milk)

Sweetened canned condensed milk has been a staple in Spain for decades. It naturally tastes fresher and more pure if you make your own—an effortless process—and you can use it to make Summer Berries with Yogurt Cream (p. 276) and Caramelized Condensed Milk (recipe follows).

Makes about 1½ cups

1 quart whole milk   1 cup sugar

In a saucepan, combine the milk and sugar and bring to a boil. Lower the heat to a high simmer and cook, stirring frequently, until thickened to the consistency of condensed milk and slightly darkened in color, about 1 hour.

LECHE CONDENSADA AL CARAMELO
(Caramelized Condensed Milk)

My husband grew up in Madrid with this artless confection and every so often develops a craving for it. There's nothing to it—just an unopened can of condensed milk cooked in boiling water—but the result is like chewy caramel candy. Few can resist it. We keep it in the refrigerator and take a spoonful every time we pass by, although you may also spread it on plain cookies, dip apple wedges in it, or serve it over ice cream. If you wish, you can make your own condensed milk, pour it into a jar in which it just fits, and cover with foil, then proceed as described below.

Caramelized Condensed Milk (continued)

> A 14-ounce can sweetened
>   condensed milk or 1½ cups
>   Dulce de Leche (p. 277)

Remove the paper label from the unopened can of condensed milk and place the can on its side in a saucepan with water to cover. If using Dulce de Leche, prepare and pour into a jar. Cover tightly with foil and place in a saucepan with water that comes up ¾ of the jar.

Bring the water to a boil and simmer about 2½ hours, adding more water as necessary (make sure a closed can is always covered by water). Remove from the water and cool (if made in a closed can, do not open until cool, and if the milk is not caramelized enough, return the open can, standing upright, to the water and continue cooking).

PASTA FLORA
(Powdered Sugar Cookies)

A requisite visit for me in Madrid is the city's oldest bakery, Pastelería del Pozo, founded in 1830. It's tiny—bakers can be seen from the street through screening, expertly patting and rolling dough—and their cakes and pastries are those that have long been traditional in Madrid.

However, I always come specifically to buy boxes of Pasta Flora, a crumbly cookie that I find addictive. It is classically made with lard, which was, and continues to be, a typical dessert shortening. Lard (available in most supermarkets, but better when homemade) gives these cookies a very special flavor, but if you wish you can substitute vegetable shortening. (See box on page 159 for more about lard.)   *Makes 30*

2½ cups flour	¼ cup dry white wine
1 tablespoon cinnamon	Confectioners' sugar for
¼ cup granulated sugar	dusting
½ pound lard, softened	

In a large bowl, mix together 2 cups of the flour, the cinnamon, and the granulated sugar. With your hands work in the lard, then mix in the wine. Add the remaining ½ cup flour or enough to make a dough that can be rolled. Roll on a floured board ¼ inch thick and cut with a 2½-inch scalloped-edge cookie cutter. Arrange on a lightly greased cookie sheet and bake at 400°F on the upper rack of an oven until well browned—about 8 to 10 minutes. Cool slightly, then coat heavily on both sides with confectioners' sugar.

MANTECADOS DE VINO CASTELLANOS
(Powdered Sugar Cookies)

START PREPARATION SEVERAL HOURS IN ADVANCE

This kind of cookie—light, delicate, and flaky— relies on flour, wine, and lard. There is no sugar in the dough, but the cookies are coated with confectioners' sugar after baking. It is a cookie basic to the sweets of central Spain.

Makes about 16

½ pound lard, vegetable short-
    ening, or butter
½ cup dry white wine

2 cups flour
Sifted confectioners' sugar for
    dusting

With an electric beater, beat the lard until light and fluffy. Beat in the wine, then gradually stir in the flour until the dough holds together. Remove the dough from the bowl and pat between your hands to make a smooth shape.

Roll the dough ⅜ inch thick and cut in 2½-inch circles (preferably with a fluted-edge cookie cutter). Arrange on a greased cookie sheet and let sit, uncovered, for several hours. Bake at 350°F for 15 to 20 minutes, or until the cookies are lightly golden. Cool, then coat heavily with confectioners' sugar.

MANTECADOS OSSA DE MONTIEL
(Flaky Sugar Cookies)

We were in the nondescript town of Ossa de Montiel in the province of Albacete putting together a picnic lunch that we would eat that afternoon by the banks of the bright turquoise Ruidera lakes, just a few minutes away. After a stop at the grocers for cold cuts, cheese, and such, we searched for the local bakery and found it tucked away off the main street in a cul-de-sac. The bread was exceptionally moist and crusty and the thick flaky cookies irresistible. Neither survived the ride to the lakes untouched. May I emphasize once more that lard, despite its unattractive connotation, is nothing but another form of animal fat, but with less cholesterol than butter (see box, p. 159). It produces short cookies and lends a distinctive flavor.

Makes about 14

¼ pound lard or vegetable shortening
¼ cup sugar
1 teaspoon anisette liqueur
1 tablespoon dry white wine
1¼ cups flour
1 egg, lightly beaten
Granulated sugar for sprinkling

Beat in an electric mixer the lard and the sugar until the mixture is light and fluffy, then beat in the anisette and wine. Stir in the flour.

Roll the dough on a floured surface ¾ inch thick. Cut with a 1½-inch fluted-edge cookie cutter and arrange on a lightly greased cookie sheet. Brush with the beaten egg and sprinkle each cookie with about ¼ teaspoon sugar. Bake in a 300°F oven for about 30 minutes, or until golden.

TORRIJAS TABERNA DE ANTONIO SÁNCHEZ
(Crisply Sautéed Bread in Honey Syrup)

Torrijas, closely related to what we call French toast, can be delightful creations when well made and, most importantly, freshly made. Too often what you find is cold and soggy and not very appealing. The bread used to make *torrijas* affects the outcome—it should be a day old and fairly fine textured. *Torrijas* are great any time of day, from breakfast to afternoon snack, to evening dessert.

La Taberna de Antonio Sánchez, a historic tavern in Madrid that has a distinctive patina of age enhanced by mahogany-colored walls, achieved fame in the first few decades of this century in part because of its memorable *torrijas*. Owned by a retired bullfighter, who became an artist and filled the tavern with his paintings and bullfight memorabilia, it was also a gathering place for Madrid's literati. Today the tavern's *torrijas* have lost their luster (although the recipe survives), but La Taberna de Antonio Sánchez is nevertheless a wonderful place that recalls Madrid of times past and serves good tapas.   *Serves 4*

1 egg
1 tablespoon sugar
⅛ teaspoon cinnamon
1 cup milk
Peel of ½ lemon, in several
    strips

4 dense but fine-textured slices
    of day-old country bread,
    approximately 3 x 4 inches
    and 1 inch thick

HONEY SYRUP

¼ cup water
2 tablespoons sugar
⅛ teaspoon cinnamon

2 tablespoons honey
Peel of ¼ lemon, in several
    strips

· · ·

Mild olive oil for frying

In a saucepan, whisk together the egg, sugar, and cinnamon. Stir in the milk and lemon peel. Heat over a medium-low flame, stirring constantly, until the mixture begins to bubble and has reached the thickness of a soft custard. Cool, remove the lemon peel, and pour into a large deep plate (the custard should not be too thick—thin if necessary with milk). Add the bread slices and let them sit 30 minutes, turning occasionally. All the custard should be absorbed.

Meanwhile, make the syrup. Combine all ingredients in a small saucepan, bring to a boil, and simmer 5 minutes. Cool and discard the lemon peel.

Transfer the bread slices to a cake rack to dry for 10 minutes. Pour oil in a skillet to a depth of ⅛ inch and heat until the oil browns a cube of bread. Add the bread slices and sauté over a medium flame until golden. Turn and brown the other side. Drain on paper towels and serve bathed in the syrup.

ALMENDRAS DE ALCALÁ
(Candied Almonds)

Visitors come to Alcalá de Henares to see the sensational Plateresque architecture of its old university, but few will leave without passing through one
of the city's many candy shops to purchase these celebrated sugar-coated
almonds.

1 cup almonds with skins	1 cup water
1 cup sugar	¼ teaspoon cinnamon

Line a cookie sheet with a greased piece of foil. In a skillet, mix together all
ingredients and boil over a high flame, stirring constantly, until the sugar
crystallizes.

Spread the mixture on the cookie tray, separating it into individual
sugar-coated almonds. Cool.

CHAPTER 6

Southeastern Coastal Spain (El Levante)

REGION OF THE RICES

e were on our way to Tasca del Puerto restaurant in the provincial capital of Castellón de la Plana with a craving for *arroz negro*, a rich dish flavored and colored by squid ink, that was so compelling we could almost taste it. It was already four o'clock, approaching the end of Spanish lunch hour, and we still had a long way to go, but there was no way we were going to forsake our black rice. We stopped to phone our good friend Chimo, co-owner of Tasca del Puerto, and he assured us that the chef would await our arrival. Finally we were there, and the *arroz negro*, served with an eye-opening garlic mayonnaise, was as stunningly good as we expected it to be.

That day of long hours and high speed driving is engraved in our minds as a symbol of the lengths to which we will go for our favorite rice dishes. There was another instance when our sights were fixed on *arroz a banda* at El Pegolí in Denia, a simple beachside restaurant we have known for years. The one-lane road we took from Valencia, our only possible route at the time, was clogged with the cars of vacationers leaving the beaches and of residents heading home for lunch. We literally inched along but refused to give up hope, and by sheer chance we arrived just before the restaurant closed, secured a table, thanks to my husband's considerable powers of persuasion, and were served the menu that everyone was eating: a platter of simply boiled and cooled shellfish from local waters, followed by *arroz a banda*, or "rice on its own," a name that certainly does no justice to this paragon of rice dishes. It is, as its name suggests, completely unadorned, with none of the tasty morsels of meat and seafood common to other paella-style dishes, and yet it is the very essence of what eating rice in this region is all about. Any self-respecting native of the Levante, as this southeastern coast of Spain is traditionally called, will tell you that the focal point of a Spanish rice dish must always be the rice.

It was the Moors who made rice growing possible in this region more than a millennium ago when they established elaborate irrigation systems to regulate the flow of water to the flat, fertile delta lands created by silting from two of Spain's major rivers, the Turia and Júcar. The Moors subsequently introduced both rice and saffron to Spain.

Indeed, irrigation transformed this warm arid region into the "Garden of Spain," where vegetables are harvested throughout the year, typically in small family plots called *huertas*. When the legendary El Cid wrested control of Valencia from the Moors in 1094, he gazed upon these very same orchards that were "lush and grand," as described in the epic poem *El Cantar de Mío Cid*. The climate is also perfect for the orange and lemon trees that yield three crops a year and stretch in endless rows not far from the shimmering Mediterranean Sea. Looming beyond the citrus groves are imposing mountains, where the grapes for Jumilla and Utiel-Requena wines find suitably cool growing conditions. Mild temperatures and boundless sunlight have made El Levante (literally "land of the rising sun") a mecca for European tourists, who flock to its beaches year round.

In El Levante it is not necessary to look very far to find a theme or product that gives the region gastronomic identity. Rice dishes obviously predominate; eating rice is a way of life, and rice fields are a striking feature of the landscape. All this is what brings me back to the Levante time and time again, to eat Spanish rice dishes at their source and to travel leisurely through the flat rice fields—an endless green expanse fed by the vast La Albufera lagoon. Charming whitewashed workers' cabins called *barracas* stand out in striking contrast, while bent laborers in wide-brimmed straw hats and rolled-up trousers tend to the crops. The scene is very much as native son Blasco Ibáñez described it at the beginning of this century in his best-selling novels. One sometimes wonders if this is really Spain or some exotic Eastern land.

I've not really talked about paella, although the black rice and *arroz a banda* that I prize are paellas in everything but name. Paella in Spain's rice country is not a single dish but a diversity of rice dishes prepared paella-style in the typical wide and shallow metal paella pan. Without doubt paella in all its variations is the crowning glory of this region's cooking, a symphony of colors and flavors in which the rice emerges al dente and admits all kinds of additions, from fish and shellfish to meat, poultry, snails, and just about any vegetable from the *huertas* of El Levante.

However, rice in El Levante does not always take the form of paella. The most traditional rice dishes are hearty, soupy rice stews, often made in earthenware casseroles, which include ingredients like dried beans, fresh vegetables, and pork. You will find recipes for many of my favorite rice dishes in this chapter, some of them treasured family recipes given to me by our friends Reme Domínguez and Chimo Boix of Tasca del Puerto restaurant, who in turn inherited them from their mothers and grandmothers. I am confident that with these recipes you will come as close as you can get to Spanish rice dishes in their homeland. The only thing missing is the satisfaction of eating local foods at their source.

Although rice dishes are by far the most outstanding feature of Levante cooking, fine fruits and vegetables grown in the region and fresh-caught seafood from the Mediterranean guarantee the quality and appeal of many other dishes. Murcia in particular is known for its sweet, intensely colored vegetables, which become distinctive first courses when grilled or boiled and dressed with olive oil, salt, and a touch of vinegar or lemon juice. Think of color as key to Levante cooking—altogether appropriate in a region where vividly painted ceramics, extravagantly fashioned Baroque sculpture, and lively fiestas are the very essence of the region's heritage.

Notes on Regional Wines

Wines reaching our shores from the Valencia region have traditionally been low-quality robust jug and bulk wines, which I have always used to make fine sangría. However, today there are several regions that hold promise, particularly the Utiel-Requena appellation of origin, with wines that range from whites to rosés and flavorful reds, and in neighboring Murcia the predominantly red wines of Jumilla are attracting attention.

Saffron: The Gift of Gold

Saffron, a precious, poetic spice more than worth its weight in gold, is as exotic and bewitching today as it was to ancient man. The early Greeks and Romans prized saffron, although it is thought to be native to the East, perhaps Persia. Writers throughout the ages—Aristotle, Homer, Chaucer, and Shakespeare, to name but a few—have referred to saffron's pleasurable qualities (it was said to produce euphoria). When sipped as an infusion saffron was credited with curing a variety of human ailments, from measles to asthma. Saffron also colored cloth a rich yellow, although that practice disappeared when more stable dyes were discovered.

The Moors, with their exquisite sensuality and good taste, rescued saffron from oblivion after the Dark Ages and reintroduced it to Europe in the eighth century by way of the Iberian Peninsula. They planted the saffron crocus in Andalucía, Valencia, and southern Castile and called it *zafaran*, referring to the yellow color saffron produces. The word was later incorporated into most European languages.

Made from the stigmas of a purple autumn crocus, the world's best saffron today comes from Spain, and more specifically from a small area centering around the town of Membrilla in La Mancha, where the ideal microclimate exists. The landscape is dry and colorless, but for a few days in October a dense carpet of purple crocus pushes forth from the parched earth, creating startling brilliance and an intoxicating scent. It is a sight to behold.

There is no time to waste, however, admiring the scene; the flowers have to be picked at dawn before the morning dew dries and the stigmas removed and roasted immediately to conserve flavor and aroma. It's all painstaking hand labor, since no machine has as yet been invented to do the job. Each crocus flower produces just three stigmas; tens of thousands of flowers yield a few ounces of fresh saffron, which may be reduced to a mere ounce after roasting.

Everyone, children and elders alike, pitch in and work through the night if necessary. Salaries are often paid in saffron, and since saffron will not spoil if kept dry and away from light, workers hoard their wealth at home, in drawers and under mattresses. With saffron prices continuing to soar (it can sell for over $6,000 a pound), it's better than money in the bank.

Although there are no bargains when it comes to saffron, fortunately a very small amount goes a long, long way. Saffron's astonishing worth, unfortunately, invites fraud, and buyers must beware of adulterations. It's a good idea to buy saffron strands instead of powder so you know what you are getting (the strands should have a uniformly deep red color), but most importantly, purchase from a reliable and knowledgeable store merchant.

Once you become acquainted with saffron at its best, nothing less will do. Its delicate pale yellow color (bright orange "saffron" rice often found in restaurants has been artificially colored) and its subtle flavor can make an ordinary dish extraordinary. In Spanish cooking a few strands are added to any number of dishes, the most famous being, of course, paella. Saffron is sure to add a touch of glamour and mystery to any meal you prepare.

Salads ❧ Soups ❧ Meals-in-a-Pot Vegetables

ENSALADA DE NARANJAS TASCA DEL PUERTO
(Orange Salad with Onion, Almonds, and Raisins)

It should come as no surprise that a sweet and sour orange salad is a dish of the Valencia region: first because the orange groves of this part of Spain's east coast stretch in mind-boggling rows as far as the eye can see, and second because this was an area where the Moors remained long after they were expelled from the rest of the peninsula. The almonds and the sweet-sour mixture of oranges, raisins, onion, and vinegar are surely a vestige of those far-off times. This version comes from one of my favorite restaurants of the region, Tasca del Puerto (see p. 283) in Castellón de la Plana.

Serves 4

4 teaspoons golden raisins

SALAD DRESSING

3 tablespoons extra virgin olive oil

2 teaspoons red wine vinegar, preferably raspberry-scented

⅛ teaspoon sugar

Salt

Freshly ground pepper

· · ·

4 small oranges, peeled, cored, and seeded, with as much of the pith as possible removed, in ¼-inch slices

20 paper-thin red onion rings

4 teaspoons finely chopped blanched almonds

Mint leaves for garnish

Soak the raisins in warm water to cover for 15 minutes. Drain.

In a small bowl, whisk together the Salad Dressing ingredients. Arrange the orange slices on 4 individual salad plates or on a serving platter. Scatter the onion slices, almonds, and raisins over the oranges and pour on the dressing. Garnish with the mint leaves.

GIRABOIX
(Cod and Vegetable Soup with Alioli*)*

START PREPARATION 3–4 DAYS IN ADVANCE

A dish of very long lineage and typical of the town of Jijona in the province of Alicante, *giraboix* is so firmly established in the region you will find few variations in its preparation. The only ones I have come across are the inclusion of cabbage instead of a vegetable of the thistle family similar to cardoon and the addition of dried white beans. There are also two styles of presentation—one as a thick soup, the other separating the fish and vegetables and serving them as an accompaniment to the soup broth (since the broth is so flavorful, I think it should be appreciated on its own, so I prefer the second method). A pungent *alioli,* which brings the dish to life, is an essential component.   *Serves 4*

½ pound dried boneless salt cod
3 cups Fish Broth (p. 175) or
  2¼ cups clam juice diluted
  with ¾ cup water
3 cups water
¾ pound new or red waxy
  potatoes, peeled and left
  whole, if very small, or cut
  in 1½-inch pieces
2 medium onions, peeled
½ pound broad green beans,
  snapped in halves
1 red bell pepper, very finely
  chopped
1 sweet dried red pepper or
  mild New Mexico style,

seeded, or another fresh
  red pepper plus 1 teaspoon
  paprika
10 cloves garlic, minced
A 2-inch piece, or to taste,
  dried red chile pepper,
  seeded
A ½-pound wedge of cabbage
2 medium tomatoes
Salt
8–12 bread slices, cut from a
  long narrow loaf, about
  ½ inch thick
Alioli (p. 302)

Cod and Vegetable Soup (continued)

Soak the cod in cold water to cover in the refrigerator for 2 to 3 days, changing water once or twice daily, until desalted to taste. Drain, then cut in 4
pieces. Add to a soup pot the Fish Broth, water, cod, potatoes, onions, green
beans, fresh red pepper, dried red pepper, garlic, chile pepper, cabbage,
tomatoes, and salt. Bring to a boil, cover, and simmer 1 hour. Meanwhile,
toast the bread on a cookie sheet in a 350°F oven about 10 minutes, or until
golden. Prepare the *alioli* according to instructions and thin with a little of
the soup broth to a thick sauce consistency.

Remove the tomatoes, dried sweet red pepper, and chile pepper, and reserve. Strain the soup, placing the fish, onions (cut in halves), cabbage (in
several chunks), and green beans on a warm platter. Press the tomato and the
dried sweet red pepper and chile pepper through a strainer, passing as much
of the solid matter as possible. Stir into the soup broth and taste for salt.

Pour the broth into 4 wide shallow bowls. Place a dollop of *alioli* on each
toasted bread slice and float in the soup right before serving. At the same time,
serve the fish and vegetables on a platter or small individual dishes and pass
the remaining *alioli* for use with the fish and vegetables (you may also like to
moisten the fish and vegetables in your soup before dipping in the *alioli*).

If you prefer to serve this dish as a thick soup, chop the fish and vegetables and add them to the broth.

POTAJE DE GARBANZOS
(Carmen Pastor's Chickpea Stew)

START PREPARATION 1 DAY IN ADVANCE

A fine family recipe from Carmen Pastor (see p. 324), a stew of chickpeas,
greens, potatoes, and almonds that is great on a cold winter's night.

Serves 6

1 pound dried chickpeas
4 cups water
6 cloves garlic, peeled
2 bay leaves

¼ pound slab bacon or salt
   pork
1 ham or beef bone
2 tablespoons olive oil

Two ¼–½-inch-thick bread
   slices from a long narrow
   loaf
¼ cup diced Spanish mountain
   cured ham or prosciutto, cut
   from a ¼-inch slice
1 medium onion, finely
   chopped
½ teaspoon paprika
1 pound greens, such as Swiss
   chard or collard greens

1 pound small red potatoes
   (about 2-inch diameter),
   peeled, whole, or larger
   potatoes halved or
   quartered
Salt
10 blanched almonds, finely
   chopped
2 hard-boiled eggs

Soak the chickpeas overnight in a large pot of cold water to cover. Drain. Combine in the pot 4 cups water, the garlic, bay leaves, slab bacon, and bone. Bring to a boil, cover, and simmer about 1½ hours.

Meanwhile, in a medium skillet, heat the oil and sauté the bread slices until golden on both sides. Remove and reserve the bread and add to the skillet the ham and onion. Sauté until the onion has wilted, stir in the paprika, and remove from the flame.

Add the onion mixture to the chickpeas, then add the greens, potatoes, and salt to taste and continue cooking 30 minutes more, or until the chickpeas and potatoes are tender.

In a mortar or mini processor combine the sautéed bread, almonds, 2 tablespoons of chickpeas from the pot, and the yolks of the hard-boiled eggs. Mash to a paste. Stir into the stew, cover, and let sit 10 minutes before serving. Divide into soup bowls and garnish with chopped hard-boiled egg white.

ZARANGOLLO RINCÓN DE PEPE
(Stewed Zucchini and Onion)

A somewhat simplified rendition of a dish that often includes tomato, peppers, and potatoes and was a favorite of field workers in Murcia, who could find all its ingredients literally within reach. This recipe comes from Rincón de Pepe (see p. 323), an excellent restaurant in the city of Murcia.

Serves 4

Stewed Zucchini and Onion (continued)

2 tablespoons olive oil	Salt
2 cloves garlic, minced	Freshly ground pepper
1 medium onion, slivered	1 tablespoon minced oregano
½ teaspoon imported sweet paprika	leaves or ½ teaspoon dried
1½ pounds zucchini, in ¼-inch slices	

Heat the oil in a shallow casserole. Sauté the garlic and onion a minute or two, then cover and cook very slowly 10 minutes. Stir in the paprika and the zucchini. Add the salt, pepper, and oregano, cover, and cook over a low flame for 10 minutes, or until the zucchini is done to taste.

CALABACÍN RELLENO DE SETAS Y TRUFAS
(Zucchini Filled with Wild Mushrooms and Truffles)

I thoroughly enjoyed this dish that our good friend Reme Domínguez, co-owner and chef at Tasca del Puerto (see p. 283) in Castellón de la Plana, insisted that I try. Its presentation was quite elegant and its preparation and ingredients seemed more haute cuisine than regional. And yet what could be more basic to the cooking of Castellón than leeks and zucchini from the famed *huertas* and wild mushrooms and truffles from the magnificent mountains of the Maestrazgo, part of which belongs to the province of Castellón. You may omit the truffles if unavailable.   *Serves 4–6*

LEEK SAUCE

1 pound leeks, well washed and trimmed	1 teaspoon butter
1 tablespoon olive oil	1 tablespoon flour
1 medium onion, chopped	2 cups milk
	Salt

. . .

2 pounds very small thin zucchini, each about ¼ pound
  or less
1 tablespoon olive oil
¾ cup finely chopped onions
2 cloves garlic, minced
½ pound wild mushrooms, such
  as shitake, stems trimmed,
  finely chopped

Salt
Freshly ground pepper
2 teaspoons minced black truffles (optional)
¼ cup chicken broth

To make the Leek Sauce, place the leeks in boiling salted water to cover and simmer until tender, about 15 to 20 minutes. Drain and chop.

Heat the oil in a skillet, add the onion, and sauté a minute or two. Cover and cook over low heat 10 minutes. Stir in the butter, then add the leeks. Sprinkle with the flour and gradually stir in the milk. Taste for salt. Bring to a boil and cook until thickened. Cool slightly, transfer to a food processor, and purée. The sauce should have a medium thickness; if too thin, return to the skillet and boil down.

Cut the zucchini in half crosswise and with a small spoon hollow out each half, leaving a scant ¼-inch shell. Finely chop the pulp. Heat the oil in a skillet, add the onions and garlic, and cook a minute or two. Cover and continue cooking over low heat about 10 minutes, until the onions have softened. Add the mushrooms, cook another minute, then stir in the zucchini pulp and cook about 2 minutes, until softened. Season with salt and pepper and stir in the truffles, if using. Stuff the zucchini halves with the mixture.

Arrange the stuffed zucchini in a baking dish and add the broth. Bake at 350°F for 15 minutes. Heat the leek sauce and spoon onto 4 dishes. Arrange the stuffed zucchini on top and serve.

GUISANTES A LA VALENCIANA
(Peas, Valencia Style)

A wonderful way to enhance the flavor of peas. *Serves 4*

1 tablespoon olive oil
1 small onion, finely chopped
2 cloves garlic, minced
1½ cups fresh or frozen peas
2 tablespoons dry white wine
2 sprigs parsley
1 bay leaf
1½ teaspoons thyme leaves or
    ¼ teaspoon dried

Few strands of saffron
2 teaspoons chicken broth
Salt
Freshly ground pepper
Pimiento strips or wedges of
    hard-boiled egg for garnish
    (optional)

Heat the oil in a saucepan and sauté the onion and half of the garlic until the onion has softened. Add the peas and cook a minute, then stir in the wine, 2 tablespoons water, the parsley, bay leaf, and thyme. Cover and simmer 2 minutes.

Meanwhile, in a mortar or mini processor mash the remaining garlic with the saffron, then stir in the chicken broth. Add this mixture to the peas, season with salt and pepper, cover, and cook about 5 minutes more, or until the peas are done and the liquid consumed.

Garnish, if you wish, with pimiento strips or hard-boiled egg.

Glorious Paellas—and Ḫow to Ẫchieve Them

Call me a purist, if you will, but I firmly believe that to merit the name "paella" a dish should bear a close resemblance to the splendid rice creations from the Levante region of Spain. Unfortunately, paella has been subjected to a host of indignities in its rise to international fame.

The problem with paella outside the Valencia region (including most other regions of Spain) is not that chefs take creative liberties, but rather that they share a general ignorance of the fundamentals that make a rice dish a paella. Most believe that as long as there is plenty of rice mixed with bits and pieces of meat, fish, and vegetables, with perhaps a lobster tail or two for show, a paella has been born. That's like saying that painting by number will magically produce a Picasso.

Paellas have always been dishes of endless possibilities, albeit within certain boundaries, that depend on the individual cook and on availability of ingredients. You might say that paella began with the Moors, who brought irrigation to Spain, planted rice and purple saffron crocuses (saffron is a common, although not essential, ingredient in paellas), and transformed the Levante region into an elaborate network of canals, without which rice growing in this flat delta land would be impossible. The Spanish words for rice (*arroz*) and saffron (*azafrán*) both derive from Arabic.

Rice has been eaten for centuries along Spain's eastern coast, but paella began as an inland dish, prepared by laborers over an open fire in the orchards or *huertas* of the region. Its ingredients included chicken, rabbit, land snails, and the exceptional garden vegetables for which the region is known. Whatever was at hand went into the pan. The elaborate creation of chicken, meat, and seafood that is now associated with paella is a relatively recent invention, and the combination of seafood and meat in the same paella, a trademark of international paellas, is still frowned upon by *levantinos* and prepared mainly for the sake of tourists. There are also several time-honored rice dishes

Glorious Paellas (continued)

included in this chapter that are not considered paellas because of their distinct cooking methods.

I can't emphasize enough that paella is not a fixed dish (and one that often does not even include the word "paella"), but a movable feast that takes many exciting and unusual twists and turns. This does not mean, however, that ingredients are thrown together indiscriminately; paella requires certain cooking techniques and there are rules to observe. Perhaps my favorite paella is the sensational *arroz negro*, made with squid and shrimp, darkened with squid ink, and served with garlicky *alioli*. An exciting paella from Castellón de la Plana is made with an abundance of fresh vegetables, then studded with wonderful mint-scented meatballs. There are all-seafood paellas, all-meat paellas, all-vegetable paellas, even a pasta dish made in the style of paella that has become popular in recent years. Certainly there is no lack of variety.

What all paellas have in common, however, is Spanish short-grain rice. Using the right kind of rice is without doubt the most important factor in creating an authentic paella (you wouldn't use Uncle Ben's rice for your favorite risotto, so why even consider using it in paella?). Short-grain rice, be it imported from Spain, Spanish style, California pearl rice, or Arborio, absorbs flavors and has a chewiness not found in long-grain, both qualities that are the very essence of a paella. After all, the rice is the principal player in this dish, and aside from whatever else goes into the paella, the rice must be extraordinarily good. The wide flat metal paella pan in which the rice cooks is also of utmost importance. A good all-purpose size for paellas serving 4 to 8 persons is 17 to 18 inches at the widest point, although it is better to have several different sizes. (I doubt, however, that you would ever have use for the paella pans some thirty feet across that are set up in public squares on festive occasions to make paellas for hundreds.)

When preparing paellas, follow cooking instructions closely, taking particular care to use the exact proportions of rice and liquid in each recipe. Spaniards are not fans of precise measurements in cooking, but paella is an exception. Pay attention also to timing. When the paella comes out of the oven, the liquid should be absorbed but the rice slightly underdone. It will finish cooking as it rests before serving.

Finally, paella has always been, and continues to be, an ideal party dish, sure to please guests with its multifaceted tastes and spectacular appearance. Since in most cases all preparation except the final cooking of the rice can be done in advance, paella is also easy on the hosts. And no accompaniment except, perhaps, a salad, is necessary.

Rice ❦ Rice Dishes

ARROZ AL AZAFRÁN CON PIÑONES
(Saffron Rice with Pine Nuts)

This is my basic all-purpose rice that I use to accompany meat, fish, and poultry dishes. Although it has flavor of its own, it takes well to sauces that the principal dish may have.   *Serves 4*

2 tablespoons butter
2 tablespoons minced onion
2 tablespoons pine nuts
1 cup short-grain rice,
    preferably Spanish
1 cup chicken broth
1 cup water

2 tablespoons minced parsley
1½ teaspoons thyme leaves or
    ¼ teaspoon dried
Few strands of saffron,
    crumbled
Salt

Saffron Rice with Pine Nuts (continued)

Melt the butter in a deep casserole, then add the onion and pine nuts and cook until the onion has wilted. Stir in the rice, coating it with the butter. Pour in the chicken broth and water, stir in the parsley, thyme, saffron, and salt, and bring to a boil. Remove from the flame, cover, and transfer to a 400°F oven. Cook for 15 minutes, remove from the oven, and let sit, covered, on top of the stove for 5 to 10 minutes before serving.

Variation

For a heartier side dish serving 4 to 6, mix in 2 cups chopped escarole when adding the broth and water, then proceed as directed.

PAELLA VALENCIANA
(*Valencian Rabbit Paella*)

Although most Americans—and even Spaniards from other regions—consider the "mixed" paella, made with meats, chorizo, and fish, to be the traditional paella, those born and bred in rice country grimace at the idea of combining meats and fish; they firmly believe it must be one or the other. So here is the "real" paella according to people of the Levante. It is, in fact, an excellent paella—and quite unusual if served with the optional mint-scented meatballs—but if you are looking for what you probably consider a classic paella, see the recipe that follows this one. If you wish to make Arroz con Pollo, simply substitute chicken for the rabbit in this recipe.

Serves 5–6

CHICKEN BROTH

6 cups water
1 pound chicken parts, such as backs or thighs, skin and fat removed
1 stalk celery
1 small leek, well washed
½ medium onion, peeled

1 carrot, trimmed, scraped, and cut in 2-inch lengths
1 bay leaf
2 sprigs parsley
1 sprig rosemary or ¼ teaspoon dried
Salt

. . .

½ cup dry white wine

¼ teaspoon crumbled thread saffron

2 ripe and flavorful medium tomatoes

A 2–2½-pound rabbit or a 3-pound chicken

Kosher or sea salt

6 tablespoons olive oil

½ cup finely chopped green bell pepper

½ cup finely chopped red bell pepper

5 scallions, chopped

5 cloves garlic, minced

2 teaspoons imported sweet paprika

½ cup lima beans, fresh or frozen

½ cup peas, fresh or frozen

¼ pound green beans, preferably broad beans, ends snapped off

2½ cups short-grain rice

Mint Meatballs (p. 310) (optional)

2 sprigs rosemary or ¼ teaspoon dried

To make the Chicken Broth, combine all ingredients in a large pot. Bring to a boil, cover, lower the heat, and let simmer about 1 hour. Strain and measure to 4½ cups (boil down if there is more). Stir in the wine and saffron.

Cut the tomatoes in halves crosswise. Squeeze gently to extract the seeds and with a coarse grater, grate down to the skin. Drain off any excess liquid. Hack or cut the rabbit into pieces of approximately 2 inches. Sprinkle with salt. If including the optional meatballs, mix and shape them as directed.

Heat the olive oil in a paella pan measuring about 17 inches at its widest point and place over 2 burners if necessary. Stir-fry the rabbit pieces about 10 minutes over high heat, until lightly browned on all sides, rotating the pan occasionally to equalize the heat. Remove the rabbit to a warm platter. Add the optional meatballs and sauté until lightly browned. Remove to the platter.

Add the green and red peppers, scallions, and garlic to the pan and cook over medium heat about 5 minutes. Stir in the paprika, then the grated tomatoes. Add the lima beans, peas, and green beans (the paella can be made in advance up to this point). Stir in the rice, coating it well with the pan mixture.

Bring the chicken broth to a boil and pour over the rice. If including the optional meatballs, add them and continue to boil until the paella is no longer soupy, but sufficient liquid remains to continue cooking the rice. Taste for

Valencian Rabbit Paella (continued)

salt and stir in the rabbit pieces. Place the rosemary sprigs over the rice and transfer to a 375°F oven for 10 minutes, uncovered, or until the rice is almost done and most of the liquid absorbed. Cover lightly with foil and let sit on top of the stove another 10 minutes before serving.

PAELLA VALENCIANA MIXTA
(Meat and Seafood Paella)

This is the paella that has traveled the world, and although most people of the Levante do not approve of it, its popularity cannot be ignored. I'm sure you would feel cheated if this recipe were not included in this book, so here it is. It is a well-prepared paella and there is no denying its great taste.

Serves 6–8

1 recipe Chicken Broth, using 6½ cups water, cooked as directed below (p. 298)

½ pound medium shrimp in their shells

A 1¾-pound lobster, split lengthwise

½ cup dry white wine

¼ teaspoon crumbled thread saffron

2 ripe and flavorful medium tomatoes

A 2–2½-pound rabbit or a 3-pound chicken, hacked or cut into 2-inch pieces

Kosher or sea salt

6 tablespoons olive oil

¼ pound sweet chorizo, in ¼-inch slices

A ¼-pound piece Spanish mountain cured ham, prosciutto, or capicollo, diced

¼ pound lean pork, cut in ½-inch cubes

½ cup finely chopped green bell pepper

½ cup finely chopped red bell pepper

5 scallions, chopped

5 cloves garlic, minced

2 teaspoons imported sweet paprika

½ cup peas, fresh or frozen

3 cups short-grain rice

1½ dozen very small mussels, thoroughly cleansed of all sand particles (p. 33)

1 pimiento, cut in strips

Combine the Chicken Broth ingredients as directed. Shell the shrimp and add the shells to the pot. Separate the tail section from the split lobster. Keeping the shell on, cut each tail piece in half crosswise for a total of 4 tail pieces. Divide each large claw in 2 parts and lightly crush the claw shells for easy removal of the meat. Add the lobster head and small claws to the pot and reserve the rest. Cook the broth according to instructions. When it is done, strain and reserve 5½ cups. Stir in the wine and saffron.

Cut the tomatoes in halves crosswise. Squeeze gently to extract the seeds and with a coarse grater, grate down to the skin. Drain off any excess liquid. Sprinkle the rabbit pieces with salt.

Heat the olive oil in a paella pan measuring at least 17 to 18 inches at its widest point and place over 2 burners if necessary. Stir-fry the rabbit pieces about 10 minutes over high heat, until lightly browned on all sides, rotating the pan occasionally to equalize the heat. Remove the rabbit to a warm platter.

Add the chorizo, ham, pork, shrimp, and lobster and stir-fry about 3 minutes. Remove the shrimp to a warm platter, and stir-fry the lobster another 2 minutes, then remove it also. Stir the chopped green and red peppers, scallions, and garlic into the pan with the meats and cook over medium heat about 5 minutes. Stir in the paprika, then the grated tomato. Add the peas (the paella can be made in advance up to this point). Stir in the rice, coating it well with the pan mixture.

Bring the Chicken Broth to a boil and pour over the rice. Boil until the rice is no longer soupy, but sufficient liquid remains to continue cooking the rice. Stir in the shrimp and rabbit and taste for salt (it should be well seasoned). Arrange over the rice the pimiento strips, the lobster pieces, and the mussels, rinsed and drained, with the edge that will open facing up. Transfer to a 375°F oven and cook, uncovered, about 10 minutes, or until the rice is almost done and most of the liquid absorbed. Cover loosely with foil and let sit on top of the stove another 10 minutes before serving.

ARROZ NEGRO TASCA DEL PUERTO
(Black Rice Tasca del Puerto)

Arroz negro, as its name suggests, is not pale gray but truly black from the squid ink in which it is cooked; it is served with an incredibly pungent garlic mayonnaise that in Castellón is called *ajo aceite.* Ever since I discovered black rice many years ago it has been my favorite among the many delicious varieties of Valencian rice dishes.

The only inconvenience in preparing black rice is emptying the squid ink sacs. However, since discovering squid ink in vacuum-sealed packets (see Marketing Sources, p. 428), I have found it is no longer a chore to prepare the dish. If you cannot find the product or would rather put together the necessary ink yourself, you will need to buy 2 more pounds of squid—large, uncleaned squid with their ink sacs intact (see p. 81 for squid cleaning instructions). You can save the extra squid for another recipe.

Serves 6–8

Ingredients for Fish Broth
  (p. 175)
½ pound medium shrimp in
  their shells
1½ pounds small cleaned (see
  p. 81) squid with tentacles

(add 2 pounds uncleaned
  large squid if you need the
  ink)
¼ teaspoon crumbled thread
  saffron

AJO ACEITE (ALIOLI)

8 cloves garlic, peeled
¾ teaspoon salt
1 egg or ¼ cup egg substitute
  made with egg white

1 teaspoon lemon juice
2 cups pure olive oil
2 tablespoons hot water

. . .

1 pound cleaned monkfish, cut
  in ¾-inch cubes
Kosher or sea salt
3 ripe and flavorful medium
  tomatoes

Six 4-gram packets squid ink
½ cup dry white wine
½ cup olive oil
1½ cups finely chopped green
  bell peppers

12 cloves garlic, minced

1½ teaspoons imported sweet
   paprika

3 cups short-grain rice

1 pimiento, cut in ½-inch strips

Combine the Fish Broth ingredients, as instructed, in a large pot. Shell the shrimp and add the shells to the pot. Cut the squid in ½-inch rings and the tentacles in half lengthwise, adding any squid scraps to the pot, then cook the Fish Broth according to instructions. When the broth is done, strain and reserve 5½ cups (if there is more, boil down for fuller flavor). Stir in the saffron.

To make the Ajo Aceite, mash to a paste in a mortar the garlic and ¼ teaspoon of the salt (or use a garlic press). Transfer to a food processor. Add the egg, the remaining ½ teaspoon salt, and the lemon juice. Blend about 30 seconds. With the motor running, drizzle in the oil and gradually blend in the water. Set aside 6 tablespoons, which will be needed to make the rice. If you make the *ajo aceite* in advance, refrigerate and bring to room temperature before serving.

Cut each shrimp crosswise into 2 pieces. Sprinkle the shrimp, squid, and monkfish with salt and let sit until ready to use. Cut the tomatoes in halves crosswise, squeeze gently to extract the seeds, and with a coarse grater, grate down to the skin, draining off any excess juices. Over a small bowl, strain the squid ink with the wine, passing it through the strainer several times.

Heat the oil in a paella pan measuring at least 17 to 18 inches at its widest point, covering 2 burners if necessary. Add the shrimp, squid rings and tentacles, and the monkfish. Stir-fry over medium-high heat about 2 minutes, rotating the pan occasionally to equalize the heat. Add the green peppers and stir-fry 2 minutes more. Stir in the garlic, cook a minute, then add the 6 tablespoons reserved *ajo aceite* and the paprika and cook another minute. Add the grated tomato, cook 3 minutes (the dish can be made in advance up to this point), then stir in the rice, coating it well with the pan mixture.

Bring the Fish Broth to a boil and pour over the rice. Stir in the ink mixture and boil over a medium-high flame for about 5 to 10 minutes, or until the rice is no longer soupy, but sufficient liquid still remains to continue cooking the rice. Taste for salt.

Arrange the pimiento strips attractively over the rice and transfer to a 375°F oven, uncovered, for 10 minutes, or until the rice is almost done and

Black Rice Tasca del Puerto (continued)

most of the liquid absorbed. Cover loosely with foil and let sit on top of the stove another 10 minutes. Serve, passing the *ajo aceite* separately.

PAELLA A LA MARINERA
(Mixed Seafood Paella)

You can vary the seafood in this paella as you please, and no matter what kind you use, the dish is sure to be excellent because of the many vegetables and seasoning, which will remain the same. I love *alioli* or *ajo aceite*, as it is often called in the Valencia region (p. 302), with just about any rice dish, so if you would like to offer it with this paella, feel free to do so.

Serves 6—8

Ingredients for Fish Broth
(p. 175)
½ pound medium shrimp in their shells
1 pound cleaned monkfish or other firm-fleshed white fish
1 pound small cleaned (see p. 81) squid with tentacles
A 1¾-pound live lobster, split lengthwise
¼ teaspoon crumbled thread saffron
½ cup dry white wine
Kosher or sea salt
3 ripe and flavorful medium tomatoes

½ cup olive oil
1½ cups finely chopped green bell peppers
12 cloves garlic, minced
2 teaspoons imported sweet paprika
3 cups short-grain rice
1 tablespoon minced parsley
1 bay leaf, finely crumbled
½ cup peas, fresh or frozen
18 small mussels, thoroughly cleansed of sand particles (see p. 33)
1 pimiento, cut in long thin strips

Combine the Fish Broth ingredients as instructed. Shell the shrimp and add the shells to the pot. Cut the monkfish into ¾-inch cubes, slice the squid into ½-inch rings, and cut the tentacles in halves lengthwise. Add any fish scraps or bones to the stockpot. Separate the tail section from the split lobster. Keeping the shell on, cut each tail piece in half crosswise for a total of 4 tail pieces. Divide each claw in two parts and lightly crush the claw shells for easy removal of the meat. Add the lobster heads and small claws to the stockpot and reserve the rest of the seafood. Bring to a boil, cover, and simmer about 1 hour. Strain and reserve 5½ cups. Stir in the saffron and wine.

Sprinkle the shrimp, monkfish, and squid with salt and let sit at room temperature until ready to use. Cut the tomatoes in half crosswise and with a coarse grater, grate down to the skin, draining off any excess juices. Have all other ingredients chopped and/or measured before beginning the paella.

Place a paella pan measuring at least 17 to 18 inches at its widest point over two burners (or one very large burner, if your stove is so equipped). Heat the oil and stir-fry the lobster pieces for 2 minutes over a medium-high flame, rotating the pan occasionally to equalize the heat. Add the shrimp, squid, and monkfish, and continue frying another 2 minutes. Remove all seafood except the squid to a warm platter.

Add the chopped peppers to the paella pan and sauté about 3 minutes, then add the minced garlic and cook another minute. Stir in the paprika, then the tomato, and cook 2 minutes (the paella can be made in advance up to this point). Add the rice, stir to coat with the tomato mixture, and mix in the parsley and crumbled bay leaf. Bring the broth to a boil and pour into the paella pan. Add the peas and boil over medium-high heat, uncovered, 5 to 10 minutes, or until the paella is no longer soupy, but enough liquid remains to continue cooking the rice. Taste for salt (it should be well seasoned).

Stir in the reserved monkfish and shrimp. Arrange the lobster pieces and the mussels, drained and rinsed (with the edge that will open facing up) over the paella. Garnish with the pimiento strips. Transfer to a 375°F oven and cook, uncovered, for 10 minutes, or until the rice is almost done and most of the liquid absorbed. Cover loosely with foil and let sit on top of the stove for 10 minutes before serving.

ARROZ A BANDA CON ALIOLI
(Rice "On Its Own" with Garlic Mayonnaise)

START PREPARATION SEVERAL HOURS IN ADVANCE

Here is a rice dish, a specialty of the province of Alicante, that is the very essence of a paella without all the decorative elements—no showy shrimp, clams, or lobster to elicit oohs and ahs from guests. And yet in many ways it is the very best of rice dishes—one of my favorites—that has all the flavors of the fish, shellfish, garlic, and peppers used to make the broth concentrated in the rice itself.

To make this dish you will need some inexpensive fish to prepare the stock (traditionally and ideally, rockfish is used to give good flavor—in this recipe I have substituted mussels and whiting), then choose whatever fish you wish to serve before, after, or alongside the rice, using the *alioli* to enhance both the rice and the fish. Since the stock is the most important element of this dish, the bulk of the work is done in advance, and the *alioli* can also of course be made ahead. Have all preparatory work done before beginning the final preparation of the rice. If at all possible use the dried sweet red peppers called for in the recipe—they really do give a distinctive flavor.   *Serves 4–6*

3 dried sweet red peppers, or
    mild New Mexico, stems
    and seeds removed (if un-
    available, use paprika as
    indicated below)

Alioli (p. 302)
½–1 pound large or jumbo
    shrimp in their shells

FISH BROTH

6 cups water
1 dozen mussels,
    thoroughly cleansed of all
    sand particles (see p. 33)
½ pound whiting, cleaned
1 medium onion, peeled and cut
    in thick slices
2 sprigs parsley

1 medium tomato, coarsely
    chopped
1½ teaspoons thyme leaves or
    ¼ teaspoon dried
8 peppercorns
Salt
1 bay leaf
1 bottle clam juice (optional)

· · ·

7 tablespoons olive oil
6 cloves garlic, peeled
⅛ teaspoon crumbled thread
    saffron
2 tablespoons minced
    parsley
1 small tomato

8 cloves garlic, minced
2 teaspoons lemon juice
Kosher or sea salt
1 pound monkfish
¼ pound cleaned squid, finely
    chopped
2 cups short-grain rice

1 teaspoon imported sweet
   paprika (2 tablespoons

paprika if the dried red
peppers are not used)

Soak 2 of the dried peppers in warm water to cover for several hours. Make the *Alioli* according to directions. Shell the shrimp. Combine the Fish Broth ingredients and the shrimp shells in a large pot. Bring to a boil, cover, and simmer 45 minutes.

Meanwhile, break the remaining dried pepper into several pieces and discard the seeds and stem. Heat 2 tablespoons of the oil in a small skillet and lightly sauté the dried pepper pieces and the 6 peeled cloves of garlic (do not let the garlic brown). Transfer the pepper pieces and garlic to a mortar or mini processor, combine with the saffron and 1 tablespoon of the parsley, and mash to a paste. Add to the Fish Broth as it is cooking.

Strain the Fish Broth, pressing with the back of a wooden spoon to extract as much liquid as possible (there should be about 5½ cups). Reserve 4 cups for the rice and return the rest to the pot (the fish will cook in it later).

Drain the 2 peppers that have been soaking and scrape off the pulp, discarding the skin. Cut the tomato in half crosswise. Squeeze gently to remove the seeds and some of the liquid and grate down to the skin with a very coarse grater. Mash the pepper pulp in a mortar or mini processor with two of the minced garlic cloves and the remaining tablespoon of parsley. Stir in a tablespoon of oil, the grated tomato, lemon juice, and ¼ teaspoon salt and reserve. Sprinkle the shrimp and monkfish with salt and let sit.

In a paella pan about 17 inches at its widest point, set over 2 stove burners if necessary, heat the remaining 4 tablespoons oil and lightly sauté the chopped squid and the remaining 6 cloves minced garlic (the dish can be made in advance up to this point). Add the rice, then stir in the paprika (the larger amount if dried peppers are not being used) and the tomato mixture and coat the rice well. Pour in the 4 cups reserved stock, boiling hot, and cook until the rice is no longer soupy but some liquid remains. Transfer to a 375°F oven and bake, uncovered, for 10 minutes. Remove from the oven, cover loosely with foil, and let sit another 10 minutes before serving. Bring to a boil the reserved fish stock, add the monkfish, and simmer about 10 minutes, or until almost done. Add the shrimp and cook a minute more. Drain the monkfish and shrimp and serve either as a first course, as an accompaniment to the rice, or following the rice. Provide a bowl of *Alioli* for both the fish and the rice.

ARROSETXAT
(Rice with Squid and Shrimp)

This is a dish peculiar to Castellón de la Plana but also found in similar preparations in Catalunya, where it is often called Arrossejat but more properly referred to as Rossejat. Both names allude to the golden color of the rice that results from sautéing the rice before stirring in the liquid in which the rice will cook. *Serves 4–6*

FISH BROTH

1 small whiting, cleaned, head on
1 small onion, peeled
6 peppercorns
2 sprigs thyme leaves or ¼ teaspoon dried
1 bay leaf
1 slice lemon

Salt
2 sprigs parsley
1 cup clam juice
3 cups water
1 medium green frying pepper, cored and seeded
1 small tomato, halved

. . .

⅛ teaspoon crumbled thread saffron
3 cloves garlic, peeled
5 tablespoons olive oil
1 pound cleaned squid with tentacles, coarsely chopped
¼ pound medium shrimp, shelled and cut in thirds

2 cups short grain rice
5 cloves garlic, minced
1 small tomato, skinned, seeded, and chopped
2 teaspoons imported sweet paprika
½ cup dry white wine
Salt

Combine all ingredients for the Fish Broth in a pot, adding the shrimp shells and any squid scraps, bring to a boil, then simmer 40 minutes. Strain and measure to 3½ cups (boil down if there is more).

In a mortar or mini processor, mash to a paste the saffron and the 3 cloves garlic. Stir in ¼ cup of the broth and reserve.

Heat the oil in a metal paella pan about 17 to 18 inches at its widest point, over 2 burners if necessary. Slowly sauté the squid and shrimp about 10 minutes, then raise the heat and add the rice, minced garlic, tomato, and paprika, and cook, stirring constantly, until the rice is lightly golden (the dish can be made in advance up to this point). Add the remaining 3¼ cups broth, the wine, and the mortar mixture. Bring to a boil and cook, stirring, until the rice is no longer soupy but enough liquid remains to continue cooking the rice. Taste for salt, then transfer to a 375°F oven and cook, uncovered, 10 minutes, or until the rice is almost done and most of the liquid absorbed. Cover loosely with foil and let sit on top of the stove 10 minutes. Serve accompanied by *Alioli* (p. 302).

ARROZ CON ACELGAS, JUDÍAS, Y ALMEJAS
(Rice with Greens, Beans, and Clams)

In Valencia, rice dishes, besides varying in their ingredients, are made two distinct ways—either in a paella pan, where the rice emerges dry and crisp around the edges, or in an earthenware casserole, where the final product is somewhat soupy. Here is one of the soupy versions that is a hearty meal, for besides the rice it includes beans and potatoes. Whether you use chicken or fish broth depends on the emphasis you wish to give to the dish.

Serves 3–4

1 cup cooked white beans, homemade or good-quality canned, cooking or can liquid reserved

About 3 cups Chicken Broth (p. 298) or Fish Broth (p. 175)

2 tablespoons olive oil

3 cloves garlic, minced

1 medium onion, finely chopped

¾ pound Swiss chard or collard greens, thick ends trimmed, finely chopped

1 small tomato, skinned and seeded

1½ teaspoons imported sweet paprika

Salt

Few strands of saffron

6 ounces new or red waxy potatoes, peeled, in ½-inch cubes

1½ cups short-grain rice

2 dozen cockles or Manila clams, or 1½ dozen small littlenecks, thoroughly cleansed of sand particles (see p. 33)

Rice with Greens, Beans, and Clams (continued)

Drain the beans and reserve some of the cooking or the can liquid. Add enough broth to make 3¼ cups plus 2 tablespoons liquid.

In a shallow casserole, preferably earthenware, heat the oil and sauté the garlic and onion until the onion has wilted. Add the greens and sauté 5 minutes, then mix in the tomato and cook 5 minutes more. Sprinkle in the paprika and salt, stir in the reserved liquid, the saffron, and the potatoes. Taste for salt. Cover and simmer 10 minutes. Add the cooked beans, rice, and clams and cook at a higher simmer, uncovered, for 25 minutes, stirring occasionally, or until the rice is just done (add more broth or water if necessary so that the dish remains a little soupy).

PAELLA DE VERDURAS Y PELOTAS
(Vegetable Paella with Mint-Scented Meatballs)

Besides being chock-full of vegetables, this rice has the added appeal of mint-flavored pork and pine nut meatballs; it is a marvelous rice creation found in Castellón de la Plana. The recipe comes from the family files of Chimo Boix and Reme Domínguez, owners of Tasca del Puerto restaurant (see p. 283).

There is a lot of chopping to do, but don't let that put you off. It should all be done in advance (the vegetables, except the tomato and garlic, can be combined in a big bowl, since they are added all at once) and the rest is easy. Commercial chicken broth is fine in this recipe (although homemade is of course better), since its flavor will be enhanced with wine, saffron, and chickpeas, but try to use fresh mint for the meatballs. Although this recipe does not call for *alioli* as some other paellas do, consider it an option.

Serves 6

PELOTAS (MEATBALLS)

3 tablespoons bread crumbs	1 teaspoon salt
2 tablespoons chicken broth	2 tablespoons finely chopped
¾ pound very lean ground	pine nuts
pork	1 clove garlic, minced
2 tablespoons chopped mint	1 tablespoon minced parsley
leaves, or 1 teaspoon dried	1 egg

. . .

6 cups chicken broth, preferably homemade (p. 298)
¼ teaspoon crumbled saffron
   strands
1 small onion, peeled, in halves
½ cup cooked chickpeas
   (canned are fine)
1 bay leaf
6 peppercorns
3 sprigs parsley
½ cup dry white wine
½ pound tomatoes
6 tablespoons olive oil
1 small zucchini, in ½-inch
   cubes
4 scallions, in ½-inch pieces
¼ pound broad green beans
8 wild mushrooms, such as
   oyster or shitake, brushed
   clean and cut in halves or
   quarters
4 medium-large cultivated
   mushrooms, brushed clean
   and cut in quarters

4 artichoke hearts, fresh or
   frozen, in halves
¾ cup lima beans, fresh or
   frozen
½ cup peas, fresh or frozen
1 red bell pepper, finely
   chopped
1 green bell pepper, finely
   chopped
1 carrot, trimmed, scraped, and
   finely chopped
2 cups spinach, well washed,
   dried, and coarsely chopped
2 tablespoons minced parsley
Salt
2 teaspoons imported sweet
   paprika
4 cloves garlic, minced
3 cups short-grain rice

To make the Meatballs, in a small bowl soak the bread crumbs in the 2 table-spoons chicken broth. In a larger bowl, combine the rest of the meatball ingredients and mix in the softened bread crumbs. Shape into 1- to 1½-inch balls.

In a deep pot combine the 6 cups chicken broth with the saffron, onion, chickpeas, bay leaf, peppercorns, and parsley. Bring to a boil, cover, and simmer at least 30 minutes. Strain, mashing the chickpeas through the strainer. Measure to 5½ cups and add the wine.

Cut the tomatoes in halves crosswise, and squeeze gently to remove the seeds and some liquid. With a coarse grater, grate down to the skin. Discard the skin and reserve the pulp.

In a large paella pan, about 18 inches at its widest point, and over 2 stove

Vegetable Paella with Meatballs (continued)

burners if necessary, heat the oil and add all the vegetables except the tomatoes and garlic. Sauté over medium-high heat for about 5 minutes, until the
vegetables cook down. Salt to taste.

Add the Meatballs and continue sautéing until the meatballs are lightly
browned. Stir in the paprika, garlic, and tomatoes and cook a minute, then
add the rice, stirring to coat with the oil. Add the broth, boiling hot, and
bring the rice to a boil. Continue cooking over a medium-high flame until
the rice is no longer soupy, but some liquid remains. Taste for salt (the rice
should be well seasoned). Transfer to a 375°F oven and cook, uncovered, for
10 minutes. Remove, cover loosely with foil, and let sit 10 minutes more
before serving.

ARROZ CON PATO
(Rice with Duck, Sausage, and Chickpeas)

The vast green La Albufera lagoon, just outside of the city of Valencia, was
once an important breeding ground for ducks, but unfortunately the ecology
of the lagoon has changed, and this is no longer true, even though ducks do
still gather here. This rice dish of duck, sausage, chickpeas, and pine nuts
is typically made during duck hunting season. However, since the duck
you are most likely to purchase is domestic, and therefore quite fatty, I
have pre-roasted it before combining with the rice to eliminate most of the
fat.   *Serves 4–6*

A 4–4½-pound duck, trussed, with the neck if available
4 cups well-flavored Chicken Broth (p. 298)
Several strands of saffron
¼ pound fresh sweet sausage, such as Italian style
3 tablespoons olive oil
1 small onion, slivered
2 cloves garlic, minced
1 cup finely chopped red bell peppers
1 teaspoon imported sweet paprika
½ pound tomatoes, skinned, seeded, and chopped
2 tablespoons minced parsley
2 cups short-grain rice

½ pound freshly cooked or
   canned chickpeas, rinsed
   and drained
½ cup peas, fresh or frozen

2 tablespoons pine nuts
Salt
1 pimiento, cut in strips

Place the duck and the neck, if using, in a roasting pan and roast at 350°F for 1½ hours, pouring off the fat occasionally. Transfer to a warm platter and cut in serving pieces. Deglaze the pan with ¼ cup of the Chicken Broth.

In a large saucepan combine the deglazed pan juices with the remaining broth and the saffron and slowly simmer on a back burner. In a shallow greased casserole, preferably Spanish earthenware, sauté the sausage until cooked. Cut in ¾-inch slices and reserve. Wipe out the pan, then heat the oil. Sauté the onion, garlic, and red peppers until the onion is translucent and the peppers softened. Stir in the paprika, then add the tomatoes and parsley and cook a minute or two. Mix in the rice, coating well with the casserole mixture, then pour in the broth. Add the sausage slices, the chickpeas, peas, and pine nuts and boil until the rice is no longer soupy, but enough liquid remains to continue cooking the rice. Taste for salt. Garnish with the pimiento strips and arrange the duck pieces over the rice. Transfer to a 375°F oven for 15 to 18 minutes, or until the rice is almost done and most of the liquid absorbed. Cover loosely with foil and let sit on top of the stove 10 minutes before serving.

ARRÒS AL FORN
(Baked Rice with Pork Ribs and Vegetables)

Recipes for similar rice dishes appear in cookbooks as far back as the four-teenth century; Ruperto de Nola's *Llibre del Cuiner*, written in the sixteenth century, has a recipe of this very name, surely making it one of the oldest rice dishes in the Spanish repertoire (paella came along much later). This exceptional version, although with a few later embellishments (such as tomatoes from the New World), is like that of Ruperto de Nola—cooked in an earthenware casserole, with a well-flavored broth and saffron. The black sausage, although not essential, adds a wonderful flavor contrast. "This is good rice," Ruperto de Nola notes in his recipe. I couldn't agree more.

Serves 4

BROTH

4 cups chicken broth
¼ cup cooked mashed chickpeas
1 small leek
1 sprig parsley
4 peppercorns

1 bay leaf
1½ teaspoons thyme leaves or
 ¼ teaspoon dried
½ onion, peeled
Several strands of saffron

. . .

2 tablespoons olive oil
¼-pound thick slice pork loin
 ribs, hacked into 1-inch
 pieces
1 small head garlic, loose skin
 removed
½ pound potatoes, peeled and
 cut in ⅛-inch slices
A ¼-inch-thick slice Spanish
 mountain cured ham or
 prosciutto, cut in a ¼-inch
 dice
¼ pound black sausage, in
 ½-inch slices (optional)

½ teaspoon imported sweet
 paprika
1 small tomato, skinned,
 seeded, and finely chopped
¼ pound yellow squash, in
 ½-inch slices
1 small tomato, cut in ¼-inch
 slices
1½ cups short-grain rice
1 cup cooked chickpeas, homemade or good-quality
 canned, rinsed and drained
Salt
1 pimiento, cut in strips

To make the Broth, combine all ingredients in a pot, bring to a boil, then simmer 30 minutes. Strain, pushing through as much of the solid matter as possible. Measure to 3 cups, boiling down if there is more.

In a shallow casserole, about 11 to 12 inches across, preferably earthenware, heat the oil and sauté the pork, garlic, and potatoes over medium heat for 10 minutes, stirring occasionally. Add the ham, black sausage, and paprika and sauté a minute or two more. Add the chopped tomato and continue cooking 2 minutes more. Mix in the squash and tomato slices, then the rice, and stir to coat the rice well. Pour in the Broth, add the chickpeas, and bring to a boil. Taste for salt. Arrange the pimiento strips on top and transfer to a 450°F oven for 25 minutes. Remove from the oven, over loosely with foil, and let sit 15 minutes on top of the stove before serving.

ARRÒS AMB FESOLS I NAPS
(Thick Rice Soup with Beans and Turnips)

Somewhere between a soup and a paella, this is a hearty age-old peasant dish, once made by workers in the *huertas* of the Levante with the vegetables and other ingredients provided by the land they tilled. Typical long before paella came into fashion, it remains a most popular comfort food.

Serves 4

Thick Rice Soup (continued)

1 pig's foot, split, then cut in halves crosswise

9½ cups water

½ celery stalk

1 small leek, well washed

1 carrot, trimmed, scraped, and cut in halves crosswise

8 peppercorns

1 bay leaf

Salt to taste

2 medium turnips (about ½ pound), peeled and cut in ¼-inch slices

1 medium tomato

3 tablespoons olive oil

A ¼-pound piece Spanish mountain cured ham, prosciutto, or capicollo, cut in ½-inch cubes

1 large red bell pepper, cored, seeded, and chopped

5 cloves garlic, sliced

2½ teaspoons imported sweet paprika

1 clove garlic, peeled

¼ teaspoon crumbled thread saffron

1 medium potato, peeled and cut in ¼-inch slices

4 black sausages, such as Spanish *morcilla*

1 cup cooked white beans, homemade or good-quality canned, rinsed and drained

1¼ cups short-grain rice

Place the pig's foot in a large pot with 5½ cups of the water, the celery, leek, carrot, peppercorns, bay leaf, and salt. Bring to a boil, cover, and simmer 3 hours (this may be done the day before). Remove the pig's foot to a platter and strain the liquid, reserving 4½ cups (boil down if there is more).

Bring the remaining 4 cups water to a boil and add the sliced turnips. Simmer 15 minutes. Remove the turnips and reserve 3¼ cups liquid, again boiling down if there is more.

Cut the tomato in halves crosswise, squeeze out the seeds, and with a coarse grater, grate down to the skin, draining off any excess juices.

In a large shallow casserole, preferably earthenware, heat 2 tablespoons of the oil, then slowly sauté the ham and the red pepper for 5 minutes. Add the sliced garlic, sauté a minute, then add the reserved pig's foot and sauté another minute. Stir in the paprika, then add the grated tomato and cook 1 minute. Pour in the reserved cooking liquid from the pig's foot and the turnips (7¾ cups total). Bring to a boil, then simmer 30 minutes, uncovered.

Meanwhile, in a mortar or mini processor, mash to a paste the whole garlic and saffron. Stir in a tablespoon of cooking liquid.

In a small skillet heat the remaining tablespoon oil and very quickly brown the potato slices (they will not be cooked through). Add the potato, turnips, black sausage, cooked beans, and the mixture from the mortar to the casserole and cook 5 minutes. Add the rice, bring to a boil, then simmer, uncovered, stirring occasionally, for 12 to 15 minutes, or until the rice is almost done. Let sit for 5 minutes, bring the casserole to the table, and serve.

FIDEUÁ ALICANTINA
(Pasta Seafood "Paella")

The Eastern coast of Spain, besides being a major rice producer and a region where rice dishes are everyday meals, also has a long tradition of cooking with pasta, so it is not surprising that a paella using pasta instead of rice has become so popular. Because of the style in which it is prepared (in a paella pan), the kind of pasta used (a pasta that resembles perciatelli—spaghetti with a tiny hole running through it—but cut in short lengths), the way it is cooked (in a fish broth and finished, uncovered, in the oven), and the way it is served (accompanied by a garlicky mayonnaise), it becomes uniquely Spanish, and invariably receives raves from my dinner guests. *Serves 6*

1 recipe *Ajo Aceite* (p. 302)
Ingredients for Fish Broth
  (p. 175)
½ pound shrimp in their shells
1 pound cleaned squid, cut in
  ½-inch rings, tentacles cut
  in halves lengthwise
½ cup dry white wine
¼ teaspoon crumbled saffron
  strands
Kosher or sea salt
2 very ripe and flavorful
  medium tomatoes
6 tablespoons olive oil

1 dozen very small littlenecks,
  or 2 dozen cockles or Manila
  clams, thoroughly cleansed
  of sand particles (see p. 33)
1 cup finely chopped green bell
  pepper
12 cloves garlic, minced
1 tablespoon imported sweet
  paprika
1 pound perciatelli #15, cut in
  1½-inch lengths with
  kitchen shears

Pasta Seafood "Paella" (continued)

Prepare the *Ajo Aceite* according to instructions, setting aside ¼ cup to be cooked with the pasta. Make the Fish Broth, adding the shells from the shrimp and any squid scraps. Strain, measure to 6½ cups (if there is less, add some water), and stir in the wine and saffron. Sprinkle the shrimp and squid with salt.

Cut the tomatoes in halves crosswise. Squeeze gently to extract the seeds and with a coarse grater, grate down to the skin. Drain off any excess juices.

In a paella pan measuring about 17 inches at its widest point, heat the oil—over two burners if necessary. Add the squid, shrimp, and clams and sauté about 2 minutes, sprinkling with salt. Remove the shrimp and clams to a warm platter. Add the green pepper and cook another 2 minutes, then stir in the reserved ¼ cup *Ajo Aceite* and the garlic and cook a minute. Add the paprika and grated tomato and cook another minute.

Add the pasta, stirring constantly to keep the pasta pieces from sticking together, and cook 2 minutes. Stir in the broth, boiling hot. Boil about 10 to 15 minutes, stirring occasionally, until the mixture is no longer soupy but some liquid remains. Return the shrimp and clams to the pan. Taste for salt. Transfer to a 375°F oven, uncovered, for 7 minutes. Remove, cover lightly with foil, and let sit on top of the stove, 10 to 15 minutes. Serve, passing the *Ajo Aceite* separately.

Fish ❧ Poultry ❧ Meats

SEPIA A LA PLANCHA CASA SALVADOR
(Cuttlefish in Garlic and Vinegar Sauce)

I have eaten shellfish in the traditional garlic, oil, and parsley sauce on innumerable occasions, but this version served with cuttlefish, which I enjoyed at Casa Salvador south of Cullera on the Valencia coast, was unusually delicious; it seemed to have some additional ingredients, which turned out to be vinegar and crushed almonds. The result was a somewhat thicker sauce of uncommon flavor, and the added touch of *alioli* served on the side made this dish outrageously good.

Salvador, a man of immense girth with a Dalí-esque mustache, who directs operations without ever rising from his front desk, owes his success in part to his mother, who still presides over the kitchen. Crowds flock to this large attractive restaurant, occupying two typical slope-roofed Valencian houses called *barracas*. It is beautifully set on the Estany lagoon, where fishermen, on shore or in old-fashioned rowboats, cast their lines from long thick poles.

It would be heresy to come to Casa Salvador without eating their excellent paellas, but this dish is a wonderful starter.

Serves 4 as a first course or tapa

10 unpeeled almonds, chopped
3 tablespoons minced parsley
Salt
¼ cup olive oil
3 cloves garlic, minced
¼ cup white wine vinegar

¾–1 pound cleaned (see
    p. 81) cuttlefish or large
    squid
Freshly ground pepper
1 recipe *Alioli* (see p. 196)

In a mortar or mini processor, mash the almonds, 2 tablespoons of the parsley, and ⅛ teaspoon salt to a paste.

In a small skillet, slowly heat the oil and garlic. When the garlic begins to sizzle (do not let it brown), add the vinegar and simmer slowly 5 minutes. Add the almond and parsley mixture and simmer 5 minutes more. Set aside.

Sprinkle the cuttlefish with salt and pepper. Brush a griddle or skillet with olive oil and heat to the smoking point. Grill the cuttlefish over high heat, about 5 minutes, turning once (don't overcook or it will toughen). Place in a serving dish (you may cut into bite-size pieces), reheat the sauce, and pour over the fish. Sprinkle with the remaining tablespoon parsley. Serve the *Alioli* on the side.

LUBINA A LA BRASA CON SALSA DE TOMATE FRESCA

(Charcoal-Grilled Striped Bass with Fresh Tomato Sauce)

We were in the city of Valencia, dining at an elegant restaurant with a large table of friends. Everyone had this striped bass, and as we tasted it, all conversation came to a halt so that we could concentrate on savoring each exquisite bite. Of course, part of the beauty of the dish is the spectacular quality and freshness of the fish, but it is also the perfect balance of the fish, its charcoal-grilled preparation, and the herb-scented bed of tomato on which it is served.

Serves 4

FRESH TOMATO SAUCE

2 pounds ripe and flavorful tomatoes, skinned, seeded, and finely chopped

2 tablespoons extra virgin olive oil

2 cloves garlic, minced

1½ teaspoons minced rosemary leaves or ¼ teaspoon dried

2 tablespoons minced parsley

1 tablespoon minced oregano leaves or ½ teaspoon dried

1 tablespoon thyme leaves or ½ teaspoon dried

1 tablespoon minced marjoram leaves or ½ teaspoon dried

¼ teaspoon sugar

Salt

Freshly ground pepper

. . .

1½ pounds striped bass fillets, skin on

Salt

Olive oil

Rosemary, thyme, or parsley sprigs for garnish

To make the Fresh Tomato Sauce, place all ingredients in a saucepan and simmer 10 minutes, uncovered.

Sprinkle the fish fillets with salt and brush on both sides with olive oil. Cook on a greased grill over hot coals or on a stovetop griddle until done, turning once, about 10 minutes to each inch of thickness. Spoon the tomato, sauce onto 4 dinner plates and place the fish, skin side up, over the sauce. Garnish with sprigs of rosemary, thyme, or parsley.

POLLO EN PEPITORIA
(Chicken in Almond and Pine Nut Sauce)

This very old recipe, appearing in a similar form in cookbooks of the sixteenth century, like *El Llibre del Cuiner* by Ruperto de Nola, was mentioned by Cervantes and other early writers. The dish is most probably of Moorish origin, and classic versions call for hen instead of chicken. The tomato, discovered in America and incorporated into Spanish cooking at a later date, is used in this especially good version that comes from an unpublished cookbook by Carmen Pastor (see p. 324).   *Serves 4*

A 3–3½-pound chicken
Kosher or sea salt
1 tablespoon olive oil
1 small onion (about ¼ pound), chopped
1 small skinned, seeded, and finely chopped tomato

Freshly ground pepper
Pinch of cinnamon
2 tablespoons minced parsley
½ cup dry white wine
½ cup chicken broth

PICADA

10 blanched almonds, finely chopped
2 tablespoons pine nuts
2 cloves garlic, minced

1 tablespoon parsley
Few strands of saffron
Salt

·   ·   ·

1 hard-boiled egg, minced

Cut the chicken into small serving pieces, discarding the wing tips, hacking off the bony ends of the legs, cutting each thigh in halves crosswise and the breast in 4 pieces. Sprinkle with salt.

Heat the oil in a shallow casserole and brown the chicken lightly on both sides. Add the onion, sauté 2 minutes, then add the tomato, pepper, cinnamon, 1 tablespoon of the parsley, the white wine, and broth. Cover and simmer 30 minutes.

Meanwhile, combine the Picada ingredients in a mortar or mini proces-

Chicken in Almond and Pine Nut Sauce (continued)

sor, and mash to a paste. Stir into the chicken and cook 15 minutes more. Sprinkle with the minced egg and the remaining tablespoon parsley and serve.

CANELONES MAMÁ
(Chicken, Veal, and Sausage–Filled Cannelloni)

In Spain *canelones* are so popular that dried pasta cut in small squares for that purpose can be found at every corner grocer. Curiously, this is one of the very few pasta dishes to become a part of traditional Spanish cooking.

Serves 4–5

1 tablespoon olive oil
1 medium onion, chopped
½ pound ground chicken or turkey
½ pound ground veal
1 tablespoon minced Spanish mountain cured ham or prosciutto
¼ pound sweet sausage meat
Salt
Freshly ground pepper
1 tablespoon dry sherry (*fino*)

1 tablespoon liverwurst or other liver pâté
4 tablespoons (¼ cup) grated Manchego or Parmesan cheese
3 tablespoons minced parsley
20 dried cannelloni, about 2½ inches square, fresh pasta cut in 4-inch squares, fresh wonton skins, or dried un-ridged manicotti
1 cup tomato sauce, preferably homemade (p. 95)

WHITE SAUCE

5 tablespoons butter
5 tablespoons flour
2 cups milk

Salt
Freshly ground pepper
Dash of nutmeg

. . .

Butter

In a skillet heat the oil and sauté the onion until wilted. Add the chicken, veal, ham, sausage, salt, and pepper (the mixture should be well seasoned). Brown, stirring and breaking up the meats as they cook. Stir in the sherry, the liverwurst, 1 tablespoon of the cheese, and the parsley.

Drop the cannelloni into a large pot of boiling salted water to which 1 tablespoon of oil has been added. Cook until al dente, about 10 to 12 minutes for dried pasta and just a few seconds for fresh pasta and wonton skins. Drain, run under cold water, and dry on paper towels.

Pour the tomato sauce into a baking pan in which the *canelones* will fit snugly. Place about 2 tablespoons of the meat filling on each pasta square. Roll and arrange seam side down in the baking pan.

To make the White Sauce, melt the butter in a saucepan. Stir in the flour and cook a minute or so. Gradually add the milk, then season with salt, pepper, and nutmeg. Cook until thickened and smooth.

Pour the White Sauce over the *canelones*. Sprinkle with the remaining 3 tablespoons cheese, dot with butter, and bake at 450°F for about 10 minutes, or until bubbly and lightly browned.

CHULETAS DE CORDERO AL AJO CABAÑIL RINCÓN DE PEPE
(Lamb Chops and Sliced Potatoes with Garlic and Vinegar)

This is a wonderful lamb dish from Murcia, as prepared by one of the region's finest restaurants, Rincón de Pepe, where Raimundo Frutos and his son and daughter take great pride in their restaurant and its regional foods. *Ajo cabañil* refers to the garlic and vinegar sauce, which seasons the meat as well as the potatoes, although the two are cooked separately. I have microwaved the potatoes instead of frying them, and the results are surprisingly similar.   *Serves 4*

Lamb Chops and Sliced Potatoes (continued)

12 cloves garlic, peeled and
    mashed to a paste in a garlic
    press
¼ cup white wine vinegar
½ cup chicken broth
½ teaspoon sugar
1 pound potatoes, peeled and
    cut in very thin slices

3 tablespoons olive oil
Salt
Freshly ground pepper
2½ pounds small rib lamb
    chops, ¾–1 inch thick

In a small bowl, combine the mashed garlic, vinegar, broth, and sugar. Arrange the potato slices in layers in a greased microwave-safe dish, sprinkling each layer with oil (a total of about 1 tablespoon), salt, and pepper. Drizzle on 2 tablespoons water, cover, and cook on high 7 minutes. Mix in half of the garlic mixture, cover, and microwave about 8 minutes more, or until the potatoes are tender. Alternatively, the potatoes can be roasted, omitting the water, covering with foil, and cooking in a 350°F oven for about 1 hour, adding the garlic mixture after 30 minutes.

When the potatoes are almost ready, heat the remaining tablespoon of oil in a skillet and sauté the chops over a high flame until browned and almost done. Sprinkle with salt and pepper and stir in the remaining garlic mixture. Simmer 10 minutes.

To serve, place the potatoes in the center of each dinner plate or a serving platter and arrange the chops around them.

GUISADO DE MELÓN
(Beef Stew with Melon)

One evening at the home of our dear friends Chalo Peláez and Mari Carmen Martín, Mari Carmen showed me a well-worn volume with the word *diario* (diary) on its cover. She handled it with care, almost reverence, for this was nothing less than the handwritten cookbook of her mother, Carmen Pastor, who had lived in Valencia and died when Mari Carmen was just a child. Inside, in a difficult-to-decipher, beginning-of-the-century penmanship, was a treasure trove of recipes, collected from the different regions in which the family had lived and from the various cooks that the family had employed over the years. One immediately caught my eye: a beef stew cooked with melon. I had never seen such a recipe before, but I assumed that since Valencia is famed for its fine fruits and vegetables and was long under Moorish domination that the sweet addition of melon was a product of those times. It turned out to be a delicately flavored creation in which the melon dissolves into the sauce and lends a haunting, hard-to-identify flavor.   *Serves 4*

2 tablespoons olive oil
2 pounds stewing beef, cut in
   2½-inch cubes
Salt
½ cup chopped onions
2 tablespoons minced parsley
½ teaspoon paprika

2 teaspoons flour
Dash of cinnamon
½ cup chicken broth
Half medium melon, such as
   honeydew, scooped into
   balls or cut in ½-inch pieces

Heat the olive oil in a deep casserole. Add the meat and brown well on all sides. Sprinkle with salt, then add the onions and sauté until wilted. Stir in the parsley, paprika, flour, and cinnamon. Cook for a minute, then add the broth and the melon. Salt to taste. Cover and simmer 1½ to 2 hours, or until the meat is tender.

Desserts

ALMENDRADOS CARMEN
(Crisp Almond Wafers)

Another recipe from my treasured source, the personal recipe book of Carmen Pastor (see p. 324). These typically Spanish cookies have no shortening and are crisp, airy, and too tempting to stop at one.

Makes 20 large cookies

Crisp Almond Wafers (continued)

1 cup sugar	2 eggs, separated
½ pound blanched almonds	1 teaspoon grated lemon peel
(about 1⅓ cups)	Cinnamon

In a food processor, beat together the sugar and almonds until the almonds are very finely chopped.

Beat the egg whites with an electric beater until stiff but not dry. Gently stir in the egg yolks and the grated lemon peel, then add the almond and sugar mixture.

Line a cookie tray with foil and grease the foil. Drop the dough, 2 tablespoons at a time, onto the tray. Leave plenty of space between the cookies since they will more than double their size during baking. Sprinkle with cinnamon and bake at 350°F for about 10 minutes, or until golden. Cool on the cookie sheet, then peel off the foil.

ALMENDRADOS
(Almond Cupcakes)

Extremely simple, light, and moist cupcakes that are cholesterol free— neither egg yolk nor shortening enters into the recipe.   *Makes 12*

¾ pound blanched almonds	¼ teaspoon cinnamon
(about 2 cups)	½ teaspoon grated lemon peel
1 cup confectioners' sugar	3 egg whites

Toast the almonds on a cookie tray in a 350°F oven until they are lightly browned, about 5 minutes. Cool, transfer to a food processor, and grind as fine as possible. Add ½ cup of the sugar, the cinnamon and grated lemon peel, and briefly process again.

Beat the egg whites until foamy, gradually beat in the remaining ½ cup sugar, and continue beating until stiff but not dry. Fold in the almond mixture, and spoon into 12 greased muffin or cupcake pans 2½ inches in diameter, filling them ¾ full. Bake at 350°F for 15 to 20 minutes, or until the cupcakes spring back to the touch.

TARTA DE ALMENDRA Y PATATA
(Almond and Potato Cake)

Here is an old family recipe that comes to me from Reme Domínguez, co-owner and culinary whirlwind of Tasca del Puerto in Castellón de La Plana. This cake relies on ground almonds rather than flour to achieve cake consistency, and in this respect is quite similar to the famous *tarta de Santiago* or *tarta de almendra* (page 120). The addition of potato makes this confection incredibly moist, besides lending subtle flavor. Its taste and texture are remarkably like a pound cake, but without a trace of butter.

Makes one 8½- to 9-inch cake

½ pound blanched almonds
   (about 1⅓ cups)
2½ cups sugar
1 pound potatoes (preferably
   Idaho), peeled

6 eggs
¾ cup flour
Confectioners' sugar for
   dusting

In a food processor combine the almonds and 1 cup of the sugar. Beat until the almonds are finely ground.

Boil the potatoes in water to cover until tender. Pass through a ricer or strainer and stir in the almond and sugar mixture.

In a large mixing bowl, beat the eggs with an electric beater at high speed for about a minute. Gradually add the remaining 1½ cups sugar and beat until the mixture is thick and pale lemon colored. Gradually beat in the flour, then the potato and almond mixture.

Grease a 9-inch, 2½-inch-deep springform cake pan. Bake at 350°F for 1 to 1¼ hours, or until a toothpick inserted comes out clean. Cool and invert onto a serving dish. Dust heavily with confectioners' sugar. Wrap and store at room temperature—it will stay fresh and moist for several days.

CHAPTER 7

Andalucía

REGION OF FRIED FOODS
AND GAZPACHOS

We were about to leave for a summer vacation in Spain, struggling, as usual, with our unwieldy luggage, when the phone rang. It was our peripatetic friend Marsha Stanton, who seems to have been to every exotic destination imaginable. "Pick me up at the airport in Jerez de la Frontera on July 1," she said. "I'm going to treat all of us to a *langostinos* feast in Sanlúcar de Barrameda." Marsha had spent a short time in Spain with us the previous summer, and we had stopped only briefly at Casa Bigote restaurant in the beachside town of Sanlúcar de Barrameda to enjoy *langostinos,* the amazingly sweet and flavorful local prawns from the estuary of the Guadalquivir River. Next to us on that occasion a large family was eating with abandon heaping platters of prawns, lobster, fried fish, fish brochettes—in short just about everything this waterfront restaurant had to offer. Even the smallest children were devouring the most expensive shellfish, and we looked on with awe and envy, feeling slightly deprived by the "sensible" portions in front of us. That afternoon became etched in Marsha's memory; when she returned to New York, she could not stop thinking about the *langostinos* and the carefree seafood feast she had witnessed.

We met Marsha on the appointed day at the airport and arrived at our hotel in nearby Cádiz just in time to order a *fino* sherry and watch the glorious sunset over the Atlantic from our terrace. It was 10:00 p.m., but the night was young and it was a local holiday as well. We walked to the fetching Plaza del Tío de la Tiza, where lightbulbs crisscrossed from one rooftop to the next and tables covered with purple and coral cloths and bright green chairs had been set up for the evening's festivities. Mackerel and sardines were grilling at the doorstep of every bar in the square. Despite the hour, tots were out in force, clambering onto a makeshift stage to stomp in flamenco rhythms with all the aplomb of seasoned performers.

The following day we drove to Sanlúcar de Barrameda for *langostinos* that had been plucked that morning from the water and for which Marsha had traveled across the Atlantic. This time our platters were piled high and we ate lavishly, savoring every exquisite bite. Cherubic-faced Fernando of Casa Bigote looked on with obvious pleasure, knowing that his beloved *langostinos* ("They are part of my very being," he likes to tell me) are the finest in the world. We relaxed after lunch on the beach to the strains of flamenco wafting from the restaurant's bar—one of many spontaneous bursts of song that a visitor is likely to come upon in Andalucía.

Andalucía is without doubt a region of enchantment. Its many miles of fine beaches face both the Atlantic Ocean and the length of Spain's southern Mediterranean shores, and year-round good weather and majestic mountain landscapes have made it a popular tourist destination. But these undeniable attributes are less important than Andalucía's flamenco music and dance, the pageantry of its bullfights, and its colorful fiestas, which are not incidental holidays but integral to the life that Andalusians enjoy to the fullest.

Then there is Andalucía's fascinating Moorish legacy; we can credit the Moors, who ruled Andalucía for almost eight hundred years, with the region's ethereal architectural creations, from the incomparable Alhambra in Granada, the Great Mosque of Córdoba, and Sevilla's Alcázar, to the delightful patios, scrupulously whitewashed houses, and unbridled displays of brightly colored flowers that light up even the most humble balcony. Much of this may sound like an overblown travel brochure, and yet Andalusians are genuinely involved in their proud and colorful heritage; the exuberance expressed in their fiestas and flamenco is part of the very fiber of their being. This special joy of life is called *alegría* and is sure to captivate and delight you, as it has me for the past thirty years.

Eating is one more manifestation of Andalusian *alegría*, and cooking is neither a chore nor a cerebral exercise. To hear an Andaluz talk about food, you might think he is describing a darling child, for cooking is a labor of love, and freshness is key. "I put my very soul into my cooking," Salvador Lucero of Bar Bahía in Cádiz often tells me, his eyes welling up with emotion. It's little wonder that tapas, which probably originated here, have become a way of life for Andalusians. Tapas may be anything from thin slices of the region's extraordinary cured ham (*jamón de Jabugo*), to glistening fresh marinated seafood salads, plump intensely flavorful shellfish, crisply fried white anchovies (*boquerones*), or Moorish spiced kabobs; they are as much an excuse for socializing as an extraordinary eating experience. What better way to complement tapas than with Andalucía's world-renowned sherry and *manzanilla* wines, made in the unique microclimates of Jerez de la Frontera and Sanlúcar de Barrameda.

The eight-hundred-year presence of the Moors in Andalucía had a pronounced effect on regional cooking. Light sauces seasoned with cumin, coriander, and saffron, and simple sweets such as *pestiños,* bathed in honey, sprinkled with sesame seeds, and scented with anise, are clear examples of Eastern influences. Certainly it is true that Andalusians excel when it comes to preparing simply fried foods—especially same-day fresh fish—that are crisp and grease-free (some regional secrets for frying are included in this chapter). It is not surprising that this skill has reached perfection in Andalucía: you need only gaze upon the never-ending rows of olive trees blanketing the mountains of Jaén province to understand the importance of olive oil in the region. Besides using their olive oil for frying (contrary to popular belief, it is ideal for that purpose), Andalusians like it for dressing their wonderfully cooling salads and for enhancing marinades. It contributes flavor and silky texture to gazpacho, the Andalusian refreshment without equal when the weather turns fiery.

By naming Andalucía the Region of Fried Foods and Gazpachos I certainly do not mean to overlook, as many do, the wonderful diversity of Andalusian cooking. Fried foods need only a handful of recipes—that's why the dishes in this chapter do not reflect a predominance of fried foods. The bulk of the recipes cover a wide range of food preparations, many of Moorish origin, with exciting flavors that reveal a more unusual side of Andalusian cooking. I firmly believe that once some of the wonderful Moorish dishes of the past, like cilantro gazpacho, lamb with honey, lamb with apricots, chicken with sesame seeds, and chicken in pomegranate sauce, become known as part of the repertoire of Andalusian cooking, this region will be considered more than a match for the better-known gastronomic regions of Spain.

Be that as it may, nothing will change the fact that enjoying life to its fullest and reveling in fine food in the company of friends are the Andalusian way of showing the world what life is really all about.

Notes on Regional Wines and Brandies

*Andalucía is celebrated for its unique sherry wine, and the majority of the wine produced here is indeed sherry, a fortified wine that runs the gamut from very pale and dry to deeply colored and syrupy sweet. Typically the dry wines—*manzanillas, finos, *and* amontillados—*are aperitifs, while the sweeter* olorosos *and cream sherries are dessert wines. The major wineries usually produce all varieties—some of the best come from Barbadillo, Domecq, Williams & Humbert, Osborne, and Emilio Lustau.*

While the largest wine production comes from the Jerez region, sherry-like wines are also made in the Montilla-Moriles area of Córdoba (most notably by Alvear), and Málaga has long been known for its sweet wines made from the Pedro Ximénez grape.

There has been some interest in diversifying into white table wines, made from the same palomino *grape grown in the chalky* albariza *soil that creates sherry. The light refreshing Castillo de San Diego from Barbadillo has met with great success.*

Seignorial aged brandies are another highlight of sherry country, and several are decidedly impressive, such as Conde de Osborne, Carlos I (Pedro Domecq), and Lepanto (González Byass).

Salads ❦ Soups ❦ Meals-in-a-Pot Vegetables ❦ Egg Dishes

ENSALADA DE ESPINACA, CHAMPIÑONES, Y JAMÓN EN VINAGRETA DE JEREZ
(Spinach, Mushroom, and Ham Salad in Sherry Vinaigrette)

Spinach, mushrooms, and ham taste unusually good together, especially when paired with the distinctive taste of sherry vinegar.   *Serves 4–6*

SHERRY VINAIGRETTE

1 tablespoon Spanish sherry vinegar or red wine vinegar
¼ teaspoon Dijon-style mustard
3 tablespoons extra virgin olive oil

1 tablespoon minced parsley
1 clove garlic, minced
1 ½ teaspoons thyme leaves or ¼ teaspoon dried
Salt
Freshly ground pepper

. . .

About 9 cups young spinach leaves, well washed
¼ pound mushrooms, brushed clean and cut in thin slices

¼ pound Spanish mountain cured ham or prosciutto, cut in ¼-inch-thick matchsticks

In a small bowl, make the Sherry Vinaigrette by whisking together the vinegar and mustard, then the oil, parsley, garlic, thyme, salt, and pepper.

Arrange the spinach leaves on 4 salad dishes, scatter the mushrooms and ham on top, and spoon on the vinaigrette.

Vineyards of La Rioja in early spring

Artfully arranged fruits and vegetables, La Boquería market, Barcelona

The native black-hoofed Iberian free-range pigs, from which exquisite jamón ibérico *is made*

Baby lamb quarters roasting in a typical brick-vaulted wood-burning oven, Posada de la Villa, Madrid

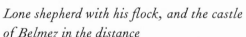

Lone shepherd with his flock, and the castle of Belmez in the distance

Purple saffron crocus breaking through the cracked soil at dawn, Membrilla, La Mancha

Paella cooked in the traditional way, over a wood-burning fire

Medicinal herbs to cure everything from low blood
pressure to hemorrhoids, in the mountain village of
Lanjarón, famed for its health-giving waters

Olive trees everywhere in narrow straight rows, Jaén province, Andalucía

Incomparable Spanish Sherry Wine Vinegar

Ranking among the world's elite vinegars, sherry vinegar from Andalucía is to common vinegar what a rare vintage wine is to sangría. Chefs have long treasured sherry vinegar for the unique flavor it imparts to food.

Sherry vinegar is worlds beyond the simple fermentation of an alcoholic liquid that is the base of all vinegars. Traditionally vinegar was just a by-product of wine making, a result of a natural process initiated when wine is exposed to light. It was not until Louis Pasteur scientifically studied fermentation that vinegar could be produced under controlled conditions. Vinegar has come a long way from its image (and its word origin) as "spoiled" wine to become today a gourmet item sought by connoisseurs.

Sherry vinegar begins with fine-quality sherry wines, made from the indigenous *palomino* grape, that have already undergone extensive aging by the *solera* system. By this method, young wine is poured into American oak wine barrels, arranged in tiers, and over a period of years, transferred from the upper to the lower casks, where the wine blends with traces of wines that may be far older.

Sherries destined to become sherry vinegar are subjected to a second *solera* system in which the wine is fermented and aged again in barrels previously used in wine making, thus imparting to the vinegar some of the wine's subtle flavors. The vinegar typically ages over a period of six years before it is ready for bottling. Like a fine wine, however, vinegar deepens in complexity if allowed to age still further, and there are older sherry vinegars that are gastronomic treasures. Nevertheless, a sherry vinegar label that reads "25-year-old sherry" generally means that the barrels from which the sherry vinegar was drawn contain a blend of vinegar, some of which may be of that age.

Use sherry vinegar whenever the taste of quality vinegar is important and most especially when cooking Spanish dishes. Although it

Spanish Sherry Wine Vinegar (continued)

usually stands out in salads and marinades, sherry vinegar is also distinctive in sauces, as today's creative chefs have discovered, and is important in some gazpachos. Remember, sherry vinegar is aged and therefore quite concentrated, so use a little less in any recipe that does not specifically call for sherry vinegar.

PICADILLO A LA GADITANA
(Tomato and Pepper Salad, Cádiz Style)

A wonderfully refreshing chopped salad that has the taste of Cádiz, where it often accompanies grilled or fried fish.   *Serves 6*

1 pound ripe and flavorful
    tomatoes, seeded, in a
    ½-inch dice
½ pound green frying peppers,
    cored and seeded, in a
    ½-inch dice
1 small onion, preferably
    Vidalia or Spanish, slivered

2 ounces light-meat tuna, in
    small chunks
¼ cup extra virgin fruity olive
    oil
2 tablespoons sherry vinegar
Salt
Freshly ground pepper

Combine in a bowl the tomatoes, peppers, onion, and tuna. In a cup, whisk together the olive oil, vinegar, salt, and pepper. Fold into the salad and taste for salt. Chill and serve in small salad bowls.

ENSALADA DE PIMIENTOS
A LA ANDALUZA
(Andalusian Pepper Salad)

In Cádiz and Sevilla, this delicious red and green pepper salad typically accompanies all kinds of simple seafood dishes (in particular, the Andalusian fish-fry, p. 359). It is often placed on the table in a bowl, allowing diners to take small amounts as they choose. *Serves 4–6*

1½ pounds green bell peppers
1½ pounds red bell peppers
Kosher or sea salt
Freshly ground pepper
4 tablespoons (¼ cup) minced
    Vidalia or Spanish onion

1 clove garlic, minced
2 tablespoons extra virgin olive
    oil
2 teaspoons sherry vinegar

Heat the oven to 500°F. Place the red and green peppers in a roasting pan and roast 20 minutes, turning once. Remove the peppers from the oven, transfer right away to a bowl, cover tightly with foil, and let sit until cool, about 30 minutes. Remove the peppers from the bowl, leaving the juices that have accumulated. Skin, core, and seed the peppers, cut into long strips about ½ inch wide, and return to the bowl. Add salt, pepper, the onion, garlic, oil, and vinegar. Gently mix with a rubber spatula. Cover and refrigerate 1 hour or more before serving.

ENSALADA ANDALUZA DE ARROZ
(Andalusian Rice Salad)

This is simple enough to be a side course with grilled meat, fish, or poultry or with any dishes that are served cool or chilled, like Marinated Trout (p. 141) or marinated quail, partridge, or chicken (p. 266). However, with its garnish of tomatoes, asparagus, peppers, and hard-boiled egg, it makes a nice summer lunch or light supper. *Serves 4*

Andalusian Rice Salad (continued)

1 cup short-grain rice
Salt
Olive oil
2 tablespoons minced cilantro
 or parsley
2 tablespoons flaked tuna
¼ cup cooked peas
2 tablespoons finely chopped
 pimento, preferably

imported or homemade (see
 p. 178)
2 tablespoons thinly sliced
 scallions
2 radishes, in thin slices
2 tablespoons chopped green
 olives

SALAD DRESSING

3 tablespoons extra virgin olive
 oil
1 tablespoon wine vinegar
Salt
Freshly ground pepper
⅛ teaspoon sugar

½ teaspoon imported sweet
 paprika
1 clove garlic, minced
1½ teaspoons thyme leaves or
 ¼ teaspoon dried

· · ·

2 hard-boiled eggs, in wedges
Pimiento strips
Cooked white or green aspara-
 gus spears

12 cherry tomatoes
Cured black olives

Bring the rice to a boil in 3 cups salted water and a splash of olive oil. Cover and cook at a high simmer until cooked slightly al dente, about 15 minutes. Pour into a strainer, rinse with cold water, and drain well. Transfer to a bowl. Fold in the cilantro, tuna, peas, chopped pimiento, scallions, radishes, and green olives.

Whisk together the Salad Dressing ingredients and fold into the rice mixture. Season with salt and pepper. Let sit 30 minutes at room temperature to blend flavors.

Transfer the salad to a serving bowl or a platter. Attractively arrange over it the egg wedges and pimiento strips, the asparagus, cherry tomatoes, and olives. Serve cooled or at room temperature.

ENSALADA DE PATATA VERANIEGA
(Summer Potato Salad in Sherry Vinaigrette)

Andalusians certainly know how to prepare foods that are appealing during the searing summers of the region. These marinated potatoes—with the addition of other refreshing ingredients like green pepper and cucumber—surely show this talent.   *Serves 6*

6 tablespoons extra virgin olive oil

2 tablespoons sherry vinegar

Salt

Freshly ground pepper

1½ pounds new or red waxy potatoes

¼ cup freshly squeezed lemon juice

½ pound tomatoes, cut in wedges

2 hard-boiled eggs, cut in wedges

¼ cup finely diced kirby cucumber, peeled or unpeeled

2 scallions, finely chopped

¼ cup finely diced green bell pepper

12 cured black olives

In a small bowl, whisk together the oil, vinegar, salt, and pepper. Boil the potatoes in salted water mixed with the lemon juice until tender. Cool slightly, then peel and cut in ⅛- to ¼-inch slices. Arrange in layers in a shallow serving bowl, drizzling each layer with a very small amount of the vinaigrette and seasoning lightly with salt and pepper.

Arrange the tomato and egg wedges over the potatoes. Scatter on the cucumber, scallions, green pepper, and olives. Pour the remaining vinaigrette over the salad. Serve chilled or at room temperature.

An Olive Oil Primer

Once upon a time Americans scorned olive oil, slathering butter lavishly on bread and using butter almost exclusively in cooking. How times have changed, thanks to scientific studies that prove what had long been conjectured: olive oil is good for you. It aids in digestion, reduces arteriosclerosis, is rich in vitamin E and carotene, and, best of all, is a mono-unsaturated fat that may prevent some forms of cancer and can actually help to lower cholesterol levels. With each new finding, olive oil consumption jumps still higher.

If you are confused by the bewildering array of olive oils, even in local supermarkets, you are not alone. Some labeling is deliberately deceptive, creating, for example, the impression that an oil is Italian, when in fact it has merely been bottled in Italy but produced elsewhere. Some oils called virgin may be far inferior in flavor to "pure" oils, and prices oscillate wildly, sometimes with little relation to quality. A fancy bottle can inflate a price significantly; many consumers, unsure how to choose an oil, associate elegant packaging with a superior product. What is beyond question is that Spain is the world's leading producer of olive oil and the country where some of the most exquisite oils are made.

Olive oil has been a "staff of life," you might say, for 6,000 years and in Spain dates back to the Romans, who brought the olive tree and the olive press to Spain. There, the tree thrived under ideal temperature and moisture conditions; ever since those early times, Spain has been a major exporter. Its olive oil traveled to ancient Rome and was brought to California by Franciscan monks, who planted olive trees in this new land similarly suited to olive oil production. Today Spain's olive oil finds its way to most of the world, but a surprisingly large portion of it still goes to Italy, where it is often bottled and shipped to the United States. Spain's olive oil production is today concentrated in Catalunya and in Andalucía, the region that produces fully 20 percent of the world's olive oil supply. Here, olive trees stretch as far as the eye can see in endless rows, their silvery leaves shimmering in the sunlight.

The use of olive oil is deep-rooted in Spain. Preferred in cooking, it is even used in making desserts. Contrary to popular belief, olive oil is ideal for deep-frying; foods fried in olive oil emerge crisper and more succulent, since olive oil quickly forms a coating around the food, thus blocking the penetration of oil. Although you might think olive oil expensive for frying, such is not the case, since it can be used repeatedly. Simply refresh before each use by frying a lemon peel and a slice of bread to remove any flavors and odors from past cooking. Store all olive oil away from light and do not refrigerate.

Olive oil is classified as pure, virgin, and extra virgin. Pure has the least quality, so it must be chemically refined, then mixed with some virgin oil for flavor. Virgin does not necessarily mean an oil tastes better, only that it has not been chemically processed. Extra virgin oils have the lowest acidity, generally use the finest olives, and are most likely to have the best flavor (and yet a technicality allows some very poor oils to be labeled extra virgin). As a rule, use pure and virgin oils for sautéing, frying, and in desserts, and reserve extra virgin oils for salads and marinades, to serve with pasta, and for drizzling on bread.

Green-tinted olive oils from early harvests are thick and fruity, while olives picked later in the season tend to be milder and have a pale yellow color. One is not necessarily better than the other; it's a question of taste and of how you plan to use it (do you like your oil to be assertive or remain in the background?). To distinguish among olive oils, your best bet is to taste them, preferably "straight" from the bottle, but otherwise on cubes of bread. See which oils please your palate (I am particularly partial to Andalucía's fruity green oils), then buy accordingly.

A small selection of Spain's best olive oils can be found at specialty food shops, or consult Marketing Sources, page 428. Among the finest extra virgin oils are Nuñez de Prado, Rafael Salgado, and Ybarra, and excellent supermarket-quality Spanish olive oils for everyday cooking, very reasonably priced, are Itálica and Sabroso pure olive oils.

GAZPACHO ANDALUZ, ESTILO SALVADOR
(Salvador's Celebrated Gazpacho)

Salvador Lucero, owner of Bar Bahía in Cádiz, has graciously provided me with any number of his simple but exceptional recipes. His silky smooth gazpacho, however, has become legendary, the standard by which all other gazpachos in Cádiz are measured. I can't remember how many times, when I have been dining with friends in Cádiz, someone orders gazpacho, tastes it, and comments, "It's very good, but doesn't compare to Salvador's." There's nothing unusual about the ingredients, save perhaps the proportions and the fine flavor of a mild golden-colored wine vinegar he uses (made in nearby Chiclana de la Frontera and with a faint flavor of sherry vinegar). I have achieved a similar taste by combining white wine vinegar with a small amount of sherry vinegar.   *Serves 8–10*

A 4½-inch length of bread, cut from a long narrow loaf, crusts removed

2 pounds ripe flavorful tomatoes, coarsely chopped

3 green frying peppers (about 6 ounces), coarsely chopped

1 kirby cucumber, about 5 inches long, peeled and coarsely chopped

1 medium onion, preferably Vidalia or Spanish, coarsely chopped

7 large cloves garlic, peeled and chopped

1 cup mild extra virgin olive oil

Salt

1 teaspoon sugar

6 tablespoons white wine vinegar

2 tablespoons sherry vinegar

2 cups cold water

Finely chopped tomato, green pepper, and/or cucumber for garnish (optional)

Soak the bread in water and squeeze dry. Place the tomatoes, peppers, cucumber, onion, and garlic in a large food processor with the olive oil, salt, sugar, vinegars, and bread. Process until as smooth as possible (do this in two steps if necessary). Pass through a strainer or chinois into a bowl, pressing with the back of a wooden spoon to extract as much liquid from the remaining solid pieces as possible. Stir in the water. Add more vinegar and salt, a little at a time, tasting after each addition, until the flavors are fully developed. Chill thoroughly. Taste again for salt and vinegar, and serve in chilled bowls with an ice cube in each, if necessary, to keep the chill (several mini ice cubes are more attractive). If you like, pass small bowls with the chopped vegetables so each diner can garnish to taste.

Andalucía's Quintessential Gazpacho

Gazpacho arouses passions in Andalucía (not at all surprising in a region where just about any subject sparks lively debate), for it is a dish uniquely *andaluz* and a source of enormous pride. Contests are held to decide the best gazpachos, and exhaustive studies on the subject abound. Everyone in every province of Andalucía has a favorite version, for the word "gazpacho" by no means denotes one specific preparation; rather, it refers to a loose grouping of soups that fall within certain recognized limits.

"Gazpacho is tradition, and that's that," declares José Briz, author of an entire book on the subject. No question that gazpacho is a supremely traditional dish, at least in its most primitive form. Although the word came into use in the seventeenth century, the original mixture of bread, garlic, salt, olive oil, vinegar, and water most likely dates to the Romans (the word is either from the Latin *caspa*, meaning fragments, or the Hebrew *gazaz*, meaning to break into pieces, both referring to gazpacho's bread base). A poor man's meal, both nourishing and refreshing, gazpacho was prepared and consumed by workers laboring in the fields under the fiery Andalusian sun. By the nineteenth century gazpacho had become considerably more sophisticated and subtle; the bread content was reduced, cucumbers were sometimes added, and the peppers and tomatoes introduced from America often incorporated. Indeed, there are lighter versions today that include neither bread nor oil.

We can thank the electric blender and a desire to eat healthy foods for making gazpacho a dish known and appreciated around the globe.

Gazpacho (continued)

Preparing gazpacho was once an arduous task that involved mashing ingredients in a mortar or passing them through a chinois. To this day many cooks consider labor-saving devices heresy; they recognize the blender's ability to finely chop ingredients, but contend that it is incapable of fusing many flavors into one.

Andalusians are masters of gazpacho and each province of the region has its distinctive style. Red gazpacho, still the favorite, is also the most celebrated worldwide. Only the finest tomatoes—deep red, juicy, and vine ripened—along with Andalusian extra virgin olive oil and local vinegar with a faint sherry flavor produce a gazpacho that meets with the approval of an *andaluz*. But there are many other versions of gazpacho, albeit sometimes with different names, among them green gazpachos, made with green vegetables and herbs; white gazpachos (*ajo blanco*), based on almonds or pine nuts; a thick sauce-like gazpacho called *salmorejo;* hot gazpachos; and *pipirrana,* which is closer to a finely chopped salad than a soup. And finally, there is a related dish by the same name found in La Mancha and Aragón—a heavy, and, to modern tastes, somewhat unappealing mix of bread and meats that Don Quixote's squire, Sancho Panza, loved to eat. Probably this gazpacho is closer to the original dish, but it most certainly has fallen out of favor today.

Don't think of cooling, delicious gazpachos as special-occasion soups. In summer I always have a jar of gazpacho in my refrigerator (there are several outstanding versions to choose from in this chapter) and we pour it by the glass whenever thirst overcomes us. One sip and we are instantly transported to Andalucía.

AJO BLANCO DE ALMENDRAS Y PIÑONES

(White Almond and Pine Nut Gazpacho with Melon)

Pure white and most refreshing, this gazpacho is more commonly made solely with almonds, but using pine nuts is one of many traditional variations. The touch of sweetness provided by the melon in the soup and used for the garnish is a lovely counterpoint to the piquant flavor of the soup.

Serves 6

2 ounces blanched almonds (about ⅓ cup)

2 ounces pine nuts (about ⅓ cup)

2 cloves garlic, peeled

1 teaspoon salt

Four 1-inch cubes of green melon, such as honeydew

4 slices good-quality sandwich or other bread, crusts removed

6 tablespoons extra virgin olive oil

1 tablespoon plus 1 teaspoon sherry vinegar

2 tablespoons white wine vinegar

4 cups iced water

Small green melon balls, 4–6 per portion

Place the almonds, pine nuts, garlic, and salt in the bowl of a food processor and beat until the nuts are as finely ground as possible. Add the cubes of melon and beat until puréed. Soak the bread in water, squeeze dry, and, with the motor running, add it, a few pieces at a time, to the processor. With the motor still running, drizzle in the oil, then beat in the sherry and white wine vinegars. Gradually pour in the water. Strain into a bowl.

Add more vinegar and salt, a little at a time, tasting after each addition, until the flavors are fully developed. Chill well. Taste again for salt and vinegar and serve in chilled bowls with the melon balls floating in the soup.

GAZPACHO BLANCO DE HABAS EL CHURRASCO
(Fresh Bean Gazpacho)

I defy anyone to identify the main ingredient in this outstanding green gazpacho from El Churrasco restaurant in Córdoba as being lima beans.

Makes 4 small portions

½ pound fresh or frozen lima beans

4 slices good-quality sandwich or other white bread, crusts removed

2 cloves garlic, peeled

Salt

3½ tablespoons wine vinegar

6 tablespoons extra virgin olive oil

1 cup chicken or vegetable broth

Small green melon balls, about 6 per portion

Place the lima beans in a microwave-safe dish with salted water to cover. Cover and cook on high for 2 minutes (or boil in a saucepan for 5 minutes). The limas will be partially cooked. Drain, reserving the cooking liquid. Measure the liquid to ½ cup, adding some water if necessary.

Soak the bread in water and squeeze dry. Put in a food processor along with the garlic, limas, salt, and vinegar, and beat until smooth. With the motor running, add the oil in a thin stream (the mixture will resemble a mayonnaise). Transfer to a bowl and stir in the ½ cup reserved cooking liquid and the broth. Add more vinegar and salt, a little at a time, tasting after each addition, until the flavors are fully developed. Chill well, taste again for vinegar and salt, and serve in chilled bowls, garnished with the melon balls.

GAZPACHO DE CILANTRO
(Cilantro Gazpacho)

Yet another take on gazpacho, this one incorporates cilantro and lettuce, which give this cold soup a totally distinct taste although it is still most certainly a gazpacho.

Serves 4

6 cloves garlic, peeled and cut
   in several pieces
1 small onion, peeled and cut in
   several pieces
1 kirby cucumber about
   5 inches long, peeled and
   cut in several pieces
1 medium green bell pepper,
   seeded and chopped
1 cup chopped cilantro

2 tablespoons chopped parsley
1½ teaspoons salt
4 slices good-quality sandwich
   bread, or other white bread,
   crusts removed
½ cup extra virgin olive oil
2 tablespoons sherry vinegar
2 tablespoons wine vinegar
2 cups water
6 tablespoons minced lettuce

Place in the bowl of a food processor the garlic, onion, cucumber, green pepper, cilantro, parsley, and salt, and process until no large pieces remain. Soak the bread in water and squeeze dry. With the motor running add pieces of the bread, then drizzle in the oil. Add the vinegars and 1 cup of the water. Strain or pass through a chinois into a bowl, pressing to extract as much liquid from the remaining solid pieces as possible. Stir in the remaining water. Add more vinegar and salt, a little at a time, tasting after each addition, until the flavors are fully developed. Stir in the lettuce and chill well. Taste again for vinegar and salt, and serve in chilled bowls.

ALBÓNDIGAS EN CALDO
(Meatballs in Broth)

We took our tour group for a fabulous tapas lunch in Córdoba at a very popular nineteenth-century tavern, Taberna San Miguel, which is set around a patio, its colorfully tiled walls filled with bullfight memorabilia. Loli, rosy-cheeked with a permanent smile on her face, has been in command of the kitchen for decades.

Although this dish is really a first course (or a light meal in larger portions), it was presented here as a tapa, in small soup bowls with two meatballs in each serving. One of our regular travelers, Lillian Seiden, took one taste and exclaimed, "Matzoh ball soup!" Indeed, she was probably right. We had just visited the fourteenth-century synagogue that functioned when Córdoba had an important Jewish community. This soup is most certainly a vestige of those times—with the difference that pork was substituted for matzoh meal. It was a common practice among converted Spanish Sephardic Jews to add pork in an effort to validate their conversion and, in many instances, to hide their continuing practice of Judaism.

This soup should be made with the broth of a chickpea stew to give it a slightly thickened consistency and a rich flavor. In lieu of this I have added some potato and mashed chickpeas to achieve a similar broth.

Serves 4

BROTH

1 pound chicken thighs, backs, and necks
6 cups water
½ pound potatoes, peeled and cut in ½-inch cubes
½ cup cooked chickpeas, homemade or good-quality canned
2 ounces Spanish mountain cured ham, prosciutto, or capicollo, in 1 piece

1 ham bone (optional)
1 small onion, peeled
1 clove garlic, peeled
2 sprigs parsley
¼ teaspoon crumbled thread saffron
6 peppercorns
1 bay leaf
Salt

MEATBALLS

⅓ cup dried bread crumbs
⅓ cup chicken broth
A 1-pound mixture ground veal and pork in equal parts
1 egg, lightly beaten
1 clove garlic, minced
1½ teaspoons salt
Freshly ground pepper
1 tablespoon minced Spanish

mountain cured ham, prosciutto, or capicollo
1 tablespoon olive oil
1 tablespoon minced parsley
Several strands of saffron, crumbled
Dash of nutmeg
Olive oil for coating

Bring all the Broth ingredients to a boil in a soup pot. Cover and simmer 1½ hours.

While the broth is cooking, make the Meatballs. In a bowl, soak the bread crumbs in the chicken broth, add the rest of the ingredients (except the olive oil for coating), and mix well. Shape into very smooth 1- to 1½-inch balls. Coat with olive oil to help prevent pieces of meat breaking off into the broth.

Strain the broth, mashing the chickpeas and potatoes through the strainer. Finely chop the ham. Return the broth to the pot and add the chopped ham. Heat the broth, drop the meatballs into the broth, cover, and simmer 45 minutes more. Serve in small soup bowls with some meatballs in each bowl.

LENTEJAS CON MELÓN
(Lentil Soup with Melon)

Here's a dish of obvious Moorish inspiration, with the characteristic sweet touch (although hardly perceptible) of melon and the lovely flavors of cumin and cilantro. Black sausage and bacon would most certainly not have been used by the Arabs, but they do add substance and greater character to the dish. *Serves 6*

3 tablespoons olive oil	preferably freshly ground in
2 large onions, peeled and chopped	a mortar or spice mill
2 cloves garlic, minced	Few strands of saffron
1 pound lentils, washed and drained	2 bay leaves
½ medium melon of your choice, seeded, skinned, and chopped	2 sprigs cilantro
2 cups chopped Swiss chard or escarole (white and green portions)	Pinch of cinnamon
Two 1-inch cubes slab bacon or salt pork	7 cups water
1 teaspoon ground cumin,	Salt

Ingredients (second column): preferably freshly ground in a mortar or spice mill; Few strands of saffron; 2 bay leaves; 2 sprigs cilantro; Pinch of cinnamon; 7 cups water; Salt; 2 tablespoons vinegar; 2 medium potatoes, peeled and quartered; 2 *morcillas* (black sausages) (optional); Chopped cilantro leaves for garnish

Heat the oil in a soup pot and sauté the onions and garlic until the onions have wilted. Stir in the lentils, melon, Swiss chard, slab bacon, cumin, saffron, bay leaves, cilantro sprigs, and cinnamon. Add the water, bring to a boil, cover, and simmer 45 minutes.

Lentil Soup with Melon (continued)

Add salt, the vinegar, potatoes, and black sausage, if using. Cover and continue cooking for 45 minutes more, until the lentils and potatoes are done. If the soup is too thick, add a little water, or if too soupy, boil down. Serve in soup bowls, sprinkled with cilantro.

MENUDILLO GADITANO SALVADOR
(Chickpea and Bean Stew with Greens)

START PREPARATION 1 DAY IN ADVANCE

Habitués of Bar Bahía in Cádiz look forward to the days when Salvador (see p. 340) cooks *menudillo,* a bean and vegetable stew which he serves in small portions as a tapa, although it is more commonly considered to be a hearty meal. I am constantly amazed by the great food that comes out of Salvador's closet-size kitchen.   *Serves 4 as a main course*

½ pound dried chickpeas
¼ pound dried large white
　beans
¼ pound celery, in 3-inch
　pieces
1 pound Swiss chard or collard
　greens, mostly the white
　portion, in 1-inch pieces
¼ pound sweet chorizo
1 pound lean pork, cut in
　4 pieces
A 2-ounce piece slab bacon,
　preferably fresh, otherwise
　cured
1 pig's foot, split in half
¼ pound black sausage,
　preferably Spanish-style
　morcilla

½ teaspoon imported sweet
　paprika
1 clove garlic, sliced
1 small onion, peeled,
　cut in pieces
6 cups water
2 tablespoons olive oil
½ medium dried sweet red
　pepper or mild New Mexico
　style, cored and seeded, or
　½ pimiento, finely chopped,
　plus ½ teaspoon paprika
3 cloves garlic, peeled
½ teaspoon cumin seeds or
　ground cumin
Dash of nutmeg
4 peppercorns
Salt

Soak the chickpeas and beans overnight in cold water to cover. Drain and transfer to a stewpot with the celery, Swiss chard, chorizo, pork, bacon, pig's foot, sausage, paprika, sliced garlic, onion, water, and olive oil. Bring to a boil, cover, and simmer 2 to 2½ hours, or until the chickpeas and beans are tender.

Meanwhile, soak the dried red pepper 10 minutes in warm water, drain, and chop finely. In a mortar or mini processor, mash to a paste the chopped red pepper (or pimiento and paprika), peeled garlic, cumin, nutmeg, and peppercorns. Stir into the stew and add salt to taste.

Cut the meats (discarding the pig's foot bones) into small portions, return to the soup, and serve.

PATATAS CAMPESINAS
(Potatoes with Walnuts and Cumin)

Here is a great dressing for boiled potatoes, with an enticing blend of walnuts, garlic, and cumin. It is equally good over other vegetables.

Serves 6

2 pounds new or red waxy
    potatoes, peeled
Salt
2 bay leaves
A few slices onion
2 cloves garlic, peeled
2 tablespoons chopped walnuts

½ teaspoon cumin seed or
    ground cumin
2 tablespoons minced parsley
2 tablespoons minced pimiento,
    preferably imported or
    homemade (see p. 178)
¼ cup extra virgin olive oil

Place the potatoes in a saucepan with salted water to cover. Add the bay leaves and onion slices and boil until tender.

Meanwhile, in a mortar or mini processor, mash to a paste the garlic, walnuts, ⅛ teaspoon salt, the cumin, and the parsley. Add the pimiento and continue mashing. Stir in the olive oil.

Drain the potatoes, reserving a few tablespoons of the water in which they have cooked. Stir enough of it into the mortar mixture to make a sauce of a mayonnaise consistency. Spoon over the potatoes or serve on the side.

PATATAS AL AJILLO
(Garlic Potatoes)

These sautéed sliced potatoes, seasoned with a mixture of garlic, cumin, paprika, and vinegar, make a splendid accompaniment for any plain meat, fish, or poultry dish.   *Serves 4*

3 tablespoons olive oil	½ teaspoon paprika
4 medium potatoes, peeled, in ⅛-inch slices	¼ teaspoon ground cumin, preferably freshly ground in a mortar or spice mill
Salt	
2 cloves garlic, minced	1 teaspoon vinegar
1 tablespoon minced parsley	2 teaspoons chicken broth

Heat the oil in a 9- or 10-inch skillet and arrange the potato slices in layers, sprinkling each layer with salt. Turn the potatoes to coat them with the oil, then lower the heat to medium-low. Cover and cook until the potatoes are tender, about 20 minutes, lifting and turning occasionally (some of the potatoes will brown).

Meanwhile, in a mortar mash to a paste the garlic, parsley, paprika, and cumin. Stir in the vinegar and broth, then sprinkle this mixture over the potatoes and serve.

BERENJENA EN SALMOREJO
(Fried Eggplant with Salmorejo *Sauce)*

Salmorejo in classic Cordoban cooking resembles a mildly seasoned, very thick gazpacho, and frankly I always found it a bit heavy as a dish in itself. But recently *salmorejo* has become popular as a dipping sauce, especially for fish and vegetables. Sprinkled with cured ham and chopped egg and served as an accompaniment to crisply fried eggplant—as it is at El Churrasco restaurant in Córdoba—its blend of flavors is exquisite. It's hard to judge yields, since the eggplant seems to disappear in the blink of an eye, so I have allowed enough sauce for double the amount of eggplant called for in the recipe. The dish may be a first course or a tapa.   *Serves 6–8*

SALMOREJO SAUCE

Three ½-inch-thick bread
   slices, cut from a round
   country bread, crusts removed (about 1½ cups
   cubed)
1 pound ripe flavorful tomatoes, skinned and seeded
1 small clove garlic, minced

¾ teaspoon salt
¼ cup fruity extra virgin olive
   oil
1 teaspoon wine vinegar
1 hard-boiled egg, chopped
¼ cup chopped Spanish
   mountain cured ham or
   prosciutto

. . .

A ¾-pound eggplant, peeled
   and cut in ⅛-inch crosswise
   slices
Milk
¼ teaspoon salt

Oil for frying
A mixture of flour and
   cornmeal for coating the
   eggplant

To make the Salmorejo Sauce, soak the bread in water and squeeze dry. Place in a processor the tomatoes, garlic, and ¾ teaspoon salt and purée. With the motor running, gradually add the bread, then drizzle in the olive oil and finally the vinegar. Transfer to a serving bowl and sprinkle with the egg and ham.

Soak the eggplant in milk to cover mixed with ¼ teaspoon salt for 10 minutes. Pour the oil into a skillet to a depth of at least 1 inch (or better still, use a deep-fryer) and heat until the oil quickly browns a cube of bread. At the moment of frying, remove the eggplant slices one by one from the milk—do not dry—and coat with the flour and cornmeal, patting with fingertips so the mixture adheres well. Immediately transfer to the hot oil. Fry until golden, turning once. Drain on paper towels and serve immediately. While cooking the remaining slices you can keep the eggplant warm in a 200°F oven. Pass the Salmorejo Sauce separately.

ALBORONÍA

(Eggplant, Peppers, and Tomatoes with Cumin and Cilantro)

Without doubt, this dish originated with the Moors and was enriched much later with New World tomatoes and peppers (and to think that the "newest" trend in cooking today is the fusion of East and West!). It took the discovery of America to bring all these ingredients together, and yet eggplant with tomato and peppers, seasoned with the Eastern spices of cumin and cilantro, is an exceptional and most natural melding of flavors.   *Serves 4*

1 pound small eggplants,
    unpeeled, in ½-inch cubes
Olive oil
2 cloves garlic, peeled
A ¼-inch-thick bread slice, cut
    from a long narrow loaf
1 medium onion, finely
    chopped
½ pound green frying peppers,
    cored, seeded, and diced
½ pound tomatoes, skinned,
    seeded, and chopped

½ teaspoon ground cumin,
    preferably freshly ground in
    a mortar or spice mill
2 tablespoons minced cilantro
A few threads of saffron,
    crumbled
Salt
Freshly ground pepper
Minced cilantro for garnish

Place the eggplant cubes on a cookie tray and brush with olive oil. Place in a 400°F oven and bake 10 minutes, turning once.

In a shallow casserole, heat 1 tablespoon of oil and sauté the garlic and the bread slice until the garlic is golden (do not overbrown) and the bread crisp. Drain on paper towels and cool, then transfer to a mortar or mini processor and mash to a paste.

Sauté the onion and peppers in the casserole (add a little more oil if necessary) for a minute or two, cover, and cook very slowly 10 minutes. Turn up the flame, add the tomatoes, and cook 5 minutes more. Stir in the cumin, cilantro, eggplant, saffron, salt, and pepper. Cover and cook for 5 minutes more. Add the mortar mix and let sit a few minutes. Sprinkle with cilantro and serve.

PISTO CORDOBÉS
(Vegetable Stew, Córdoba Style)

There are versions of this vegetable stew in most regions of Spain and generally all are based on tomato, peppers, and zucchini. I found this *pisto* from Córdoba while browsing through a marvelous booklet issued by the producers of olive oil from the Baena appellation of origin. The recipes are written in script in a folksy style and couldn't be more down to earth.

Served with crisp garlic bread rounds, this pisto has beaten eggs stirred into the mixture right before serving. The eggs greatly enhance the flavor, but unfortunately do not give a very pretty appearance. You may delete the eggs, but I don't recommend doing so. *Pisto* is an excellent supper dish.

Serves 4–6

2 cloves garlic, mashed to a paste in a mortar or garlic press

5 tablespoons extra virgin olive oil

8–12 bread rounds, ¼ inch thick, cut from a long narrow loaf

1 onion, coarsely grated

2 cloves garlic, minced

1½ pounds zucchini, in ¾-inch cubes

2 pounds potatoes, peeled and cut in 1-inch cubes

2 large green bell peppers, cored, seeded, and cut in ½-inch strips

2 tablespoons minced parsley

1½ pounds tomatoes, halved crosswise, seeded, and coarsely grated down to the skin

¼ teaspoon sugar

¾ cup water

Salt

Freshly ground pepper

4 eggs

In a cup, combine the mashed garlic and 2 tablespoons of the oil. Place the bread rounds on a cookie tray and brown lightly in a 350°F oven for about 8 minutes, turning once. Brush with the oil and garlic mixture and reserve.

In a large sauté pan, heat the remaining 3 tablespoons oil, add the onion and minced garlic, and cook until the onion has wilted. Stir in the zucchini, potatoes, peppers, parsley, tomatoes, and sugar, then add the water. Add salt and pepper to taste, cover, and simmer 25 minutes.

Lightly beat the eggs in a bowl and season with salt. Pour over the stew and stir until the egg is set. Serve accompanied by the garlic toast.

CEBOLLAS CON MIEL
(Onions Coated with Honey and Spices)

L. Benavides Barajas, in his interesting book on the foods of Moorish Andalucía, writes that for the Moors it was prohibited to eat raw onion, for religious reasons and because of the characteristic breath it left behind. He presents a recipe, however, for cooked onions with honey and spices, from which the following recipe has been adapted. They are spectacularly good and accompany pork particularly well. Since the onions have a strong flavor, a small amount goes a long way. You can vary the amounts of spice to taste.

Serves 4

12–16 small onions about
   1½ inches in diameter
4 teaspoons butter
2 tablespoons honey
A few strands of saffron,
   crumbled
Dash of ground cloves

⅛ teaspoon ground cumin,
   preferably freshly ground in
   a mortar or spice mill
Dash of nutmeg
Salt
Freshly ground pepper

Trim the stem end of the onions and make an incision in the shape of a cross at the same end. Plunge the onions into boiling water and boil 1 minute. Remove from the water and slip off the onion skins, then return the onions to the water, cover, and simmer 20 minutes more.

Pour off all but 2 tablespoons of the water, stir in the butter, honey, and all the remaining seasonings. Cook at a high simmer, uncovered, until the liquid is absorbed and the onions golden, stirring constantly (watch carefully to prevent scorching).

PURÉ DE GARBANZOS CON MIGAS
(Chickpea Purée with Crisp Bread Bits)

START PREPARATION I DAY IN ADVANCE

Chickpea purée is an exceptional side dish, especially with the additions of cumin and cilantro and contrasted with crunchy toasted bread cubes. For a quick version, use canned chickpeas, purée them, and combine with the sautéed onion and garlic and the seasonings, as directed below.

Serves 4

½ pound dried chickpeas
1 ham or beef soup bone
1 cup chicken broth
1 cup water
2 bay leaves
1 tablespoon plus 2 teaspoons
    olive oil
¼ cup minced onion
2 cloves garlic, minced
½ teaspoon imported sweet
    paprika
2 tablespoons minced cilantro
2 tablespoons minced parsley

Several strands of saffron
2 tablespoons dry white wine
¾ cup bread cut in ½-inch
    cubes
1 clove garlic, mashed to a
    paste
½ plus ⅛ teaspoon freshly
    ground cumin
Salt
Freshly ground pepper
1 hard-boiled egg, chopped
    (optional)

Soak the chickpeas overnight in cold water to cover. Drain.

Put the chickpeas in a soup pot with the soup bone, broth, water, and bay leaves. Bring to a boil, cover, and simmer 1 hour. Meanwhile, heat 1 table-spoon of the oil in a skillet and sauté the onion and garlic until the onion has softened. In a mortar or mini processor, mash to a paste the paprika, cilantro, parsley, and saffron. Stir in the wine.

Add the onion and mortar mixtures to the chickpeas and cook about 1½ hours more, or until the chickpeas are tender, adding more liquid during cooking if necessary. Boil down any remaining liquid when the chickpeas are done.

To make the toasted bread, combine the remaining 2 teaspoons oil with

Chickpea Purée (continued)

the mashed garlic and ⅛ teaspoon of the cumin. Place the bread cubes on a cookie sheet and drizzle or brush with the garlic mixture. Bake at 350°F about 5 minutes, or until crisp and golden.

Discard the bay leaves and soup bone and purée the chickpeas, seasoning with the remaining ½ teaspoon cumin, salt, and pepper. Serve, scattering the optional chopped egg and the toasted bread cubes over the purée.

MIGAS ESTILO ANDALUZ
(Sautéed Bread Bits with Peppers, Grapes, and Fried Eggs)

It was a glorious October day in southern Spain when we left Úbeda with our tour group after seeing its extraordinary assemblage of architectural works from the Renaissance period and having dined the night before at the sixteenth-century palace of our old friend Natalio Rivas. We were heading to the nearby ranch of another friend, Juan Pablo Jiménez, where fighting bulls, destined for the bull ring, are raised. There we were treated to an outdoor country meal of *migas* with all the trimmings: sautéed peppers, fried eggs, and grapes. We basked in the sunlight and joined in song with our hosts to the accompaniment of guitars. In this setting, no meal could have been better than this one.

As we prepared to leave, Juan Pablo instructed two ranch hands to mount their horses and round up the bulls, which we had not yet seen. We were warned to stay close to our bus and to be absolutely still—the bulls are accustomed to their keepers and will do them no harm, but anything out of the ordinary brings out their inbred fighting instincts. As we stood transfixed, dozens of the majestic creatures came into view and approached us. Someone inadvertently emitted an exclamation. The bulls raised their mighty heads; their eyes, as one, focused on us. We beat a hasty retreat to the safety of the bus and continued on our way.

Migas must be made with day-old bread and then moistened so that when they are crisped in the skillet they will remain tender within. Nothing tastes better with them than peppers and fried eggs, and the grapes provide a refreshing contrast. *Migas* are one of the great comfort foods of Spain.

Serves 4

8 cups day-old good-quality
  crustless torn bread pieces,
  about ½-inch size
Kosher or sea salt
3 tablespoons olive oil
¼ cup fresh slab bacon,
  pancetta, or cured slab
  bacon, in ½-inch cubes
3 sweet chorizos (about 6
  ounces), sliced or in a
  ½-inch dice
¼ pound Spanish mountain
  cured ham, prosciutto, or

capicollo, cut ¼ inch thick
  and diced
6 cloves garlic, minced
2 tablespoons minced onion
2 teaspoons imported sweet
  paprika
1½ pounds small green frying
  peppers, left whole
2 cloves garlic, lightly smashed
  and peeled
8 fried eggs, Spanish style
  (p. 254)
24 peeled seedless green grapes

Place the bread pieces in a bowl. Combine ½ cup water with ¼ teaspoon salt, and with your hands gradually work the salted water into the bread, dampening it evenly. Set aside.

In a large skillet heat 1 tablespoon of the oil and sauté the slab bacon slowly until its fat is rendered. Add the chorizos, ham, garlic, and onion and cook slowly until the onion has softened and the meats are lightly crisped. Add the bread pieces, sprinkle with the paprika, and stir to coat. Continue cooking until the bread is golden and crisp, about 20 minutes.

To make the peppers, heat the remaining 2 tablespoons oil in a skillet. Add the peppers and peeled garlic cloves and slowly brown the peppers, turning occasionally, until softened to taste. Sprinkle with salt.

Prepare the fried eggs according to instructions. Serve the sautéed bread scattered with the grapes and served with the peppers and the fried eggs on the side.

HUEVOS A LA FLAMENCA
(Baked Eggs, Flamenco Style)

Although considered a typical dish of Sevilla, Huevos a la Flamenca is said to have originated in the late eighteenth century at a meal attended by Charles IV in Aranjuez in the province of Madrid at an estate called La Flamenca.

Another theory which seems more plausible is that *a la flamenca* makes reference to the colorfulness of the dish. Whatever its origin, this is one of my favorite one-dish meals.

Serves 4

2 tablespoons olive oil
1 medium potato, peeled and
    cut in a ½-inch dice
1 cup finely chopped onions
2 cloves garlic, minced
¼ pound Spanish mountain
    cured ham, prosciutto, or
    capicollo, cut in ¼-inch
    slices, then diced
6 tablespoons cored, seeded,
    and finely chopped green
    frying peppers
¼ teaspoon imported sweet
    paprika
½ pound tomatoes, skinned,
    seeded, and chopped
2 tablespoons minced parsley
¼ cup cooked peas

¼ cup cooked green beans cut
    in 1-inch pieces
2 tablespoons chopped
    pimiento, preferably
    imported or homemade
    (p. 178)
¼ pound sweet chorizo, in
    ⅛-inch slices
2 teaspoons tomato sauce
    (optional)
½ cup chicken broth
Salt
Freshly ground pepper
8 eggs
¼ pound small cooked
    asparagus tips
Pimiento strips for garnish

Heat the oil in a skillet and slowly fry the potatoes, covered, until tender. Remove the potatoes to a warm platter and add to the skillet the onions, garlic, ham, and green peppers. Sauté until the onions have softened. Stir in the paprika, tomatoes, and parsley and cook two minutes. Add the peas, green beans, pimiento, chorizo, optional tomato sauce, broth, salt, and pepper and cook 2 minutes more. Mix in the reserved potatoes.

Divide into 4 individual ovenproof casseroles, preferably Spanish earthenware. Break 1 egg at a time into a cup and slide over the vegetable mixture, 2 eggs to each casserole. Sprinkle the eggs with salt and pepper. Arrange the asparagus and pimiento strips attractively in the casseroles and transfer to a 450°F oven for about 8 minutes, or until the eggs are just set (be careful not to overcook, since the eggs will continue to cook in the hot dishes once they are removed from the oven).

Fish

PESCADO FRITO A LA SANLUQUEÑA
(Fried Fish, Sanlúcar Style)

I had despaired of ever being able to reproduce the incredibly crisp and greaseless fried fish that I so enjoy eating all over Andalucía. But thanks to a few tips from Fernando Hermoso (see p. 329) of Casa Bigote in Sanlúcar de Barrameda, I have finally reproduced it to my satisfaction. You will of course have to find just-caught fish (perhaps catch it yourself!) to completely duplicate the dish, then follow Fernando's instructions: wet the fish before salting and coating with flour, use a very coarse flour, and fry in very hot oil.

You can use just about any kind of whole fish (as long as it is very small) or fish fillets for this recipe. For a classic Andalusian fish-fry, combine several kinds of whole fish, like baby flounder, whiting, and/or snappers (if you can find tiny whitebait, by all means use it also). For variety include fried squid (p. 42) and Marinated Fried Fish (p. 46). Some classic accompaniments are sautéed green peppers (p. 357), the chopped salad *picadillo* (p. 334), or pepper salad (p. 335). You might also wish to offer a dipping sauce like Garlic Mayonnaise (p. 196), and serve the fish with a very dry chilled sherry, like *manzanilla* from Sanlúcar or *fino* from nearby Jerez de la Frontera.

The typical way to eat these fried fish is to pick them up, nibble the meat along one side right down to the bone (as if playing the harmonica, my husband likes to say), turn to the other side, and repeat. Eat the tails—they will be crunchy like potato chips—and if you have left the heads on, bite on the crispy lips. Whitebait, if included, can be eaten whole, bones and all.

Serves 4

1½ pounds whiting, smallest available, cleaned, heads on or off
4 very small whole flounders, cleaned, heads off, or flounder fillets, cut in halves lengthwise
1 pound very small smelts or snappers, cleaned, heads on or off

Fried Fish, Sanlúcar Style (continued)

Freshly squeezed lemon juice
Salt
¾ cup flour
¾ cup cornmeal
Mild olive oil or salad oil for
   frying

Parsley or radish leaves for
   frying
Lemon wedges

Wet the fish thoroughly with water and sprinkle with lemon juice and salt. Combine the flour and cornmeal and dredge the wet fish in this mixture.

Heat the oil in a skillet to a depth of 2 inches (or better still, use an electric fryer set at 375°F) until it reaches the smoking point. Shake off any loose flour from the fish and fry in the oil over high heat, turning once. Fry in several steps if necessary. (Adding too much fish to the oil will cause the oil temperature to drop.) Figure about 8 minutes to each inch of thickness. The fish should be lightly golden and very crisp. Drain on paper towels.

Plunge the parsley or radish leaves into the hot oil and fry until just crisp—it shouldn't take more than a few seconds. Drain on paper towels and use to garnish the fish. Serve the fish with lemon wedges.

PESCADO A LA SAL
(Fish Baked in Salt)

I cannot think of a more succulent way than this to prepare whole fish, and it's hard to believe that a fish so plain can nevertheless be so memorable. Pescado a la Sal has in recent years caught on all over Spain, but I still associate it with Andalucía, where I have eaten it in Cádiz at the western extreme of the region, as well as in the port of Garrucha in the eastern province of Almería.

Don't be put off by the large amount of salt needed to make this dish; it acts only as an insulator, keeping the fish moist and giving it a firmer texture. Since the fish scales are not removed (this is very important), the salt is blocked from the fish (the skin and scales are removed before serving). Sea salt the size of pebbles is best, but kosher salt can also be used. Likewise, this cooking technique may be used for jumbo shrimp in their shells. Follow this same recipe (you may need less salt) and figure 1½ pounds shrimp for 4 servings. Bake at the same temperature for about 10 minutes, brush off all the salt, and serve the shrimp in their shells accompanied by the same dipping sauces.

You will want the freshest possible fish, and to ensure perfectly cooked fish, a meat thermometer is most helpful. It is customary to serve this dish with one or more sauces on the side. The garlicky parsley sauce on page 362 is ideal, but red or green *mojo* (p. 401 or 402) and/or cilantro mayonnaise (p. 404) are also favorites of mine. *Serves 4*

½ teaspoon *each* of dried thyme, oregano, rosemary, and marjoram
Two 1¾-pound fish, such as red snapper, cleaned (head on), scales left on
4 sprigs parsley
2 bay leaves
About 4 cups very coarse sea salt or kosher salt
Olive oil

Mix together the dried herbs. Sprinkle the mixture in the cavities of the fish, reserving ½ teaspoon. Also place 2 parsley sprigs and 1 bay leaf in each cavity.

In a bowl, combine the salt with 2 tablespoons water. Sprinkle a thin layer of the salt over the bottom of a shallow baking pan in which the fish just fits. Arrange the fish in the pan, brush with olive oil, and sprinkle with the reserved herb mixture. Coat the fish heavily with the salt—it should be completely covered. Pat the salt over the fish to secure.

Place in a 400°F oven and check after 20 minutes. A meat thermometer inserted in the thickest part of the fish should read 145°F. If it has not yet reached that temperature, return it to the oven, but watch carefully since the temperature will rise rapidly. If you do not have a meat thermometer, calculate about 25 minutes total baking time.

Bring the fish in the baking pan to the table for diners to see, then return to the kitchen, crack the salt, and discard. Transfer the fish to a work surface, brush off any remaining salt, and peel off the skin on the upper side. Fillet the fish and transfer to a warm platter or warm individual dishes. Pass the sauces separately.

SALSA DE AJO Y PEREJIL

(Garlic and Parsley Sauce)

Makes about ½ cup

6 tablespoons minced parsley
4 cloves garlic, mashed to a
    paste
6 tablespoons extra virgin olive
    oil

A squeeze of lemon juice
Salt

Mix together thoroughly all ingredients in a small serving bowl.

MERLUZA AL ACEITE CON PICADILLO EL FARO

(Steamed Hake with Olive Oil, Tomato, and Picadillo)

El Faro restaurant—the finest in the city of Cádiz and, I daresay, in the entire region of Andalucía—is always under the watchful, restless eye of owner Gonzalo Córdoba. He never ceases in his efforts to elevate his restaurant yet another notch, while at the same time broadening his horizons. He now has two more excellent restaurants in Cádiz province, El Faro del Puerto and El Ventorillo El Chato, each featuring one of his talented sons in the kitchen.

In his perpetual attempt to restrain his ever-expanding waistline, swelled by gourmand habits and an insatiable sweet tooth, Gonzalo has come up with this fish preparation. It takes choice ingredients of Andalucía and combines them into a healthy low-calorie dish with a sauce that closely resembles *salmorejo,* from the province of Córdoba.

Since there is nothing in this recipe to mask less-than-the-best ingredients, be sure to use the freshest fish, superior olive oil, and tomatoes that are, if possible, vine-ripened.

Serves 4

1½ pounds ripe, flavorful toma-
    toes, skinned and seeded

1 clove garlic, minced
Kosher or sea salt

¼ cup fruity extra virgin olive
    oil
1 teaspoon sherry vinegar

1½ teaspoons white or red wine
    vinegar

PICADILLO

2 tablespoons minced carrot
    cooked al dente
2 tablespoons minced unpeeled
    zucchini cooked al dente
1 teaspoon minced cured black
    olives
1 teaspoon minced green olives
1 teaspoon minced Vidalia or
    Spanish onion

1 tablespoon minced parsley
1 tablespoon finely chopped
    tomato
2 teaspoons fruity extra virgin
    olive oil
1 teaspoon freshly squeezed
    lemon juice
Salt

. . .

Fish Broth (p. 175) or clam
    juice diluted with ¼ part
    water

2 pounds hake or scrod, about
    1 inch thick and cut in
    4 serving pieces

In a food processor, blend the tomatoes, garlic, and a little salt until smooth. With the motor running, gradually add the ¼ cup oil and the vinegars. Transfer to a small saucepan and simmer 5 minutes. Adjust the salt and vinegar to taste.

In a small bowl, combine the Picadillo ingredients. Pour enough Fish Broth into a steamer or large pot so that it almost reaches the level of the rack that will be inserted to steam the fish. Cover the pot and bring the liquid to a boil. Arrange the fish on the rack, cover, and steam over medium-high heat about 8 minutes, or until the fish is just done.

Heat the tomato mixture and spoon it onto 4 dinner plates. Place a piece of fish on each plate and garnish with the Picadillo. Serve immediately, accompanied, if you wish, with boiled potatoes.

PESCADO EN AMARILLO
(Fish in Saffron Sauce)

START PREPARATION 1 HOUR IN ADVANCE

A specialty of the province of Cádiz, this fish is exceptionally tasty, with a very light sauce that hints of vinegar and saffron. It is called *en amarillo* because of the sauce's slightly yellow tinge. I have often enjoyed this dish, with the fish cut in cubes, as a tapa at my favorite tapas bar in the city of Cádiz—Bar Bahía.   *Serves 4*

4 teaspoons wine vinegar
¼ cup dry white wine
5 tablespoons olive oil
2 bay leaves
1 tablespoon thyme leaves or
    ½ teaspoon dried
1 tablespoon minced marjoram
    leaves or ½ teaspoon dried
Salt
Freshly ground pepper
2 pounds firm-fleshed fish, such
    as swordfish, shark, monk-
    fish, or halibut, about 1 inch
    thick

¼ teaspoon cumin seeds or
    ground cumin
Several strands of saffron
2 cloves garlic, peeled
2 tablespoons minced parsley
Flour for dusting
¼ cup minced onion
¼ cup minced green frying
    peppers
¼ cup skinned, seeded, and
    finely chopped tomato
1¼ cups Fish Broth (p. 175) or
    1 cup clam juice diluted
    with ¼ cup water

Combine in a shallow bowl the vinegar, wine, 2 tablespoons of the oil, the bay leaves, thyme, marjoram, a little salt, and pepper. Add the fish, turn to coat, and marinate 1 hour.

Meanwhile, in a mortar or mini processor mash as finely as possible the cumin, saffron, and ⅛ teaspoon salt. Add the garlic and parsley and mash to a paste.

Drain and dry the fish, reserving the marinade. Dust the fish with flour. In a shallow casserole, heat another tablespoon of the oil and sauté the fish, turning once, about 2 minutes to each side (the fish will be partially cooked). Transfer to a warm platter and wipe out the pan. Heat the remaining 2 tablespoons oil in the casserole and sauté the onion and peppers a minute or two. Cover and cook slowly about 15 minutes, until the vegetables have softened. Turn up the flame, add the tomato, and cook a minute or two, then pour in the reserved marinade, the Fish Broth, and the mortar mixture. Bring to a boil, then simmer 10 minutes, uncovered, adding a little water if the sauce becomes too thick. Add the fish, spoon some of the vegetables over it, cover, and simmer about 5 minutes, or until the fish is just done.

RAPE MOZÁRABE EL CABALLO ROJO
(Monkfish with Carrots and Raisins)

In an ongoing effort to revive the cooking of Andalucía's Moorish past, Córdoba's fine restaurant El Caballo Rojo offers this dish on its menu. I cannot vouch for its authenticity—brandy would most likely not have been used by Muslims—but it does taste wonderful.   *Serves 4*

2 pounds monkfish or scrod, about 1 inch thick
Kosher or sea salt
Flour for dusting
2 tablespoons olive oil
¼ cup finely chopped onion
1 small carrot, trimmed, scraped, and cut in ⅛-inch slices
2 tablespoons brandy
2 tablespoons raisins
1 cup Fish Broth (p. 175) or ¾ cup clam juice diluted with ¼ cup water

Sprinkle the fish on both sides with salt and let sit 5 minutes. Dust with flour. In a shallow casserole, heat 1 tablespoon of the oil and sear the fish on both sides. Remove to a warm platter and wipe out the pan.

Heat the remaining tablespoon of oil in the casserole and slowly sauté the onion and carrot until both have softened. Add the brandy and cook away. Return the fish to the casserole and add the raisins and Fish Broth. Bring to a boil, cover, and simmer about 15 minutes, or until the fish is just done.

CABALLA A LA PARRILLA CON PICADILLO DE TOMATE Y PIMIENTO

(Grilled Mackerel Topped with Tomato and Pepper Salad)

Whenever I think of Cádiz, a tantalizing image comes to mind: a warm summer night, a cozy square crammed with tables, smoke rising from outdoor restaurant grills, and whole mackerels that barely fit on platter-size dinner plates, smothered in a chopped tomato and pepper salad. Even when the setting is not Cádiz, I cannot think of a more perfect summer meal.

After grilling, I like to fillet the fish (leaving the skin on) for easier eating, then I spoon the salad over the boned fish. Trout is also delicious prepared in this manner.

Serves 4

5 tablespoons extra virgin olive oil

1 tablespoon white or red wine vinegar

Salt

Freshly ground pepper

¾ teaspoon sugar

1 small Spanish or Vidalia onion, slivered

1½ medium cored and seeded green bell peppers, in a ½-inch dice

Mackerel or trout, either four ¾-pound fish or two 1¼–1½-pound fish, cleaned, heads on

¾ pound ripe and flavorful tomatoes, in a ½-inch dice

In a bowl, whisk together 4 tablespoons of the oil, the vinegar, salt, pepper, and sugar. Stir in the onion and peppers. Reserve at room temperature.

Brush the fish on both sides with the remaining tablespoon oil and grill, preferably over charcoal—otherwise, on a stovetop griddle—until done, turning once, about 10 minutes to each inch of thickness.

Add the tomatoes to the salad. Carefully fillet the fish and arrange the fillets on a platter or individual dishes. Spoon on the salad.

Capers and Caperberries: Pungent Culinary Accents

Known to earliest civilizations, the caper bush (*capparis spinosa*) has grown wild in the Mediterranean for millennia, for it thrives in bright sunlight and in warm dry climates. Today it is also successfully culti-vated, and Spain's ideal growing conditions, especially in the regions of Andalucía, Murcia, and the Baleares, make Spain the world's largest producer of capers.

The caper bush bears graceful white flowers that send forth dozens of delicate pistils, but you're not likely to see the bush in bloom; while its flowers are still tightly closed buds the size of pellets, they are plucked and pickled to become highly prized nonpareil capers. Perfect timing, tedious hand labor, and close vigilance (not unlike that needed to harvest saffron, see p. 286) account for the high price of these elite capers.

All the buds, however, are not seized at this early stage of develop-ment, and those that have begun to unfurl are also harvested. These are far less costly, even though a caper's size is unrelated to its taste and quality. The difference is that the tiny and elegant nonpareils can be scattered whole into a sauce or over foods, while larger capers are usu-ally chopped to distribute their flavor more evenly.

The piquance of capers makes them ideal for marinades, especially those for shellfish, and as a good counterpoint to smoked fish and caviar. But certainly the usefulness of capers does not end here. Try ca-pers in a sauce for fresh tuna (p. 368), capers in beef stew (p. 154), in a marinade for quail eggs (p. 19), puréed with olives, garlic, and anchovy (p. 27), or scattered over Mallorcan-style bread (p. 24).

From the same caper bush comes the caperberry, which is the fruit that forms once the caper flowers have faded. They too are pickled, but are somewhat less pungent, so they can be eaten on their own as a light tapa or, in a role similar to the pickle, as a sharp accent to other foods. Caperberries are still somewhat novel and as such are sure to be tasty conversation pieces at any gathering.

ATÚN CON SOFRITO DE TOMATE Y ALCAPARRAS

(Fresh Tuna with Tomato Sauté and Capers)

The tomato and onion mixture for this sautéed tuna—light yet piquant with capers and vinegar—is exceptional, and also works well with salmon.

Serves 4

2 pounds fresh tuna steaks, about 1 inch thick
Kosher or sea salt
2 tablespoons capers, preferably nonpareil
2 tablespoons olive oil
1 medium onion, slivered
1 pound tomatoes, skinned, seeded, and chopped
2 tablespoons minced parsley
2 tablespoons wine vinegar
2 tablespoons Fish Broth (p. 175), diluted clam juice, or water

Sprinkle the tuna with salt on both sides. Place the capers in a cup and add cold water to cover.

In a shallow casserole, heat the oil to the smoking point and sear the tuna on both sides. Remove to a warm platter. Add the onion to the casserole, sauté a minute, then cover and cook very slowly 15 minutes, or until the onion has softened.

Turn up the heat and add the tomatoes, parsley, vinegar, and the capers, drained. Cook 5 minutes, then add the Fish Broth and taste for salt. Place the tuna steaks over the tomato mixture, cover, and continue cooking until the tuna is done, about 5 minutes. Serve the tuna with the tomato mixture spooned over it.

ATÚN MECHADO

(Baked Tuna with Onion and Sherry Sauce)

Fernando Hermoso exudes warmth and hospitality, taking inordinate pleasure and pride in his Casa Bigote in Sanlúcar de Barrameda, which he owns with his brother Paco. His eyes sparkle and his enthusiasm bubbles over as he tells me about the food he prepares in his restaurant and his efforts to provide the finest that Andalucía has to offer. This baked tuna is a specialty.

Tuna is particularly good in this part of western Spain. It is caught in the Atlantic off the coast of Cádiz province in a yearly rite that takes place in spring when the tuna migrate from colder waters to the Mediterranean in search of spawning grounds. They are captured in *las almadrabas,* intricate centuries-old underwater traps that cover the coastal ocean beds. Still protected by a layer of winter fat, these are the tuna that gourmets prize, and following closely on the heels of the tuna are Japanese businessmen, here to snap up the best of the catch and transport it to Japan ("Our tuna brings them to their knees," declares Fernando).

I am especially fond of this somewhat unusual tuna preparation, in which the fish is baked in one large piece, seasoned with Sanlúcar's famed pale dry *manzanilla* sherry, then sliced and served in its sauce at room temperature. It makes a distinctive appetizer or first course. Ask your fishmonger to save 2 whole pieces of tuna cut from 2 narrow tail portions (they will look somewhat like meat tenderloin).   *Serves 6–8 as a first course*

Two 1-pound pieces of fresh tuna (about 3 inches thick), cut from the tail portion	4 cloves garlic, lightly smashed and peeled
Salt	1 medium onion, thinly sliced
2 tablespoons coarsely ground pepper	½ cup extra virgin olive oil
2 bay leaves	1 cup *manzanilla,* or other very dry Spanish sherry

Place the tuna in a roasting pan, sprinkle with salt, and, with the heel of your hand, press the ground pepper over it to form a crust. Scatter the bay leaves, garlic, and onion around the pan. Pour in the oil and *manzanilla* and sprinkle the vegetables with salt.

Bake at 300°F for 45 minutes, or until the tuna is cooked (reaching an internal temperature of 140° to 145°F). Remove the tuna to a platter and cool. Transfer the contents of the roasting pan to a saucepan and simmer slowly, uncovered, until the onion has softened and the sauce is reduced, about 15 minutes. Discard the bay leaves.

Transfer to a food processor and pulse briefly—the sauce should still have small pieces. Cut the tuna crosswise into ¼-inch slices. Pass the sauce separately in a bowl.

Poultry ❀ Rabbit ❀ Meats

POLLO AL AJILLO CON JAMÓN
(Garlic Chicken with Cured Ham)

In Andalucía cured ham often enhances simple garlic sauces. This version of garlic chicken incorporates another common Andalusian ingredient—sherry—as well.

Serves 4

A 3–3½-pound chicken
3 tablespoons olive oil
6 large cloves garlic, peeled
Kosher or sea salt
2 tablespoons diced Spanish
    mountain cured ham or
    prosciutto, cut from a
    ⅛-inch-thick slice

2 tablespoons medium-dry
    sherry (*amontillado*)
1 tablespoon minced parsley
A 1-inch length dried red chile
    pepper, seeded
¼ teaspoon imported sweet
    paprika

Cut the chicken into small serving pieces: chop off the bony ends of the legs, cut each thigh in half crosswise, cut the whole breast in 4 pieces and the wings in two pieces, discarding the tips.

Heat the oil in a shallow casserole, add the garlic, and sauté until golden. Remove the garlic and reserve.

Salt the chicken pieces and place in the hot oil, frying until well browned and almost done, about 15 minutes. Add the ham and sherry, cook a minute, then stir in the parsley, chile pepper, paprika, and the reserved garlic, lightly pressing the garlic with the back of a wooden spoon to release its flavor. Cover and continue cooking 10 minutes more, adding a little chicken broth or water if the pan dries out. Serve each chicken portion with a little sauce spooned over it and garnished with the garlic cloves.

POLLO AL AJILLO EN SALSA DE VINO SALVADOR
(Chicken in Garlic and Wine Sauce)

Salvador of Bar Bahía in Cádiz uses this recipe interchangeably for chicken or rabbit. Our good friend Pepe Delfín likes nothing better on a Sunday afternoon than to stop at the central market, purchase a chicken, and take it to Salvador. While Salvador prepares the chicken as in this recipe, Pepe relaxes at the bar over a frosty beer and chats with friends who drop by.

Serves 4

A 3–3½-pound chicken
Kosher or sea salt
2 tablespoons olive oil
1 small head garlic, peeled and
   minced
2 bay leaves
½ cup dry white wine

1 small tomato, skinned,
   seeded, finely chopped, and
   drained of excess liquid
1 sprig thyme or ¼ teaspoon
   dried
¼ teaspoon dried oregano

Cut the chicken into small serving pieces, detaching the wings and legs and dividing the breast in 4 pieces and each thigh in half crosswise. Sprinkle on both sides with salt. Heat the oil in a large shallow casserole and sauté the chicken until golden on both sides. Stir in the garlic and bay leaves, and cook until the garlic begins to color. Stir in the wine, tomato, thyme, and oregano and taste for salt. Cover and cook 45 minutes.

POLLO AL AJONJOLÍ
(Chicken with Ginger and Sesame Seeds)

This dish was once a part of Andalusian cuisine and serves as a delicious reminder of what the cooking of southern Spain must have been during the nearly eight centuries that the Moors ruled and influenced both culture and cuisine. Ginger, saffron, cumin, and sesame seeds were all brought to Spain by the Moors and gave a decidedly Eastern taste to cooking. Recipes such as this one are among those that have been discovered and are being revived. The seasonings in this chicken dish are wonderfully subtle and understated, and quite difficult for the diner to identify.   *Serves 4*

A 3–3½-pound chicken
Kosher or sea salt
Freshly ground pepper
2 tablespoons olive oil
¾ cup finely chopped onions
1 garlic, minced
½ teaspoon flour
2 tablespoons minced parsley

½ teaspoon grated fresh ginger
Few strands of saffron
½ teaspoon ground cumin,
    preferably freshly ground in
    a mortar or spice mill
2 teaspoons sesame seeds
¾ cup chicken broth

Cut the chicken into small serving pieces, detaching the wings and legs and dividing the breast in 4 pieces and each thigh in half crosswise. Sprinkle on both sides with salt and pepper. Heat the oil in a shallow casserole and brown the chicken on all sides. Add the onions and garlic and sauté until the onions have wilted. Stir in the flour, then sprinkle in 1 tablespoon of the parsley, the ginger, saffron, cumin, and sesame seeds. Add the chicken broth, cover, and simmer about 50 minutes. Sprinkle with the remaining parsley and serve.

The Pomegranate: Fruit of Fertility and Symbol of Granada

From earliest times when Phoenicians occupied the hills of Granada, a cult worshiped the ancient god Rimmon, whose name in Hebrew signifies pomegranate. Then the Moors arrived in Granada and named it Medina Garnata, or "red town" because of the ruddy color of the earth. Granada's Alhambra, the breathtaking palace of the Moors, means "the red one," alluding to the reddish-gold brick and stone used in its construction. And although the Latin derivation of pomegranate, *granatum,* refers only to the fruit's seeds, or "grains," by extension the word became associated with the color of pomegranate juice. Still further interweaving the fruit and the city is the Spanish word for pomegranate, *granada;* thus we have the somewhat tangled connection between Granada the city and *granada* the fruit.

However this association came to be, the pomegranate has for centuries been closely linked to Granada. The conquest of Granada by the Catholic Kings in 1492 signaled the unification of Spain, and the pomegranate became a symbol of the reign of Fernando and Isabel and a common motif in the decorative style named Isabelline, in honor of the queen. Today the pomegranate appears in the coat of arms of Granada and in Spain's national coat of arms. It is also traditionally represented in Granada's beautiful blue pottery.

Quite apart from its symbolic significance, the pomegranate, which thrives in hot dry climates like that of southern Spain, was favored in the Moorish diet. It was considered a passion fruit that contributed to good health and had extraordinary curative powers. With their penchant for sweet-sour flavors, the Moors were particularly fond of the pomegranate in cooking. And during the intensely hot Granada summers, the Moors loved to drink the pomegranate's refreshing juice; they even prepared pomegranate sorbets by collecting snow from the highest peaks of the Sierra Nevada.

The pomegranate continues to have passionate fans who cannot get enough of it when the season arrives in the fall. The sudden burst of sweet juice when biting into the seeds that make up most of the pomegranate (this profusion of seeds made the pomegranate an ancient symbol of life and fertility) is the best part, although many detest the hard dry seeds left behind.

Little remains in Spanish cooking of the Moors' love for pomegranate, save a handful of dishes. Try the chicken and pork recipes made with pomegranate juice (pp. 374 and 210) and a refreshing green salad sprinkled with pomegranate seeds (page 233) that ideally accompanies the chickpea stew *cocido.*

POLLO EN SALSA DE GRANADAS
(Chicken in Pomegranate Sauce)

START PREPARATION 2 HOURS IN ADVANCE

In this recipe pomegranate juice, boiled to a syrup and mixed with Eastern spices like cumin, clove, nutmeg, and cinnamon, makes a wonderful marinade and sauce for a chicken dish that has all the flavors of Moorish Andalucía.

Serves 4

A 3–3½-pound chicken
Kosher or sea salt
2 large pomegranates
4 teaspoons cumin seeds or
    ground cumin
2 cloves
2 teaspoons peppercorns

¼ teaspoon ground nutmeg
Dash of cinnamon
4 cloves garlic, peeled
2 tablespoons extra virgin olive
    oil
Chicken broth

Cut the chicken into small serving pieces, detaching the legs and wings and dividing the breast in 4 pieces and each thigh in half crosswise. Sprinkle with salt.

Quarter the pomegranates and remove the seeds. Place the seeds in a food processor and beat a few seconds, just until the seeds are crushed and the juice extracted. Strain (there should be about 1½ cups juice). Pour into a small saucepan and boil down to a syrup—you should have about ½ cup. Cool.

In a mortar or mini processor, mash to a paste the cumin, clove, peppercorns, nutmeg, cinnamon, salt, and garlic. Stir in the pomegranate juice and the oil.

Arrange the chicken pieces in a shallow bowl, skin side up, and spread the marinade over the chicken with a rubber spatula. Marinate 2 hours.

Transfer the chicken with its marinade to a roasting pan and pour ¼ cup chicken broth into the pan. Roast at 350°F for about 45 minutes, adding more broth as the pan dries out.

POLLO CON MANZANAS Y PASAS
(Chicken with Apple and Raisins)

The recipe from which I adapted this tasty chicken dish originally appeared in a Granada newspaper and was contributed by a local housewife. I would bet that the recipe has been in her family for generations; because of its sweet-sour flavor, combining wine and onions with fruits, it is most likely of Arab origin.

Serves 4

A 3–3½-pound chicken
Kosher or sea salt
2 tablespoons olive oil
2 medium onions, finely
   chopped

2 medium apples, peeled,
   cored, and cut in ⅛-inch
   wedges
4 tablespoons (¼ cup) raisins
¾ cup dry white wine

Cut the chicken into small serving pieces, detaching the wings and legs and dividing the breast in 4 parts and the thighs in half crosswise. Sprinkle with salt.

Heat the oil in a shallow casserole and brown the chicken on all sides. Add the onions and sauté until softened. Stir in the apples, raisins, white wine, and salt to taste. Cover and simmer about 45 minutes.

POLLO AL ANDALUS
(Chicken with Almonds and Honey)

A preparation from Andalucía's Moorish past that includes many of the most characteristic ingredients of Moorish cooking of those times: almonds, honey, cilantro, ginger, saffron, and cumin.   *Serves 4*

A 3–3½-pound chicken
Kosher or sea salt
Freshly ground pepper
2 tablespoons plus 1 teaspoon
    olive oil
1 medium onion, finely
    chopped
1 tablespoon minced cilantro
1 tablespoon minced parsley
¼ teaspoon grated fresh ginger
Few strands of saffron,
    crumbled

¼ teaspoon ground cumin,
    preferably freshly ground in
    a mortar or spice mill
⅛ teaspoon nutmeg
½ cup chicken broth
¼ cup dry white wine
2 tablespoons chopped
    blanched almonds
1 tablespoon honey

Cut the chicken into small serving pieces, detaching the wings and legs and dividing the breast in 4 pieces and each thigh in half crosswise. Sprinkle on both sides with salt and pepper. Heat 2 tablespoons of the oil in a shallow casserole and lightly brown the chicken on all sides. Add the onion and cook until it has wilted. Sprinkle in the cilantro, parsley, ginger, saffron, cumin, and nutmeg. Stir in the chicken broth and wine, cover, and simmer 40 minutes.

In a very small skillet, heat the remaining teaspoon oil and lightly brown the almonds over a medium flame. Add the honey and 2 tablespoons water and cook away most of the liquid. Spoon over the chicken, cover, and cook 5 minutes more.

CONEJO CON MORAS Y AZÚCAR MORENO
(Rabbit with Blackberries and Brown Sugar)

If you have any misgivings about serving rabbit, try to overcome them—it is a delicious low-fat white meat that is cooked without its skin. (But chicken, too, works very well in this recipe.) This is a dish that reflects the many centuries of Arab rule in Andalucía and is a prime example of the Moorish culinary influence. It comes, most appropriately, from Las Alpujarras, a magnificent isolated mountain area where the Moors took refuge after they were expelled from their beloved Granada in 1492. It can be found on the menu, in a somewhat more elaborate version, at Ruta del Veleta restaurant in the Sierra Nevada town of Cenes de la Vega.   *Serves 4*

½ cup dry white wine
A 3-pound rabbit or chicken,
   cut in small serving pieces
Kosher or sea salt
Freshly ground pepper

½ teaspoon imported sweet
   paprika
3 tablespoons thyme leaves or
   1½ teaspoons dried
½ cup chicken broth

SAUCE

2 tablespoons packed light
   brown sugar
2 tablespoons mashed blackberries or blackberry preserves
2 tablespoons wine vinegar,
   preferably white
2 cloves garlic, minced

1 teaspoon olive oil
¼ teaspoon imported sweet
   paprika
¼ teaspoon ground cumin,
   preferrably freshly ground
   in a mortar or spice mill

·   ·   ·

½ cup blackberries (optional)

Pour ¼ cup of the wine into a roasting pan. Arrange the rabbit pieces in the pan (do not crowd) and sprinkle them with salt, pepper, paprika, and thyme. Bake at 375°F for 35 minutes, adding the remaining wine as it evaporates and then adding the chicken broth so that the pan does not dry out. Brush the chicken occasionally with the pan juices.

   Meanwhile, in a bowl mix together the Sauce ingredients and spoon them over the rabbit. Continue cooking and basting with the pan juices for 10 minutes more. Serve, spooning on some sauce and garnishing with the optional blackberries. Saffron Rice with Pine Nuts (p. 297) is an excellent accompaniment.

CONEJO AURORA
(Rabbit in Almond and Olive Sauce)

The outstanding sauce of almonds, olives, and white wine makes this a particularly good preparation for rabbit and also works well with chicken. Aurora, wife of our old friend Pepe Sanz, lives in Madrid, but her family roots are in Jaén—an Andalusian province blanketed with olive trees. She tells me this dish is always a big hit with her guests, and I was similarly impressed by it.   *Serves 3–4*

3 ounces pitted green olives, cut
   in half crosswise
1½ ounces (about ¼ cup)
   blanched almonds
A 2½–3-pound rabbit, cut in
   serving pieces
Kosher or sea salt
Flour for dusting

3 tablespoons olive oil
3 cloves garlic, lightly crushed
   and peeled
1 large onion, finely chopped
¾ cup dry white wine
½ cup chicken broth
Freshly ground pepper

Put the olives in a small saucepan with water to cover. Boil 5 minutes, drain, and reserve. Place the almonds on a cookie tray and brown in a 350°F oven about 5 minutes. Cool and transfer to a mortar or mini processor.

Sprinkle the rabbit with salt and dust with flour. Heat the oil in a shallow casserole and brown the rabbit on all sides. Remove to a warm platter. In the same oil, lightly brown the garlic and transfer to the mortar. Mash the almonds and garlic to a paste. Add the onion to the casserole and sauté 2 minutes, then add the rabbit, wine, broth, salt and pepper, the reserved olives, and the mortar mixture. Bring to a boil, cover, then simmer about 1½ to 2 hours.

CHULETAS DE CERDO ALIÑADAS Y EMPANADAS
(Marinated Breaded Pork Chops)

START PREPARATION SEVERAL HOURS IN ADVANCE

These chops are first marinated with herbs, garlic, and olive oil, then breaded and sautéed. The result is moist, tender, and subtly flavored meat.

Serves 4

MARINADE

¼ cup extra virgin olive oil
1½ tablespoons freshly
    squeezed lemon juice
1 clove garlic, mashed to a
    paste
1 bay leaf, crumbled
1½ teaspoons thyme leaves or
    ¼ teaspoon dried

¾ teaspoon minced oregano
    leaves or ⅛ teaspoon dried
¾ teaspoon minced marjoram
    leaves or ⅛ teaspoon dried
1½ teaspoons minced rosemary
    leaves or ¼ teaspoon dried
Salt
Freshly ground pepper

. . .

1½ pounds boneless lean loin
    pork chops, cut ½–¾ inch
    thick
1 egg, lightly beaten with
    1 teaspoon water

Dried bread crumbs seasoned
    with salt and pepper
2 tablespoons olive oil

In a shallow bowl in which the chops will fit in one layer, combine the Marinade ingredients. Add the chops, turn to coat well, cover, and marinate several hours at room temperature or overnight in the refrigerator.

Remove the chops from the marinade and dry on paper towels, then coat with the egg and cover well with bread crumbs. Heat the 2 tablespoons oil in a skillet and sauté the chops over a medium flame until golden and just cooked through, about 4 minutes on each side.

LOMO DE CERDO A LA PLANCHA, BAR BAHÍA
(Lemon and Garlic Marinated Grilled Pork Fillets)

START PREPARATION I HOUR IN ADVANCE

I remember the raves our friend Salvador received from the Americans in the group we had brought to his bar for lunch when he presented this ever-so-simple dish that is so appealing to all, no matter what their culinary bent. You can serve these thin fillets as a main dish or cut them into smaller pieces and present as tapas (in which case there will be 6 to 8 servings).   *Serves 4*

1 pound boneless pork loin, in slices ¼ inch or less in thickness	4 cloves garlic, minced
	Dried oregano
	Salt
½ lemon	Freshly ground pepper

Arrange the meat in one layer on a platter and sprinkle with lemon juice and garlic. Cover with foil or plastic wrap and let sit at least 1 hour.

Grease a griddle and heat to the smoking point. Cook the meat quickly on both sides and sprinkle with oregano, salt, and pepper.

LOMO DE CERDO ESTOFADO CON PATATAS
(Stewed Pork Loin and Potatoes)

A touch of nutmeg gives the sauce of this pork stew a special flavor, often found in Andalusian cooking. It is a taste that transports me to Bar Bahía (see p. 340) in Cádiz, where this stew is served in small portions as a tapa. The dish calls for a head of garlic, but the garlic mellows as it cooks and lends a splendid flavor to the sauce.   *Serves 4*

2 tablespoons olive oil

1½ pounds pork loin, in
    1½-inch cubes

1 head garlic, peeled and finely
    chopped

1 medium onion, finely
    chopped

3 bay leaves

1 medium tomato, skinned,
    seeded, and finely chopped

Generous grating of nutmeg

Freshly ground pepper

1 cup dry white wine

¼ cup chicken broth

Salt

1 pound new or red waxy
        potatoes, peeled and cut in
    1-inch cubes

Heat the oil in a stewpot and sauté the pork until browned on all sides. Add the garlic, onion, and bay leaves and sauté until the onion has wilted. Stir in the tomato, cook a minute or two, then add the nutmeg, pepper, white wine, broth, and salt. Bring to a boil, cover, and simmer 30 minutes. Add the potatoes and cook 30 minutes more, or until the potatoes are tender.

ALBÓNDIGAS SALVADOR
(Meatballs Salvador)

The recipes of Salvador Lucero of Bar Bahía in Cádiz are invariably simple, using very basic ingredients, and yet they always taste uncommonly good. These meatballs can also be served as tapas. *Serves 4*

¾ cup dried bread crumbs

¾ cup chicken broth

1 pound mixture of ground
    pork and veal in equal parts

4 cloves garlic, minced

2 tablespoons minced parsley

7 tablespoons minced onion

Generous grinding of pepper

⅛ teaspoon nutmeg

½ teaspoon salt

1 small egg, lightly beaten

2 tablespoons olive oil

Flour for dusting

1 bay leaf

1 small tomato, skinned,
    seeded, and chopped

¼ cup dry white wine

In a large bowl, soak the bread crumbs in ½ cup of the chicken broth. Lightly mix in the meat, 2 of the minced garlic cloves, 1 tablespoon of the minced

Meatballs Salvador (continued)

parsley, 3 tablespoons of the onion, the pepper, nutmeg, salt, egg, and 1 tablespoon of the oil. Shape into 1½-inch balls and dust with flour.

Heat the remaining tablespoon of oil in a shallow casserole and brown the meatballs on all sides. Add the remaining 2 cloves minced garlic, 4 tablespoons onion, and 1 tablespoon parsley, and the bay leaf. Sauté until the onion has softened. Add the tomato, the remaining ¼ cup broth, the wine, and season with salt and pepper. Cover and simmer 45 minutes, adding more chicken broth or water if necessary.

ALBÓNDIGAS AL-ANDALÚS
(Lamb Meatballs, Moorish Style)

Ginger and cilantro never appear in traditional Spanish cooking, yet under the Moors they were common. Certain ingredients, many totally unfamiliar to Spaniards today, and unexpected food combinations have added an entirely new dimension to the cuisine of Spain, enriching it immeasurably. These wonderfully scented meatballs include almonds and a punch of garlic and saffron (La Picada), added when the meatballs are almost done.

Serves 4

2 tablespoons olive oil
1 large onion, finely chopped
2 pounds ground lamb
1 egg, lightly beaten
1 teaspoon finely chopped
  ginger
3 tablespoons minced cilantro
½ teaspoon ground cumin,
  preferably freshly ground in
  a mortar or spice mill
2 tablespoons minced parsley
1½ teaspoons salt
Freshly ground pepper

1½ teaspoons thyme leaves or
  ¼ teaspoon dried
1½ teaspoons minced marjoram
  leaves or ¼ teaspoon dried
1½ teaspoons minced basil
  leaves or ¼ teaspoon dried
Flour for dusting
3 tablespoons finely chopped
  onion
¾ cup beef broth or a mixture
  of beef and chicken broth
½ cup water

LA PICADA

2 cloves garlic, minced	Few strands of saffron
⅛ teaspoon salt	8 blanched almonds, finely
1 tablespoon minced cilantro	chopped

Heat 1 tablespoon of the oil in a large shallow casserole and sauté the onion slowly for 5 minutes. Cover and continue cooking slowly until the onion is tender but not browned, about 10 minutes.

Meanwhile, in a bowl combine the lamb, egg, ginger, 2 tablespoons of the cilantro, the cumin, parsley, salt, pepper, thyme, marjoram, and basil. Mix in the sautéed onions. Form into small balls, 1½ to 2 inches, and dust lightly with flour.

Heat the remaining tablespoon of oil in the casserole and brown the meatballs all over. Add the 3 tablespoons onion and continue cooking until the onion has softened. Stir in the broth and water. Cover and simmer 40 minutes.

Meanwhile, place La Picada ingredients in a mortar or mini processor and mash to a paste. When the meatballs are done, stir in La Picada and cook another 5 minutes. Serve, sprinkled with the remaining tablespoon cilantro.

CHULETAS DE CORDERO Y CHAMPIÑONES ALIÑADOS
(Marinated Lamb Chops and Mushrooms)

START PREPARATION 2 HOURS IN ADVANCE

An excellent marinade that produces tender and well-seasoned chops and flavorful mushrooms. *Serves 4*

¼ cup wine vinegar	½ teaspoon salt
¾ cup extra virgin olive oil	Freshly ground pepper
¼ teaspoon celery seed	1 small onion, slivered
2 tablespoons minced parsley	2 pounds lamb chops
½ teaspoon imported sweet paprika	½ pound mushrooms, brushed clean, stems trimmed

Marinated Lamb Chops and Mushrooms (continued)

In a shallow bowl, whisk together the vinegar, oil, celery seed, parsley, paprika, salt, and pepper. Stir in the onion, then add the chops and mushrooms, turning them to coat well with the marinade. Scatter the onion over the chops and mushrooms and marinate 2 hours, turning occasionally. Drain and cook the chops and mushrooms on a stovetop griddle or under the broiler until done to taste, allowing more time for the chops than the mushrooms.

CORDERO A LA MIEL
(Lamb with Honey)

José García Marín, owner of Córdoba's classic El Caballo Rojo restaurant, is tireless in his efforts to rekindle the city's Jewish and Moorish culinary past. In the tenth century Córdoba was the capital of Moorish Spain, the cultural mecca of Europe, and a melting pot of Jews, Arabs, and Christians.

This slowly simmered lamb, seasoned with saffron, paprika, honey, brandy, and wine (although the original preparation was not likely to have contained alcohol), is one of the finest examples of age-old Spanish cooking brought up to date. I think you will be surprised to find how beautifully a slightly sweet-sour sauce complements lamb.   *Serves 4*

1 tablespoon olive oil	1 teaspoon paprika
3–3½ pounds lamb stew with bone, cut into 1½–2-inch pieces	1 tablespoon brandy
	⅓ cup dry white wine
	Few strands of saffron
Salt	½ cup chicken broth
⅔ cup finely chopped onions	2 tablespoons wine vinegar
⅓ cup very finely chopped green bell pepper	1½ tablespoons honey

In a stewpot, heat the oil and brown the lamb well on all sides. Sprinkle with salt. Add the onions and green pepper and sauté until slightly softened. Stir in the paprika, then the brandy, wine, and saffron, and simmer 5 minutes. Add the chicken broth, bring to a boil, cover, and simmer 1 to 1½ hours more, or until the meat is tender. Stir in the vinegar and honey, taste for salt, and simmer 10 minutes more before serving.

CORDERO CON FRUTAS SECAS
(Lamb Stew with Raisins and Apricots)

An exceptional dish of pronounced Eastern flavors—tender stewed lamb cooked with dried apricots, raisins, and coriander.   *Serves 4*

1 tablespoon olive oil	20 dried apricots
2 pounds boneless lamb stew meat, in 1½-inch cubes	2 tablespoons raisins
	Dash of cinnamon
Salt	½ teaspoon crushed coriander seeds
Freshly ground pepper	
1 medium onion, finely chopped	1½ cups chicken broth
	Chopped cilantro for garnish

Heat the oil in a deep stewpot and brown the meat, sprinkling it with salt and pepper as it cooks. Add the onion and sauté until it has wilted, then stir in the apricots, raisins, cinnamon, and coriander and sauté a minute or two. Pour in the broth, bring to a boil, cover, and simmer 1½ to 2 hours, or until the meat is tender. Sprinkle with cilantro and serve over or with rice.

ESTOFADO DE CORDERO CON MANZANA
(Lamb Stew with Apples)

Clearly this is a dish of Moorish origin. The slightly sweet sauce combines beautifully with the flavor of lamb.   *Serves 4*

1 tablespoon olive oil	1 apple, peeled, cored, and chopped
3–3½ pounds lamb stew meat (with bone), cut in 1½-inch pieces	1 medium onion, chopped
	1 medium tomato, skinned, seeded, and chopped
Salt	
Freshly ground pepper	2 cups dry white wine

Lamb Stew with Apples (continued)

Heat the oil in an ovenproof casserole and brown the meat well on all sides. Sprinkle with salt and pepper. Stir in the apple, onion, and tomato, cook a minute, then pour in the wine and adjust the seasoning. Bring to a boil, cover, and transfer to a 350°F oven. Cook 1½ hours, adding some chicken broth or water if the liquid cooks away.

CALDERETA DE TERNERA AL COMINO
(Veal Stew with Cumin)

START PREPARATION 1 HOUR IN ADVANCE

The distinctive taste of cumin in the sauce of this tender and flavorful veal stew is one reason why this dish is out of the ordinary.   *Serves 4*

1¾ pounds boneless veal, in
   1½–2-inch pieces
Kosher or sea salt
Freshly ground pepper
2 cloves garlic, minced
1 tablespoon minced parsley
2 tablespoons olive oil
1 small onion, finely chopped
1 small tomato, peeled, seeded,
   and chopped

1 medium green frying pepper,
   cored, seeded, and cut in
   ½-inch strips
½ cup chicken broth
¼ teaspoon cumin seeds or
   ground cumin
¼ teaspoon imported sweet
   paprika

Mix together in a bowl the veal, salt, pepper, 1 minced garlic clove, and the parsley. Let sit 1 hour.

In a stewpot, heat the oil and brown the meat over a medium flame. Add the onion, tomato, and pepper and cook until the onion and pepper have softened. Stir in the broth and bring to a boil. Cover and simmer 45 minutes.

Meanwhile, in a mortar or mini processor, mash to a paste the cumin, the remaining garlic, the paprika, and ⅛ teaspoon salt. Add to the stew and continue cooking about 20 minutes more, or until the meat is tender.

CARNE ESTOFADA CON AJO Y VINAGRE
(Beef Stew with Garlic and Vinegar)

A down-to-earth beef and potato stew, made exceptionally tasty by the addition of vinegar, a head of garlic, and a large amount of slivered onion, all of which combine to provide the only moisture the stew will need to slow-cook.

Serves 4

2 tablespoons olive oil
1¾–2 pounds boneless beef
    chuck, in 1½-inch pieces
Salt
2 large onions, slivered
1 head garlic, loose outer skin
    removed

2 tablespoons wine vinegar
2 bay leaves
1 pound potatoes, peeled and
    cut in ¾-inch cubes

Heat the oil in a stewpot and brown the meat on all sides. Sprinkle with salt, then add all the remaining ingredients except the potatoes. Cover and simmer 45 minutes.

Sprinkle the potato cubes with salt and add to the stew. Cover and continue cooking 45 minutes more. Squeeze the garlic flesh into the stew, discard the skin, and serve.

RABO DE TORO AL ESTILO PEDRO ROMERO
(Oxtail Stew, Pedro Romero Style)

START PREPARATION I DAY IN ADVANCE

Restaurante Pedro Romero, which bears the name of one of the greatest figures in bullfighting history, is in the spectacular town of Ronda set above an awesome gorge. The restaurant, appropriately adorned with bullfighting memorabilia, is situated next to Ronda's legendary bullring, among the oldest and most beautiful rings in Spain. This rendition of oxtail stew is a very traditional one. In Spain, not surprisingly, it goes by the name "bull's tail stew."

Serves 4

Oxtail Stew (continued)

4 pounds oxtail, cut in 2-inch-
  thick rounds
1½ teaspoons thyme leaves or
  ¼ teaspoon dried
1½ teaspoons minced oregano
  leaves or ¼ teaspoon dried
1½ teaspoons minced rosemary
  leaves or ¼ teaspoon dried
4 peppercorns
1 bay leaf
Salt
5 cloves garlic, lightly crushed
  and peeled
2¾ cups dry white wine

¼ cup dry red wine
1 medium onion, coarsely
  chopped
1 medium carrot, trimmed,
  scraped, and cut in ¼-inch
  slices
1 small leek, well washed
¼ pound green frying peppers,
  cored, seeded, and diced
½ pound tomatoes, skinned,
  seeded, and diced
½ teaspoon imported sweet
  paprika
Dash of nutmeg

Place the oxtail in a stewpot with the thyme, oregano, rosemary, pepper-corns, bay leaf, salt, and garlic. Pour in the white and red wine and refriger-ate overnight.

Add the onion, carrot, leek, green peppers, tomatoes, paprika, and nut-meg to the pot, bring to a boil, then cover and simmer 2½ hours. Uncover and boil for about 30 minutes, until the sauce is reduced and thickened. If you wish to remove some of the fat, cool the stew and refrigerate. When the fat has congealed, remove it, then reheat the stew.

Desserts

CABELLO DE ÁNGEL
(Spaghetti Squash Marmalade)

A typically Spanish filling or topping for pastries that you will find in most regions of the country. Sweetened spaghetti squash is a wonderful and quite unusual alternative to the typical fruit fillings to which we have become accustomed.   *Makes about 1 cup*

A 1-pound piece of spaghetti squash, seeded and cut in quarters

½ cup plus 2 tablespoons honey
1 cinnamon stick
Peel of ½ lemon

Place the spaghetti squash in a saucepan with water to cover. Bring to a boil, cover, and simmer about 15 to 25 minutes, or until tender. Drain and scratch down to the rind with a fork to form thread-like strands of the pulp.

Return the pulp to the saucepan. Mix in the honey, 2 tablespoons warm water, the cinnamon stick, and lemon peel. Bring to a boil, then simmer, uncovered, for about 35 minutes, or until thickened to a marmalade consistency.

BUÑUELOS DE FRESONES EN PASTA DE JEREZ
(Strawberries Fried in Sherry Batter)

This batter is especially good for small whole fruits or fruit wedges, but is at its best when used to coat strawberries or whole fresh figs. For an elegant presentation, serve these fruit puffs over a raspberry purée.   *Serves 4*

¼ cup Spanish cream sherry
¼ cup milk
½ cup flour
2 tablespoons plus 1 teaspoon sugar
1½ teaspoons oil
Pinch of salt
1 egg white
Oil for frying, preferably mild olive oil

16 medium strawberries with stems and leaves if possible, or 4 fresh figs or other fruits, cut in ½-inch wedges
Flour for dusting
¼ teaspoon cinnamon
Mint leaves for garnish

In a bowl, mix together the sherry, milk, flour, 1 teaspoon of the sugar, the oil, and salt. In a separate bowl, beat the egg white until stiff but not dry, then fold into the batter.

Pour the oil into a skillet to a depth of at least 1 inch (or better still, use a deep-fryer) and heat until the oil quickly browns a cube of bread (about

Strawberries Fried in Sherry Batter (continued)

365°F). Dust the strawberries with flour, coat with the batter, and fry until golden. Drain on paper towels. Combine the remaining 2 tablespoons sugar and the cinnamon and coat each strawberry with this mixture. If using figs, after frying cut each fig vertically into four sections, without completely separating the sections, and open out (it will look like a flower). Garnish with mint leaves and serve right away.

NATILLAS CON BORRACHUELOS
(Pastries in Soft Custard)

START PREPARATION SEVERAL HOURS IN ADVANCE

I always remember this dessert in connection with the restaurant of Úbeda's outstanding parador, a sixteenth-century palace in a town in which Renaissance buildings abound. The pastries and custard combine into one exceptional dessert, but they can be, and often are, eaten separately. In this case the pastries are somewhat crunchier than other similar ones so that the custard will not make them soggy. The recipe makes extra pastries which I'm sure will vanish in no time.   *Makes 30*

THE PASTRIES

1 egg yolk	1 tablespoon *aguardiente*
1 tablespoon sugar	(grappa) or brandy
¼ teaspoon ground anise	¼ cup white wine
⅛ teaspoon cinnamon	¼ cup mild olive oil
⅛ teaspoon vanilla	1 strip lemon peel
1 tablespoon orange juice	1¼ cups flour

SOFT CUSTARD   *Serves 4*

2 cups milk	4 tablespoons (¼ cup) sugar
4 egg yolks	½ teaspoon vanilla

· · ·

Oil for frying, preferably mild olive oil	Sugar for dusting

In a bowl mix together with a wooden spoon the egg yolk and sugar. Stir in the anise, cinnamon, vanilla, orange juice, *aguardiente,* and white wine.

In a small skillet heat the oil with the lemon peel until the peel turns black. Discard the peel and cool the oil, then combine with the egg mixture. Gradually stir in the flour to make a smooth dough. Cover with plastic wrap and let rest for several hours.

Meanwhile, prepare the custard. Bring the milk to a boil, then cool slightly. In a large saucepan or the top of a double boiler, whisk the egg yolks until lemon colored. Whisk in the sugar and gradually stir in the warm milk. Cook over hot water, stirring constantly, until thickened to a soft custard consistency. Remove from the heat and add the vanilla, stirring frequently as the custard cools.

Roll the dough on a floured surface ⅛ inch thick. Cut in 1½- to 1¾-inch-wide strips. Then cut across at a 45-degree angle to form rhombuses.

Pour the oil into a skillet to a depth of at least ½ inch (or better still, use a deep-fryer) and heat until the oil quickly browns a cube of bread. Add as many pastries as will comfortably fit and brown them on both sides (they should puff up while cooking). Drain on paper towels, then dust with sugar.

Serve the custard in wide shallow bowls (typically earthenware) and float several pastries on top.

TOCINILLOS DEL CIELO
(Rich Little Custards with Caramelized Sugar)

My husband rarely eats desserts, but I have never known him to pass up these marvelous little caramelized custards whenever they are offered in Spanish restaurants. Think of this dessert as being closer to candy; since it is quite rich, a small portion is more than enough.

We can thank Spanish wine makers and convent nuns of centuries past for *tocinillos* and other sweets that rely on egg yolks (like *yemas*—candied egg yolks reshaped into yolks). It was the custom for wine makers to donate egg yolks to the convents after using the whites to clarify their wines. From the sixteenth through the eighteenth century, when convents flourished, such sweets, whose recipes were closely guarded secrets, were given as gifts to convent benefactors, and when hard times came to the religious orders in the nineteenth and twentieth centuries, convent sweets became a means of support, as they remain today.

Fashionable restaurants in Spain often dress up these custards with artfully swirled raspberry sauces, but I think such additions only distract from—and often clash with—the pure and simple taste of this classic Spanish dessert.   *Serves 6–8*

1⅓ cups sugar	6 egg yolks
1 cup water	¼ teaspoon vanilla
1 recipe Caramelized Sugar Syrup (p. 220)	¼ teaspoon grated lemon peel

Combine the sugar and water in a saucepan and bring to a boil. Simmer about 15 to 20 minutes, or until a drop of syrup lengthens to a thread when placed in a glass of cold water. Cool. Lightly coat the sides of about fifteen 1¼-inch mini muffin tins or individual mini custard molds with some syrup.

Make the caramelized sugar according to instructions and divide among the custard cups. In a bowl, whisk the egg yolks with the vanilla and grated lemon peel. Gradually whisk in the cooled syrup. Fill the muffin pans to the rim with this mixture (about 2 tablespoons in each). Place on a rack over—not in—boiling water, cover, and cook about 13 minutes, adding more water if it evaporates, until the custard is just set (do not overcook). Cool. To serve, loosen the sides, invert, and serve at room temperature.

LECHE FRITA
(Fried Custard)

START PREPARATION SEVERAL HOURS IN ADVANCE

One of my fondest memories is of our stay in Cortijo Faín, a private home surrounded by olive groves near Arcos de la Frontera, where owner Soledad Gil has turned family bedrooms, filled with personal mementos, into guest rooms. Dinner is prepared by the longtime family cook, and coffee is served in the family living room, accompanied by this delicious rendition of a Spanish favorite (and a great favorite of mine) which literally translates as "fried milk." It is a custard without eggs, thickened only with cornstarch and flour, which solidifies when refrigerated and can then be deep-fried or sautéed.   *Serves 6–8*

3 cups milk	2 teaspoons cinnamon
1 cinnamon stick	Oil for frying, preferably mild
Peel of 1 lemon	olive oil
¼ cup cornstarch	Flour for coating
¼ cup flour	2 eggs, lightly beaten with
10 tablespoons sugar	1 teaspoon water

Bring 2½ cups of the milk to a boil in a saucepan with the cinnamon stick and lemon peel. Simmer 30 minutes. Discard the cinnamon stick and lemon peel.

Grease an 8-inch-square baking pan. In a large bowl, combine the cornstarch, flour, and 6 tablespoons of the sugar. Gradually stir in the remaining ½ cup cold milk, then stir in the hot milk. Return this mixture to the saucepan and cook for about 15 minutes over a medium flame, stirring constantly, until the custard is thickened and just begins to bubble. Pour the custard directly into the baking pan and cool 5 minutes. Do not stir. Chill several hours or preferably overnight until the custard is firm.

In a cup or small bowl mix together the remaining 4 tablespoons sugar and the cinnamon. Cut the custard diagonally at 1½-inch intervals, then repeat in the opposite direction, crisscrossing to form rhombus shapes. Pour oil to a depth of ¼ inch in a large skillet and heat until it quickly browns a cube of bread (you can also use a deep-fryer). Coat the custard pieces with flour, dip in the beaten egg, and fry in the oil, browning on all sides. Drain on paper towels. Coat with the sugar and cinnamon and serve warm.

PESTIÑOS CORDOBESES
(Córdoba's Sugar-Coated Fried Pastries)

START PREPARATION 2 HOURS IN ADVANCE

You will find *pestiños* all over Spain, in a variety of shapes and sizes, some coated with honey and others, such as these typical to Córdoba that are wonderfully flaky, subtly scented with spices, and heavily coated with sugar and cinnamon.   *Makes about 36–40*

Sugar-Coated Fried Pastries (continued)

2 cups flour

Pinch of salt

1½ teaspoons ground anise seeds

1½ teaspoons sesame seeds

1 clove, crushed to a powder

½ teaspoon grated lemon peel

3 tablespoons lard or vegetable shortening, softened

¼ cup mild olive oil

¼ cup dry white wine

Oil for frying

½ cup sugar

¼ teaspoon cinnamon

Mix together in a bowl the flour, salt, anise, sesame seeds, clove, and grated lemon peel. Add the lard and, working with your fingers, incorporate it into the flour mixture. Stir in the olive oil and white wine, turn out onto a work surface, and knead lightly until smooth. Shape into a ball, wrap in plastic wrap, and let sit at room temperature for 2 hours.

Flour a work surface, briefly knead the dough again, then roll to the thinness of a nickel. With a sharp knife or pizza cutter, cut into strips 2 by 4 inches.

Pour the oil into a skillet to a depth of at least 1 inch (or better still, use a deep-fryer) and heat until the oil quickly browns a cube of bread. Double over the dough rectangles, moisten the edges with water, and press to seal. Fry in several batches (do not crowd) until golden brown, turning once. Drain on paper towels. Mix the sugar and cinnamon together and dredge the pastries. Arrange on a platter and coat heavily with more of the sugar mixture.

FLORES DE MIEL
(Flowers Coated with Honey)

To make these crisp, gossamer-light fried pastries you will need a rosette iron, a flower-shaped device with a long handle, to dip into the batter and then into the hot oil. *Flores* are almost too easy to eat—the yield in this recipe is not likely to be excessive. *Makes about 60*

3 eggs	Oil for frying, preferably mild
1 cup milk	olive oil
¼ teaspoon grated lemon peel	Peel of ½ lemon, cut in strips
¼ teaspoon cinnamon	½ cup honey
Pinch of salt	2 tablespoons water
1 cup flour, preferably bread flour	Confectioners' sugar

In a bowl, beat the eggs with an electric beater until foamy. Add the milk, grated lemon peel, cinnamon, and salt and beat a minute, then add the flour and beat at a low speed until smooth—the batter should be quite thin.

Pour the oil into a skillet to a depth of at least 1 inch (or better still, use a deep-fryer) and heat until the oil quickly browns a cube of bread (about 365°F). Add the strips of lemon peel and cook until they blacken. Discard.

Place the rosette iron in the oil until the metal becomes very hot, then dip in the batter. Be careful to coat the mold only to the top of the rim—if the batter goes over, it will be more difficult to separate the pastries when done. Transfer immediately to the oil. Hold the mold in the oil until the batter becomes golden. Remove from the oil—the pastries should slip off easily from the mold; otherwise use the point of a knife to gently loosen them. Drain on paper towels. Repeat, immersing the mold in the oil briefly each time before dipping in the batter.

Combine in a small saucepan the honey and water. Heat until the mixture is thin and smooth. Drizzle over the flowers and dust with confectioners' sugar.

PASTEL CORDOBÉS
(Puff Pastry Pie with Spaghetti Squash Marmalade)

We were not expecting to have dessert at the end of a tapas lunch enjoyed with one of our travel groups at the charming Taberna San Miguel (see p. 345) in Córdoba, but as a special treat this pastry had been ordered from a local bakery and was the hit of the meal. I think you will be pleasantly surprised to find how delicious spaghetti squash is as a pastry filling.

Remember that puff pastry must always be chilled and firm—if it becomes soft after rolling out, refrigerate for a few minutes before continuing.

Serves 8

¾ pound puff pastry, prefer-
    ably homemade (p. 22)
½ cup Spaghetti Squash
    Marmalade (p. 388)

1 egg, lightly beaten with
    1 teaspoon water
Granulated sugar

On a floured surface, roll the prepared pastry dough to an 18- by 10-inch rectangle. Cut into two 8½-inch squares, then trim each square into an 8½-inch circle. Place one circle on a baking tray that has been dampened with water.

Spread the Spaghetti Squash Marmalade with a rubber spatula to within 1½ inches of the edge. Cover with the other pastry round and seal the edges. Make several slits with a sharp knife, brush with egg, and bake at 425°F on a middle to upper rack until golden, about 25 minutes. Turn off the oven and leave in the oven 20 minutes more to dry the inner pastry layers. Cool and sprinkle heavily with sugar.

CHAPTER 8

Canary Islands

REGION OF THE *MOJOS*

The Canary Islands, hundreds of miles from Spain near the northwestern coast of Africa and blessed by eternal spring, arose from the sea in volcanic eruption eons ago. Some believe the seven major islands that form the archipelago—Tenerife, Gran Canaria, La Palma, La Gomera, Lanzarote, Fuerteventura, and El Hierro—are actually the exposed peaks of the sunken continent of Atlantis. Volcanic cones and craters dominate the landscape, creating startling heights and unfathomable abysses. Exuberant subtropical vegetation has largely erased the bleak volcanic landscape on most islands, while more recent eruptions have turned the island of Lanzarote, for example, into a virtual desert of surreal beauty. Scenically the Canaries are entirely distinct from mainland Spain, and since geography and climate play such an important role in food supply, the foods are also dissimilar.

Canary Island cooking merits its own chapter because it is not closely related to any of Spain's regional cuisines. It is a fascinating culinary hybrid that traces its roots to Africa (from which its indigenous people, the Guanches, are thought to have originally come), was enriched by Spanish products when Spain took control of the islands, and transformed once again by foods arriving from the New World (the Canary Islands were directly along early shipping routes that followed the trade winds and the last stop before crossing the Atlantic). *Gofio,* toasted grain perhaps related to couscous, was a staple of the Guanche diet that took the place of bread. Although in recent years the popularity of *gofio* has greatly diminished, it is still used in a polenta-like mix to accompany meat dishes, as a breakfast cereal, as a thickener for soup, and, when sweetened, as a dessert.

When Spaniards claimed the Canary Islands in the fifteenth century the Guanches were still living in the Stone Age, and their foods were primitive and few. Spain introduced wheat and many subtropical crops that adapted remarkably well, in particular bananas and sugar cane (the islands subsequently became Spain's chief provider of these two products). Goats, pigs, and chickens brought from Spain became the principal sources of meat, along with game animals like rabbit. Conditions on some islands were appropriate for grapevines, and by the sixteenth century the Canary Islands were producing wines of international acclaim; in Shakespeare's England, Canary Island *malvasía* wine was in great demand.

After the discovery of the New World, native American foods were brought to the Canary Islands. The climate proved ideal, and once more culinary horizons were expanded. Potatoes grew in dozens of varieties; tomatoes were exceptionally sweet and juicy, and corn, which in Spain was strictly feed for livestock, effortlessly became a part of Canary Island cooking, as did the avocado, papaya, and pineapple. In turn, cilantro, which had been favored by the Moors in Spain (contrary to popular belief, cilantro is a product of the East, introduced to America through Spain; see box, p. 403), disappeared there once the Moors were expelled, but blended wonderfully well with foods of the New World and also survived in the Canary Islands. Watercress, another herb of the East rarely found in Spain today, was similarly embraced on the islands, and both contribute to the distinctive flavors of Canary Island cooking.

Mojos—uncooked dipping sauces made with olive oil, vinegar, garlic, peppers, such spices as cumin and paprika, and often including an abundance of cilantro—have become a signature of island cookery. *Mojo* ingredients also create exciting marinades and cooking sauces. Because *mojos* in all their various styles are so much a part of typical Canary Island cooking, I have called the islands Region of the *Mojos*.

Besides devising their own dishes by combining foods brought to the islands from three continents, Canary Islanders took traditional Spanish dishes and gave them a personal stamp. To Spain's classic chickpea stew, sweet potatoes and pears were added; raisins and sweet potato were incorporated into Spanish black sausage; and the Spanish potato omelet received the addition of sautéed bananas. An abundance of sugar cane made sweets an important feature of Canary Island cooking, and they take some uncommon forms. There are cheese desserts, pastries with sweet potato fillings, sweetened chickpea croquettes, and candied squash.

In short, Canary Island cooking is a fascinating blend of several cuisines that came together to produce flavors that are singularly "Canary Island." For a cooking style that in reality is exceedingly limited, it includes a disproportionate number of preparations that I thoroughly enjoy, among them *mojos;* little "wrinkled" potatoes; simple meat and fish dishes well seasoned with herbs and spices, such as tuna in spicy red pepper and cumin sauce (*bonito en salmorejo*); and the almond and honey dessert sauce, *bienmesabe.* They have all become part of my everyday cooking—certainly not a small accomplishment for a region that until quite recently had little culinary identity of its own.

Notes on Regional Wines

Canary Island wines are not well known today in mainland Spain or in any other countries, although in centuries past they were held in highest esteem. Nevertheless, the light and fruity dry and semi-dry white malvasía *wines of the island of Lanzarote, where grapevines grow in soil of volcanic ash, certainly have potential. So too the fresh young red wines from the Tacoronte appellation of origin on the island of Tenerife.*

Mojos Canarios:
Tantalizing Tastes
from the Canary Islands

Mojos, from the Spanish word *mojar*, to wet or dunk (it can refer to taking a swim as well as sopping up a sauce with a piece of bread), are the typical dipping sauces of the Canary Islands, and are related to similar sauces from Cuba and Portugal. Based upon an abundance of garlic, a variety of herbs and spices, red or green peppers, olive oil, and vinegar, they come in endless subtle variations. Although usually mild, they are occasionally quite spicy. Rare is the restaurant in the Canary Islands that does not as a matter of course place bowls of red and green *mojo* on every table.

Sometimes referred to as the "king of *mojos*," red *mojo*, made from sweet and spicy dried red peppers, is usually the hotter of the two. When thinned it becomes a sauce for several chicken, rabbit, and fish dishes. Green *mojo* relies on cilantro or parsley, is well seasoned but usually mild, and most often accompanies fish. Other tasty but less common *mojos* include mayonnaise and cilantro *mojo* and the "aristocrat" of *mojos*, *mojo de almendra*, made with toasted almonds.

No matter where or what you eat in the Canaries, *mojos* provide a distinctive and delicious accent, be it with simply grilled meats, fish, or poultry, "wrinkled" potatoes, or with cheese. I'm sure you will find ample use for *mojos* at home, so prepare one or two and keep them on hand in the refrigerator.

Mojos (Dipping Sauces)
Salads ❀ Soups
Meals-in-a-Pot ❀ Vegetables

MOJO PICÓN
(Spicy Red Dipping Sauce)

This slightly spicy and very garlicky mixture is also called "a bitch of a sauce" when plenty of chile pepper is used. The recipe comes from the fine restaurant El Drago (see page 31) on the island of Tenerife. I consider this the best of all possible *mojos,* especially good with meats, poultry, and potatoes.   *Makes about 1 cup*

1 sweet dried red pepper, or mild New Mexico style, cored and seeded, or 1 pimiento plus 1 teaspoon paprika
A 1-inch piece, or to taste, dried red chile pepper, seeded
¼ cup red wine vinegar
12 cloves garlic, minced
¼ teaspoon kosher or sea salt
½ teaspoon cumin seeds or ground cumin
¾ teaspoon thyme leaves or ⅛ teaspoon dried
¾ teaspoon minced oregano leaves or ⅛ teaspoon dried
1 teaspoon minced parsley
½ teaspoon imported sweet paprika
½ cup extra virgin olive oil

Break the sweet and hot dried peppers into several pieces and soak them for 10 minutes in the vinegar. Meanwhile, in a mortar or mini processor, mash to a paste the garlic, salt, cumin, thyme, oregano, and parsley.

Remove the peppers from the vinegar, reserving the vinegar. Finely chop the peppers (or pimiento) and add to the mortar or processor and continue mashing until no large pieces remain. Stir in the paprika (½ teaspoon if using dried peppers, 1½ teaspoons with the pimiento), oil, and reserved vinegar.

MOJO DE CILANTRO
(Cilantro and Green Pepper Dipping Sauce)

This splendid *mojo* and the parsley dipping sauce that follows are used mainly with fish or "wrinkled" potatoes. Green *mojo* is also an outstanding marinade for fresh cheese (see p. 7).   *Makes about 1¼ cups*

½ teaspoon salt
6 cloves garlic
½ medium green bell pepper
1 cup finely chopped cilantro
    (stems trimmed)

⅔ cup extra virgin olive oil
3 tablespoons wine vinegar

Mash to a paste in a mortar or mini processor the salt, garlic, green pepper, and cilantro. Stir in the oil and vinegar.

MOJO VERDE DE PEREJIL
(Parsley Dipping Sauce)

Makes 1½ cups

1 teaspoon cumin seeds or
    ground cumin
8 cloves garlic, minced
1 teaspoon kosher or sea salt
1 cup minced parsley leaves
1 medium green bell pepper,
    minced

2 teaspoons, or to taste, minced
    fresh hot green pepper
½ cup extra virgin olive oil
3 tablespoons wine vinegar

In a mortar or mini processor crush the cumin seeds. Mash in the garlic and salt, then add and mash to a paste the parsley and the sweet and hot green peppers. Gradually stir in the oil and vinegar.

Cilantro, Culantro, Coriander, Chinese Parsley: Birds of a Feather

Have you ever gone to a garden center in spring to buy potted cilantro, only to be told they don't have it? Chances are they do, but it is called coriander.

Cilantro, culantro, and Chinese parsley are nothing more than three ways to identify the aromatic leaf of the *coriandrum sativum* plant. Coriander, on the other hand, usually refers to the plant itself or to the seed from that plant.

Contrary to popular thinking, coriander, a plant related to the carrot, is not Mexican; rather, its origins go back to ancient Egypt and Babylon, and it was the Spaniards who introduced coriander to the New World. Popular for culinary as well as medicinal purposes, coriander was also frequently maligned, for many found its scent quite unpleasant, likening it to that of bedbugs. The word, in fact, means bedbug in Ancient Greek, but I must confess, I have never seen a bedbug nor do I know how bedbugs smell.

Introduced to Spain by Moorish invaders, who were great fans of coriander as an herb and as a spice, coriander virtually vanished from Spanish cooking in later centuries, replaced by parsley, although vestiges remain in Andalusian cooking in recipes that are of direct descent from the Moors. Only in the Canary Islands is cilantro commonly used today, probably as a result of the islands' close connections with the former Spanish colonies in the New World.

Fresh coriander leaves are of course better than dried, and because of the popularity of Mexican cooking they are commonly available in supermarkets. If a recipe calls for crushed coriander, try to buy the whole seeds and crush them yourself for fuller flavor.

For the sake of clarity and to follow common usage, I have referred in recipes to coriander seeds as coriander and coriander leaves as cilantro.

MOJO DE MAYONESA Y CILANTRO
(Mayonnaise and Cilantro Dipping Sauce)

This is excellent with any simple fish dish. If you are not making your own mayonnaise, add a little extra virgin olive oil to the commercial mayonnaise to improve its flavor. This recipe will make enough dip to accompany 4 to 6 main-course dishes.

Makes about ½ cup

6 tablespoons mayonnaise, preferably homemade (p. 302; omit garlic)
3–4 tablespoons minced cilantro

2 cloves garlic, mashed to a paste
2 teaspoons freshly squeezed lemon juice

Whisk together all ingredients and transfer to a small serving bowl.

MOJO DE ALMENDRA
(Almond and Garlic Dipping Sauce)

Not as all-purpose as the other *mojos,* this one is much richer (maybe that's why it is sometimes referred to as the "aristocrat of *mojos*"), but can be used with fish and "wrinkled" potatoes just like any other *mojo*. It also makes a terrific salad dressing.

Makes about 1 cup

½ cup plus 2 tablespoons extra virgin olive oil
Four ¼-inch slices day-old bread cut from a long narrow loaf
1½ ounces (about 25) blanched almonds
1 teaspoon ground cumin, preferably freshly ground in a mortar or spice mill

10 cloves garlic, peeled
1 sweet dried red pepper, mild New Mexico style, seeded and finely crumbled, or 1 pimiento plus 1 teaspoon paprika
½ teaspoon imported sweet paprika
⅛ teaspoon salt
1 tablespoon wine vinegar

In a skillet, heat 2 tablespoons of the oil and sauté the bread and almonds, removing them as they become golden. Transfer to a food processor and beat the almonds and bread as fine as possible. Beat in the cumin, garlic, dried red pepper (or pimiento), paprika (½ teaspoon if using dried peppers, 1½ teaspoons with the pimiento), and salt. With the motor running, gradually beat in the remaining ½ cup oil, then the vinegar.

ENSALADA SAN ANDRÉS
(Cabbage Salad, San Andrés)

We had spent the morning strolling the extraordinarily beautiful and well-preserved Old Quarter of Santa Cruz de La Palma, capital of the island of La Palma, and were now driving to see the northern extreme of this exceptional island. We came upon San Andrés and found it to be a delightful cobblestone village that rises steeply from the sea. On this glorious spring day we chose an outdoor table at Restaurante San Andrés in the singular setting of the town's palm-filled church courtyard. Besides a well-prepared potato omelet and fried squid rings, we tried this exceptional shredded cabbage salad that includes pineapple, hearts of palm, green pepper, and corn.

Serves 4

SALAD DRESSING

6 tablespoons extra virgin olive oil

2 tablespoons freshly squeezed lemon juice

Salt

Freshly ground pepper

1 clove garlic, mashed to a paste

¼ teaspoon ground cumin, preferably freshly ground in a mortar or spice mill

2 tablespoons minced parsley

Cabbage Salad (continued)

. . .

1 pound green cabbage, finely
  shredded
16 hearts of palm, in ¼-inch
  slices
Two ¼-inch slices pineapple,
  cut in small wedges
8 thin slices tomato

8 very thin rings green bell
  pepper
8 very thin onion rings
4 tablespoons (¼ cup) cooked
  corn
1 cup shredded carrot
Salt

In a small bowl, whisk together the Salad Dressing ingredients. Arrange a bed of cabbage on a serving platter, and scatter over it the hearts of palm, pineapple, tomato, green pepper, and onion. Sprinkle on the corn and shredded carrot and a little salt, then pour on the dressing.

ENSALADA DE REPOLLO Y BERROS
(Cabbage and Watercress Salad)

I think this is one of the best salads I have ever tasted, with a wonderful mix of flavors typical of the Canary Islands.   *Serves 4*

1½ tablespoons freshly
  squeezed lemon juice
3 tablespoons extra virgin olive
  oil
Salt
Freshly ground pepper
½ cup finely chopped watercress, thick stems trimmed
1 small onion (preferably
  Vidalia or Spanish), slivered

1 small carrot, trimmed,
  scraped, and coarsely grated
2 cups finely shredded green
  cabbage
1 cup finely shredded red
  cabbage
8–12 cherry tomatoes
1 tablespoon finely chopped
  cilantro leaves

To make the salad dressing, whisk together the lemon juice, olive oil, salt, and pepper. In a salad bowl, toss together all the remaining ingredients. Fold in the dressing, taste for salt, and chill before serving.

POTAJE DE BERROS

(Watercress, Bean, and Potato Soup)

START PREPARATION 1 DAY IN ADVANCE

Apart from the Canary Islands, watercress was an unknown ingredient in Spanish cooking until recently, when proponents of "nouvelle" cooking adopted it. This soup, a Canary Island twist, you might say, on the famous *caldo gallego* of Galicia, has become a favorite of mine and makes a lovely light dinner. *Serves 6*

½ pound dried white beans
A ¼-pound piece salt pork
4 cups chicken broth, prefer-
    ably homemade (p. 298)
4 cloves garlic, minced
½ teaspoon salt
Freshly ground black pepper
½ teaspoon imported sweet
    paprika
½ teaspoon ground cumin,

preferably freshly ground in
    a mortar or spice mill
2 teaspoons olive oil
2 bunches (about 1 pound)
    watercress, leaves and stems
    finely chopped
1½ pounds peeled new pota-
    toes, left whole if small or
    cut in 1-inch cubes

Soak the beans overnight in cold water to cover. Drain, place in a soup pot with the salt pork, 1 quart water, and the chicken broth. Bring to a boil, then cover and simmer 1½ to 2 hours, or until the beans are almost tender.

Meanwhile, in a mortar or mini processor mash the garlic with the salt, pepper, paprika, and cumin. Stir in the olive oil.

Add the watercress and potatoes to the beans. Dilute the mortar mixture with a little liquid from the pot and stir into the soup. Continue cooking until the potatoes are tender, about 30 minutes. Turn off the flame, cover the pot, and let sit 5 to 10 minutes. Serve the soup with a piece of salt pork in each portion.

BUÑUELOS DE BUANGOS
(Zucchini Puffs)

These zucchini fritters are seasoned with onion, parsley, and thyme. They make a fine accompaniment to meat dishes, or can be served as tapas.

Makes 14

1 tablespoon olive oil
1 medium onion, finely
   chopped
1 clove garlic, minced
¼ pound zucchini, unpeeled
   and coarsely grated
2 tablespoons minced parsley
1½ teaspoons thyme leaves or
   ¼ teaspoon dried
Salt
Freshly ground pepper

1 tablespoon chicken broth or
   water
6 tablespoons flour
1 teaspoon baking powder
¼ cup milk
1 tablespoon grated cured
   Manchego or Parmesan
   cheese
1 egg white
Olive oil for frying

Heat the oil in a skillet and slowly sauté the onion and garlic until the onion is translucent. Stir in the zucchini, parsley, thyme, and a little salt and pepper. Cover and cook 5 minutes. Add the broth, cover, and continue cooking over a low flame 10 minutes more.

Stir together the flour and baking powder in a bowl. Add the milk and mix until smooth, then add the zucchini mixture and the cheese and salt to taste. Beat the egg white until stiff but not dry, and fold into the batter.

Pour the oil into a skillet to a depth of at least 1 inch (or better still, use a deep-fryer), and heat until it quickly browns a cube of bread. Drop the zucchini mixture by the tablespoon into the oil and fry until golden. Drain on paper towels and serve.

PAPAS PANADERAS
(Oven-Roasted Potatoes)

Simple sliced roast potatoes, beautifully seasoned with onion, garlic, herbs, and spices.

Serves 4

2–2½ pounds potatoes, peeled and cut in ¼-inch slices
1 medium onion, in thin slices
8 cloves garlic, peeled and sliced
Salt
Freshly ground pepper

½ teaspoon imported sweet paprika
1½ teaspoons thyme leaves or ¼ teaspoon dried
2 tablespoons olive oil
2 bay leaves
1 tablespoon minced parsley

Grease a large baking pan and arrange the potatoes in layers, scattering each layer with onion and garlic, sprinkling with salt, pepper, paprika, and thyme and drizzling with olive oil. Place the bay leaves between the layers and drizzle with 3 tablespoons water. Bake at 400°F about 45 minutes. Garnish with the parsley and serve.

PAPAS ARRUGADAS
("Wrinkled" Potatoes)

Although "Wrinkled" Potatoes are cooked in a disproportionate amount of salt, don't be put off—the potatoes are not at all salty. The salty water draws water out of the potatoes by osmosis but the salt cannot penetrate the potato skin, and the potatoes acquire a distinctive "meaty" consistency without a trace of mealiness. Papas Arrugadas are made with tiny potatoes (often less than an inch across) that grow on the islands and come in dozens of varieties, including prized black potatoes. They are commonly served as an appetizer, dipped in *mojos,* and also accompany just about every main course.

Serves 4

"Wrinkled" Potatoes (continued)

1 pound very small potatoes in
their jackets (preferably
"new," and not more than

1½–2 inches), washed and
scrubbed
¾ cup kosher or sea salt

Place the potatoes in a saucepan with abundant water to cover. Add the salt and stir until dissolved. Bring to a boil and cook, partially covered, over a medium-high flame until tender.

Drain off the water, leaving the potatoes in the pan, and continue to cook over a low flame, shaking occasionally, until the potatoes are dry and the skins slightly wrinkled, about 10 minutes.

Fish

CHURROS DE SAMA
(Red Snapper Fish Sticks)

My fishmonger looked at me somewhat perplexed—and dismayed—when I asked him to skin and fillet a lovely large red snapper he had on display. I was trying to reproduce the delicious fish sticks I ate in the Canary Islands (called *churros* because of their resemblance to Spain's long thin breakfast fritters of the same name), and red snapper seemed to me to be the closest equivalent to an island fish called *sama*. My guess was good, for these were the best fish sticks I have ever tasted, and great with a green *mojo* (p. 402) on the side.

Serves 4–6

Two 1½–1¾-pound red
snappers, filleted and skin
removed
Kosher or sea salt

2 eggs, lightly beaten with
1 teaspoon water
Flour for dredging
Olive oil for frying

Cut the fish fillets in ¾-inch crosswise strips, about 2½ to 3 inches long. Sprinkle on both sides with salt and let sit 30 minutes.

Coat the fish with egg, then dredge in flour seasoned with salt. Pour the oil into a skillet to a depth of at least 1 inch (or better still, use a deep fryer) and fry until golden. Drain on paper towels and serve right away, accompanied by green *mojo*.

PESCADO AL CILANTRO CHO ZACARÍAS
(Fish Fillets with Cilantro)

Cho Zacarías, on the island of Gran Canaria in the town of San Mateo, is a delightful and most unusual restaurant that has preserved several centuries-old village houses, filled them with greenery, and amassed a magnificent collection of antique farm tools, utensils, and ceramics that record the peasant ways of times past.

Often made with an island fish somewhat similar to grouper, called *cherne,* this quick-to-prepare, delicate, and quite exceptional dish that includes cilantro, garlic, and wine is great with many kinds of fish. I particularly like it with red snapper. *Serves 4*

Two 1½-pound red snappers, groupers, or bass, filleted, skin on
Salt
Freshly ground pepper
Olive oil
Freshly squeezed lemon juice
½ cup Fish Broth (p. 175) or diluted clam juice
¼ cup dry white wine
2 tablespoons minced cilantro
2 cloves garlic, peeled

Sprinkle the fish fillets on both sides with salt and pepper. Arrange skin side up in a shallow baking dish, brush with olive oil, and sprinkle with lemon juice. Let sit 15 minutes.

In a small saucepan, combine the Fish Broth and wine and boil down to half. To make the sauce, in a mortar or mini processor, mash to a paste the cilantro, salt, pepper, and garlic. Stir in the broth and wine mixture. Pour over the fish and bake at 350°F about 7 minutes, or until the fish is just cooked through. A nice accompaniment is a roast tomato, which you might season with salt, pepper, thyme, and slivered onion.

BONITO EN SALMOREJO
(Fresh Tuna in Spicy Red Pepper and Cumin Sauce)

There are several dishes in Canary cooking that use the term *salmorejo* to refer to a sauce well scented with herbs and spices and containing wine and vinegar (see Conejo en Salmorejo, p. 415). I tasted this version at Bar Lucas on the island of Tenerife at the San Marcos beach, a place I hadn't been to in many years. So much had changed in Tenerife, and yet here was the tiny black volcanic sand beach, enclosed by tiers of green-covered cliffs, just as we remembered it.   *Serves 4*

2 dried sweet red peppers, stems removed and seeded, or 2 pimientos and 2 teaspoons paprika

2 pounds fresh tuna steaks, about 1½ inches thick, in 1½-inch cubes

Kosher or sea salt

8 black peppercorns

8 cloves garlic, peeled

2 tablespoons minced parsley

2 tablespoons thyme leaves or 1 teaspoon dried

2 teaspoons cumin seeds or ground cumin

2 tablespoons minced oregano leaves or 1 teaspoon dried

1 teaspoon imported sweet paprika

7 tablespoons olive oil

2 tablespoons wine vinegar

¾ cup dry white wine

Soak the dried peppers in warm water for 20 minutes, then drain and chop finely. Sprinkle the fish cubes with salt and let sit while preparing the sauce.

In a mortar or mini processor, mash to a paste the dried red peppers (or pimientos), peppercorns, garlic, parsley, thyme, cumin, and oregano. Mix in the paprika (1 teaspoon if using dried peppers, 1 tablespoon if using pimientos), then 6 tablespoons of the oil, the vinegar, white wine, and salt to taste.

Heat the remaining tablespoon oil in a skillet to the smoking point. Sear the fish on all sides, lower the heat, and add the mortar mixture. Continue cooking, uncovered, until the fish is done, about 3 to 4 minutes, turning the fish in the sauce occasionally. Serve with "Wrinkled" Potatoes (p. 409).

Meats ❧ Poultry ❧ Game

POLLO EN SALSA DE CEBOLLA
(Chicken Braised with Onions)

There are no unusual ingredients in this dish and yet the taste is sensational—one of the best chicken preparations I have ever found.

Serves 4

A 3–3½-pound chicken, cut in
   serving pieces
Salt
Freshly ground pepper
Flour for dusting
2 tablespoons olive oil
2 medium onions, finely
   chopped

⅔ cup dry white wine
6 tablespoons chicken broth
1 head garlic, loose skin
   removed
1 bay leaf
Several strands of saffron,
   crumbled

Sprinkle the chicken pieces with salt and pepper, then dust with flour. Heat the oil in a shallow casserole and brown the chicken on both sides. Stir in the onions and sauté until translucent, then add the wine and broth.

Slash the garlic head halfway through vertically and add to the casserole along with the bay leaf, salt, pepper, and saffron. Cover and simmer about 40 minutes, adding more broth if necessary (the sauce should be fairly thick). Squeeze the garlic flesh into the sauce, discard the skin, and serve.

POLLO CON MIGAS Y LIMÓN
(Chicken with Bread Bits and Lemon)

A most tasty chicken dish with the added interest of croutons, which will soak up the flavors of the sauce.

Serves 4

Chicken with Bread Bits (continued)

1 cup bread without crusts, torn
  roughly into ½-inch pieces
2 tablespoons plus 1–2
  teaspoons olive oil
A 3–3½-pound chicken, cut in
  serving pieces
Salt
Flour for dusting
1 medium onion, chopped

¼ cup chopped Spanish mountain cured ham, prosciutto,
  or capicollo (about 2
  ounces)
¾ cup dry white wine
¼ cup chicken broth
½ lemon, in thin slices
Minced parsley for garnish

Place the bread pieces on a cookie tray and drizzle with 1 to 2 teaspoons oil.
Bake at 350°F until golden, about 5 minutes.

Sprinkle the chicken with salt, then dust with flour. Heat the remaining
2 tablespoons oil in a shallow casserole and brown the chicken on all sides.
Add the onion and ham and sauté until the onion has wilted. Pour in the wine
and broth and scatter in the lemon slices. Bring to a boil, then transfer to a
350°F oven and cook, uncovered, 45 minutes, adding more broth or water if
necessary. When ready to serve, sprinkle with the bread pieces and parsley.

POLLO AL ROMERO Y LIMÓN
CON PATATAS
(Rosemary and Lemon-Scented Chicken with Potatoes)

A chicken dish that tastes outstanding and out of the ordinary despite the
utter simplicity of its ingredients and its preparation.   *Serves 4*

2 tablespoons olive oil
A 3–3½-pound chicken, cut in
  serving pieces
12 cloves garlic, skin on, lightly
  crushed
Salt
Freshly ground pepper
¾ pound baking potatoes,

peeled and cut in ¾-inch
  cubes
4 lemon slices, cut in halves
3 sprigs rosemary or
  ½ teaspoon dried
¼ cup dry white wine
¼ cup chicken broth

Grease a roasting pan with 1 tablespoon of the oil and arrange the chicken pieces, skin side up, and the garlic cloves in the pan. Brush the chicken with the remaining oil and sprinkle with salt and pepper. Roast at 450°F for 10 minutes, lower the heat to 350°F, add the potatoes, and sprinkle them with salt.

Scatter the lemon slices and rosemary sprigs around the pan (or sprinkle the chicken and potatoes with the dried rosemary) and cook 5 minutes. Add the wine and roast 10 minutes more, then stir in the broth and cook 30 minutes, adding more broth or water if needed to keep some liquid in the pan.

CONEJO EN SALMOREJO
(*Rabbit in Spicy Wine and Vinegar Sauce*)

START PREPARATION 2 HOURS IN ADVANCE

Mesón El Drago, a restaurant set in a charming old country house with terra-cotta floors and wood-beamed ceilings, takes its name from the impressive dragon tree—a phantasmagorical tree indigenous to the Canary Islands—that stands in its patio. Owner and chef Carlos Gamonal has garnered many prestigious awards for his fine renditions of traditional island dishes, including this rabbit in a marinade piquant with vinegar.

The marinade becomes the sauce for this dish (similar to the *mojos* but less concentrated). You may substitute chicken, but the results are far better with rabbit. And don't forget the ideal accompaniment, "Wrinkled" Potatoes (p. 409).   *Serves 3–4*

SALMOREJO

8 cloves garlic
½ dried sweet red pepper, or mild New Mexico style, seeded and crumbled or minced, or ½ pimiento, finely chopped, and ½ teaspoon paprika
1 teaspoon salt
5 teaspoons imported sweet paprika

½ cup red wine vinegar
1½ cups dry white wine
½ cup olive oil
2 sprigs thyme or ¼ teaspoon dried
2 sprigs oregano or ¼ teaspoon dried

Rabbit in Spicy Sauce (continued)

. . .

A 2½–3-pound rabbit, cut in serving pieces

2 tablespoons olive oil

To make the Salmorejo, mash to a paste in a mortar or mini processor the garlic, dried red pepper, and salt. Stir in the paprika (5 teaspoons if using dried peppers, 5½ teaspoons if using pimientos) and vinegar and transfer to a bowl. Mix in the wine, olive oil, thyme, and oregano.

Arrange the rabbit pieces in a shallow bowl. Pour on the Salmorejo and turn the rabbit pieces to coat well. Cover with foil and let marinate 2 hours.

Drain the rabbit pieces, reserving the marinade, and dry on paper towels. Heat the 2 tablespoons oil in a shallow casserole and brown the rabbit lightly on all sides. Remove to a warm platter and pour off the oil. Add the marinade, bring to a boil, and boil down by half. Taste for salt. Return the rabbit to the casserole, cover, and simmer 1 hour.

COCHINO EN ADOBO A LA PARRILLA
(Seasoned Grilled Pork Chops)

START PREPARATION A FEW HOURS IN ADVANCE

The appealing marinade called for in this recipe works equally well with lamb and chicken and is traditional for grilled baby goat, called *baifito*. At Las Grutas de Artiles, a restaurant in Santa Brígida on the island of Gran Canaria, set in a grotto overlooking the beautiful Angostura valley, *baifito* is a specialty.   *Serves 4*

3 tablespoons minced oregano leaves or 1½ teaspoons dried
1½ teaspoons thyme leaves or ¼ teaspoon dried

6 peppercorns
1 bay leaf, crumbled
¼ teaspoon cumin seeds or ground cumin
¼ teaspoon kosher or sea salt

2 cloves garlic, minced
¼ teaspoon imported sweet
   paprika
A 1-inch piece fresh hot green
   pepper, seeded and minced

¼ cup extra virgin olive oil
1 teaspoon red wine vinegar
4 loin pork chops, 1 inch thick
3 tablespoons dry white wine

In a mortar or mini processor, mash together the oregano, thyme, pepper-corns, bay leaf, cumin, salt, garlic, paprika, and hot green pepper. Gradually stir in the oil and vinegar.

Arrange the pork chops in one layer in a shallow bowl, pour the mortar mixture over them, and marinate for a few hours or overnight. Drain the chops; place the marinade in a small saucepan and stir in the wine. Simmer while the chops are cooking.

The chops are best when barbecued over hot coals, but they may be broiled or pan-fried as well, about 5 minutes to each side. When the chops are done, spoon some of the marinade over them and serve, accompanied by "Wrinkled" Potatoes (p. 409).

Desserts

MERMELADA DE CALABAZA
(Squash Marmalade)

This sweetened squash accompanies the fried pastries on page 425, but could also be a filling for baked dessert turnovers.

Makes about 1½ cups

1½ pounds orange winter
   squash, cut in large pieces
¾ cup sugar

5 tablespoons water
Peel of ½ lemon
1 cinnamon stick

Place the squash in a saucepan with water to cover. Bring to a boil, cover, and simmer about 15 minutes, or until tender. Cool, scrape the pulp from the shell, and mash.

Squash Marmalade (continued)

In a saucepan heat the sugar, water, lemon peel, and cinnamon until the sugar dissolves, then add the squash and bring to a boil. Cook over a low flame, uncovered, for about 35 minutes, stirring frequently, or until the mixture has the consistency of marmalade.

BIENMESABE
(Rich Almond Sauce)

You will need only a small amount per portion of this deliciously rich candy-like sauce (whose name literally means "It tastes good to me") which in the Canary Islands is often served by itself as a dessert. I love it with vanilla ice cream or with Frozen Almond Cream (p. 427). To make coconut *bienmesabe,* simply incorporate 6 tablespoons of flaked coconut.

Serves 8

½ pound blanched almonds	1 teaspoon grated lemon peel
1 cup sugar	½ teaspoon cinnamon
1 cup water	4 egg yolks
½ cup honey	

Grind the almonds and sugar in a food processor until the nuts are as fine as possible. Transfer to a saucepan and add the water, honey, grated lemon peel, and cinnamon. Bring to a boil and cook at a lively simmer until thickened, about 15 minutes, stirring frequently. Cool slightly.

Whisk the egg yolks in a small bowl and gradually whisk in a few tablespoons of the almond mixture. Add this to the saucepan and cook over a medium-high flame until the mixture begins to bubble, stirring constantly. Cool, stirring occasionally, and serve at room temperature. *Bienmesabe* should have the consistency of a thick custard; thin with water if necessary.

To serve with ice cream, spoon about 3 tablespoons onto each dessert dish or bowl and put a scoop of ice cream over the sauce.

CREMA DE PLÁTANO CON ALMENDRA
(Banana and Almond Cream)

This typical Canary custard dessert should be served the same day, otherwise the banana will discolor.   *Serves 4*

¼ cup (about 1¾ ounces)
   blanched almonds
3 tablespoons cornstarch
2 cups plus 2 tablespoons milk
Pinch of salt
Peel of ½ lemon
1 cinnamon stick

2 eggs
⅓ cup sugar
2 medium bananas, peeled,
   mashed, and sprinkled with
   lemon juice
Strawberry wedges for garnish

Place the almonds on a cookie tray and bake at 350°F for about 5 minutes, or until lightly golden. Cool, then grind the almonds. Dissolve the cornstarch in 2 tablespoons of the milk. Bring the remaining 2 cups milk to a boil in a saucepan with the salt, lemon peel, and cinnamon. Simmer 20 minutes. Discard the peel and the cinnamon.

In another saucepan, whisk together the eggs, sugar, bananas, the cornstarch mixture, and the ground almonds. Stir in the milk and bring to a boil over medium heat, stirring constantly. Remove from the heat and transfer right away to individual dessert bowls (do not stir). Serve garnished with the strawberries.

QUESILLO
(Flan, Canary Style)

PREPARE 1 DAY IN ADVANCE

A creamy flan—somewhat richer because it is made in part with condensed milk—with the added flavor and texture of ground almonds. I found it at the delightful Restaurante Los Abrigos, a lively local fish restaurant overlooking the port of Los Abrigos in the south of Tenerife, where diners scrutinize the fresh fish display before making meal selections.   *Makes 5*

Flan (continued)

Caramelized Sugar Syrup
  (p. 220)
3 eggs
½ cup condensed milk, homemade (p. 277) or canned

2 cups fresh milk
⅓ cup ground blanched
  almonds

Prepare the Caramelized Sugar Syrup according to instructions and pour into 5 custard cups.

In a large bowl, lightly whisk the eggs, then whisk in the condensed and fresh milks and stir in the almonds. Pour into the custard cups and place in a pan of warm water. Bake at 350°F for 30 minutes, or until a knife inserted in the custard comes out clean. Remove from the water and cool. Refrigerate overnight—the custard will settle and the air pockets will disappear. To serve, unmold onto dessert dishes.

GALLETAS DE NATA
(Cream Cookies)

An excellent cookie—short, buttery, with a touch of cream, a little coconut, and lots of lemon peel—that is often kept on hand in Canary households and a fine example of the celebrated sweets of La Gomera.

Makes about 18

6 tablespoons unsalted butter
1 egg yolk
5 tablespoons sugar
½ teaspoon grated lemon peel
2 tablespoons heavy cream
¼ teaspoon cinnamon
1 tablespoon flaked coconut

⅛ teaspoon ground anise
1 cup plus 3 tablespoons flour
¼ teaspoon baking soda
1 egg, lightly beaten with
  1 teaspoon water
Granulated sugar for sprinkling

In a bowl, cream the butter with an electric mixer. Beat in the egg yolk and sugar, then beat in the grated lemon peel, cream, cinnamon, coconut, and anise. Combine the flour and baking soda and stir into the butter mixture to form a smooth dough. Roll out on a floured surface to ¼ inch, and cut with a cookie cutter (about 2½-inch size) into desired shapes. Brush with the beaten egg and sprinkle with sugar. Bake at 350°F for 10 to 12 minutes, or until well browned.

BOLLOS DE CUAJADA
(Fresh Goat Cheese Fritters)

When *carnaval* is in full swing in the Canaries, these delicious puffs of fresh cheese, flavored with lemon and cinnamon and bathed in honey, are holiday treats. They will not keep for long, so eat and enjoy right away.

Makes 24 (serves 6–8)

1 pound fresh goat cheese or
    farmer cheese
½ teaspoon grated lemon peel
½ teaspoon cinnamon
3 tablespoons sugar
1 tablespoon melted butter
½ teaspoon brandy
⅛ teaspoon salt

⅛ teaspoon baking powder
4 eggs
¼ cup flour
Oil for frying
½ cup honey
1 teaspoon lemon juice
Cinnamon for dusting

In a bowl, mash the cheese with a fork. Stir in the grated lemon peel, cinnamon, sugar, butter, brandy, salt, and baking powder, then beat in the eggs with an electric mixer. Stir in the flour until well blended.

Pour the oil into a skillet to a depth of at least 1 inch (or better still, use a deep-fryer) and heat until the oil quickly browns a cube of bread. Drop the batter by tablespoons into the oil and fry until golden and crisp (do not crowd). Drain on paper towels. Keep the fritters warm in a 200°F oven while preparing the honey mixture.

In a saucepan, heat the honey with 2 tablespoons water and the lemon juice. Bathe the fritters in the honey sauce, arrange on a dish, and dust with cinnamon.

BUÑUELOS DE GARBANZOS
(Sweetened Chickpea Fritters)

From the island of Lanzarote come these fritters with a nice cake-like texture. They are best warm, but good also eaten at room temperature, if made the same day.   *Makes about 20*

½ pound cooked chickpeas,
  freshly made or good-
  quality canned, rinsed
  and drained
2 eggs, separated
⅛ teaspoon salt
1 tablespoon anisette liqueur
1 tablespoon mild olive oil or
  vegetable oil

¼ cup sugar
¼ teaspoon cinnamon
¼ teaspoon grated lemon peel
7 tablespoons flour
Oil for frying
Confectioners' sugar

Purée the chickpeas in a food processor. Beat in the egg yolks, salt, anisette, and oil until smooth. Add the sugar, cinnamon, grated lemon peel, and flour and pulse to blend.

In a bowl, beat the egg whites until stiff but not dry. Fold in the chickpea mixture. Pour the oil into a skillet to a depth of at least 1 inch (or better still, use a deep-fryer) and heat until the oil quickly browns a cube of bread. Drop the chickpea mixture by the tablespoon into the oil and fry until golden on both sides. Drain on paper towels and dust with powdered sugar.

QUESADILLAS CANARIAS
(Goat's Milk Cheese Tartlets)

Because of the Canary Island terrain, most of its fine cheeses are made from goat's milk. Many are used to make a variety of cheese desserts, such as these pastry tartlets filled with sweetened goat's milk cheese. Fresh goat's milk cheese has more flavor than that of cow's milk, and anise adds to the distinctive taste of the *quesadillas*.   *Makes 12*

PASTRY DOUGH

⅔ cup flour
2 tablespoons butter, softened
2 teaspoons sugar

2 teaspoons beaten egg
⅛ teaspoon grated lemon peel

FILLING

¼ pound fresh goat cheese or
     farmer cheese
2 tablespoons sugar
1 tablespoon honey
1 egg, lightly beaten

¼ teaspoon ground anise
⅛ teaspoon cinnamon
¼ teaspoon grated lemon peel
Pinch of salt

Mix together all the Pastry Dough ingredients with your fingers in a bowl.

To make the Filling, put the cheese in another bowl and work in the sugar. Stir in the honey, egg, anise, cinnamon, grated lemon peel, and salt.

Roll the dough out less than ⅛ inch thick and cut in 2½-inch circles. Fit the dough into twelve 1¾-inch tartlet pans. Fill each with 1 tablespoon of the filling. Bake at 350°F for about 25 to 30 minutes, or until the filling is set. Serve chilled.

TRUCHAS CANARIAS
(Sweet Potato Dessert Turnovers)

START PREPARATION 2 HOURS IN ADVANCE

These turnovers, made with a flaky pastry and an unusual filling of sweet potato (or, more precisely, batata), almonds, and a hint of anise, are Canary Island Christmas treats. Why they are called *truchas*—trout—is a mystery, for there are no real rivers in the islands and certainly no trout. You can also make these turnovers, if you prefer, with puff pastry (p. 22). The *truchas* can be fried or baked, although I think they are better when fried.

Makes about 25

Sweet Potato Turnovers (continued)

PASTRY DOUGH

¼ cup mild olive oil or
    vegetable oil
¼ cup dry white wine
⅛ teaspoon salt

3 tablespoons lard or vegetable
    shortening, softened
2 cups flour

SWEET POTATO FILLING

1 pound sweet potatoes or
    batatas, unpeeled
2 egg yolks
¼ pound ground almonds
¼ cup sugar

1 teaspoon cinnamon
¼ teaspoon grated lemon peel
2 teaspoons anisette liqueur
¼ teaspoon ground anise seed

. . .

Oil for frying
A mixture of granulated
    sugar and cinnamon
    for sprinkling

To make the Pastry Dough, in a bowl mix with a fork the oil, wine, salt, and lard. Stir in the flour, then turn out on a floured surface and knead lightly until smooth. Cover with plastic wrap and let sit 2 hours.

Meanwhile make the Sweet Potato Filling. Boil the potatoes in a pot of water. Cover and cook about 30 minutes, or until tender. Drain and peel, transfer to a bowl, and mash with a fork. Stir in the egg yolks, almonds, sugar, cinnamon, lemon peel, anisette, and anise. Cover and let sit 1 hour.

Roll out the dough to ⅛ inch and cut in 3½-inch rounds. Place 2 teaspoons filling in the center of each, bring up the sides, press together, then place flat on the work surface and seal with the tines of a fork.

Pour the oil into a skillet to a depth of at least 1 inch (or better still, use a deep-fryer) and heat until the oil quickly browns a cube of bread. Fry the turnovers until golden, turning once. Drain on paper towels, sprinkle with the sugar and cinnamon mixture, and serve at room temperature.

To bake instead of fry, brush with beaten egg and bake at 350°F for about 15 minutes, then sprinkle with the sugar and cinnamon mixture.

TORRIJAS CON MERMELADA DE CALABAZA Y MIEL
(Pastries with Squash Marmalade and Honey)

START PREPARATION 1 DAY IN ADVANCE

Of all the unusual desserts I have sampled in the Canary Islands, this is among my favorites. It comes from La Era, an inviting Canary country restaurant, laden with rustic antiques, on the island of Lanzarote, which serves nothing but beautifully prepared island specialties.

Makes about 15

2¾ cups flour
¼ teaspoon cinnamon
¼ teaspoon ground anise
1 teaspoon baking powder
⅛ teaspoon salt
6 eggs, lightly beaten

2 tablespoons milk
¼ teaspoon grated lemon peel
1 recipe Squash Marmalade
   (p. 417)
Oil for frying
Honey

In a bowl, combine the flour, cinnamon, anise, baking powder, and salt. Stir in the eggs, milk, and grated lemon peel to form a soft dough.

Turn out onto a work surface and knead briefly until smooth, adding a little more flour if the dough is too sticky. Wrap loosely in oiled plastic wrap and leave at room temperature overnight. Make the Squash Marmalade according to instructions.

Divide the dough into 1½-inch balls and roll each on a floured surface into roughly a 6- by 3-inch oval. Pour the oil into a skillet to a depth of at least 1 inch (or better still, use a deep-fryer) and heat until the oil slowly browns a cube of bread (about 340°F). Fry the dough pieces very briefly, turning once, until slightly puffed but not browned. Drain on paper towels.

Serve right away (or keep warm briefly in a 200°F oven), drizzled with honey and topped with a dollop of Squash Marmalade.

BIZCOCHO DE NARANJA
(Orange Yogurt Cake)

The tiny volcanic island of La Gomera, blanketed by forests, is mentioned in history books because it was here that Columbus stayed in the company of his supposed mistress (read more in my *Discovering Spain: An Uncommon Guide*) before setting out for the New World. And it is this diminutive island that is famous all over the Canaries for its outstanding desserts. I have sampled La Gomera's cakes, tarts, and cookies and, indeed, all were excellent. Here is a moist and dense orange, almond, and yogurt cake that is wonderful for tea.

Makes an 8–9-inch cake

3 cups flour
½ teaspoon salt
2¼ teaspoons baking powder
5 eggs, separated
1½ cups sugar
Grated peel of ¼ lemon
Grated peel of 1 orange

½ cup orange juice
¼ pound (1 stick) butter, melted
¾ cup yogurt, preferably made from whole milk
¼ cup ground blanched almonds

Grease a deep 8- to 9-inch springform pan with butter and dust with flour. Sift together the flour, salt, and baking powder. In a large bowl, beat the egg yolks with an electric mixer until light colored, then beat in the sugar, grated lemon and orange peel, orange juice, butter, and yogurt. Gradually stir in the flour mixture.

In a separate bowl beat the egg whites until stiff but not dry, then gently stir into the batter. Pour the batter into the prepared springform cake pan and sprinkle with the almonds. Bake at 350°F for about 55 minutes, or until a toothpick inserted in the cake comes out clean. Cool briefly, then remove the sides of the springform pan and cool completely.

BISCUIT DE ALMENDRA
(Frozen Almond Cream)

This frozen dessert tastes much richer than it is, considering it has no egg yolks and a relatively small amount of cream. If you don't wish to use uncooked egg whites, use instead an egg substitute made with egg whites. *Biscuit* is at its best served with Bienmesabe almond sauce (p. 418).

Serves 8

¼ pound blanched almonds
½ cup sugar
8 egg whites, or 1 cup egg substitute made with egg whites

⅔ cup heavy cream
Pinch of salt
½ teaspoon vanilla

Toast the almonds on a cookie tray in a 350°F oven for 3 to 4 minutes, or until golden. Cool, transfer to a food processor with ¼ cup of the sugar, and grind as fine as possible.

Beat the egg whites or egg substitute until frothy, then beat in the remaining ¼ cup sugar and continue beating until the egg whites are stiff but not dry (if using egg substitute the mixture will be very thick, but not stiff). In a separate bowl whip the cream with the salt and the vanilla. Stir in all but 2 tablespoons of the almond mixture, then fold in the egg whites.

Grease a loaf pan and coat with the remaining 2 tablespoons of the almond mixture. Pour in the egg white–cream mixture, cover with foil, and freeze. To serve, cut in slices.

MARKETING SOURCES

The availability of Spanish foods and kitchenware in most food specialty shops is spotty at best. The following are the sources I have found that stock the finest Spanish products. Call for more complete product information. Several accept mail and phone orders and credit cards.

Dean & Deluca   560 Broadway, New York, New York 10012; (800) 221-7714 (for mail order), (212) 431-1691 (store). Spanish paella rice, fine virgin olive oils, *piquillo* peppers, top-quality saffron, Spanish honey, and an excellent selection of cheeses. Also paella pans and chorizo sausage. Catalog available. Mail and phone orders and credit cards accepted.

La Española   25020 Doble Avenue, Harbor City, California 90710; (310) 539-0455. The largest selection of Spanish products, including a complete line of exceptional homemade Spanish sausages, squid ink, prepared partridge, quail, rabbit, and pheasant, many Spanish cheeses, *turrón* candy, and Spanish cookies. Also paella pans and earthenware casseroles in many sizes. Catalog available. Mail and phone orders and credit cards accepted.

Zingerman's   422 Detroit Street, Ann Arbor, Michigan 48104; (313) 769-1625 (for mail order), (313) 663-3400 (store). An exceptional selection of top-of-the-line imported Spanish foods, including the best of Spanish cheeses, olive oils, vinegars, marinated olives, and rice. The only source for authentic *piquillo* peppers from the Lodosa appellation of origin. Paella pans in a variety of sizes and chorizo sausage. Catalog available. Mail and phone orders and credit cards accepted.

Two sources for baby eels (*angulas*) imported frozen from Spain, among many other Spanish specialties, are:

Despaña Brand   86-17 Northern Boulevard, Jackson Heights, New York 11372; (718) 779-4971. Product list available.

España Specialties   41-01 Broadway, Astoria, New York 11103; (718) 932-9335.

INDEX

A NOTE ON THE TYPE

This book was set in Fournier, a typeface named for Pierre Simon Fournier *fils* (1712–1768), a celebrated French type designer. Coming from a family of typefounders, Fournier was an extraordinarily prolific designer of typefaces and of typographic ornaments. He was also the author of the important *Manuel typographique* (1764–1766), in which he attempted to work out a system standardizing type measurement in points, a system that is still in use internationally.

Fournier's type is considered transitional in that it drew its inspiration from the old style, yet was ingeniously innovational, providing for an elegant, legible appearance. In 1925 his type was revived by the Monotype Corporation of London.

Composed by Americomp, Brattleboro, Vermont
Printed and bound by R. R. Donnelley & Sons,
Harrisonburg, Virginia
Map by David Cain
Designed by Virginia Tan